The dBASE Book Plus

A Companion to The dBASE Book

Ken Mayer

Version 1

The dBASE Book Plus
A Companion to <u>The dBASE Book</u>

by Ken Mayer

Copyright © 2015 by Kenneth *(Ken)* J. Mayer
ISBN: 978-0-9892875-6-2 (soft cover printed)
         978-0-9892875-7-9 (electronic pdf file)

First Printing, 2015
Printed in the United States of America

Trademark and Copyright acknowledgments:
- ➢ *dBASE, dBASE PLUS, dQuery* and variations of these product names and words are registered trademarks of dBase, LLC.
- ➢ *Borland Database Engine, BDE,* are registered trademarks of Borland International, Inc. and/or Embarcadero.
- ➢ *Firebird* is a registered trademark of Firebird Foundation Corporation.
- ➢ *Microsoft, Windows 7, Windows 8, Windows 10* (and all other forms of the names of the Windows operating system) are registered trademarks of Microsoft Corporation.
- ➢ *Inno Setup* is copyrighted by Jordan Russel and Martijn Laan
- ➢ *glyFX* is a division of PerthWeb.
- ➢ *FotoGrafix* is copyrighted by L. Madhaven
- ➢ *Fugue* images are copyrighted by Yusuke Kamiyamane.
- ➢ *PhotoShop Pro* is copyrighted by Corel Corporation
- ➢ Ultimate Grid (GridEX) is part of "The Ultimate Toolbox" project, open source code

No attempt has been made to designate as trademarks or service marks all personal computer words or terms in which proprietary rights might exist. The inclusion, exclusion or definition of a word or term is not intended to affect, or express any judgement on, the validity or legal status of any proprietary right which may be claimed in that word or term.

Disclaimer: The author and publisher have used their best efforts in preparing this book, and the programs contained herein. However, the author and publisher make no warranties of any kind, express or implied, with regard to the documentation or programs contained in this book, and specifically disclaim without any limitations, any implied warranties of merchantability and fitness for a particular purpose with respect to program listings in the book and/or the techniques described in the book. In no event shall the author or publisher be responsible or liable for any loss or profit or any other commercial damages, including but not limited to special, incidental, consequential or any other damages in connection with or arising out of furnishing, performance, or use of this book or the programs.

Cover: Word Cloud created by using: http://www.tagxedo.com; layout done in Microsoft Publisher.

Table of Contents

Index

About the Author

Ken Mayer has used dBASE both as a hobbyist and as a professional coder for many years, starting with dBASE III+ and working up to dBASE PLUS.

Ken worked for Borland, Intl. for two years as a Senior Quality Assurance Engineer on the Intrabuilder and dBASE products (Intrabuilder 1.0, Visual dBASE 7.0 and 7.01), and also worked for five years for dBASE Inc. as a Senior Quality Assurance Engineer, also working on dBASE (Visual dBASE 7.5, dB2K and dBASE PLUS, as well as dQuery). Ken was a contributing editor to dBASE Advisor magazine for the one and a half years or so it was in publication.

He served on Borland's TeamB (volunteer technical support) when Borland owned dBASE, and has helped many in the dBASE developer community. At this time he is a member of the dBVIPS for dataBased Intelligence, Inc., doing the same things he did with TeamB. He authored a good portion of the Knowledgebase articles that ship with dBASE PLUS, and authored the original dBASE PLUS tutorial. Some of the material in this book will look suspiciously familiar to any who have used the Knowledgebase.

Ken has also been the librarian of a freeware library of code made available to all dBASE developers called the dBASE Users' Function Library Project (dUFLP) for so long he's lost count. He has been a speaker at Borland and other conferences on dBASE, speaking about coding techniques.

Ken is the author of The dBASE Book, and The dBASE Reports Book.

At the time the book is being published Ken is looking for full-time work – the school he was working at for 8 years shut down suddenly due to a variety of issues we don't need to get into here (let's not open those wounds again).

When not working, Ken is very active in the Society for Creative Anachronism, Inc. (http://www.sca.org), and enjoys cooking, movies, games, and reading.

Ken lives in Walnut Creek, CA with his wife Carolyn Eaton.

(Photograph of the author is by Sandra Linehan, December, 2012)

Introduction

Between dBASE II and Visual dBASE 5.x, a great number of books were written about dBASE. With the 32-bit versions of dBASE (Visual dBASE 7.x, dB2K and dBASE PLUS), even data became objects, ruled by object-oriented programming. In order to deal with these new data objects (data modules, queries, rowsets, and even field objects) a new language was created: OODML. This has created a steep learning curve for developers fluent in the 16-bit versions of dBASE, as well as those new to dBASE. When books were needed more than ever, only one book was published *(until I wrote mine)* about the 32-bit versions of dBASE (Ted Blue's courseware book <u>The dBASE Developer – Book 1: Getting Started</u>).

I wrote three editions of <u>The dBASE Book: Developing Windows Applications with dBASE PLUS</u>, the last in 2013. The third edition was a pretty comprehensive edition, up-to-date at the end of the life cycle of dBASE Plus 2.8. The problem was: at the time I was finishing the third edition, the developers at dBASE were about to release dBASE Plus 8, which added a lot of new features. I decided to stop at that time. *(This was really simply a bad timing issue, and no one's "fault".)*

<u>The dBASE Book Plus: A Companion to The dBASE Book</u> is basically meant to be an enhancement to the third edition of <u>The dBASE Book</u>. The use of this book assumes you have the third edition handy (both volumes), as it will not repeat information in those books except as necessary to explain new functionality, new features, or changes to the software.

Since the third edition of <u>The dBASE Book</u> was published, the developers at dBASE have released dBASE Plus 8 (and updates/fixes), dBASE Plus 9 (through 9.5.1), and dBASE Plus 10.

There will be further updates of course to dBASE Plus, and over time I may chronicle them. In the meantime, keep your eyes on the dBASE Plus support newsgroups, ask questions, make suggestions (the wishlist group), report bugs, and good luck with your coding!

It should be noted to developers that dBASE, LLC is releasing a major release every year – this is not to mess with you, the people who rely on it, it is a revenue issue for a small company. They are producing a great product that many developers rely on to make a living. The difficulty is that they also need to make a living *(and their investors need to see a positive revenue stream or they will stop investing)*. I have seen users of dBASE cry out in anger or frustration that there's a new build and they have to pay for it, but do keep in mind that without you paying for the new builds, they cannot afford to keep fixing issues that you may have with the software or enhancing the software with new features and functionality. It's a two-way street. *(Also keep in mind I haven't worked for dBASE for many years, and they did not ask me to write this … I'm just trying to be fair and get you to think equitably about this.)*

Acknowledgments and Thanks

I would like to thank the people who have helped make this book possible. While I cannot thank by name every single person who may have contributed indirectly to the writing of this book, I would like to thank the following specifically.

The dBASE Community

Thanks to the dBASE community for the encouragement which helped me to decide that writing this book was a good idea. I cannot possibly name everyone who sent me "Please do this!" messages, either in private email or in the newsgroups, but my thanks to you all.

In addition, when I posted messages asking for ideas or specific information in the dBASE newsgroups many people came forward with their thoughts, advice, and assistance, sometimes providing code samples. Some of these folk are mentioned by name in the book, where I have referenced posts by them in the dBASE newsgroups, code I am using of theirs, etc. Again, thanks to you all.

Contributors

Others who have contributed to this book in some fashion, and who have given me permission to use or reference materials of their own – in no specific order: Mervyn Bick, Andre Knappstein, Ronnie MacGregor, Bruce Beacham, Heinz Kesting, John Noble, Bernard Mouille, Ivar B. Jessen, Jan Hoelterling, Rick Miller, Omer-Pitou, and Gerald Lightsey.

At dBASE, LLC

Michael Rozlig, CEO of dBASE, Inc. Michael has ensured I was part of the Beta team, meaning I had access to current versions of the software, and was able to stay on top of things.

Marty Kay, head of R&D has always been pretty straightforward, although quite politic, when dealing with issues. I worked with Marty when the company was dBASE, Inc., all those years ago. The interesting thing is that I have never met him. Suffice it to say that when I bring an issue to his attention he is usually very fast to turn things around, even it if it means telling me I forgot something or made a stupid error in my own code.

Kathy Kolosky, a woman of many talents. Again I have never met Kathy, but she's always tried her best to be helpful, whether in a Tech Support position, QA (my old job), or working on the Project Explorer and trying to provide as much help as she can. She has tried hard to provide assistance as I stumbled through aspects of this edition of the book.

My Wife

Last, but far from the least, I need to thank my wife of twenty-one years *(as of the time this version of the book becomes available)*, Carolyn Eaton, for being supportive of pretty much everything I do. When I wrote the 1st and 2nd Editions of the <u>The dBASE Book</u>, it was a tough time financially. However, she supported this effort despite the difficulties with nary a complaint. All the time I worked on the book I was also looking for work, and trying to pick up some paying contracts. Now she puts up with me muttering and mumbling while I work on the text, and sometimes cursing and swearing when a code example doesn't work. And of course, I am now looking for full-time employment again and she's supporting me again *(sigh)*. She has always been supportive – how can you ask for more? There are simply not enough words to thank her ... except to say "I love you!"

Terminology

A minor note about terminology throughout the book ...:

When I write I tend to sound things out in my head. When I discuss things like file extensions, I tend to pronounce the period as "dot". Hence you will see interesting syntax such as:

"A .INI file"

In this case, if you pronounce the period as "dot", using the letter "A" is correct. If you do not, and instead pronounce it without, then correct English would be to state:

"An .INI file"

I prefer the former option. The editors of the 3rd Edition of <u>The dBASE</u> Book questioned this in various places throughout the book, and I chose to leave the text as is in these cases. I hope this does not offend anyone's sensibilities *(although if it does, well, it's my book ...)*! And many thanks to my editors for putting up with my quirks and helping me correct my English, making this book easier to read.

Part I: Getting Started

The folk at dBASE have made some major updates to the way that dBASE looks, and the way parts of it work. This is to make the software look more modern, rather than just an update to a product from the 80s. The first part of this section of the book will deal with showing the updates.

Chapter 1: Setup and Parts of the Environment

These days, dBASE Plus usually arrives in a downloaded executable, which when run will install the software. In older versions it came on a CD, but that seems to be in the past, although I suspect if you contacted the folk at dBASE, Inc., you might be able to still receive a CD.

Once you run the installation, many things get installed for you, including dBASE itself, the runtime engine, the Borland Database Engine, and new to dBASE Plus 8, new images from GlyFX and some new resource files containing images that can be used in your applications. The image and resource libraries are buried deep in the folder structure of Windows, and in Chapter 7 we'll discuss how to find and use these.

This chapter is aimed at getting you started, so – away we go.

Getting Started

In The dBASE Book, 3rd Edition, a lot of effort was put into Chapter 1 to discuss the way that the Windows User Account Control works, and how dBASE applications work with it. This has not changed in Windows 7, Windows 8, or Windows 10. It is not necessary to go back over all that again here, so we will move on and discuss dBASE itself.

Starting dBASE Plus

When you run dBASE the first time, you should see a routine "InitUser" execute, this should only run the first time, but if you upgrade dBASE from 8 to 9, or 9 to 10, etc., this will run again. It is used by dBASE to ensure that various settings are created – all in the background. dBASE Plus now opens on the IDE (Integrated Developer Environment) directly *(see "dQuery" below)*, with the usual Navigator and Command Windows open.

Look and Feel

One of the big things is that the overall appearance of dBASE has changed. This is due to changes in the use of the Microsoft Foundation Classes, and a complete change to the dBASE codebase. The look and feel of dBASE *(which you have some control over)* has changed, and there are a lot of change to the way windows are handled *(docking, and more)*.

Some changes are fairly basic. The toolbar in dBASE has changed to use new graphics, has a more modern appearance, that kind of thing. Other things include a new Tabbar under the toolbar. Forms that are open in the IDE have tabs, and you can use this functionality in your own code *(handy for an MDI application with multiple forms open)*.

Figure 1-1

Figure 1-1 above shows the titlebar, menubar, speedbar or toolbar, and the new tabbar *(the tabbar is the part with two tabs at the bottom of the image showing the Navigator window currently has focus)*.

TabBar

You can turn the TabBar on or off using *_app.TabBar*. The default setting for this property is *true*. In the IDE the tabs can be set to appear at the bottom of the dBASE frame window ("View" menu, "MDI Tabs", "On Bottom"). This is of course a developer preference issue. This might be useful in your application as well, you can set the *_app.TabBar* property to false, and in your application the *TabBar* will not appear. This will be discussed again in Chapter 15 (deploying an application), as you may or may not wish to use these in your own programs.

Application Theme

The Application Theme allows the developer to work with a variety of color themes. You can see and select different themes from the "View" menu, and from there "Application Theme". These are pre-defined, and while there is a "Customize Theme…" option, it is currently disabled. This hints that in some version of dBASE in the future the developer may have the ability to select colors, maybe even fonts for the application.

You can specify a theme for your own application by adding information in the .INI file – this will be discussed in Chapter 15 (deploying an application) in more detail.

dQuery – No Longer the Startup Program

In older versions of dBASE (up through dBASE Plus 2.8), dQuery was the "startup" program. I usually suggested turning it off, as a developer. dBASE Plus versions 8, 9 and 10 do not start with dQuery anymore.

In current versions of dBASE, dQuery is gone. In its place is a Data Module Designer (which will be discussed in a later chapter). It is my understanding that in a future release of dBASE Plus, there may be a new version of dQuery, whether or not it will be the "startup" program is another story. At the time this book is being completed, with dBASE Plus 10 released to market, this has not changed.

Some Basic Setup

dBASE PLUS has quite a few defaults that are set up for you when the program is installed. You may wish to alter the behavior of dBASE, however.

To that end, you should become familiar with the Desktop Properties Dialog, which we are now going to look at (briefly – focusing on changes). If you wish to follow along and look at this dialog at the same time, feel free to do so.

For the time being, start dBASE PLUS.

To get to the Desktop Properties, click on the "Properties" menu in dBASE, and select "Desktop Properties". Note that you can also type the word "SET" in the Command Window and press the Enter key, and you should see the same.

The Desktop Properties dialog has not changed a *lot* since dBASE Plus 2.8, however, to the right of the Source Aliases tab are a couple more. We need to discuss those tabs in particular.

Figure 1-2

The User BDE Aliases tab of this dialog can be gotten to by using the arrow buttons on the upper right corner of the dialog (circled in red in Figure 1-2 above). The purpose of this is to allow you to add your own User BDE Aliases, a topic that is discussed heavily in the 3rd Edition. These will be stored in the Plus.ini file.

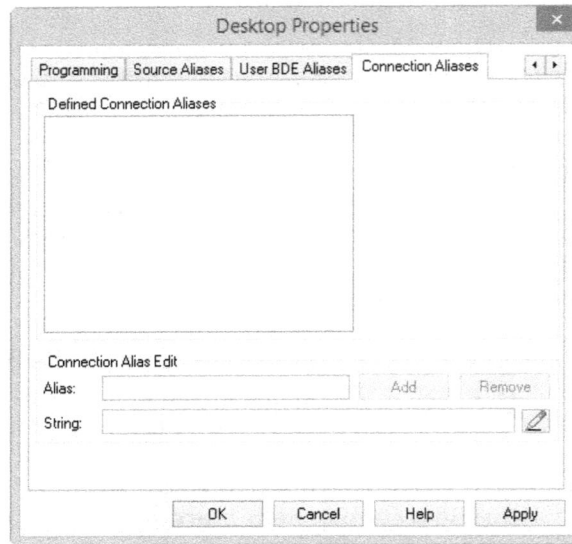

Figure 1-3

The Connection Aliases dialog is used to set up database connections for use with ADO. This will be discussed more in Chapter 2 of this book.

If you have made any changes, clicking "Apply" will cause them to go into effect now, and "OK" will do the same and close the dialog. If you have not made any changes, you can click "OK" and have no effect, or you can click "Cancel" to close the dialog, and you can click "Cancel" if you made changes you don't wish to save.

The Command Window

The Command Window does not *appear* to have changed much, but there are some new capabilities added in. These might be a little confusing at first. The big one is *dComplete*, a feature added in dBASE to help you build commands. As you start typing a command, dBASE pops up a window with options – this follows as you type, and if you find the item you want, you can just press the Tab key – it will be entered into the command for you. This functionality also appears in the Source Code Editor.

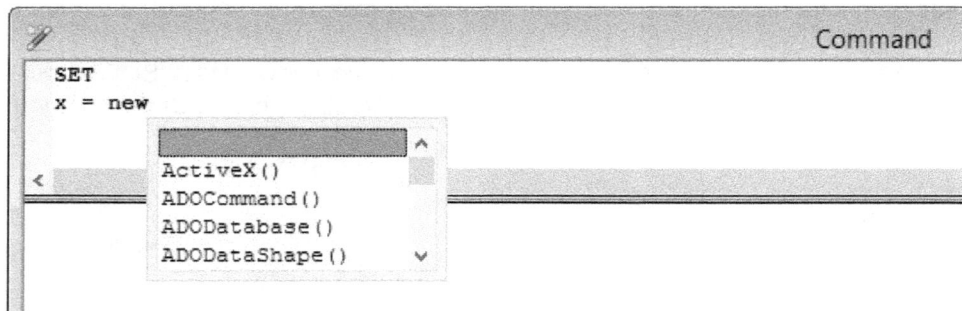

Figure 1-4

This may take some getting used to working with (*I still get a little frustrated with it at times, but I'm getting better*).

The Designers

The Designers for Forms and Reports (and Labels) have not changed a lot. You will see that the palette windows tend to be docked to the frame window. You can drag them out of "docking" mode by holding the mouse on the titlebar and dragging them to a new location. You can resize the various palettes as well.

One thing that is very handy – when working on a Form (or Report, or …), the form is added to the TabBox (discussed earlier in the chapter) with its own tab. If you click on the Navigator (or Command) window to give it focus, the new form will fall behind that window. However, rather than moving things around, digging in menus, whatever to find the window for the form to give it focus again, click the Tab in the Tabbox and the form will reappear on top.

SQL and Data Module Designers

There have been some major changes in these tools, and they will be discussed in other chapters of this book.

The Source Code Editor

A lot of effort has been put into the Source Code Editor for dBASE starting with dBASE Plus 9. Included in the new Source Code Editor are such features as:

- dComplete
- dLocator
- dBabble
- dBlocks

In addition, you have the ability to see Line Numbers and much more. Some features you can turn on and off. From the Source Code Editor Properties dialog (right click in the editor and select "Source Editor Properties"):

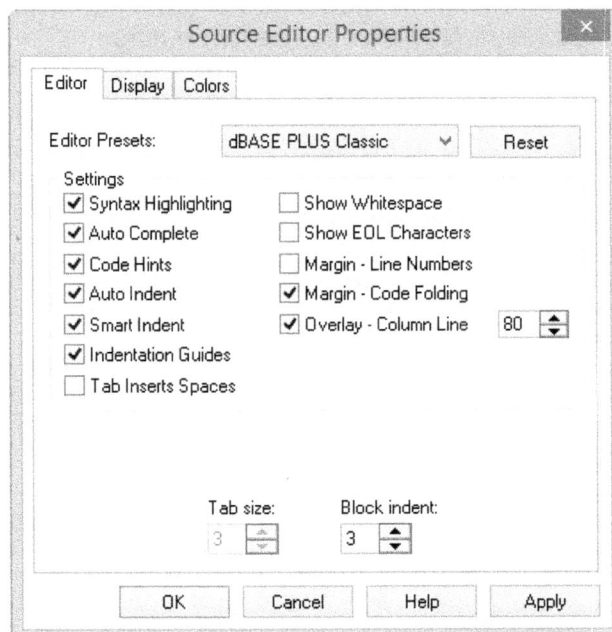

Figure 1-5

I tend to turn on "Tab Inserts Spaces", which is useful at least for this book, because it requires that I get spaces instead of tab characters *(when copy and pasting code into the book this was very handy – it meant a lot less reformatting)*. I also really like having line numbers, so I turn that on. Many of these features will take getting used to, but once you do, you may wonder how you ever coded without them!

dComplete

As mentioned in the section on the Command Window, this really handy feature assists you by helping find the command, avoiding typos, etc. Interestingly enough it will find the names of objects and variables in the current code you are working on, and help there as well.

One thing that to note is that you may want to use "Tab" to accept the current item in the list, otherwise sometimes you may end up with either the wrong selection, or worse, a blank solution, which defeats the purpose.

dLocator

The following is from the OLH discussing the Source Code Editor.

> dLocator (Find in File) is a new search engine for finding text in multiple files and producing the results of this search to quickly open files associated with the search.

> The dLocator pane (bottom pane) can be sized to make room for more or less of the code. Use the mouse to hover over the divider and move the line to view more or less of the top or bottom pane. NOTE: this pane will not be visible until you do a Find in File search, at which time it will open with the search results.

> The dLocator pane will show the results of searches when doing a Find in File search (Edit | Search | Find in File). The Find in File search option uses a search engine to search through many files. The results in the dLocator pane can then be used to open any file that is found with the search parameters. To open one of the files in the results just double click on the line in the results and it will open the file in the Code view pane above.

Selecting (as noted) the menu options, filling in some information (I told it to search for "Test"), you can see what happens here:

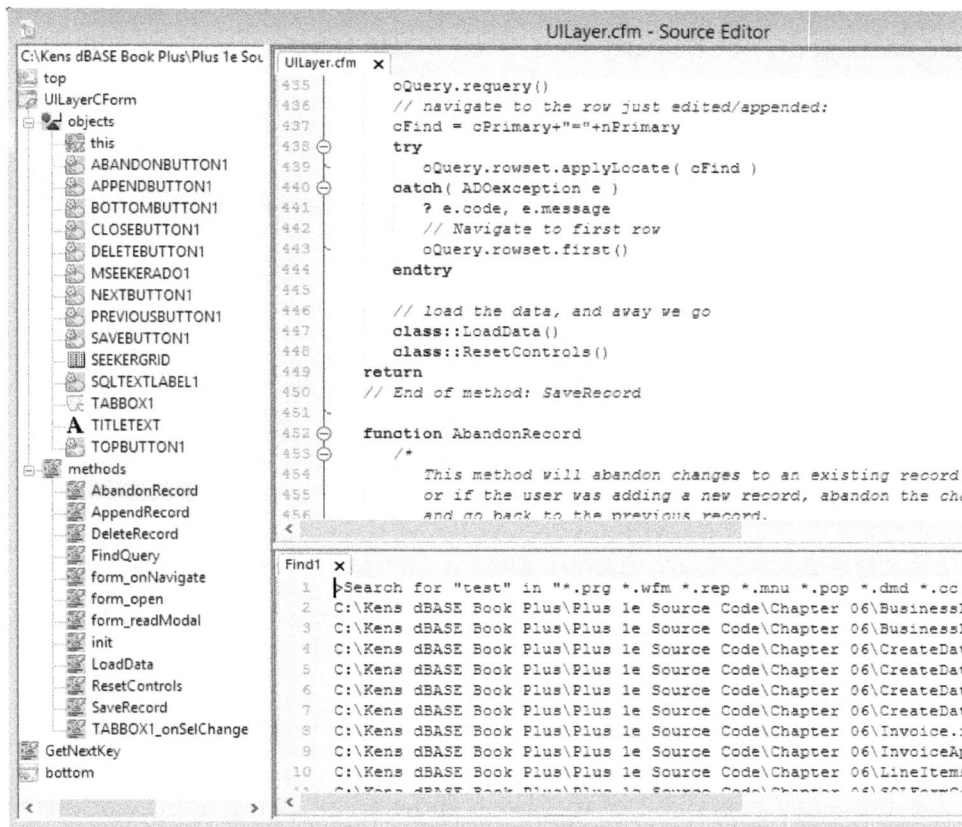

Figure 1-6

Selecting a file will open it in the Source Code Editor with its own tab ...

dBable

This feature of dBASE allows you to add other programming languages that the Source Code Editor can work with. You can also define your own properties file for use with this. Currently this recognizes Java, HTML, C++, PHP, SQL, XML and others. What does that mean? It means that you can use the Source Code Editor in dBASE to edit source code for other programming languages. For example, if you wanted to work on a .PHP file (a web programming language), you could open that file in the dBASE Source Code Editor, and many of the features of the Source Code Editor should work.

With all that in mind, please understand that dBASE itself has *no* idea how to actually compile or execute these files – this is only for use in the Source Code Editor. *(I mention this because I know at least one developer thought they could build C++ applications using dBASE, and had to have that explained ...)*

dBlocks

Added to dBASE Plus 10, this functionality, also called *abbreviations*, allows you to define blocks of code that can be inserted into your own code, by typing a key word that you define, and then either typing Ctrl+B or using the "Edit" menu and selecting "Expand Abbreviation". The idea is that if you have specific code that you use consistently throughout your applications, you can have dBASE fill it in for you.

A couple of examples of this are shown below – in the Source Code Editor, if you type:

```
ifelse
```

and then press **Ctrl+B**, the Source Code Editor would expand this out:

```
if

else

endif
```

If you type:

```
trye
```

and press **Ctrl+B**, the Source Code Editor would expand it out to:

```
try

catch (exception e)

endtry
```

There is a table in Appendix 3 of this book showing all of the abbreviations that are in the standard abbreviation file for dBASE – stored here as a text file:

```
C:\Users\UserName\Documents\dBASE\Plus10\Properties\abbrev.properties
```

There is also an example of adding your own abbreviations into the file.

Other New Features

There are a lot of interesting coding features built in to the Source Editor. Here are a few you might like:

Code Folding

With a large amount of code, there are always blocks of code that are marked at the beginning and end by specific words: IF/ENDIF, DO/WHILE/UNTIL, and so on. The Source Code Editor allows you to collapse *(dBASE uses the term "fold", but in my head I am seeing the code collapse)* that code while working –if you have a set of code that is working but you don't need to see it right now so you can focus on another set of code, you can fold it:

```
461
462 ⊖    if form.append
463 ⊖        if not form.rowset.next(-1) // previous record -- if we error
464             form.rowset.first()       // first record
465             // form_onNavigate event handler calls LoadData method
466         endif // navigate
467 ⊖    else
468 ⊖        // If here, user was not appending, but editing, re-load the
469         // current row's data from the table:
470         class::LoadData()
471     endif // form.append
472
473 ⊖    // reset appearance of controls and some of the
474     // custom properties:
475     class::ResetControls()
476 return
477 // End of method: AbandonRecord
```

Figure 1-7

Note the red circled "-" symbol on the left next to line 462? If you click this, notice that the code down to the "else" statement at 467 will collapse:

```
459     form.append = false
460     endif
461
462 ⊕    if form.append
467 ⊖    else
        // If here, user was not appending, but editing, re-load the
469     // current row's data from the table:
470     class::LoadData()
471     endif // form.append
472
473 ⊖    // reset appearance of controls and some of the
474     // custom properties:
475     class::ResetControls()
476 return
477 // End of method: AbandonRecord
```

Figure 1-8

Note that the "-" has changed to "+" – clicking that will expand (or "unfold") the collapsed (folded) code.

This is not permanent, and it you close the Source Editor and reopen the same file, the lines that were collapsed are not collapsed.

Auto Comment

You can select a set of code, and tell dBASE to comment it out – multiple lines at once. Selecting a set of lines of code, you can then go to the "Edit" menu and select "Comment Lines". There is also an option to "Uncomment Lines" in the menu:

```
285
286             // not found, assign null value ...
287         if not bOK
288             form.aSQLControls[ nControls ].value := null
289         endif
290
291 //      // set some custom properties:
292 //      form.aSQLControls[ nControls ].newValue := null
293 //      form.aSQLControls[ nControls ].oldValue := ;
294 //          form.aSQLControls[ nControls ].value
295 //      form.aSQLControls[ nControls ].modified := false
296 //      form.aSQLControls[ nControls ].error    := false
297 //      // set colors (constants in SQLFormControls do not carry over):
298 //      form.aSQLControls[ nControls ].colorNormal    := "WindowText/Window"
299 //      form.aSQLControls[ nControls ].colorHighlight := "WindowText/0x80ffff"
300         next // nFields
301     next // nControls
302
```

Figure 1-9

This might be useful when testing some code, not executing part of it, and then coming back, highlighting the same code and uncommenting it.

Notice that there are some lines in the example in Figure 1-9 that were already commented. If you select Edit | Uncomment Lines, the comments at the far left are removed, but the others are not, leaving the comments intact.

dExtract

This one is mentioned in and has its own topic in the OLH – it allows you to take an existing file, and save it to another file type. Example, you might wish to take a .TXT file and save it as a .HTM file. You can do that by opening the .TXT file in the Source Editor, going to the "Edit" menu, and selecting "Copy to File". This will give you the option(s). The folk at dBASE do not guarantee that the new document will run properly – if you convert a .txt file to a web page (.htm or .html) it would need to have the appropriate HTML tags in it, for example.

There are other features but most of them you should be able to figure on your own. I wanted to highlight a few just to give you a feel for the changes.

Online Help

The OLH has been enhanced starting with dBASE Plus 8, to include links to the Knowledgebase, FAQs (Frequently Asked Questions) and the newsgroups, which means you don't have to remember where they are on the dBASE website!

dPreview

This is a new feature that allows you to preview something before printing it, and you can print from the preview window. It allows zooming in and out, changing the view from one to two page view, and more.

This can be used within the IDE from the File menu, and selecting "Print Preview". You can even do a print of the Command Window. A specific file must be open in some fashion if you wish to preview it, so for example, if you open a program in the Source Editor, and then select File | Print Preview from the menu, you might see:

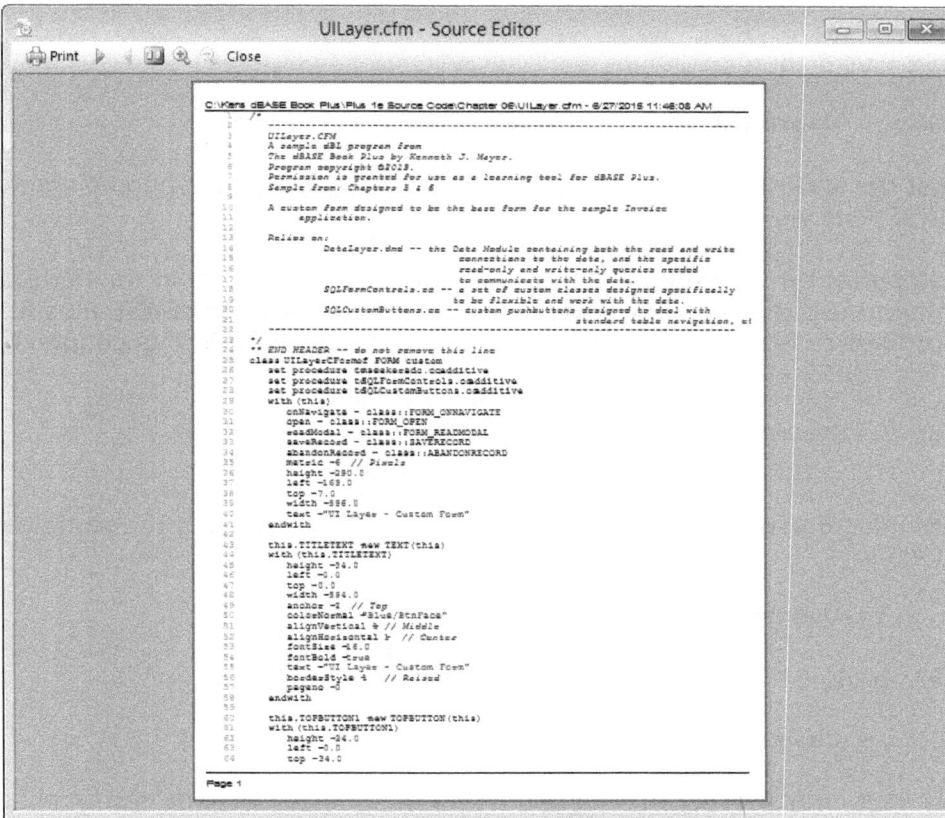

Figure 1-10

You can toggle to two page view, you can zoom in and see the text in a larger view, you can scroll through the pages, and of course you can print this.

Compiler

The dBASE Plus code compiler has been improved in several ways. Many users will not see some of this, but in dBASE Plus 10, the compiler is faster, and the symbol table has been improved. For some applications the symbols table could not handle the number of variables and objects that developers were using. The current symbol table is substantially larger and the beta testers were able to verify that their large applications were not having these problems anymore. This is discussed in a little more detail in Chapter 14.

File Locations

In dBASE Plus 2.8 and later, the developers have put a lot of effort into placing sample files, images, and other documents that come with dBASE in appropriate locations, based on MicroSoft's UAC and other specifications.

It is useful to know what files are stored where, so below are some basics breaking things out for dBASE Plus 8 & 9 and 10. It should be noted the file locations are the same for dBASE Plus 8 and 9, but dBASE Plus 10 has changed the file locations dramatically. Another thing to note is that the files may be in multiple locations (this is part of the Microsoft requirement), but the location you should *access* the files in may not be the obvious one.

BIN Folder –PLUS.INI
In dBASE Plus 8 through 10:

```
C:\Users\UserName\AppData\Local\dBASE\Plus9\Bin
```

Note that the **UserName** will be the Windows username of the person logged in. The dBASE Plus version number will vary as well.

This is important if you wish to check settings, change settings in the PLUS.INI file (or if you use the Debugger, the PLUSDEBUG.INI file), for dBASE Plus 8 and 9, the properties files used by the Source Editor (see earlier in this chapter), and so on. For dBASE Plus 10, the properties files are here:

```
C:\Users\UserName\Documents\dBASE\Plus10\Properties
```

Samples
In dBASE Plus 8 and 9, the Samples files are stored here (using the same caveats as above):

```
C:\Users\UserName\AppData\Local\dBASE\Plus9\Samples
```

However, in dBASE Plus 10, the Samples files are stored here:

```
C:\Users\UserName\Documents\dBASE\Plus10\Samples
```

This information is **important** – if you upgrade an application to dBASE Plus 10, and you use any of the sample code in your application (files such as Seeker.cc, Registry.prg, DataButtons.cc, etc.), you **need** to change the paths in your Project file – see also "Classes Files" below.

INCLUDE (Header Files)
The location of the "INCLUDE" files, which is important when using the dUFLP, as well as other tools, varies depending on the version of dBASE. In dBASE Plus 8 and 9:

```
C:\Users\UserName\AppData\Local\dBASE\Plus9\Include
```

In dBASE Plus 10:

```
C:\Users\UserName\Documents\dBASE\Plus10\Include
```

Classes Files
The "Classes" files are actually normally referenced via the Source Code Aliases :FormControls: and so on, but the physical locations vary from version to version of dBASE *(see note about Samples files above)*. In dBASE Plus 8 and 9:

```
C:\Users\UserName\AppData\Local\dBASE\Plus9\dBLClasses
```

In dBASE Plus 10:

```
C:\Users\UserName\Documents\dBASE\Plus10\dBLClasses
```

Labels Table
The Labels table is used by the Labels designer. There is even code in the dUFLP that works with this. In dBASE Plus 8 through 10:

```
C:\Users\UserName\AppData\Local\dBASE\Plus9\Designer\label
```

Images (glyFX and other) and Media Files
The location of the image files is very different in the different versions of dBASE. Again, you can get to these a little bit easier by using the Source Code Aliases, such as :GlyFx: and so on. In dBASE Plus 8 and 9:

```
C:\ProgramData\dBASE\Plus9\Media\
```

And in dBASE Plus 10:

```
C:\Users\Public\Documents\dBASE\Plus10\Media
```

This last is a rather dramatic change in the location of the files.

Knowing that all these differences exist will help a lot when you go to find specific files that are installed with dBASE.

Deployment
We will discuss deployment issues for deploying your own files in a later chapter of this book *(this will include where to place the .INI file, and so on)*.

Reports

The developers at dBASE, LLC have not really done much with reports in the latest versions. However, there are hints that in the future some interesting things may occur. I only mention it to whet your appetite. If you are familiar with reports in dBASE Plus, nothing dramatic has happened in this area, so your current reports will work fine.

Windows XP?

If you have users/clients still working with Windows XP, you cannot develop your applications in dBASE Plus 9.x or 10.x. Once Microsoft announced that they were done supporting Windows XP, the folk at dBASE decided to do the same. This actually makes it easier to move forward, with a goal (once a new database engine is created) of being able to create a full 64-bit version of dBASE, which Windows XP cannot handle. While dBASE is not at this point, there are aspects of Windows XP that current versions of dBASE cannot run on. The only reason to stay with dBASE Plus 8 (or earlier) is because you need to work with Windows XP.

Summary

For the most part, the dBASE IDE has changed mostly in appearance, but it definitely has a more modern feel to it, which was the goal. It can make your applications feel more modern as well.

The changes to the Source Code Editor are bound to be welcome to most developers, some of the features are ones that have been requested on and off for years.

Don't forget that Appendix 3 has a listing of all the "standard" abbreviations that can be used with dBlock in the Source Code Editor, and that you can modify the definitions or add your own.

Part II: Data

Working with data is what a database software package such as dBASE is all about. In <u>The dBASE Book</u> a lot of discussion is involved in working with the Borland Database Engine, and working with both local tables (.DBFs) and with SQL Server databases.

In <u>The dBASE Book Plus</u> the focus for this section of the book is going to be on SQL Server databases, and using ADO (<u>A</u>ctiveX <u>D</u>ata <u>O</u>bjects) to connect to them. The ADO database classes are a version of the OODML classes in dBASE designed to work with data – specifically bypassing the Borland Database Engine. This should allow for a deployment of an application that doesn't rely on the BDE as well.

Chapter 2: SQL Server Databases

dBASE has, since the Windows version was created at Borland, International all those years ago, relied heavily on the Borland Database Engine (BDE). The developers at dBASE, Inc. have been telling us that they are working on a new data engine to replace the BDE, but this is a difficult task at best, and we do not have a projected date at this time for when we might see it.

In the meantime, dBASE, Inc. has implemented ADO (ActiveX Database Objects) in dBASE (starting with dBASE Plus 8, and improved on over time), which work combined with OLE DB (Object Linking and Embedding Database) and ODBC (Open Database Connectivity) database drivers, and bypasses the BDE completely.

ADO is a Microsoft™ Technology, and you can of course research it in some detail on the web. For our purposes we will focus on the implementation in dBASE, and attempt to find the best methods for most applications.

For the purpose of this book we will focus on one (free) database server – Firebird, and how to set up a Firebird database, then connect to it using dBASE. I will be walking through a complete setup of Firebird, creating a database from scratch, and so on. I considered *(and started)* to work with MySQL, but found it to be particularly difficult/confusing to work with. This is not to say it cannot be done – there are developers in the dBASE community working with MySQL, and I have included the work I did for setup in the appendices. The goal for the book, however, is *not* a focus on Firebird – I am not endorsing any specific database product (other than dBASE, of course). Most of what is done in the book should be similar to what can be done in most or all of the database servers available.

SQL Databases

One of the first things that really needs to be discussed is why would you want to use a SQL Server Database, when dBASE works quite well with local tables (.DBFs, etc.).

The first issue is the BDE itself – it is quite outdated, as Borland stopped working on it many years ago – and the folk at dBASE, LLC cannot *(by contract)* modify the code for the BDE. They can't even update the codebase to 64-bit.

DBFs are limited in size – this is an old limitation that doesn't really make sense except that it is built into the table specifications and into the BDE. If you need really large tables, huge amounts of data, then at some point you may run into issues. Now that said, there are people who have had applications running for years with DBFs – there are many ways to deal with the limitations, and many applications never hit those limits in the first place. *(In other words, I am not shooting down the use of DBFs for an application, my own preference is to use them, DBF tables are what I am most comfortable with …)*.

In addition, you may need to use databases produced by others, you may want to create web-based applications or move your data to web-based applications at some point, etc.

So what is involved in working with SQL Databases?

The Basic Architecture of SQL Databases
The basics are:

- The Database Server
- Connections to the Data
  - Outside of dBASE
  - Inside of dBASE
- An Understanding of SQL

The Database Server is required to handle the processing of the data. With dBASE local tables, the database server is the database engine. So in this aspect, you might consider the database server to be equivalent to the BDE *(however, even if you use the BDE with SQL databases, you must have access to a database server AND the BDE)*. When you use a SQL database from dBASE, whether via the BDE or ADO, you are passing instructions to the database server, which then acts on them and returns what you need, updates the data as specified, etc.

If you are working independently, you need to have a database server set up so you can work with that specific software. In this book I will be using Firebird. There are many other databases out there, including (but not limited to):

- Oracle
- MSSQL
- Interbase
- Sybase
- Informix
- MySQL
- SQL Lite

These are the ones that immediately come to mind, I know there are others out there.

If you are working in a situation where the database server is already installed (for another business, for a company as a coder, etc.), then you may not need to install the server. You will need a username and password, which would need to be provided to you by the database administrator, as well as the name of the database so you can connect to it. If you are working on a web-based application, the odds are the server is probably already installed, and again you would need a username and password, as well as information on how to create/set-up/connect to the data.

Connections to the Data in Windows are created via ODBC and/or OLE DB, and are used to communicate from your software to the database server. These are necessary whether or not you need to install a database server. There are two parts to this – connections created via Windows *(this is the ODBC or OLE DB setup – two parts – you have to have the ODBC (or OLE DB) drivers, and you have to set up connections in Windows – drivers to the data)*, and connections *inside* dBASE. If not using ADO you need to set up BDE (or User) Database Aliases – these are discussed in some detail in <u>The dBASE Book</u>. For ADO you need to set up a connection that will allow the ADO classes to work with the data.

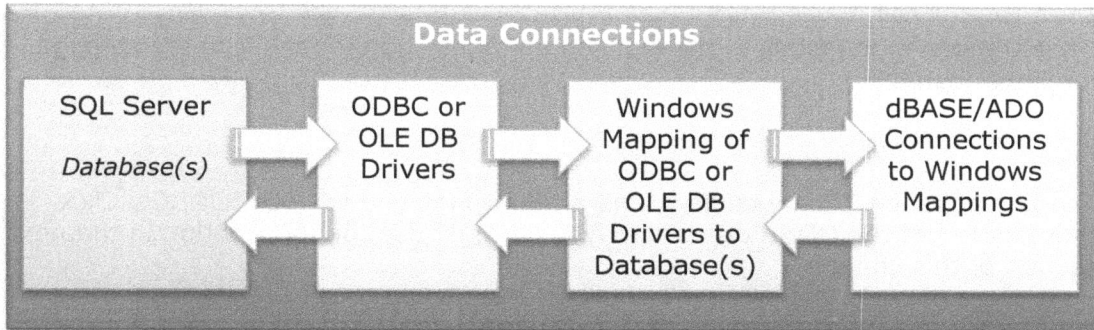

Data Connections			
SQL Server *Database(s)*	ODBC or OLE DB Drivers	Windows Mapping of ODBC or OLE DB Drivers to Database(s)	dBASE/ADO Connections to Windows Mappings

Figure 2-1

An understanding of the database language *SQL* is required to work with SQL databases. Much of the work you will be doing will require using SQL commands in more depth than if you work with the local DBF tables in dBASE. The dBASE OODML objects use SQL, so you may be familiar with some SQL, but you will be doing much more with SQL if you use SQL servers. Again, this topic is covered in some detail in <u>The dBASE Book</u>, so will be discussed only as needed in this one.

Firebird – A Free SQL Database Server

Why Firebird when there are many database servers available? Firebird works pretty well with dBASE, and always has, going back to Interbase *(which is now a separate, commercial, product)*, when dBASE was still a product belonging to Borland. In addition, Firebird is an open source database, which means that developers from around the world help improve it. <u>The dBASE Book</u> gives instructions for installing Interbase so it can be used with dBASE Plus, I chose to work with Firebird this time around.

If you have a different database server and have installed it, you can skip over the installation parts of the instructions here. However, you may want to look at the ODBC setup, some details will be different, but there are concepts you need to try to understand.

The main reason for installing the Firebird Server is if you need to be able to create your own database from scratch, and/or are not connecting to a different Firebird server. If, for example, the database server is installed on your company's network servers, you should not need to install the Firebird Server on your own computer to manipulate it. You would need a username *(which would be provided to you by your company's database administrator)*, information about the database itself *(name, where it is at, etc.)*.

Installing the Firebird Server
First you must download the Firebird Database Server software from:

```
http://www.firebirdsql.org/en/firebird-2-5-4/
```

Scroll down this web page and download the installer. There are 32-bit and 64-bit versions, depending on your version of Windows.

Installation is pretty straightforward, I opted to use all the defaults for the 64-bit version, as I am working with the 64-bit version of Windows.

Once the server is installed, the last screen takes you by default to a web page for "AfterInstall":

```
http://www.firebirdsql.org/en/afterinstall/
```

There is a link for "Connectivity", and on that page you will see "ODBC". Click that link to get the ODBC drivers. Or you can just use the information in the next section of this chapter.

Installing ODBC Drivers for Firebird

The ODBC drivers are based on the version of Windows (32-bit or 64-bit) you are using, you can get the drivers from this page:

```
http://www.firebirdsql.org/en/odbc-driver/
```

Once it is downloaded (this was pretty fast on my connection), find where it was downloaded to and run the executable. I chose a "Typical" install, from the screen with the options for different types of installation.

The ODBC driver has a couple of important options:

- Developer Install
- Deployment Install

We need the "Developer" install for starters, but if you intend to deploy an application, you will most likely need the latter.

Once you have installed the ODBC driver(s), you need to set up the ODBC side of things before you try to work with Firebird in dBASE.

ODBC Setup

For this example we're going to set up the default "Employee" database in Firebird. Later details will be given on creating your own database, with your own database name, and the ability to save the database where you want it to be stored.

Find the Control Panel in your version of Windows (in Windows 8, bring up the charms on the right side of the screen, go to "Settings", and then "Control Panel").

📝 NOTE

If you are using Windows 7, clicking the "Start" button, and selecting from the "All Programs", the "dBASE Plus" option, you will see a shortcut to the 32-bit ODBC Administrator. As Windows 8 and Windows 10 has changed the functionality of the "Start" button, you will need to use the instructions above if using that version of Windows. In Windows 10, "Search the web and Windows" – if you type "ODBC" the ODBC administrator will come up.

In the Control Panel, select "System and Security", and then "Administrative Tools". Select "ODBC Data Sources", and if you are running 64-bit Windows, select the 64-bit version.

> **📋 NOTE**
> According to sources at dBASE, the recommendation is that if you have a choice, you should use 32-bit ODBC drivers. The DSN is created as both 32 and 64-bit, and shows up in both 32-bit and 64-bit Administrator screens.

You should see a window very much like:

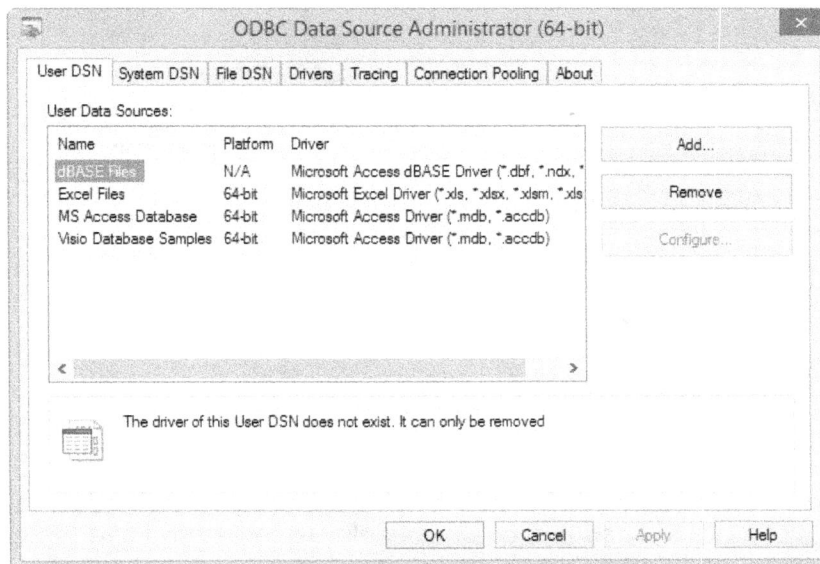

Figure 2-2

Click the "Add..." button to add a new ODBC Data Source.

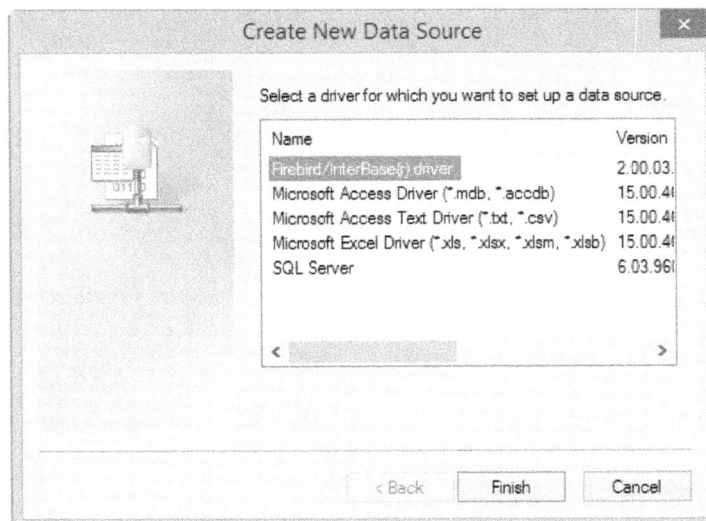

Figure 2-3

Select the "Firebird/Interbase(r)" driver, and click "Finish".

When you select the driver and then click "Finish" you will be asked for more information:

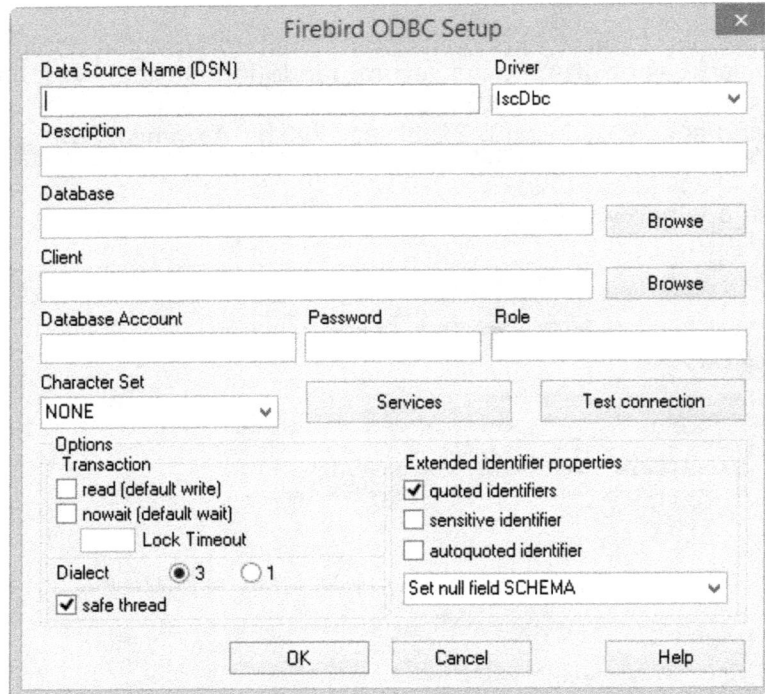

Figure 2-4

Data Source Name (DSN): The help for Firebird's ODBC drivers states that this is the name of the server, so it should probably be something like FBServer, although you can name it whatever makes sense to you.

Description: This is a useful when you have multiple database servers.

Database: Click the "Browse" button and drill down to here:

```
C:\Program Files\Firebird\Firebird_2_5\examples\empbuild
```

(Or the appropriate folder path on your installation), and find the EMPLOYEE.FDB file. Click that, and click "OK".

Client: is only required if you are using the embedded version of Firebird.

Database Account: The default username is *SYSDBA* in Firebird. If not used here, when you connect to the server to access the data you will be asked for a username and password.

Password: The default password is *masterkey*. See above.

Role: Not required.

Character set: Not required. What is not specified is what the recommended character set is. For this test I chose to use the *UNICODE_FSS* character set.

Figure 2-5

The screen should look like Figure 2-4 (above).

Before you click "OK, you should click the "Test connection" button. You should get the message: "Connection successful!" Click "OK".

The ODBC Data Source Administrator should now include your connection:

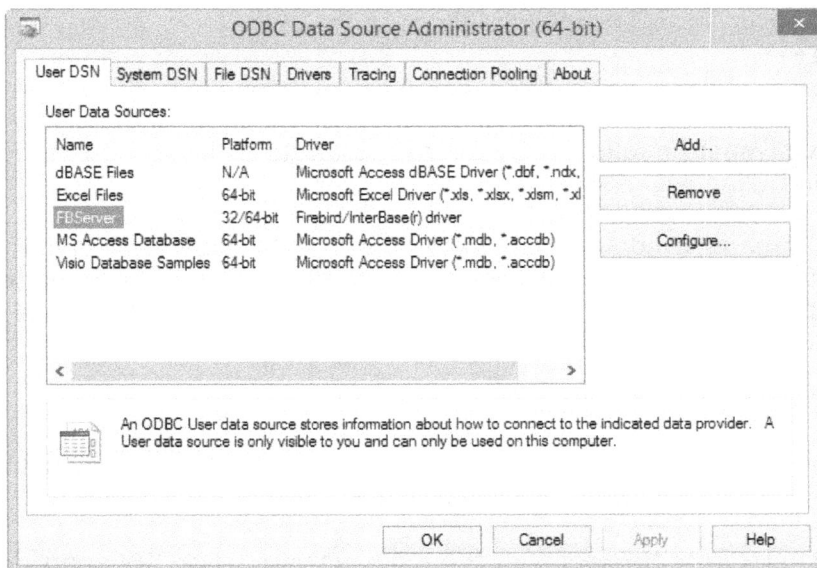

Figure 2-6

Clicking "OK", will close the ODBC setup screen.

The next section of this chapter will deal with setting up your own database, with your own name. By having this control, you can create multiple databases, give them names appropriate for the applications you are developing, and quite importantly, back them up easily. Again, if you are using a different database server, the instructions would obviously be different, but check for some concepts in these instructions (in the ODBC setup, if nothing else).

Create a Firebird Database

Firebird does not have a graphical user interface (GUI) for Windows. Without using a third-party tool, to create your own database you need to open a Command Window in Windows. In Windows 8, this is done by moving the mouse to the right, selecting "Search", and typing "cmd" in the search box and press Enter. *(In Windows 10, on the task bar in the "Search the web and Windows" box, simply type "cmd".)*

Navigate to the Firebird folder using the "CD" command *(this will be slightly different based on your own version of Windows, and how this was installed …)*, press the Enter key at the end of each line:

```
C:\Windows\System32>cd "\Program Files\Firebird\Firebird_2_5\bin"
C:\Program Files\Firebird\Firebird_2_5\bin>isql
SQL>
Use CONNECT or CREATE DATABASE to specify a database
SQL>create database 'C:\MyData\BookSample' page_size 8192
CON>User 'SYSDBA' password 'masterkey';
```

According to the Firebird manual, you can verify the database exists, by typing at the SQL> prompt:

```
SELECT * FROM RDB$RELATIONS;
```

This will show a lot of data in the Command Window – it is where the metadata is stored by Firebird. In the Command Window, type:

```
CON>exit;
C:\Program Files\Firebird\Firebird_2_5\bin>exit
```

The first "exit" must be followed by the semicolon to exit ISQL, the second closes the Command Window.

The DOS Command Window based method feels extremely "old school". The dBASE newsgroups are quite helpful, and from there Mervyn Bick pointed me at IBExpert, and noted there are both free and paid versions, but the free version will work for most people:

```
http://www.ibexpert.net/ibe/
```

He also mentioned a program called FlameRobin but finds while more intuitive than IBExpert, that it is not as powerful, either.

For the free version of IBExpert, on the main website, click "IBExpert download center", create a user account *(since that appears the only way that you can download this software)*, go through the process, and download the Personal Edition. The downloaded program is "setup_personal.exe". Like any tool, it will take getting used to, you will need to register any database that already exists that you wish to work with, then connect to it. Then you can use this interface to create tables, you can create new databases, and more.

WARNING: When I checked the folder the database was created in, ISQL did not add the file extension ".FDB", so I had to rename the database to include the extension (this was done using "File Manager" in Windows 8 *(which in earlier versions of Windows is "Windows Explorer")*.

Once the database has been renamed, you need to create **two** ODBC connections to it, following the steps given in the previous section, however, one of them needs to be set as "read-only". The reason for this will be explained early in Chapter 4.

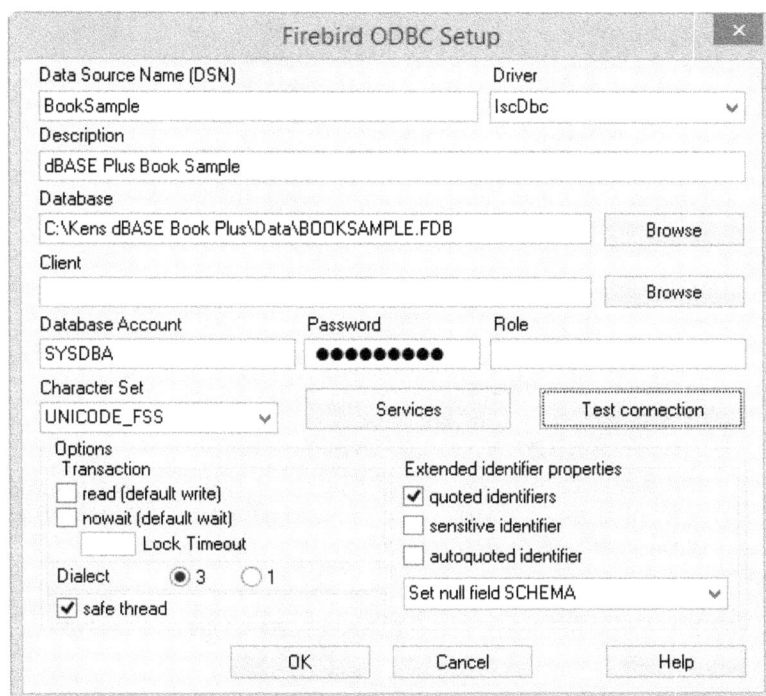

Figure 2-7

To set the second one, again, follow the same instructions as given earlier, but name the source "BookSample_RO" ("RO" for "Read-Only"), and check the box shown below:

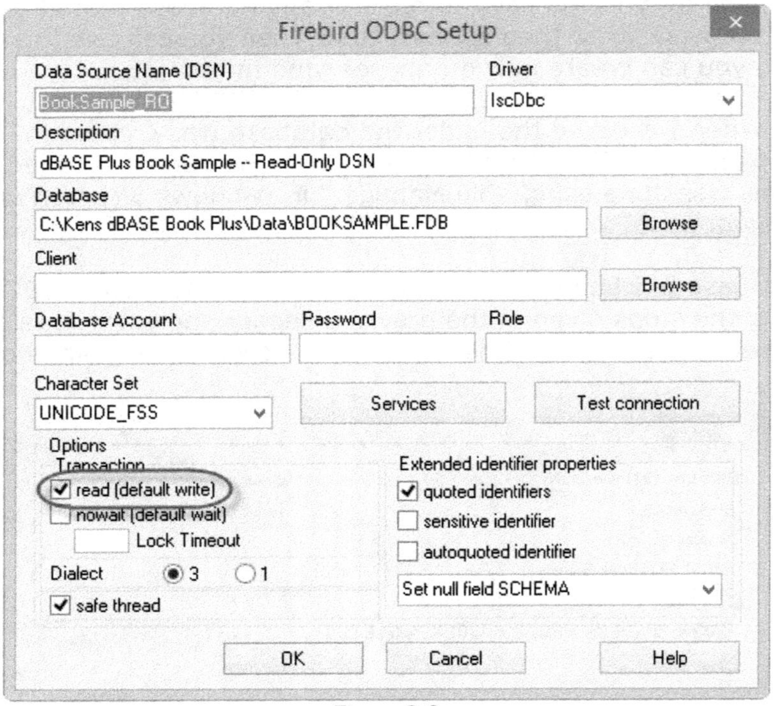

Figure 2-8

I left out the "Database Account" and "Password" here, which will be discussed in the discussion of users in this chapter.

Setup Connection Aliases in dBASE

At this point you still need to tell dBASE about your database. You will need to create two "Connection Aliases" here, one for each of the DSNs you created earlier. *(One is "read-only", the other allows for "write" access.)*

Start dBASE Plus *(8, 9, 10 …)* and select the "Properties" menu, select "Desktop Properties". Select the tab for "Connection Aliases".

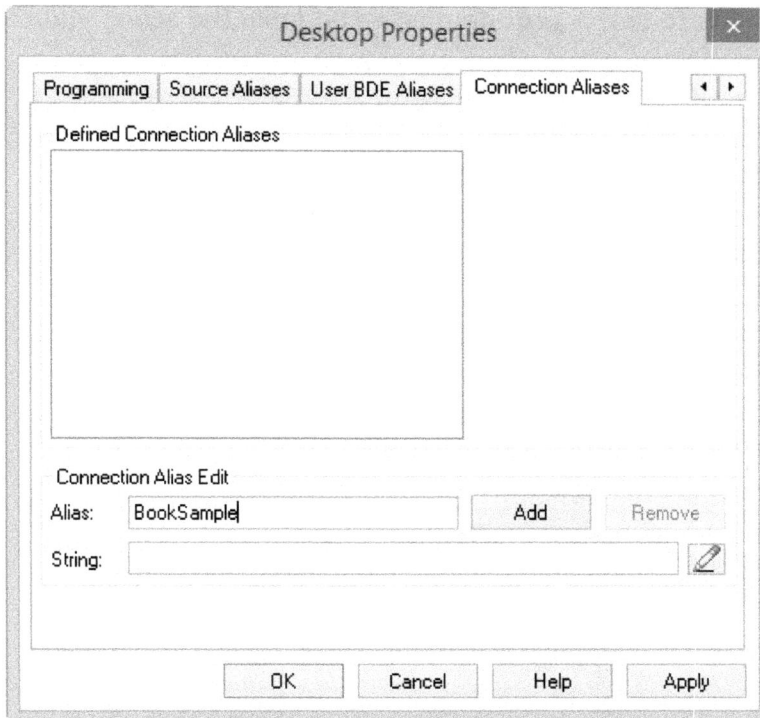

Figure 2-9

Enter the name of the alias, and then click the "Pencil" icon next to "String". A new dialog will appear:

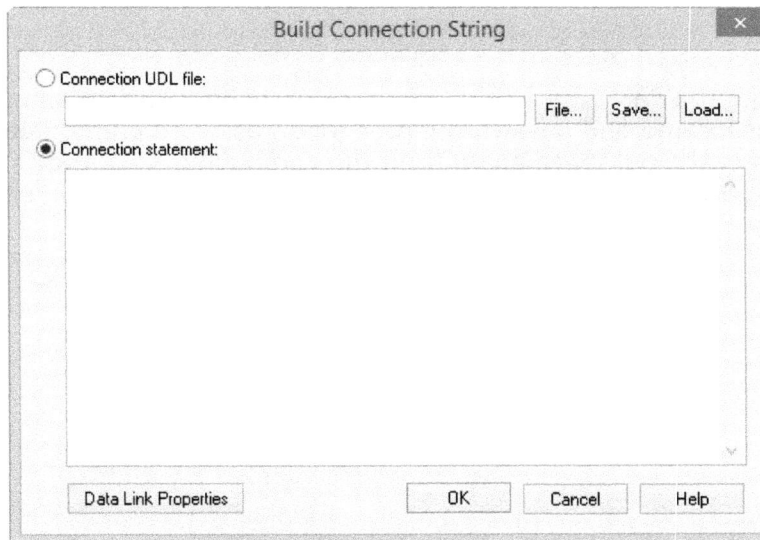

Figure 2-10

Select the "Connection statement:" radiobutton (if necessary), and then click the "Data Link Properties" button.

This will allow you to select your database and build the string and connection information needed.

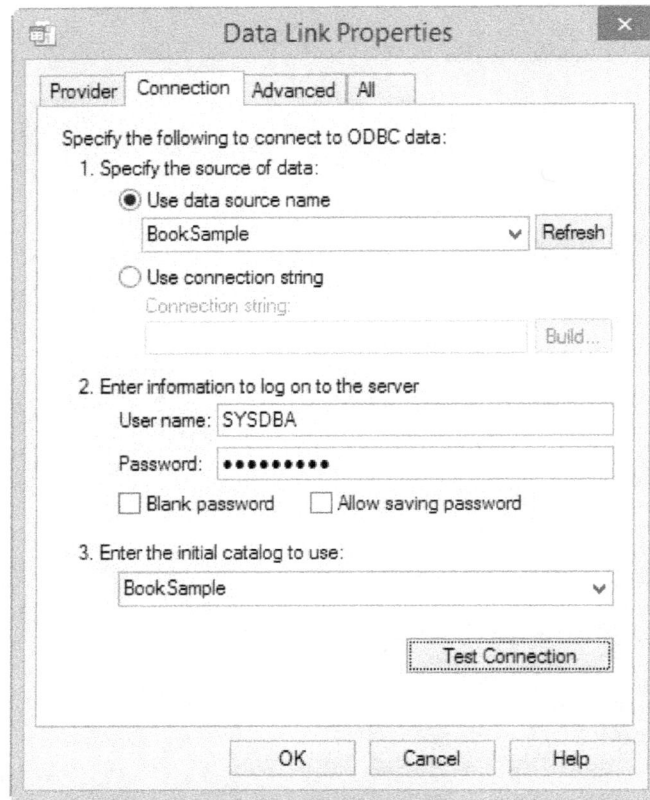

Figure 2-11

In part 1, select the database name from the combobox ("BookSample"), in part 2, enter the username and password ("root" and password created earlier), and for part 3, select the database again from the combobox. Click the "Test Connection" button. If you are able to connect, click "OK", and you should be back here:

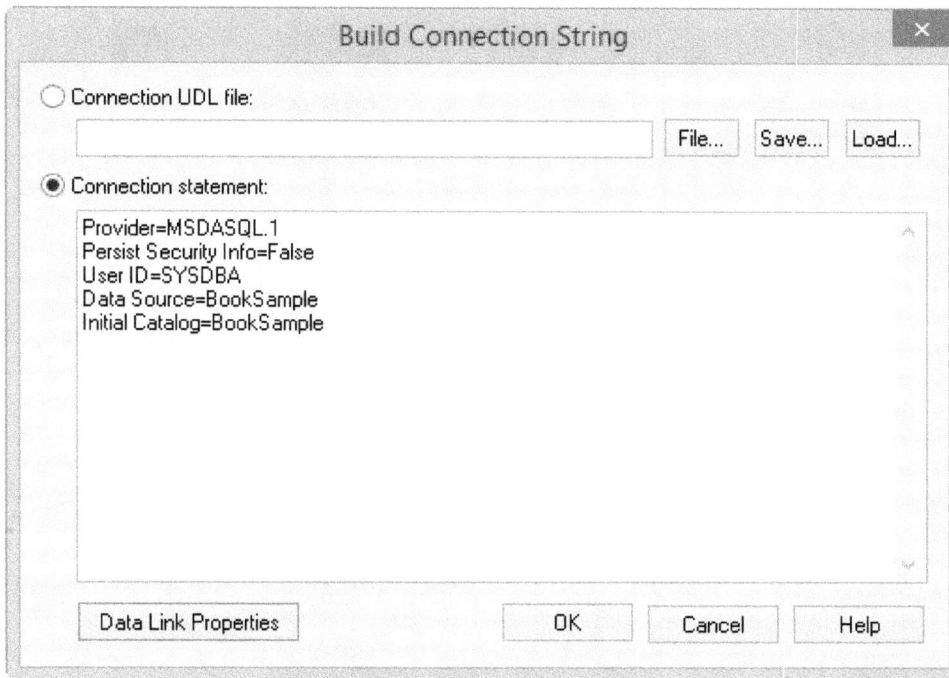

Figure 2-12

Click "OK". On the "Desktop Properties" dialog, click "Add". If dBASE already recognizes the alias *(if you used the same name as the ODBC driver, for example)* you will need to change the alias name (I added the text "_ADO" to "BookSample", which avoids confusing between the ADO Connection and the "normal" ODBC driver).

Click "Add", and the screen should look like *(Figure 2-13)*:

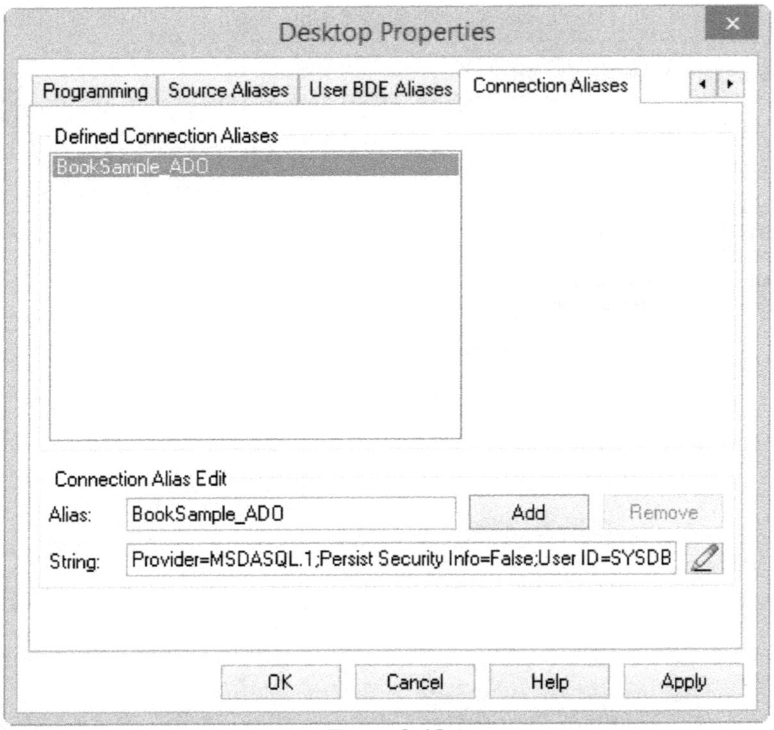

Figure 2-13

Click "OK", and now you have a connection you should be able to use with the ADO database classes.

Remember that you need to repeat this for the read-only Connection Alias. Make sure you select the read-only ODBC connection, and a name like "BOOKSample_ADO_RO" to avoid any confusion.

Users

As a developer it is likely you are going to need to have users, and with users you may need to deal with different permissions levels (you may want to have, for example, some users who are "read-only" – meaning they can view data, but not edit it, and so on).

Users can be added via IBExpert *(as well as other tools)*. Using IBExpert, connect to the database. On the "Tools" menu (or the toolbar) select the "User Manager" option.

Figure 2-14

Click the "Add User" button. Fill in the appropriate information. For example, I created a new user called "TestUser", with a new password of "User123". Note that as with most software, passwords are case-sensitive. In this example, obviously "User123" is not an ideal password, but for our purposes, it is easy to remember.

Figure 2-15

Once you have this, click "OK". The user will be created. However, by default, this user has limited permissions in the database.

Rather than using IBExpert (or some other GUI), the developers of Firebird have added some SQL statements you can use to add or remove users from a database, which can be passed to the server through the *database* or *ADOdatabase* objects, via the *executeSQL* method. These can only be executed by the SYSDBA user:

```
create user username password 'password'
alter user username password 'password'
drop user username
```

The password must be in quotes. The second statement above would let you change the password for the user.

You can also use parameters for Firstname, Middlename, and Lastname:

```
create user MyUser password 'MyPass' Firstname 'Fred' Middlename
'J' Lastname 'User'
```

This would create the user with the various fields filled in. It is a single statement, no wrapping of text. It should be noted that these are specific to Firebird, and I cannot guarantee that other database servers will have equivalent commands.

User Permissions

Unfortunately, the way to change permissions in IBExpert requires the use of the "Grant Manager", which is only available in the "Full" (paid) version of IBExpert, which I am not paying for at this time.

You can use the command line program "gsec" as mentioned earlier ("Create a Firebird Database"), which is tricky, or you can use SQL commands via the *executeSQL* method of the *database* or *ADODatabase* objects (an example will be shown in a later chapter).

```
create user User2 password 'NewUsr' grant admin role
alter user User3 grant admin role
alter user User3 revoke admin role
```

The GRANT and REVOKE parameters, as noted in the Firebird documentation, are parameters in this case to the CREATE USER and ALTER USER commands, not separate commands.

Co-Administrators

Administrator rights here are really what is called in Firebird "Co-Administrator" – the true administrator is the SYSDBA account.

The documentation for Firebird notes a few things:

- A Co-Admin can CREATE, ALTER or DROP a user, but they must, in the login screen, enter the role: RDB$ADMIN
- This is for the specific database only (meaning if the user has access to other databases, they are not automatically a co-administrator there …).

SYSDBA Account ,

If you are deploying an application, using it on a network (or on the web), you should change the default password from "masterkey" to something harder to crack. The default password is documented all over the place, and anyone could figure it out.

Database Security

One issue with databases is security. It is a good idea to not automatically log into the data. However, this does have its issues.

If you wish to set your database up so that it is *not* automatically logged into, you will need to make a couple of changes to the setup created earlier in the chapter.

First, the ODBC driver needs to have some changes made:

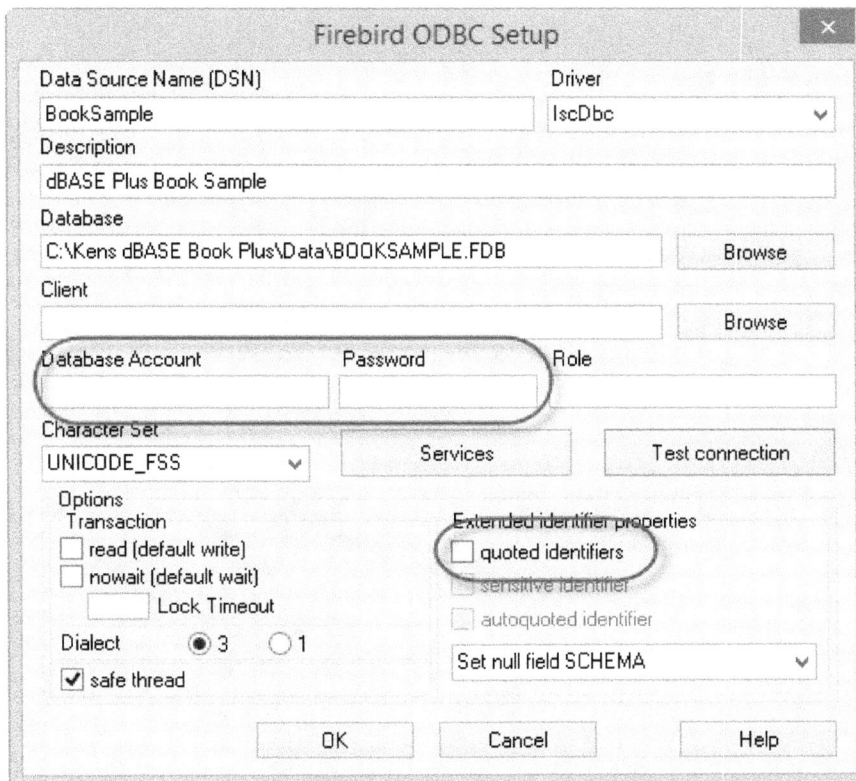

Figure 2-16

Open the ODBC driver *(when you get to the screen that lists your various drivers, select the one you wish to modify, and click the "Configure" button)*. On this screen, empty the "Database Account" and "Password" fields, and uncheck "quoted identifiers" as shown in Figure 2-16.

Click "OK" *(my attempt to "Test connection" failed here, because the Database Account and Password were empty)*. Close the ODBC Setup screen.

Close the other screens from the Control Panel, and then in dBASE, open the Desktop Properties dialog. In the "String" entryfield, enter:

```
Provider=MSDASQL.1;Persist Security Info=False;Data
Source=BookSample
```

With no quotes *(and do not press enter – the text above should be entered into the form in one line)*. Click the "Apply" button.

If you then attempt to open the database you will need to enter the Username and Password manually *(for Firebird, you can leave the "Role" entryfield empty)*. In code you can embed the *loginString* in the ADODatabase object, but otherwise your user will need to enter an appropriate Username/Password.

Note that if you are using two Connections as recommended, you will need to do the same change for the Read-Only connection. The string shown above for the second connection would be:

```
Provider=MSDASQL.1;Persist Security Info=False;Data
Source=BookSample_RO
```

Turning the Server On/Off

If you wish, you may turn the Firebird server off, or turn it on, manually. To do this, you need to get to the Control Panel in Windows. Select "System and Security", and from there, "Administrative Tools".

You need to open the "Services" option (double-click it), and in that window, you will see a list of all services available on your computer, and their current status.

If you scroll down the list you should see the Firebird server (or whatever server you have chosen to use).

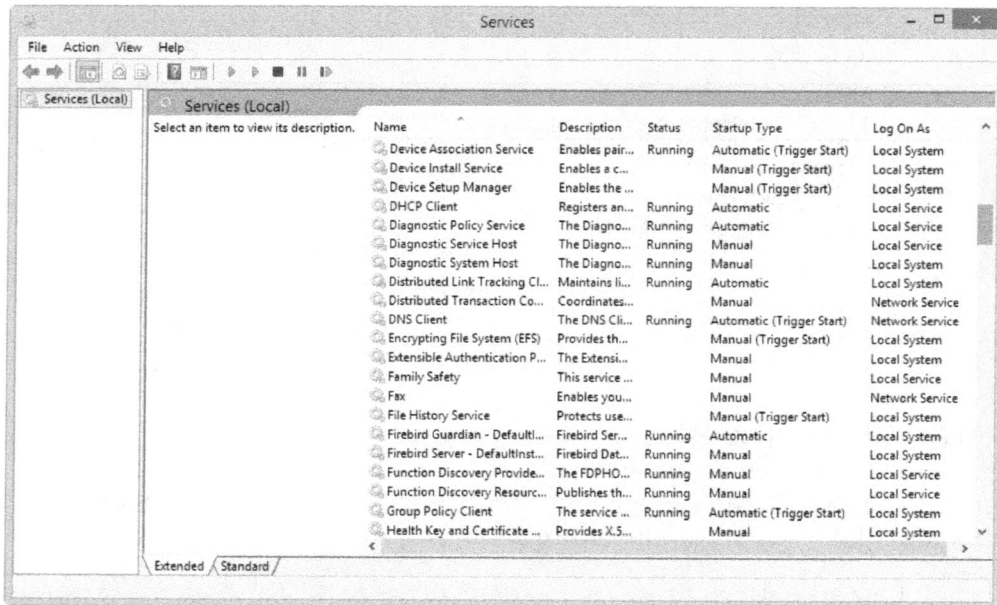

Figure 2-17

You can change the status / settings by double clicking the service, which will open this window:

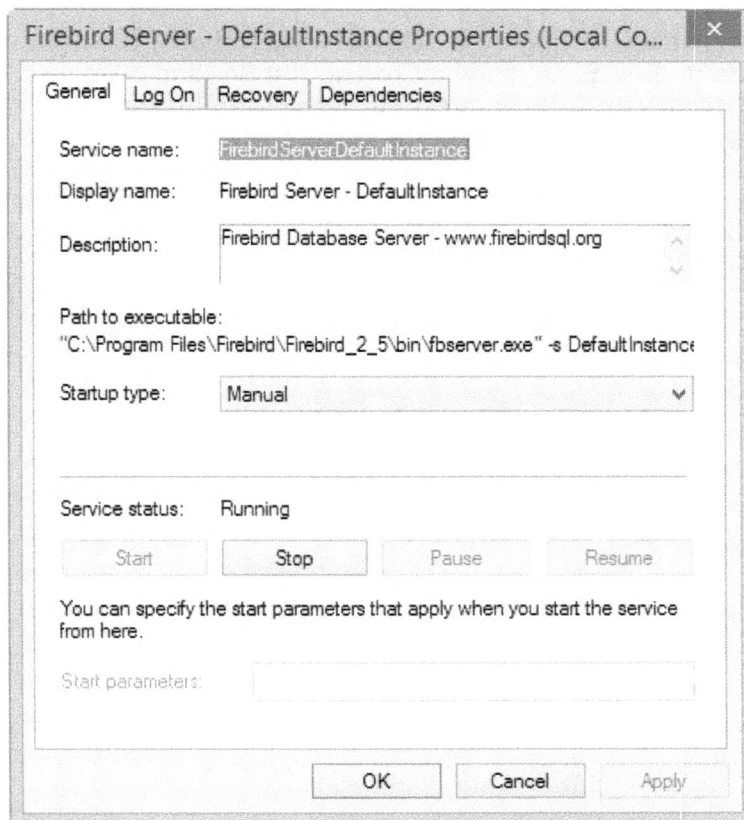

Figure 2-18

On this screen you can "Stop" the service, "Start" the service if it is stopped, you can change it from "Automatic" to "Manual" so that you can start it only when you want to work with your data (in which case you would need to start it before working ...), and so on. Windows is pretty flexible with this.

You may also want to turn off the Firebird Guardian service as well if you are turning off the server.

Summary

This chapter was about setting up a SQL Server database, the next will delve into the ADO objects in dBASE. If you want to use the Borland Database Engine, once you have the Server and ODBC drivers set for your database, the details are in <u>The dBASE Book</u> *(3rd Edition)*, Chapter 5.

In addition, the users in the dBASE Newsgroups are, as always, helpful and love to jump in with advice, information, etc. *(and I write this with as much awe and pleasure as I can put into words on a page – the helpful nature of the newsgroups is, I believe, one of the reasons dBASE has survived all these years).*

Chapter 3: ADO Database Classes

In Chapter 2 setting up the Firebird Database Server and connections was the primary focus. This chapter is going to emphasize using the *new-to-dBASE Plus 8* ADO Database Classes. These are based on the standard Microsoft ADO ActiveX controls, but are incorporated into dBASE itself. I will focus on the most common ADO Database Classes, as there are *many*, and some of them will be used less often than others.

Why Use ADO?

One issue that I have seen in the dBASE newsgroups is developers attempting to use the ADO database classes with local tables, because there is a perceived issue with the Borland Database Engine, with the idea that they should not rely on it.

This is the wrong way to look at all of this. The Borland Database Engine is not perfect, <u>but it works</u>. Until the developers at dBASE produce a different data engine, if you are using local tables the BDE will work fine for your applications. If you are considering using *only* DBF or Paradox tables, **do not** use ADO. It is not worth the frustration *(if, however, you are designing an application you intend to move to a SQL Server using ADO, then you can certainly use the local tables as a way to model the data and test your application)*.

If, however, you are using SQL Server databases, this is the reason for ADO, and is a way to work with the features of SQL Servers.

Basic ADO Concepts

The acronym ADO stands for <u>A</u>ctiveX <u>D</u>atabase <u>O</u>bjects. By definition *(as noted in the previous chapter)* these work with OLE DB providers either directly to the database or through an ODBC layer. In other words, ADO uses OLE DB by definition, and sometimes needs the ODBC driver to make this possible. If your database engine has OLE DB *and* ODBC drivers it would be more efficient to use the OLE DB drivers.

For the examples in this book I will keep most of the table structures and data fairly simple. I won't cover *all* the ADO database objects, because there are a lot. The primary focus will be equivalencies to the OODML database objects, which most dBASE developers are fairly used to working with.

If you did the steps in Chapter 2 of this book *(setting up your server, ODBC or OLE DB drivers, and the Connection in dBASE using the Properties Dialog)*, you are ready to get started. The next chapter will actually start working with the classes (building an application), but we need to examine them and get an understanding of them.

As with the OODML Database objects, the ADO Database objects are often containers, which contain other objects (see Figure 3-1).

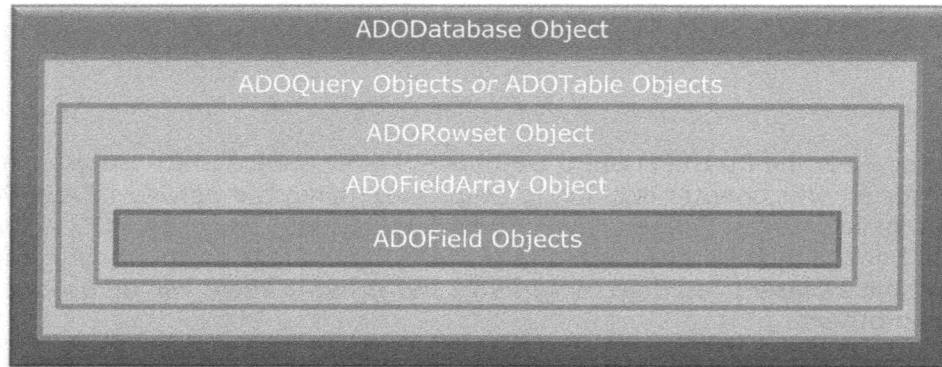

Figure 3-1

It should be noted from looking at the above image, that the primary *ADODatabase* Object can contain multiple *ADOQuery* or *ADOTable* objects. The *ADOQuery* or *ADOTable* Objects, can only contain one *ADORowset* object, which can contain only one *ADOChapterArray* object, and only one *ADOFieldArray* object. However, these last two can contain multiple objects.

There are a *lot* of ADO database objects, not all of them will be discussed here.

The ADO Connection Alias

When you set up the ADO Connection Alias (in Chapter 2) using the Desktop Properties dialog, this information is stored in the main PLUS.INI file. You can find the *connectionString* information by querying this:

```
? _app.connectionAliases["BookSample_ADO"]
```

Which will return the connection string for the database. It appears the only way to add a connectionAlias is to use the Desktop Properties dialog, so you couldn't add one programmatically (there is no "add" method). For your application you would need to enter the information into the .INI file for the executable.

Most of the rest of this chapter will discuss the basic ADO database classes needed to create an application.

The ADODatabase Class

The first class you will need to work with is the ADODatabase class, which is used to make the connection to your database.

This object is pretty much equivalent to the standard Database class in the dBASE OODML *(Object Oriented Database Manipulation Language)*.

At its most basic, the ADODatabase class can be used to create a data object connecting to the BookSample database in a very similar manner to how you would do this with the OODML equivalent:

```
d = new ADODatabase()
```

```
d.databaseName := "BookSample_ADO"
d.active       := true
```

If you removed the Username/Password *(in the discussion about users and security in Chapter 2)*, at this point the user will be required to enter a valid Username and Password. If you preferred to leave the username and password in the connection, these will be assumed here.

You could modify this so that the user does not have to log in with the application *(but if they attempt to access the data outside of the application they could not)*:

```
d = new ADODatabase()
d.databaseName := "BookSample_ADO"
d.loginString  := "SYSDBA/masterkey"
d.active       := true
```

You can also login as a different user than the default in the application this way *(remember the standard user in Firebird is SYSDBA.)*.

Keep in mind that the *SYSDBA* user has full administrator rights, other users do not, so some code may not work if a user does not have the correct rights to perform a task.

The *ADODatabase* object has many of the same properties, events and methods of the standard OODML *Database* object. However, there are some that are specific to the *ADODatabase* object, and some do not work as well with SQL Server data as they do for local tables – they were left in for compatibility, **but should be avoided**. We will examine just a few. If you are familiar with the OODML *Database* object, there is no need to go back over some of the functionality.

My goal here is to help get you on your feet and running, and hopefully at some point the developers are dBASE will provide better documentation for the ADO classes.

Properties

The *ADODatabase* class has a few properties that are new to a dBASE developer who has worked with the OODML classes. The following are a few that might be useful:

connectionString: This property accepts the information for a connection, if you have not already set a database property (as in my examples on the previous page). You can provide the information in a single string, or you can build the string in a way that is pretty common for dBASE:

```
d.connectionString := "Provider=MSDASQL.1;"
d.connectionString += "Persist Security Info=False;"
d.connectionString += "Data Source=BookSample;"
```

If you set the *databaseName* property to a valid (OLE DB or ODBC) database instead, the *connectionString* property is set to read-only.

> **NOTE**
> If you need assistance determining what details need to go into your connection string, you may wish to visit this website:
>
> ```
> https://www.connectionstrings.com/
> ```

databaseName: The *databaseName* property is the name of the ADO connection set up using the Desktop Properties dialog. If you choose not to use that dialog, you will probably need to use the *connectionString* property as above.

loginString: This property allows you to enter the username and password with a slash separating them. This allows you to set these before activating the database, without requiring the user to enter that information.

```
d.loginString := "SYSDBA/masterkey"
```

mode: The *mode* property allows you to specify available permissions. This is going to rely heavily on the SQL Server database you use.

The available modes are:

Mode	Meaning
0	Unknown *(Permissions have not been set or cannot be determined)* (Default)
1	Read *(Read-only permission)*
2	Write *(Write-only permission)*
3	Read Write *(Read/write permissions)*
4	Share Deny Read *(Prevents others from opening a connection with read permission)*
5	Share Deny Write *(Prevents others from opening a connection with write permission)*
6	Share Exclusive *(Prevents others from opening a connection)*
7	Share Deny None *(Allows others to open a connection with any permissions. Neither read nor write access can be denied to others.)*

In Firebird all 8 of these seem to be available for use.

state: The *state* property is read-only, but can be queried to check the current state of a database (very much like the OODML *rowset* object's *state* property). This might be useful when determining if there is an issue with the server, etc.

Events

The ADODatabase object comes with more events that you can attach code to than the OODML Database object. The only one they have in common is the *onExecute* event.

Events here are much like events in other parts of dBASE, the ones that have a name that begins with the word *can* normally return a logical value (*true* or *false*), you can add code to be executed, you can prevent a method from firing, because events and methods are interrelated that way (example: the *close* method is related to the *canClose* event handler – if your code determines there is a reason to not close the object, you can assign a return value of *false*, and the *close* method will not fire, even with an explicit call to the method).

canClose: This event is fired when an attempt is made to close the database – by setting the *active* property to *false*. If an event handler is created, and the code returns *false* the *ADODatabase* object will not be closed and the *active* property is returned to a state of *true*.

canOpen: The opposite of *canClose*, this event is fired with the *active* property is set to *true*.

canTransact: This is useful when using transaction processing methods. This event has three states:

State	Meaning
0	Begin new transaction
1	Commit current transaction
2	Abort current transaction

The state returned determines what the ADODatabase class should do if a *beginTrans* method is called. If you already have a transaction in action, you should provide information for what should be done. *(I do not spend any time on transaction processing in this book …)*

onClose: This event fires when the *active* property is set to *false*. You might want to add some code that should fire when the *ADODatabase* is closed.

onOpen: Fired after the *ADODatabase* object's *active* property is set to *true*.

onProgress: This event is called to display information for a long process. It can be called every so often (in a loop, perhaps), to display information as below:

percent – the approximate percent complete of the operation, from 0 to 100.

type – the process type based on this table:

Type	Explanation
0	Unknown
1	Connecting with database
2	Executing a command
3	Begins transacting logging
4	Fetching records
5	Updating records

process status – from the following table:

Status	Explanation
0	Unknown
1	Failed
2	Succeeded
3	Begins
4	Pending
5	Cancelled
6	Timeout

message – a text message returned from the event.

To obtain this information you must create an event handler, as in the sample code below (this is super simplistic):

```
d = new ADODatabase()
d.databaseName := "BookSample_ADO"
d.loginString  := "SYSDBA/masterkey"
d.onProgress   := TestProgress
d.active       := true

function TestProgress( nPercent, nType, nProcess, cMsg )
   ? "Percent: "+nPercent
   ? "Type:    "+nType
   ? "Process: "+nProcess
   ? "Message: "+cMsg
return
```

When run the code above you will see something like *(in the output pane of the Command Window)*:

```
Percent: 0
Type:    1
Process: 3
Message: Connecting to database ...
Percent: 100
Type:    1
Process: 2
Message: Connection to database is successful.
```

Using the *percent* parameter can be useful to monitor a long process with the use of the *progress* object on a form.

onTransact: This event is fired after a transaction method is successfully called. The return values are:

State	Explanation
0	Begin new transaction
1	Commit current transaction
2	Abort current transaction

Methods

Methods, like most objects in dBASE, can be called explicitly, and they can be overwritten. One must be careful when doing so however.

open: opens a database connection. When this is called, if an event handler for *canOpen* is set, that code is called first. Once the *open* method completes, the ADODatabase object's *onOpen* event handler (if there is one) is then executed.

close: closes a database connection.

cancel: cancels the execution of a pending, asynchronous method call. If for example, you passed an instruction to the database server via *executeSQL* (see below) and it is taking too long (perhaps via a timer, or some other method), you could cancel the attempt. This could occur because the server was very busy, etc.

executeSQL: this method passes a SQL command directly to the SQL server, bypassing the standard database object methods. In some of the examples in this book, I use this to create tables on the server. This adds the ability to pass not only the SQL statement, but to allow a row-returning query, which can be returned to a new *ADORowset* object.

getSchema: this method returns information about the database, including what tables are included, columns in the tables, and the data types supported. The value returned can be placed in a string or ADORowset. An example might be as shown below, to determine the names of all tables in the database:

```
// example assumes database is named "d":
oTables = d.getSchema("tables")
//inspect(oTables)
oTables.first()
do while not oTables.endOfSet
    ? oTables.fields["Table_Name"].value
    oTables.next()
enddo
```

This will give you a lot of tables that are meta-data for the database, anything beginning with "RDB$" or "MON$" is probably not useful. You could of course filter that out with some simple code added.

```
// example assumes database object is named "d":
oTables = d.getSchema("tables")
oTables.first()
do while not oTables.endOfSet
    if left( oTables.fields["Table_Name"].value,4 ) # "RDB$" and ;
       left( oTables.fields["Table_Name"].value,4 ) # "MON$"
       ? oTables.fields["Table_Name"].value
    endif
    oTables.next()
enddo
```

beginTrans, **rollback**, **commit**: standard transaction processing.

The ADOQuery Class

The *ADOQuery* class creates an object very similar to the standard OODML *query* class. At the most basic:

```
q = new ADOQuery()
// standard OODML syntax:
q.database := d // where d references an ADODatabase
q.sql       := "select * from Invoices"
q.active    := true
```

The difficulty is that when working with a LARGE table, you would be passing the whole table across the server (or the Internet), which can noticeably slow down your processing times.

In many cases it is a good idea to use the SQL select's *where* clause. For example, if using an Invoice table, something like:

```
select * from Invoices where InvoiceDate >= '04/15/2015'
```

This would limit the *rowset* (or in SQL server terminology, the *cursor*) to the records from April 15, 2015 to the present. *(The date is being passed as a string, because of the way that SQL works – in many places you cannot use the standard dBASE date objects, such as {04/15/2015}, unless you convert them to strings …)*

If your table has a lot of fields, you could limit the number of fields that are brought across from the server – only the ones you needed for a specific operation, for example *(replace the asterisk with fieldnames, separated by commas)*.

When the query's *active* property is set to *true*, the query creates, automatically, an *ADORowset*, which contains an *ADOFields* object.

Properties
As with the ADODatabase class, not all properties (events, methods) will be listed here.

cacheSize: Number of result rows that are cached locally in memory. This allows for fast processing through a set of rows, as they are all local when the data is on a server. As you navigate through the data, when you reach the end of the cache, the current rows are released back to the server and the next number of rows specified are cached. A lower number will actually slow down processing. Much depends on the nature of your database and your server.

connected: This is a read-only property that returns a logical value of *true* or *false*, depending on whether or not the data object is connected.

cursorLocation: This allows you to choose between cursors being client-side or server-side, the property is a number from the table below:

Location	Explanation
0	Client *(use the Microsoft client cursor)* (Default)
1	Server *(use the cursor support supplied by the data provider)*
2	None *(Do not use the cursor services)*

cursorType: This allows the developer to specify the type of cursor that should be used when opening the data object. The property uses a numeric value from the following:

Type	Explanation
0	Unspecified
1	Forward Only *(can navigate the cursor forward-only, best performance)*
2	Keyset *(operations on data, without additions by other users are visible)*
3	Dynamic *(operations on data by other users are visible)*
4	Static *(Create a fully scrollable snapshot of all the records)* (Default)

lockType: Lock type that will be placed on rows during editing. Not all providers may support all types. Available locks:

LockType	Explanation
0	Unspecified
1	Read Only (Default)
2	Pessimistic – record by record; lock records immediately after editing.
3	Optimistic – record by record; lock records only when updated.
4	Optimistic Batch – batch updates, required for batch update mode (Transaction processing)

masterSource: Reference to data object that acts as a master query and provides parameter values. However, depending on your needs, it may be easier to use the SQL SELECT statement to set up relationships between tables. We'll take a look at this in more depth in the next chapters.

parameters (or params): This is an object reference to the *ADOParametersArray* object, which contains *ADOParameter* objects. Parameters are a way to pass information into a SQL statement such as SELECT or INSERT. If you inspect the *ADOQuery* object, you will only see *parameters* (not the shorter *params*). This has a few properties that may be useful:

decimalLength – number of decimal points, useful for a numeric value.

direction – a numeric value from the following list:

Direction	Meaning
0	Unknown
1	Input (default)
2	Output
3	Input Output
4	Return Value

length – for a character type the length defaults to 20, if you need to input a larger value, you must specify the length (see below). If you have a value that is 21 characters or more and you do not specify the length, you will receive an error.

type – the type of input, this should match the field.

Example:

```
q.parameters[ "Email" ].type   := "Char"
q.parameters[ "Email" ].length := 60
q.parameters[ "Email" ].value  := "SomeAddressOrOther@AnISP.com"
```

rowset: Reference to *ADORowset* object, which contains the rows returned by the server.

sql: SQL statement that describes the query. This typically is a SELECT statement that describes the data to be returned. A simple default might be something like:

```
sql := "select * from "Invoices"
```

You can limit the data returned using the WHERE clause of the SELECT statement:

```
select * from Invoices where InvoiceDate >= '04/15/2015'
```

However, this requires hard-coding the date *(in this example)*. Another suggestion might be to use the *parameters* array to make this more flexible:

```
q = new ADOQuery()
// standard OODML syntax:
q.database := d // where d references an ADODatabase
q.sql       := "select * from Invoices where InvoiceDate = :dDate"
q.parameters["dDate" ].value = '04/15/2015'
q.active    := true
```

This would allow you to change the value in the parameter either in code, or perhaps in a form, and use the *ADODatabase* or *ADOQuery* object's *requery* method to refresh the data.

Events
canClose, canOpen, onClose, onOpen, close, open: very much like the ADODatabase object.

Methods
close, open: As with the *ADODatabase* object.

requery: This is used to re-execute the statement in the *sql* property of the *ADOQuery* object, retrieving the data from the server again. This has the special use of allowing you to change the filter conditions in the WHERE clause, or restating the SELECT statement:

```
q.sql := "select * from Invoices where InvoiceDate = '01/01/2015'"
q.requery()
```

If, instead, you use the *params* property of the *ADOQuery* object you have the flexibility to restate the *value* of the parameter, and then call the *requery* method, rather than restating the SQL property which can be more complex.

```
q.sql := "select * from Invoices where InvoiceDate = :dDate"
q.parameters[ "dDate" ].value = '01/01/2015'
q.active := true
// do some code
q.parameters[ "dDate" ].value = '01/15/2015' // new date
q.requery()
```

The ADOTable Class

The *ADOTable* class is very similar to the *ADOQuery* class. One might ask (I did), "What's the point?" The differences are minor: The *ADOQuery* class is designed to pull a set or subset of data from the server. The *ADOTable* class is designed to pull the **whole** table from the server so you can work on it. It is designed to work with a single table only, where an *ADOQuery* can *(through the proper SQL*

SELECT statement) combine tables, and do more. For a large table do NOT use the *ADOTable* class.

The ADORowset Class

This object represents the data returned by the *ADOQuery* or *ADOTable* classes when they are activated. This object cannot be created by itself, it is automatically created by the *ADOQuery* or *ADOTable* classes. In addition, this creates the *ADOChapter* object, and *ADOField* object upon activation.

As with the OODML *rowset* class, a dBASE developer will do a lot with this class to manipulate data, to navigate through the data, and more.

Properties

endOfSet: this is a read-only property that can be checked by a developer to see if the local row cursor is at the end of the rowset. This returns a value of *true* or *false*. A simple example might be:

```
if not q.rowset.endOfSet
    q.rowset.next() // navigate to next row
endif
```

fields: created automatically when the rowset is created, this is an object reference to the *ADOField* object array.

filter: the filter property is used with standard SQL type filters – anything that is legal in the WHERE clause of a SQL SELECT statement *should* work. It is recommended that you use the WHERE clause most of the time, however. This is mostly useful for local database tables. There is a note in the documentation that states this property cannot be set if the *indexName* property has a value.

filtered: A logical property that can be queried to see if the rowset has a filter set using the filter property above. This returns a value of *true* or *false*. This will not be useful if you used the WHERE clause of the SQL SELECT statement.

indexName: The name of the index tag on the table. The difficulty here is that most SQL Server databases do not use indexes the same way the local .DBF table types do. This property cannot be set if a *filter* has been set on the rowset.

live: this is another read-only property that returns a value of *true* or *false*. It is used to determine if the data can be modified.

marschalOptions: Options that can be used to determine how data changes are sent back to the server. The default is to send all data in the local rowset back to the server:

Option	Effect
0	All rows *(the results in all rows are sent back to the server)* (Default)
1	Modified rows *(only rows that have been changed in the local rowset are sent to the server)*

masterRowset: This and related properties (*masterFields*, *masterChild*) are only useful for local tables. For SQL Server tables, use the ADOQuery's *masterSource* property.

modified: Indicates whether or not the current row has been modified (returns *true* or *false*).

notifyControls: This logical property can be set to notify dataLinked controls (on forms and such) or not. This can be useful when processing a large amount of data (set the property to *false*, complete update, set it back to *true*).

optimizeFields: One or more field names that will be optimized. This can be used with a local *cursor* to create temporary indexes for specific operations.

sort: One or more field names on which the rows are sorted. Each fieldname is separated by a comma, and optionally followed by a keyword ("ASC" for ascending; "DESC" for descending). If no keyword is listed the field will be sorted in ascending sequence. By using this a temporary index will be created for each field specified in the sort property, if an index does not already exist. This property requires that the *cursorLocation* property be set to 0 (Client side).

Example:
```
q.sort := "CompanyName", "PostalCode" DESC
```

tableDriver: Returns a character string indicating the name of the driver currently being used to access the table.

tableName: Returns the name of the current table.

Events
The events for the *ADORowset* object are very much the same as the ones for the OODML *Rowset* object.

Methods
As with the events, many of the methods associated with the *ADORowset* are similar to the ones in the OODML *Rowset* object. Those listed below need a bit of attention.

clone: This method creates a duplicate rowset. When doing this, it creates two different rowset objects that point to the same source data. However, it allows you to navigate to a different row in the clone than the one in the original rowset (or vice versa). This is more efficient than creating a new rowset object with the same source definition. If you change data, the changes will appear in all clones. If you, however, requery the original rowset, any clones will not be synchronized to the original. You can only clone an ADORowset object that supports bookmarks.

saveToFile: Saves the contents of a rowset to a file. This uses two parameters (the second is optional):

<cFile>: The name of the file where the rowset is to be saved.

<cFormat>: The name of the format in which the rowset is to be saved, using this information (if omitted, the method will use ADTG):

Format	Explanation
XML	Extensible Markup Language
ADTG	Microsoft Advanced Table TableGram (Default)
PROVIDER	The current database provider will use its own format.

saveToStream: Saves the contents of a rowset to an *ADOStream* object. This uses two parameters (the second is optional):

<oStream>: The pointer to the stream object.

<cFormat>: The name of the format in which the rowset is to be saved (as the *saveToFile* method above).

The ADOFieldArray Class

The *ADOFieldArray* object is created when the *ADORowset* object is created, which in turn is created when the *ADOQuery* or *ADOTable* object is made active. This is an array of the fields contained in the table or cursor.

This object is addressed from the *fields* property of the *ADORowset*.

Properties
size: The number of fields in the table.

Methods
add: In theory, you can add a custom field to a table (using the ADOField class) however, the *name* property is read-only, which implies that you cannot, at least at this time.

delete: This allows you to remove a field from the array.

The ADOField Class

The ADOField objects are created for each field in a table. These individual objects are created automatically. Unlike local tables using OODML, you cannot create a custom field with the *ADOField* class. For custom fields, you will need to work with the SQL SELECT statement. Examples will be given in the next chapter.

The *ADOField* class has some standard properties, but there are also properties defined by the SQL server, which can be accessed via the *properties* property.

Properties
Some of the properties for the ADOField class are not explained below. As with other objects, we'll use them in code in various places.

properties: An associative array of dynamic properties – these are ones that belong to a specific field type based on the database engine (for example, a text field in Firebird may have different properties from a text field in MSSQL).

readOnly: This logical property allows you to set the field to *readOnly* or fully editable. The default value is *false*.

required: A logical property that lets you specify that the field is required, it must contain a value.

lookupRowset: A reference to an existing rowset object that can be used for a lookup. Returns the first field in the SQL statement.

lookupSQL: Rather than using *lookupRowset*, using *lookupSQL* specifies the SQL SELECT statement to use for a lookup.

Methods

copyToStream: Copies the contents of a BLOB field to an *ADOStream* object.

replaceFromStream: Replaces the contents of a BLOB field from an *ADOStream* object.

originalValue: Returns the original value of the field (before any changes have been committed).

underlyingValue: Returns the *current* value of the field

The ADOError Class

The ADO Error class is used with the *ADOException* class and the standard *try/catch/endtry* code construction to return information about errors when invoking or using your *ADODatabase* objects. The *ADOError* object returns some specific properties, but also returns an object reference for the *ADOErrorArray* object that is created when an error occurs.

The ADOErrorArray Class

The *ADOErrorArray* class is an array of errors returned from the SQL Server if errors occur when processing data. This is created automatically when an *ADOError* object is created, and there is an object reference to this object in the *ADOError* object.

The ADOException Class

The ADOException class is used with the try/catch/endtry code to help a developer handle errors in their code in a more elegant manner than having dBASE errors pop up on the screen and possibly crash an application.

See the example below, where the wrong password is used with the database.

Sample code:

```
/*
    Connect to the database:
*/
try
    d = new ADODatabase()
    d.databaseName := "BookSample_ADO"
    d.loginString  := "SYSDBA/master" // pwd is masterkey
    d.active       := true
    ? "Database is active!"
catch( ADOException e )
    // the error object itself:
    ? "Code:      "+e.code
    ? "Filename: "+e.filename
    ? "LineNo:   "+e.lineNo
    ? "Message:   "+e.message

    aError = e.errors
    // loop through error array
    for i = 1 to aError.size
        ? // blank line
        ? "message:      "+ aError[i].message
        ? "code:         "+ aError[i].code
        ? "source:       "+ aError[i].source
        ? "nativeCode: "+ aError[i].nativeCode
        ? "sqlCode:      "+ aError[i].sqlCode
    next

    return
endtry
```

If this code is run, the following output will appear in the Command Window output pane:

```
Code:      239
// for the book I shortened the path by inserting an ellipsis:
Filename: C:\Kens dBASE Book Plus\...\ADODatabaseTest.prg
LineNo:    41
Message:  Database Engine Error.

message:    [ODBC Firebird Driver]Your user name and password are
not defined. Ask your database administrator to
set up a Firebird login.
code:        3661
source:      Microsoft OLE DB Provider for ODBC Drivers
nativeCode: 64634
sqlCode:    08004
```

In the sample code I used most of the properties except for the *className* and *baseClassName* properties, to attempt to show the options for both the *ADOError* object and the *ADOErrorArray* object.

The ADOStream Class

The *ADOStream* object can be used on its own, or created from an *ADORowset* object (see above). This can be used to stream data out to a file in whatever format you wish. In the documentation by Hans-Peter Neuwirth, there is some sample code that can be quite instructional. It assumes you have an ADORowset object defined *(passed as a parameter to the function)*:

```
function RowsetToCSVFile( oRow, cFile )

    oStream = new ADOStream()
    oStream.type          := 0 // Text
    oStream.lineSeparator := 0 // CRLF
    oStream.open() // open empty stream

    // Output the fieldnames:
    nCount = oRow.fields.size
    for n = 1 to ncount
        oStream.write( oRow.fields[n].name )
        if (n < nCount )
            oStream.write( "," )
        else
            oStream.write( "", true ) // write line separator
        endif
    endfor // loop through fieldnames

    // loop through the data:
    oRow.top()
    do
        for n = 1 to ncount
            oStream.write( oRow.fields[n].value )
            if (n < nCount)
                oStream.write( "," )
            else
                oStream.write( "", true ) // write line separator
            endif
        endfor
    while oRow.next()

    // write the data:
    oStream.saveToFile( cFile )

return
```

The sample code above is specifically streaming out a .CSV file, which can be ready by Excel, and most database software.

The *ADOStream* object has the following unique properties, etc.:

Properties

charSet: a string that defines the character set used when streaming data. The default is "Unicode".

eos: Is the *position* (see property below) at the end of stream? Returns a logical value of *true* or *false*.

lineSeparator: This is a numeric value referencing the type of line separator in the output file:

Type	Meaning
0	CRLF (Carriage Return and Line Feed) (Default)
1	CR (Carriage Return)
2	LF (Line Feed)

mode: A numeric value referencing the permissions for the data stream:

Mode	Meaning
0	Unknown *(Permissions have not been set or cannot be determined)* (Default)
1	Read *(Read-only permission)*
2	Write *(Write-only permission)*
3	Read Write *(Read/write permissions)*
4	Share Deny Read *(Prevents others from opening a connection with read permission)*
5	Share Deny Write *(Prevents others from opening a connection with write permission)*
6	Share Exclusive *(Prevents others from opening a connection)*
7	Share Deny None *(Allows others to open a connection with any permissions. Neither read nor write access can be denied to others.)*

position: The current position in the stream object.

size: The size of the stream in bytes.

source: Specifies the source for the stream object.

type: The type of data contained in the stream object:

Type	Meaning
0	Text
1	Binary

Methods

clear: Clears the contents of the current stream object.

copyToStream: Copies the current stream object to another stream object.
Parameters:
<oStream> -- object reference for new stream object.
<nBytes> -- optional, number of bytes to be stream. If left out, the whole stream object will be copied.

flush: Flushes the current stream object to the destination.

loadFromFile: Loads the contents of a file into the current stream object. The parameter is the name of the file being read.

read: Reads a specific number of bytes of data into the stream object. If no value is given, the *read* method will read to the end of file in the input file. If a specific number is given, it can be the number of bytes, or it can be one of these:

Value	Meaning
-1	Reads all characters to the end of file from the current position.
-2	Reads all characters to the end of line reading to the *lineSeparator* from the current position.

saveToFile: Saves the contents of the stream object to an output file by the name given.

skipLine: Skips a line when reading a stream file.

write: Writes specific characters to the output stream. Uses two parameters:
<cExp> -- the value to be written.
<bSep> -- output the line separator, logical value (*true* or *false*). If left out, no line separator will be written (default value is *false*).

Other ADO Database Classes

There are a large number of other ADO database classes available for use. As we work through later chapters of the book, we may end up using some of these other classes, and some explanation will be included at that point. Some of the classes are similar to OODML classes, such as the *ADOTableDef* or *ADOUpdateSet* classes. Others are specific to ADO and SQL Server databases.

Sample Code for This Chapter

The following is a listing of the sample code in the "Chapter 03" folder, if you downloaded it from my website. You may use the code contained in these programs for your own applications if you desire, with the caveat that credit be given appropriately.

- **AddUser.prg** – Example code to add a user to the Firebird database example.
- **RowsetToCSVFile.prg** – Sample code to show how to use the ADOStream class to output data to a CSV file.

Summary

The whole point of this chapter is to give an overview of the ADODatabase Classes in dBASE and a few basic examples. Chapters 4-6 will focus on actually using these classes in code, and starting to build an application.

As with other chapters in this book, I must thank developers in the dBASE support newsgroups for their assistance, viewpoints, and experience in helping sort out all of what is in this chapter, and Kathy Kolosky at dBASE (support and QA), who comes into the newsgroups and helps where/when she can. Without them this would not make anywhere near as much sense as it does now.

Chapter 4: Using ADO Database Classes in an Application, Part 1

In this chapter we will be starting a *simple* application (I use the word "simple" with some caution – it will take us three chapters to complete) using ADO Database objects, as opposed to OODML database objects. This will include a variety of code samples, from programs, to custom classes, to data modules, and so on. It should be noted that if you are already somewhat familiar with ADO, while you might learn something from these chapters, they are really aimed at a beginner, and are really "how to get started" chapters.

As noted in earlier chapters, my focus is on the Firebird database because it is free and relatively easy to work with. I would also like to point out that many of the concepts discussed here can apply to working with SQL Servers in dBASE using the more standard OODML database objects. For example we will be discussing working with two data connections, this concept should apply whether or not you use ADO or just access the data through ODBC drivers and use the BDE in dBASE. *(Some or all of these concepts would apply to building a web-based application as well!)*

> **NOTE**
> One of the developers in the dBASE Newsgroups points out constantly that each SQL Database engine has its own way of handling certain things, and that a truly generic example isn't possible. While I understand that concept, I am doing my best to create a **starting point** for the average dBASE developer here, not a "this is the one true way" type of document. As with many aspects of database design and programming, there is no "one true way" that is absolutely perfect and bullet-proof. This – and all the other chapters in this book – are aimed at concepts more than anything else, and helping the dBASE coder get past them and be productive more quickly.

Data on the Server vs. Local Data

The following is fairly simple, compared to all the permutations, and variations that are available. I do not wish to turn this into a book on SQL Servers.

Most dBASE developers who have worked with local tables (DBFs, Paradox .DBs, etc.) have a difficult time changing the way they look at data. Local tables are interactive, and most of the time fairly fast, and updates are pretty much automatic. One drawback is that typically when working with large tables over a network, the interactions can slow down. This is because most dBASE applications tend to access the whole table *(and in some cases, because of the way the commands work this is the only method to build the application; in others, using filters and such limit what the user can do with a table).*

> **NOTE**
>
> It should be noted that a developer working with local tables *can* design an application that simulates the way a SQL Server works. If the ultimate goal for an application is to migrate the data to a SQL Server, then this is a good idea. However, if all the data is using local tables and the developer does not anticipate moving to a SQL server, then it is not necessary.

SQL Servers (or as some call them "Back-End Servers") work quite differently. When you tell the server you want to work with the data, you bring some of the data to your computer "locally" using a SQL SELECT statement. These are called *cursors*. We won't spend a lot of time on some of the concepts involved with a cursor, because that's a *huge* topic and most of it is handled automatically. Basically to summarize the idea: the cursor is the set of data that is available *at this time* to your user(s).

With local tables, most dBASE developers *(myself included)* are used to relying on indexes. Indexing works quite differently with SQL Servers. An index on a rowset cursor only affects the data in the cursor, and does not affect the data on the server itself. In addition, changing indexes on the fly, something that many developers are used to doing with local tables, does not work the same with SQL Servers. You often have to requery the data after changing the sort sequence.

If you work on the data in a rowset cursor, any changes will not be apparent to others on your network until the changes are posted back to the server and the data is brought back down to the other clients *(by requerying the tables)*. In addition, the user who is working with data locally won't see changes posted by other users until the data is requeried. This kind of thing can be quite confusing to a developer who has only worked with local tables.

Two Connections?

There is a lot of discussion on the dBASE newsgroups about working with two connections to the data – one being a read-only connection, one being a write connection. This applies when accessing the data via ADO *(as discussed here)* or accessing the data via the BDE (ODBC). Since the application we are building for the next few chapters is based on this concept, here's a summary:

Read-Only connections should be used for downloading and reading the data, searching for a specific record, etc. This connection can be left open, because by definition you are only accessing the server as needed.

Write connections should only be used to write to or change the data (using INSERT, UPDATE, DELETE ...). The write connection should be opened and closed as quickly as possible to avoid using more resources than necessary, and to avoid conflicts in the data. The larger the application, the more users with simultaneous access to the data, the more important this is.

The big reason for all of this is server resources. If you are serving data in a write mode, when the user only needs to read the data, you are tying up services (handling locking of records and such) that are unnecessary on the server side, and can ultimately slow down processing.

This type of processing adds layers of complexity for a developer, because basically you have to find a way to create an interface for the user that is easy to work with, but doesn't overload the server. To do that requires creating your own record buffering method or methods, so that you can examine the data, see what has changed, and so on. This will be described in the application as we build it.

Using SQL

As you hopefully understand by now, SQL is a programming language all its own, and it has specific rules. One thing that comes up in all the discussions in the newsgroups, is the fact that every SQL Server has its own implementation of SQL. There are standard elements, but there are going to be extra features available. I mentioned in Chapter 2, for example, that Firebird has SQL commands to work with user accounts (creating, modifying, etc.). This is not guaranteed to be something available in *all* SQL Server databases, or the same commands may have different parameters, options, etc.

In this book my goal is goal focus on common features that most, if not all, SQL Server databases have in their implementation of SQL. I do not want to spend a lot of time on a feature that is not fairly standard, because then you would need to figure out how to do that thing using the SQL Server you are working with. That said, I will be careful to mention when using a Firebird specific command or option and we will be spending some time on one Firebird specific feature.

Creating Tables in Your Database

If you are familiar with dBASE tables, you will find SQL Server databases (including Firebird) use different field types, and some field types you may be pretty familiar with using either don't exist or don't work exactly the same way.

The table below shows a list of equivalencies comparing dBASE fields to Firebird field types:

dBASE (Level 7) Field Types	Firebird Equivalent
Character	CHAR or VARCHAR
Numeric(x,y)	NUMERIC(x,y)
Memo	BLOB(10,1) or VARCHAR
Logical	INTEGER or CHAR(1)
Date	DATE
Float	FLOAT
OLE	*No match, use* BLOB(10,2)
Binary	BLOB(10,2)
Long	SMALLINT
Timestamp	TIMESTAMP
Double	DOUBLE
AutoIncrement	BIGINT, *but with code ...*

Field equivalencies will vary from SQL Server to SQL Server, so the equivalencies shown above may not work for your database server, indeed, you may need to experiment, check the documentation, ask in the newsgroups if needed.

Firebird has other field types, and you can find out more about each in the documentation. I will not get involved in trying to use every single field type.

The Sample Data

To get started, we need to create a set of tables, populate them, and then be able to manipulate them.

For the example application we will use a *simple* Invoice database. The database will start with the following structure (Figure 4-1):

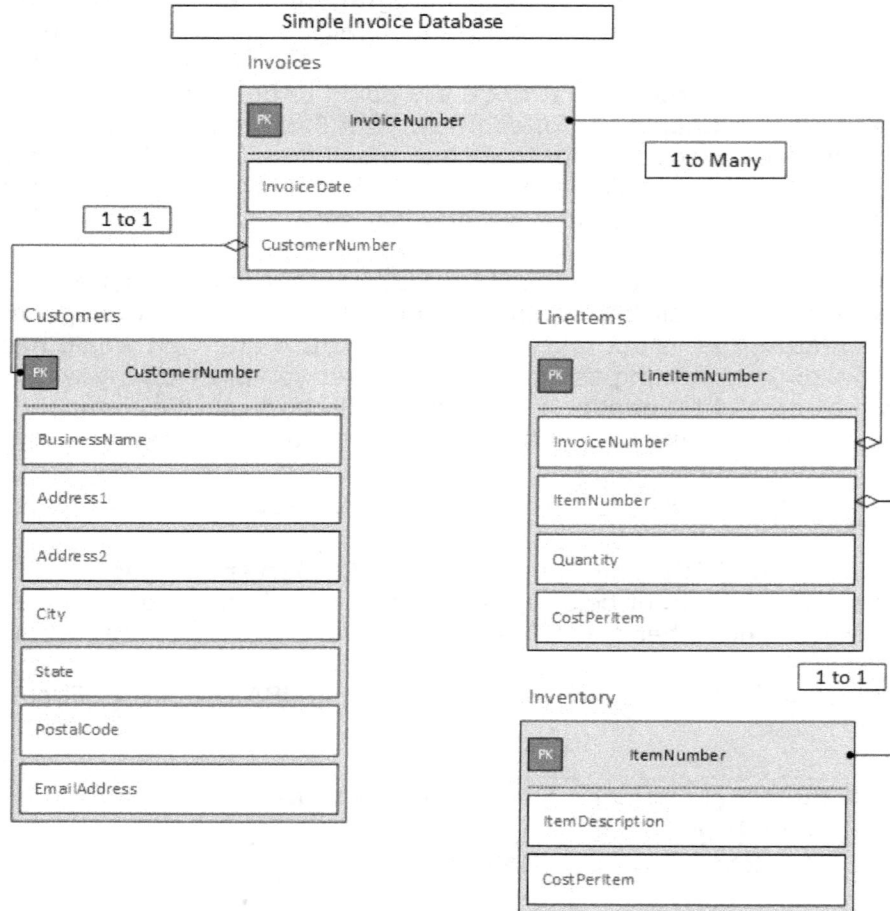

Figure 4-1

This is not as complicated as many Invoicing systems tend to be, but this book is not about designing complex databases. Any competent developer will be able to take this and expand it to where it needs to be, and any business will have their own peculiar needs that a "generic" database could not plan for.

Most of the field types are character, except where they need to be other, for example, the Primary Key fields are Integer (BIGINT), the "CostPerItem" field in the Line items and Inventory tables is numeric with 2 decimal places, etc.

This table structure will be used in examples in the chapters involved with building the sample application, as well as some of the other examples throughout the book. There is a program included in the source code for the book that creates some basic sample data. As we go I may add other tables and/or fields for demonstration purposes.

Creating tables in Firebird can be done with the IBExpert or FlameRobin software *(discussed in Chapter 3)*. You can also create tables by passing the SQL *CREATE TABLE* command through a database (or *ADODatabase*) object to the server, which is what is used here *(the goal being to do most of the work in dBASE)*.

> 📋 **NOTE**
>
> You should not assume that you can use the Table Designer in dBASE to create viable tables for your database. Worse, Firebird and Interbase *used* to work with the designer (pre dBASE Plus 8), but the changes in the software have made it difficult or impossible to create tables that are usable by either the database engine or by dBASE itself.
>
> The Table Designer works great for dBASE tables (.DBF, .DB), just don't try to use it for your SQL Server tables.

There is a program in the Sample Code that was used to create the tables and populate them, called: CreateDatabase.prg. It uses the write Connection Alias set in Chapter 2. The program uses a combination of techniques, including using the *ADODatabase* object's *executeSQL* method to perform the work needed.

The following code is used to create the Invoice table:

```
// use a character variable
cBuildTable = [create table Invoices (]+;
                            [ InvoiceNumber integer,]+;
                            [ InvoiceDate    date,]+;
                            [ CustomerNumber integer, ]+;
                            [ Primary Key (InvoiceNumber ) )]

// build the table:
d.executeSQL( cBuildTable )
```

An attempt to populate the tables using the SQL INSERT INTO command using parameters caused some frustration, but with help from developers in the dBASE newsgroups, possibly uncovering some bugs in the software, I was able to get it to work properly.

The following is how I populated the first row of the Invoice table *(this code gets modified later in the chapter, after the discussion on AutoIncrement fields)*:

```
/*
    Connect to a table using the ADOQuery object:
*/

qInvoices = new ADOQuery()
qInvoices.database := d

// add data here
local nRows

// Adding invoices here, but we haven't yet set up the
// triggers or other code for autoincrement fields.
// SO, we're going to manually do this.
nRows = 0
```

```
// first row:
nRows++
qInvoices.sql := "insert into Invoices ;
              ( InvoiceNumber, InvoiceDate, CustomerNumber ) ;
              values ( :InvNum, :InvDate, :CustNum )"
qInvoices.parameters["InvNum"].value  := nRows
qInvoices.parameters["InvDate"].value := {12/23/2014}
qInvoices.parameters["CustNum"].value := 1
qInvoices.active := true // activate and execute the command
qInvoices.active := false // deactivate
```

The more interesting aspect, which was mentioned in the previous chapter, is that in order to get a character value that is larger than 20 characters to work, you have to put more effort in. This was discovered with email addresses in the Customers table. The first record for the customer table is added in a similar fashion to that above, but is more involved:

```
qCustomers.sql := "insert into Customers ;
        (CustomerNumber, ;BusinessName, Address1, Address2, ;
        City, State, PostalCode, EmailAddress );
        values ( :CustNum, :BusName, :Addr1, :Addr2, ;
                :City, :State, :Postal, :Email )"
// here's where it gets tricky, if the character value can
// be > 20, we should specify the length for the parameters,
// but in theory, just this once:
qCustomers.parameters[ "CustNum" ].value  := nRows
// Business name could be longer than 20:
qCustomers.parameters[ "BusName"].type    := "Char"
qCustomers.parameters[ "BusName" ].length := 30
qCustomers.parameters[ "BusName" ].value  := ;
                        "A Very Fine Business"
// Address1, Address2, City could be longer than 20:
qCustomers.parameters[ "Addr1"].type    := "Char"
qCustomers.parameters[ "Addr1"].length  := 25
qCustomers.parameters[ "Addr1"].value   := "111 Main Street"
qCustomers.parameters[ "Addr2"].type    := "Char"
qCustomers.parameters[ "Addr2"].length  := 25
qCustomers.parameters[ "Addr2"].value   := ""
qCustomers.parameters[ "City"].type     := "Char"
qCustomers.parameters[ "City"].length   := 30
qCustomers.parameters[ "City"].value    := "Anytown"
qCustomers.parameters[ "State"].value   := "CA"
qCustomers.parameters[ "Postal"].value  := "99881-1234"
// Email can be up to 60 characters in length:
qCustomers.parameters[ "Email"].type    := "Char"
qCustomers.parameters[ "Email"].length  := 60
qCustomers.parameters[ "Email"].value   := ;
                        "AVFB@FineBusiness.com"
qCustomers.active := true
qCustomers.active := false
```

When adding the other records, we do not need to define the *type* and *length* properties again, only the *value* property is needed as this changes for each record, so the set of commands is shorter for additional data.

Later in this chapter we will take a look at working with AutoIncrement fields using the Firebird *Sequence (there should be something similar for most SQL Server databases)*.

Creating an Application with SQL Server Data

The goal of this and the next chapters is to create a simple application using the data described above. This application will have basic functionality, adding records, editing records, deleting records, navigating through tables, and so on.

Application Concepts

Many developers will tell you there are lots of ways to get to the final goal, but they will often point out that a "properly" defined application makes management of the application easier" (or words to that effect). I see lots of guidelines out there that talk about having layers for an application, such as:

Figure 4-2

This is based on the concept that the UI layer doesn't know anything about the Business Layer, and the Business Layer doesn't know anything about the Data Layer. The Business Layer is actually a tricky one, because it is where the business rules for the *specific* application lie, and often ends up being merged with the Data Layer, no matter how hard the developer tries to keep them separate.

All of this sounds great, but it can make things more complicated to build an application from scratch. By the time we are done with the chapters on developing the application, however, you will have a framework that you can base other applications on – copying and making minor modifications as needed.

That said, you need to have some basic ideas of how you want the application to work.

The Data Layer

In the data layer you need to be able to:

- Find records (search, filter the data to see only specific records)
- Edit records
- Delete records
- Add new records

This will be the same for most tables in a database. There may be other functionality required, but these are the basics. *(The User Interface actually has to interact with this to some extent, because you have to have the ability to tell the software what you want to do …)*

With a parent/child relationship, you probably will need to have the ability to:

- Cascade delete child records

63

- Cascade update child records *(only if you allow your users to change a primary key field ...)*

What this means is if your application allows the user to update the linking field *(which in theory you should not do)*, you will need code to ensure that the child records that are linked to the parent table are not abandoned (or orphaned). When a parent record is deleted, does the application need to delete child records *(in some cases yes, in others maybe not)*?

The Business Layer

You may have specific processing for the application you are building that is not required for another application. These are often called the "Business Rules" for the application. When saving a record, you may need to check for valid values in the data, for example *(which is why the Business Layer and the Data Layer often blur lines ...)*.

Some error checking is more straight-forward than others – as an example, when entering the Invoice Date for a new invoice, you most likely do not want to allow dates prior the current date, or you could even enforce this by automatically using today's date.

The User Interface Layer

The UI Layer is how the *user* will actually interact with the data. The Business Layer and the Data Layer should, for the most part, be invisible to the user – most users don't care about all that, as long as the application does what it needs to do.

Most users want to be able to enter and edit the data as required, generate reports as required, and not have to think about what is going on behind-the-scenes.

The Data Layer

To get things started, let's work with the data layer. This is going to be set up to be granular, meaning it will be in multiple parts. The data layer is going to contain the connections to the data (using *ADODatabase* objects) in one *data module*. A *data module* is an object in dBASE specifically designed to work with data objects – it is a container. The advantage to these is that you can design code that is re-usable, without having to copy and paste it into different forms or reports, etc.

Create a Data Module

The Data Module Designer in dBASE Plus 8 through 10 is really simple.

We will start with a custom Data Module that contains just the database objects that we need. For the sample application we will be using *ADODatabase* objects, but if you were just using ODBC connections via the BDE, the same concepts should work here – you would set up *Database* objects instead.

In the Navigator in dBASE click the "Data Modules" tab, and then double-click the "[New Data Module]" icon. The designer, as noted, is pretty simple:

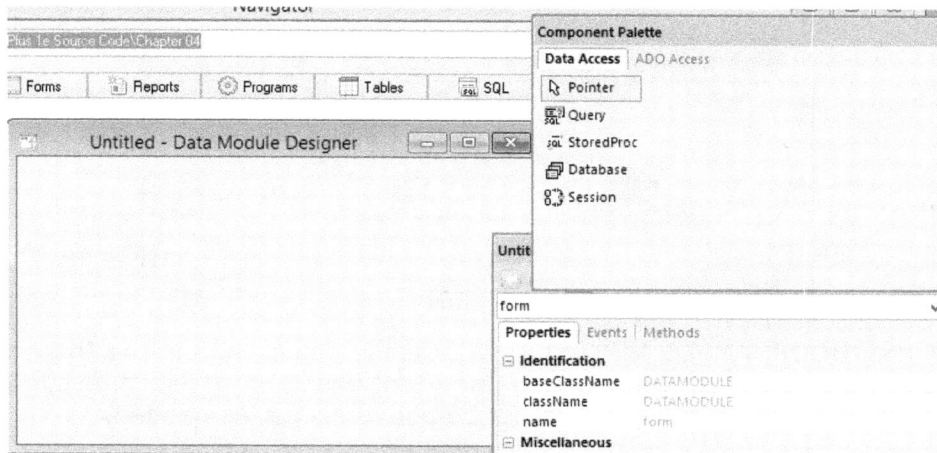

Figure 4-3

We are working with ADO, so on the Component Palette select the "ADO Access" tab, and drag an *ADODatabase* object to the surface. In the Inspector window, select the "Name" property, which should say "ADODatabase1". Change this to the name of your Read-Only connection, for the book: "BookSample_RO" – we are adding the "_RO" part so we know this is the Read-Only connection. Change these properties as well:

- *databaseName*: BookSample_ADO_RO
- *loginString*: SYSDBA/masterkey
- *active*: true

Repeat all of the above, but instead we want the writeable version, so set these properties:

- *name*: BookSample_Write
- *databaseName*: BookSample_ADO
- *loginString*: SYSDBA/masterkey
- *active*: true

Because you are providing the *loginString* value, you (or a user) are not required to log in. Once you have completed this, save the Data Module by pressing Ctrl+S or using the toolbar, etc. We're going to name this "DataLayer". This is going to be the starting point for the application. I resized it a bit because there are only the two objects, it should look something like:

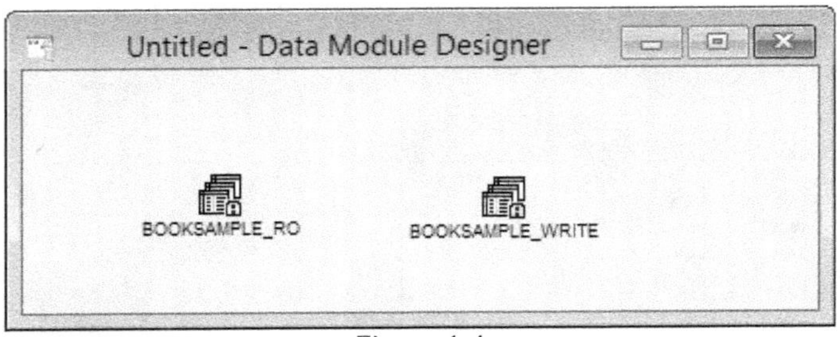

Figure 4-4

Click on the "BOOKSAMPLE_WRITE" *ADODatabase* object, and in the Inspector set the *active* property to *false*. This is important based on previous discussions – the Write enabled connection should not be active except as needed.

Save and Exit the Data Module Designer (Ctrl+W). At this point, right click the new Data Module and select the "Open in Source Editor" option.

Your code should look like this:

```
class DataLayerDataModule of DATAMODULE
   this.BOOKSAMPLE_RO = new ADODATABASE(this)
   with (this.BOOKSAMPLE_RO)
      left = 41.0
      top = 42.0
      databaseName = "BOOKSAMPLE_ADO_RO"
      loginString = "SYSDBA/masterkey"
      active = true
   endwith

   this.BOOKSAMPLE_WRITE = new ADODATABASE(this)
   with (this.BOOKSAMPLE_WRITE)
      left = 177.0
      top = 45.0
      databaseName = "BOOKSAMPLE_ADO"
      loginString = "SYSDBA/masterkey"
   endwith

endclass
```

Close the Source Code Editor (Ctrl+W works great for this).

Test the Data Module by double-clicking the icon, and it should open right up in the designer.

Add the ADOQuery Objects

For our purposes the Data Module is going to be handling all of the data layer, so we're going to add the query objects we need for the tables.

We have four tables in our database *(well, five – but one is a "dummy" table that is only used for a single purpose)*, so we're going to add all four to the Data Module. When you place the first *ADOQuery* object on the surface, set the following properties:

- *name*: Invoices
- *database*: BookSample_RO
- *sql*: select * from Invoices

- *active*: true

If the *active* property will not change, check the Read-Only database object to be sure that the *active* property is set to *true*. If not, set it, and then click back on the query object, and repeat.

Add three more *ADOQuery* objects, setting these properties:
- *name*: Customers
- *database*: BookSample_RO
- *sql*: select * from customers
- *active*: true

and:
- *name*: LineItems
- *database*: BookSample_RO
- *sql*: select * from LineItems
- *active*: true

and:
- *name*: Inventory
- *database*: BookSample_RO
- *sql*: select * from Inventory
- *active*: true

Add one more *ADOQuery* object, and set these properties:
- *name*: WriteQuery
- *database*: BookSample_Write

Note that we did not set the SQL or active properties. These will be set as needed.

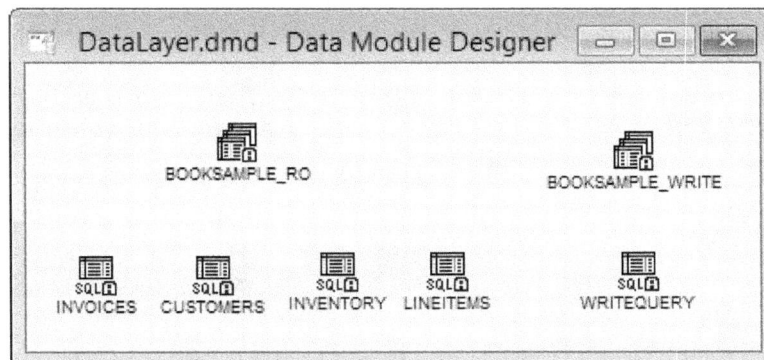

Figure 4-5

When we use the read-only queries, we will modify the SQL property as needed, and requery the data the same way. The write query is going to be used for all our "writing" needs – adding new records, updating data, and deleting records. It *(and the ADODatabase)* will be made active when we require it to be used, and then the *active* property will be set back to *false*.

> **📋 NOTE**
>
> It is very important that you use the names of the tables as the names of the *ADOQuery* objects on the Data Module. The *ADORowset* object does not have a (working) *tableName* property, even though it appears in the Inspector. The difficulty then becomes retrieving the correct query in the User Interface layer to obtain data. If you name the ADOQuery objects the names of the tables, and you are consistent throughout the application, all should work as designed in this application. One developer in the newsgroups wrote some fairly complex code to do this, but it can get more difficult when your SQL statement works with multiple tables.

Adding Code

For all of this to work, we will need to add some code into the Data Module. We also need to deal with the concept of AutoIncrement fields.

Autoincrement

An autoincrement field is one that, as the name implies, increments the value automatically. The difficulty is that every SQL Server does this differently, if the ability is built in at all. AutoIncrement fields are often used for Primary Key fields, as they are created automatically, not by the user, and are by definition unique values, which is an important consideration for Primary Key fields.

dBASE Code for AutoIncrement

What I have done is to take code from the dBASE Users' Function Library Project (dUFLP – a shareware library of code) called SeqValue.cc and modified it.

In the source code for the book you will see ADOSeqValue.cc and SQLSeqValue.cc. The only differences between the two are the first works with the ADO database classes. The other uses standard OODML database classes.

The advantage to using these classes is that they should work with most or all SQL Server databases with no modification. To use the ADOSeqValue class and increment the InvoiceNumber field:

```
set proc to ADOSeqValue.cc
oSeq = new SeqValue( "BookSample_ADO", "SYSDBA/masterkey" )
nValue = oSeq.Increment( "Invoices", "InvoiceNumber" )
oSeq.release()
```

This creates a table in the database if it doesn't exist, called "SEQVALUE", and assumes a starting value of 1. If you need to set a new starting value, there is a method of this class that will allow that, called "reset". This code *was* initially called from the program "CreateDatabase.prg" mentioned earlier in this chapter *(see discussion below about using Sequences in Firebird)* and later taken back out.

In the Data Module, when adding new rows to the different tables, you could make calls to this class as well, so you have a valid value for the new rows.

If you know that you will always use Firebird, or you will always use some other specific SQL Server database, you can take the time to learn how to set up a generator or sequence, and call it instead as needed. Some of them will, once created, automatically increment your primary key field when adding records to the table *(like the local DBF or Paradox table Autoincrement field type)*.

Firebird Generator (Sequence)/Trigger for AutoIncrement

After all of the above, Firebird has what are called Generators and Triggers, which combined can be used to *natively* create an autoincrement field that acts like the DBF version. The value is created but not saved until the record is actually saved, and so on.

The first part is the Generator or Sequence – this part is easy. It should be noted that current versions of Firebird include a more SQL-compliant option – SEQUENCE instead of GENERATOR:

```
CREATE GENERATOR invnum_gen
// or:
CREATE SEQUENCE invnum_seq
```

The name of the generator should not be the same as a field name, and using "_gen" or "_seq" as part of the name is a generally good practice, but not required *(there is a note at the end of the chapter about this as well)*.

The harder part of this is creating the trigger:

```
// Based off an example provided for Interbase by Bowen Moursund
// many years ago:
CREATE TRIGGER invnum_trigger FOR invoice ACTIVE BEFORE INSERT
POSITION0 AS BEGIN new.InvoiceNumber = GEN_ID( invnum_seq, 1);
END
```

Using "BEFORE INSERT" for a generator causes this to act just like the autoincrement field in a DBF, as noted above. The value does not appear in a form if you datalink to it (we will not) until the row is saved to the table. *(There is a discussion in the next pages about why Triggers may not be ideal in some cases …)*

It should be noted there are a couple of other commands that you can use with generators and triggers:

```
// set a different value in the generator – the next
// number generated would be nValue+1
SET GENERATOR generatorname TO nValue
// or:
ALTER SEQUENCE generatorname RESTART WITH nValue
```

The Firebird documentation notes both commands, and recommends the latter.

```
// delete generator
DROP GENERATOR generatorname
// or:
DROP SEQUENCE generatorname
```

In the code above, the second statement, according to the documentation provided by Firebird, is the preferred method.

```
// delete trigger
```

```
DROP TRIGGER triggername
```

Will, as the name suggests, remove the trigger from the database.

The documentation for Firebird notes that the use of *SEQUENCE* is preferred over *GENERATOR*, the impression I have is that this is a compatibility issue with other SQL Server Database engines.

In dBASE all of these commands should be executed through the *ADODatabase*'s executeSQL*()* method.

> ### 📋 NOTE
>
> **Very important:** The Generator/Trigger code shown here for Firebird will most likely not work exactly the same way in another SQL Server Database. Each of them is different, as is constantly being noted throughout the book. If you work with another SQL Server you will either need to figure out how to create an autoincrement field for that server, or use the ADOSeqValue (or SQLSeqValue) class shown above.
>
> **WARNING:** There is a potential drawback to these classes, however. With a large number of concurrent users, you *might* run into a situation where duplicate values are created for your primary key. Ultimately it is best to try to use the native techniques for the SQL Server engine you are working with.

After a lot of effort, trial-and-error, and tinkering to work around an odd bug in dBASE Plus 9.51, Mervyn Bick, Andre Knappstein and I have worked out how to work with the Firebird Sequences (or Generators) without using Triggers. The difficulty with using Triggers is that until the record is saved you cannot access the value used for the number. While building part of the application in the next chapters, I discovered that when you add a new record to the table, you cannot display the new record properly *(due to the nature of how the code is written)*. By avoiding the use of the Trigger, and using a call to the Firebird *Gen_ID()* function, we can return the value, display it, and save it into the record at the time we need to. This allows, after a *requery* of the data, the ability to navigate to the new record and display it on the form right after it was appended to the table.

The code in the program "CreateDatabase.prg" is written to show this, but the code originally used as I started writing everything has been commented out *(as opposed to deleted)*, to show the use of both the sequences (generators) and the use of the ADOSeqValue code, in case you wish to use that instead.

Add Records

Creating code that is "generic" *(meaning it works with most or all tables in a database)* is not always easy. It requires some special work to pull everything together. The fun part is that the code here should not know anything about the user interface, so it requires that the User Interface has the ability to pass information to the code in the Data Layer.

For this particular set of code, we will need to have the following information passed to the method of the Data Module we are creating:

- Name of the table
- Array with two columns:
  - Fieldname
  - Fieldvalue

In order to test the code we are building, a small program was created called "TestAddRow.prg", shown below. The code creates an array, then creates an instance of the datamodule, and calls the addRow method.

```
aMyData = new array(1,2)
aMyData[1,1] = "InvoiceNumber"
aMyData[1,2] = GetNextKey( "InvNum_Seq" )
aMyData.grow(1)
aMyData[2,1] = "InvoiceDate"
aMyData[2,2] = date()
aMyData.grow(1)
aMyData[3,1] = "CustomerNumber"
aMyData[3,2] = 3

set procedure to DataLayer.dmd
oDMD = new DataLayerDataModule()
oDMD.addRow( "Invoices", aMyData )
? "New Row Added"
release object oDMD
oDMD := null
close procedure DataLayer.dmd
```

This is very simple, but the idea was to make sure the method works. I chose to test with the simplest table in the database, but by the time the book is published, this will have been thoroughly tested. Note the function "GetNextKey()" shown in the code above – this sets and retrieves the next value from the Sequence for the table. This is added into the "TestAddRow" program, and is also in the Data Module:

```
function GetNextKey( cGenName )
    private dGen, qGen, nVal, cCmd
    dGen = new ADODatabase()
    dGen.databaseName := "BookSample_ADO_RO"
    dGen.loginString  := "SYSDBA/masterkey"
    dGen.active       := true

    qGen = new ADOQuery()
    qGen.database     := dGen
    cCmd = "Select Gen_ID("+cGenName+",1) from MyGen"
    qGen.sql           = cCmd
    qGen.requestLive := false
    qGen.active       := true
    qGen.rowset.first()

    // next key value:
    nVal = qGen.rowset.fields[1].value

    // deactivate:
    qGen.active := false
    dGen.active := false
return nVal
```

In the Data Module, we can add code as methods of the object after all the instantiation code (creating the objects) but before the *endclass* statement. If you open the Data Module in the Source Code Editor, and navigate to the bottom, you can add the code that way.

The code for the addrow method of the Data Module is shown below, except for the comments at the top of the method:

```
function AddRow( cTable, aData )
   local cCmd, nField, oSeq, nPrimary, cFields, cValues
   private xValue, cVal

   // check for both parameters:
   if pCount() < 2
      msgbox( "This method requires two parameters: cTable and aData."+;
              "See comments in InvoiceDataLayer1.dmd.",;
              "AddRow Method Error", 16 )
      return
   endif

   // create the strings needed for the fields
   cFields = ""
   cValues = ""
   for nField = 1 to aData.size/2 // two columns
      cFields += aData[ nField, 1 ]
      if nField < (aData.size/2)
         cFields += ", "
      endif // nField

      // add fieldname to list:
      cFields += aData[ nField, 1 ]
      // add values to value list:
      xValue = aData[ nField, 2 ]
      xValue = aData[ nField, 2 ]
      if type( "xValue" ) # "N"
         if type( "xValue" ) == "C" or type( "xValue" ) == "V"
            cVal = ReplaceApostrophe( aData[ nField, 2] )
            cValues += [']+cVal+[']
         else
            cValues += [']+aData[ nField, 2 ]+[']
         endif
      else // numeric
         cValues += aData[ nField, 2 ]
      endif // type
      if nField < (aData.size/2)
         cValues += ", "
      endif // nField
   next // nField

   // okay, actually build the string
   cCmd  = "insert into "+cTable
   cCmd += " (" + cFields + ") "
   cCmd += "values (" + cValues + ")"

   // activate the database, execute the command,
   // deactivate ...:
   try
```

```
                this.BookSample_write.active := true
                this.BookSample_write.executeSQL( cCmd )
                this.BookSample_write.active := false

            catch( ADOException e )
                // the error object itself:
                ? "Code:      "+e.code
                ? "Filename: "+e.filename
                ? "LineNo:    "+e.lineNo
                ? "Message:   "+e.message

                local aError, i
                aError = e.errors

                for i = 1 to aError.size
                    ? // blank line
                    ? "message:    "+ aError[i].message
                    ? "code:       "+ aError[i].code
                    ? "source:     "+ aError[i].source
                    ? "nativeCode: "+ aError[i].nativeCode
                    ? "sqlCode:    "+ aError[i].sqlCode
                next
                return
            endtry
        return
```

The trick with the code above is in building the SQL INSERT INTO command correctly. This code does not *(at this time)* handle binary fields, and there may be some field types that don't work properly. There is also an issue with delimiters – SQL databases typically prefer single quotes for many situations, and if the data contains a single-quote in a character field, we have to change the way it is handled by changing it to two single-quotes *(there is a function in the Data Module that takes care of this, discussed later in this chapter)*. Next, we need to have code to update an existing record …

Update Records

Updating records can be a little tricky, because with a SQL Server you typically don't want to save all the fields in the table, which is what the default would be. If you have a table with 200 fields, and there is a lot of editing of data happening, then you are taking up server time processing fields that haven't changed, which can slow down the server. It is a good idea to keep track of which fields have changed, which we will do in the User Interface layer.

For our purposes we will be doing something similar to the code for adding a new record. The interesting thing about the code given above is that it is actually fairly flexible. If you wanted to, in the User Interface or Business Rules layers, you could decide that some of the fields do not need to be saved (or added with the new record), and therefore you simply don't pass them along to the method, and they won't be added/updated.

We will do the same type of processing with the Update option. However there is one extra part – we need to find the record that is to be updated. So in addition to passing along the name of the table and the array of data, we also need to pass along the primary key value of the record that needs to be changed. The code will have to try to find that record – if it cannot be found *(perhaps it has been deleted?)* the user will need to be notified.

```
function UpdateRow( cTable, cKey, nKey, aData )
   local cCmd, nField, oSeq, cString
   private xValue, cVal

   // check for both parameters:
   if pCount() < 4
      msgbox( "This method requires four parameters: "+;
              "cTable, cKey, nKey and aData."+;
              "See comments in InvoiceDataLayer1.dmd.",;
              "UpdateRow Method Error", 16 )
      return
   endif

   // create the strings needed for the fields
   cString = ""
   for nField = 1 to aData.size/2 // two columns
      // add fieldname to list:
      cString += aData[ nField, 1 ]
      // need the = sign:
      cString += "="

      xValue = aData[ nField, 2 ]
      if type( "xValue" ) # "N"
         if type( "xValue" ) == "C" or type( "xValue" ) == "V"
            cVal = ReplaceApostrophe( aData[ nField, 2] )
            cString += [']+cVal+[']
         else
            cString += [']+aData[ nField, 2 ]+[']
         endif // character
      else // numeric
         cString += aData[ nField, 2 ]
      endif // type
      if nField < aData.size/2 // no trailing commas
         cString += ", "
      endif
   next // nField
   // okay, actually build the string
   cCmd  = "update "+cTable
   cCmd += " set "
   cCmd += cString
   // this is necessary because executing from the
   // database, not the query ...
   cCmd += " where "+cKey+" = "+ nKey

   // open the database and query:
   this.BookSample_Write.active := true
   this.WriteQuery.sql          := "select * from "+cTable+;
                                   " where "+cKey+"="+nKey
   this.WriteQuery.active       := true

   // find the key field:
   if this.WriteQuery.rowset.count() # 1
      // if we didn't find it:
      msgbox( "Could not find value '"+nKey+"' "+;
              "in primary key field '"+cKey+"'!",;
              "UpdateRow Method Error", 16 )
      return false
```

```
      endif

      // close the query
      this.WriteQuery.active        := false

      // if we're here we found the record,
      // execute the command, deactivate database ...:
      try
         this.BookSample_write.executeSQL( cCmd )
         this.BookSample_write.active := false

      catch( ADOException e )
         // same execption code as in other parts of the application
         // trimmed out of here to shorten the code …
      endtry
   return
```

Delete a Record

Deleting data is a little tricky, because you need to confirm that the user meant to choose that option *(this should not be in the Data Layer, however)*. You also need to deal with parent/child relationships, and orphaning records.

This database is simple, but a good programmer can enhance the code shown below to handle a parent table with multiple child tables *(think of using arrays)*. This version handles a single child table and cascade deletes.

```
   function DeleteRow(cTable,cKey,nKey,bCascade,cChildTable,cChildKeyfield)
      local cCmd

      // check for appropriate parameters:
      if pCount() < 3
         msgbox( "This method requires three parameters: "+;
                 "cTable, cKey, and nKey."+;
                 "See comments in InvoiceDataLayer1.dmd.",;
                 "DeleteRow Method Error", 16 )
         return
         // if we did not get the bCascade parameter,
         // assume false:
         if pCount() == 3
            bCascade = false
            // if the cascade parameter is true, but we don't
            // have a child table reference, we cannot perform
            // a cascade delete.
         elseif bCascade == true and pCount() < 6
            msgbox( "If you wish to perform a cascade delete, you must "+;
                    "provide the name of the child table and the name of "+;
                    "the key field in the child table.",;
                    "DeleteRow Method Error", 16 )
            return
         endif // pCount() == 3
      endif // pCount() < 3

      // build the command string:
      cCmd  = "delete from "+cTable
      cCmd += " where "+cKey+" = "+nKey

      // open the database and query and find the record to see if
      // it actually exists:
```

```
        this.BookSample_Write.active := true
        this.WriteQuery.sql          := "select * from "+cTable+;
                                        " where "+cKey+"="+nKey
        this.WriteQuery.active        := true

    // find the key field:
    if this.WriteQuery.rowset.count() # 1
        // if we didn't find it:
        msgbox( "Could not find value '"+nKey+"' "+;
                "in primary key field '"+cKey+"'!",;
                "DeleteRow Method Error", 16 )
        return false
    endif

    // close the query
    this.WriteQuery.active      := false

    // if we're here we found the record,
    // execute the command, deactivate database ...:
    try
        this.BookSample_write.executeSQL( cCmd )

        // only try to perform cascade delete IF we have
        // told the method we want it:
        if bCascade
            // cascade delete doesn't really need another method:
            // build the command string:
            cCmd  = "delete from "+cChildTable
            cCmd += " where "+cChildKeyfield+" = "+nKey

            // open the query and see if there are any child records:
            this.BookSample_Write.active := true
            this.WriteQuery.sql          := ;
"select * from "+cChildTable+" where "+cChildKeyfield+"="+nKey
            this.WriteQuery.active        := true

            // find the key field:
            if this.WriteQuery.rowset.count() < 1
                // if we didn't find it:
                msgbox( "Could not find value '"+nKey+"' "+;
                        "in field '"+cChildKey+"' of table '"+;
                        cChildTable+"'.",;
                   "No Child Records -- Cascade Delete Failed", 16 )
                return
            endif // count()
        endif // bCascade

    catch( ADOException e )
        // Same as other ADOException code, trimmed here …
    endtry
return
```

Apostrophes

Apostrophes or single-quotes in the data are a problem, as they are also used as delimiters for SQL commands. Interestingly, the way to resolve this is to put two of them next to each other. So if you wanted to add a Business named "Fred's

Widgets", you would actually enter it as "Fred''s Widgets". This looks almost like a double-quote, but it is two apostrophes (or single-quotes).

Ronnie MacGregor posted this code *(included in the sample code)* to handle them. The code is not actually a method of the Data Module class, so it needs to be added after the *endclass* statement:

```
function ReplaceApostrophe(cText)
    // Function by Ronnie MacGregor -- posted in the dBASE
    // newsgroups.

    // Adds a second Apostrophe for SQL handling purposes

    local nCount
    for nCount = 1 to len(cText)*2 step 2
       nPos = at( ['], cText, nCount)
       if nPos == 0
          exit
       else
          cText := stuff( cText, nPos, 1, "''" )
       endif
    endfor // next
return cText
```

Once the code is put together, you can save and close the Data Module in the Source Code Editor.

A Bit More Code

While working on the UI Layer, I realized there needed to be a way to reference the ADOQuery objects based on the name of the table, so we need to add a bit more code in the Data Module.

We need an array that contains object references for each of the read-only queries. The way the Data Module is designed, when writing to the table, we only need the one *ADOQuery*, but when reading the data there should be an *ADOQuery* object for each table. There are several approaches, the one that makes the most sense is similar to something that you will be doing with the UI Layer – each *ADOQuery* object will add a reference to itself to the query, this way when building your application you don't have to know the names of the various objects.

Open the Data Module in the Designer (double-click it), and click on the Invoices query. In the Inspector click on the "Events" tab, and find the *onOpen* event. Click this, and click on the small button to the right. The Source Code Editor will open with this code:

```
function INVOICES_onOpen()

    return
```

Insert into the code this statement:

```
class::Common_OnOpen( this )
```

Followed by a statement that assigns a custom property to the rowset called "Sequence", which is going to be used when we need to call the Firebird *Gen_ID()* function:

So the event handler looks like:

```
function INVOICES_onOpen()
   // add this query to custom array
   class::Common_OnOpen( this )
   // add custom property to rowset:
   this.rowset.Sequence = "InvNum_Seq"
return
```

You will need to repeat for each of the read-only queries (Customers, Inventory, and LineItems). For the other three tables, the name of the sequence is "CustNum_Seq", "ItemNum_Seq", and "LINum_Seq".

Then while the Source Code Editor is open, add this additional method (before the *endclass* statement):

```
function Common_OnOpen( oQuery )
   // check for array, if it doesn't exist, create it
   if type("this.parent.aROQuery") = "U"
      this.parent.aROQuery = new array()
   endif
   // add object reference for this query to array
   this.parent.aROQuery.add( this )
return
```

Once you have this save and close the Source Code Editor and the Data Module Designer.

For the time being we should be done with the Data Layer. However, we may need to come back to it. One thing that a developer learns early is that you are very seldom done.

📝 **NOTE**

When I started working with this code my inclination was to use the query object's *canOpen* event handler – the idea being to do everything before the query opened, the Data Module was done, etc. The difficulty is that with most objects if they are not open, in this case the *active* property is not set to *true* –they are not instantiated yet, the object reference is not valid. When I worked with the code what was being added to the array was not a valid object reference, but a logical value of *false*. This was, understandably, disconcerting and confusing. Using the *onOpen* event handler works great, as the object is instantiated at this point. **Understanding the sequence events occur in is important to a developer.**

The Business Layer

The Business Layer is where the application deals with any rules for the specific application. These rules can be simple, such as validating the Invoice Date, it can be more complicated, including perhaps performing some calculations to ensure the data is correct, etc.

Every application is different, and every programmer is likely to approach this differently.

You may want to use:

- Field-level validation
- Record-level validation
- Form-level validation
- Mixed – a combination of all three

For the application we are working on, we're going to create a custom code file (.CC) in dBASE, and set up a series of validation functions. These will return a logical (or Boolean, if you prefer) value – if they return a value of *true*, the data is valid, if they return a value of *false*, the data is considered to be invalid.

The following is an example of field-level validation from the file BusinessLayer.cc:

```
function InvoiceDateValid( dDate )
   // Validate an Invoice Date field:
   local bOK
   bOK = true

   if dDate > date() // Invoice in the future?
      msgbox( "The date '"+dDate+"' is in the future. "+;
              "This is not acceptable.",;
              "Invalid Date", 16 )
      bOK := false
   endif

   if dDate < date() // Invoice date in the past?
      // ask user if this is intended/okay --
      // they might be updating the record due to
      // an error when the record was created:
      bOK = msgbox( "The date '"+dDate+"' is in the past. "+;
                    "If this is okay, click 'CK', otherwise "+;
                    "click 'Cancel'.",;
                    "Date May Be Invalid", 32+1 ) == 1
                    // 1 = OK, 2 = Cancel
   endif
return bOK
```

Interestingly, after all this work, I ended up not using this in the application, so consider it an exercise. The code does function, but it is not being used.

Discussing the concepts of data validation in the dBASE newsgroups, while one will typically get many answers that all seem to make sense, one developer posted a really good comment that should be kept in mind *(used here with his permission)* – this concept is germane to all database types – local, SQL Server, etc.:

> "You might argue that good data validation is for the purpose of data integrity and quality, however the reality in today's world is that it allows the dumbing down of the user to a cheaper grade.
>
> The biggest problem with really tight data validation, is that if your data validation code has not dealt with an unforeseen set of circumstances, then the user cannot save a record with perfectly "valid" data for that scenario. Experience would support the view that in these circumstances, a user will find a way of "tweaking" the data in order to save the record and move on. The problem will generally not be reported, and your efforts to ensure good data have actually produced bad data!!!
>
> So there is a balance to be struck …
>
> Validate data that is absolutely critical, and apply a degree of flexibility for less important data." – *Ronnie MacGregor*

Further discussion of the Business Layer and data validation will occur toward the end of Chapter 6, once we have the forms all worked out.

Sample Code for This Chapter

The following is a listing of the sample code in the "Chapter 04" folder, if you downloaded it from my website. You may use the code contained in these forms for your own applications if you desire, with the caveat that credit be given appropriately.

- **ADOSeqValue.cc** – Code to handle working with an ADO type database and autoincrement fields, if your database does not have a mechanism for this functionality.
- **BusinessLayer.cc** – The BusinessLayer class for the sample application.
- **CreateDatabase.prg** – Program to create the tables and set up the sequences, add some data, and more. This is the table design for the sample application.
- **DataLayer.dmd** – The DataLayer for the sample application.
- **SQLSeqValue.cc** – Code to handle working with a SQL type database and autoincrement fields, if your database does not have a mechanism for this functionality. This would work for non-ADO, but could work with ADO as well, depending on your database design.
- **TestAddRow.prg** – A simple program to show how to add a row to one of the tables using the techniques shown in this book.
- **TestDeleteRow.prg** – A simple program to show how to delete a row …
- **TestUpdateRow.prg** – A simple program to show how to update data in a table …

Summary

This chapter, and the next few, are quite involved. The reason I split them into multiple chapters was because of this complexity. In the next chapter we will start to discuss the User Interface part of the application.

Thanks to the following for a lot of assistance with the code here:

- Andre Knappstein
- Mervyn Bick
- Ronnie MacGregor
- John Noble

> ### 📝 NOTE
>
> One of the folk who has helped me a *lot* with all of this is Andre Knappstein, a German developer who works with Firebird as a database administrator. He points out that many developers recommend using a specific naming sequence for Sequences (or Generators):
>
> ```
> Seq_InvNum
> Seq_CustNum
> ```
>
> etc. By using "Seq_" first, you are assured that, when examining the metadata in the Firebird database, all the Sequences are listed together, and so on. For a simple database like the example here, I have chosen to use the naming sequence shown in these chapters, but if you expect you may need to use the metadata of the database, this may be a consideration in your naming patterns.

Chapter 5: Using ADO Database Classes in an Application, Part 2

In this chapter we will be continuing the simple *application* using ADO Database objects that we started in Chapter 4 *(we will finish in Chapter 6!)*.

In chapter 4 we completed some of the basics of setting up the Data and Business Layers of the application, in this chapter the goal is to get a working User Interface. This chapter is going to be a bit complex, as we are building a custom form, a set of controls, adding code and there is a lot of back-and-forth work here *(modifying code created in Chapter 3 to interact properly with the code here, and so on)*.

The User Interface Layer

As noted earlier, the User Interface (UI) should not know anything about the details of the Business Layer or the Data Layer. However, it must be able to communicate with them, as the UI is how the end-user interacts with the data.

This is where things can get tricky, and as a coder who has, for years, advocated using all those nifty properties, events, and methods in the *query*, *rowset,* and *field* objects, I am now going to have to tell you that many of them do not work properly, or at least reliably, with SQL Server databases *(don't despair, they work great with local tables)*.

The hardest thing to wrap your head around is the concept that a datalink on any of the User Interface controls is a bad idea to rely on. To me, that feels almost like stepping backward in time. In the early days of dBASE for Windows, and the DOS versions of dBASE, in order to handle what is called a record buffer, we had to write a lot of code. Then along came the OODML database objects, and the buffer was built-in, and we got kind of spoiled.

The difficulty is that we have two data connections, one for reading the data, and the other for writing the data, and they don't talk to each other. What is happening in the read connection is completely unknown in the write connection, and vice versa.

This is where having a primary key field for every table in your database becomes vital. This is also where dBASE's object-oriented programming becomes a great boon to the programmer. Properly defined controls that use custom properties, overwritten methods, and event handlers can make things much easier.

All that said, it will still take some work to write code that can be used in a "generic" application.

When building your User-Interface *(and all parts of an application, really)*, particularly forms and form controls, there is the question of "Which came first, the chicken or the egg?" You could jump right in and start building your forms, but then you need the controls, and you need the code behind the controls, so where do you start? I find that this is really a back-and-forth process. You have to start with an idea, build on it, test it, build a control, put it on a test form, figure out how to set up the custom properties for the control, which will be needed, and then build code in the custom form, and test that. It is a time-consuming process. The code that is in these chapters *(and the sample app)* has been put through its paces, and it all works. Lots of trial-and-error *(and much cursing by this author)* occurred while doing so, and a lot of help was given by folk in the dBASE Newsgroups to get this working. If you use this code to build your own ADO applications, you will find I've done much of the work for you.

Application Assumptions

For this application to work properly, or any application based off this code, there are some assumptions being made. You will see discussion of some of them throughout the chapters involved in building this application. However, I need to make sure two of them are discussed up-front:

- All tables *must* have a Primary Key Field.
- The Primary Key Field *must* be the first field of any table.

Any code that deals with the Primary Key is assuming that it is the first field of the table ... it makes it easier to program for, it means not having to add some custom property to something that specifies the name of the Primary Key. The way the code is written, it also means not having to use a default Primary Key name of some sort.

The reason I am adamant about this is that it is easy to just place the Primary Key anywhere in the table structure, but that can cause difficulties as noted. Normally as a coder I am pretty "free-form" about some things, to the dismay of some of my fellow developers at times. But for this application this is important.

Create a Custom Form

A custom form is a "base" class, as defined in my other books. It is one that is the basis for other forms. Code that is set in the custom form class is *inherited* by other forms that are based on it, which means you are not having to rewrite (or copy and paste) code across multiple forms. This allows for great flexibility in your programming.

For the custom form, we know we are going to need code to:

- Load the data into the controls from the read-only query
- Handle passing record-level and/or form-level validation to the business class
- Save the data from the controls back to the write query

To get started, create a custom form in dBASE, using the Custom Form Designer. In the Navigator, click the tab for "Forms", and double-click the "[New Custom Form]" icon.

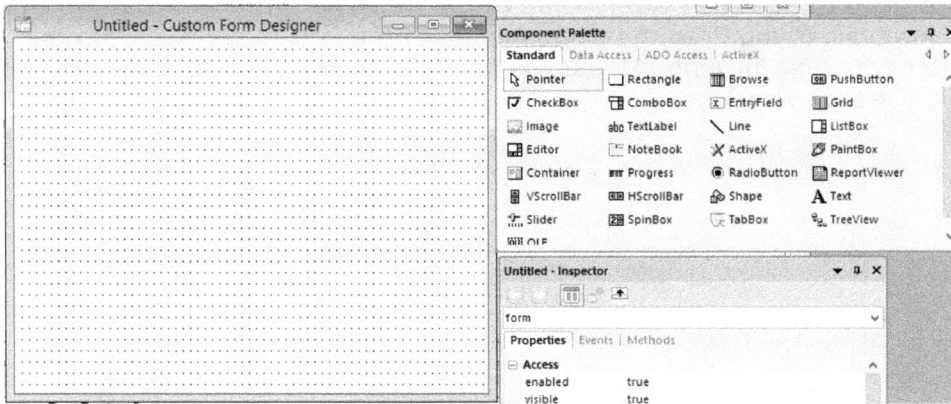

Figure 5-1

I have included the Component Pallete and part of the Inspector in the screen shot in Figure 5-1, although we will be focusing on the design surface.

I always work with a form metric of Pixels because this is how Windows itself works. For the custom form set the *metric* property to *6 – Pixels*. Then I suggest setting the form's *text* property to: "UI Layer - Custom Form" (without the quotes).

It is a good idea to save the custom form now – use Ctrl+S and name this "UILayer". If you don't save this early in the process, the class name may be saved as UntitledCForm, which is a bit weird, and might make other code more difficult.

We'll start with a couple of basics – I always prefer a title at the top of every form (not just in the form's titlebar), so I add a text control by dragging it from the Component Palette to the design surface, then change the following properties in the Inspector:

- *name:* TitleText
- *anchor*: 2 – Top
- *alignment:* 4 – Center
- *borderStyle*: 2 – Raised
- *fontSize:* 16
- *fontBold:* true
- *height:* 155
- *colorNormal*: Blue/BtnFace
- *pageNo*: 0
- *text*: UI Layer – Custom Form

> 📋 **NOTE**
> The title text at the top of the form, like many things, is a personal style issue – you can use it or not for your own applications. If you use all of the sample code to base your own applications on and do not wish to use this control, you would need to remove the title text control from the UILayer custom form, and then remove references to any other forms in the constructor code *(modify them in the Source Code Editor)*.

Then we need to add the Data Module to the form, so we have access to the data itself. However, if you drag the Data Module to the design surface from the Navigator *(my first inclination)* you will find you cannot change some properties you might need to change.

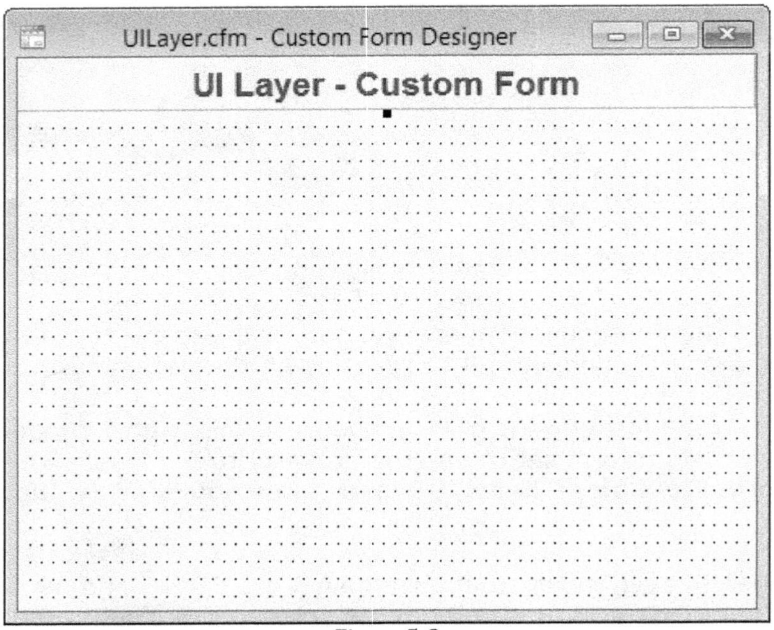

Figure 5-2

For the custom form, the next thing is some code. We need to override two standard methods of the form and add our own code to them. These two are the ones that deal with opening the form. We don't know if any specific form based on this one will be opened with the *open* or *readModal* methods, so we are going to override both of them, and call a separate function of our own called *init*. (While testing we often open the forms with *open*, where for the application most of them are opened with *readModal* ...)

To do this, in the Inspector, click the "Methods" tab, find the *open* method. Click this method, then click the button that appears on the right. When you do the Source Code Editor will open and you will see this section of code inserted:

```
function form_open()

        return FORM::open()
```

I usually rearrange the code a little (moving the return statement), but that is just a preference. All we need here is to add one line of code above the return statement:

```
function form_open()
    class::init()
return FORM::open()
```

Repeat this for the *readModal* method:

```
function form_readModal()
    class::init()
return FORM::readModal()
```

Then add the function *Init* (above the *endclass* statement):

```
function Init
   // code that executes before the form opens
   // first thing we need is to set up the DataModule:
   set procedure to DataLayer.dmd
   form.DataLayerDataModule1 = new DataLayerDataModule()
return
```

The only code in the method right now is the code that sets up the Data Module for use. We will add more code later. Close the Source Code Editor. You can close the Custom Form Designer (Ctrl+W) for now.

At this point we are going to *start* working with custom controls, and then we will come back to the custom form.

Create Custom Controls

As mentioned earlier, there are many different things that need to be done with the controls, including communicating with the custom forms, and more. The following are some of the tasks that must be dealt with:

- Display the data
- Allow the user to interact, unless a specific field is read-only *(such as a primary key)*
- If data is changed, it may be a good idea to show that
- Handle field-level validation (if any)
- Allow the user to decide if they are going to save changes, abandon changes, etc.
- Navigation through the data may be necessary depending on individual forms

And there is probably more.

To get started, we will work with the most commonly used control to interface with data, the *entryfield*. Create a new class file in dBASE by going to the Command Window and typing:

```
modify command SQLFormControls.cc
```

Note that I named this "SQLFormControls.cc" because these controls should work with either ADO database objects or standard OODML database objects. There is nothing about them that is specific to ADO ...

In the Source Code Editor, we will start with a custom entryfield: Enter the following:

```
class SQLEntryField( oParent ) of Entryfield( oParent ) custom
   with (this)
      borderStyle   := 7
      colorNormal   := "WindowText/Window"
      colorHighlight := "WindowText/0x80ffff" // yellow background
      fontName      := "WindowText"
      metric        := 6  // Pixels
      height        := 22
      selectAll     := false
```

```
        value            := "SQLCustEntryField"
     endwith
  endclass
```

This gives us the basic control that we need, with some preferences *(for example, when the control has focus, the color will change to one with a yellow background).*

From here we need to decide how the information on the form is going to be loaded, how the custom form will interact with it, and more.

This is where use of custom properties becomes ideal. To properly interact between the data and the control, with local tables we could just set the *datalink* property, and a lot of things would be handled for us. However, it's not quite that simple here.

For this application we really need, at a minimum the following custom properties:

- tableName
- fieldname
- oldValue
- newValue
- defaultValue

The first two are self-explanatory. The second two are used to interact with the control's *value* property. We can save the current value to the *oldValue*, then when the user leaves the control, we store the *value* property in the *newValue* property, and we can compare to see if they changed anything. If they did, we can use that information ... The *defaultValue* property is important when a user is appending a new row to the table, so among other things the controls know the type of data (character, numeric, date ...) that is allowed. *(A developer can also use* picture, *and other properties for these controls, such as* maxLength *for character values.)* With experimentation I realized there were some other properties that were useful:

- includeInQuery
- modified
- readOnly
- error

To use these, we have to work with code. Some of the code can be executed before an instance of this control is created (before the form opens), including creating the custom properties:

```
this.tableName      = null
this.fieldName      = null
this.oldValue       = null
this.newValue       = null
this.includeInQuery = true
this.modified       = false
this.readOnly       = false
this.error          = false
```

We also need to have a way to communicate information to the form, and after some testing, this works:

```
   // add this item to form's aSQLControls array
   // (if array doesn't exist, create it, then
   // add this ...)
   if this.includeInQuery
      if type( "form.aSQLControls" ) == "U"
         form.aSQLControls = new array()
      endif // type(...)
      // add control to array
      form.aSQLControls.add( this ) // object reference
   endif // this.includeInQuery
```

If you examine the code, you will see that if the control's *includeInQuery* property is *true*, we need to add it to an array that is part of the form. What if the array does not exist? Rather than relying on the developer (you or someone else) to create this custom array, we create it here. Then we add an object reference to the control.

Why is there an *includeInQuery* property in the first place? Don't you want all controls attached to data in the table? Well, maybe … maybe you don't. This property allows for some flexibility.

The beauty of this is that we don't need to know the names of the controls, we can just pass an array of control references to the form. The form then, before it opens, can read the data into the *value* property of the controls, and we're almost there. We have one thing that needs to happen when the form opens *(which then opens each control on the form, firing this event handler)*:

```
   function onOpen
      // is this a read-only control?
      SetReadOnly( this ) // function in the .CC file

      // set the "old" value to value currently in field
      // this is "datalinked" to:
      if this.fieldName # null
         this.oldValue := this.value
      endif // not empty

      // Suggested by Heinz Kesting:
      this.ModTimer = new timer()
      this.ModTimer.interval := 0.5 // half second
      this.ModTimer.onTimer  := class::IsModified
      this.ModTimer.parent    = this
   return // onOpen event
```

If the *fieldname* property is not empty, the code then sets the value of the *oldValue* property to that of the *value* property. This way, if the user changes the value, we can act on it.

The use of the timer shown above *(suggested by Heinz Kesting)* is designed to verify that the value has been modified, which will *(when the rest of the application is coded properly)* be useful when navigating *(ask if the user wishes to save changes, etc.)*. For this to work, we need to modify the *onGotFocus* event handler and add an *onLostFocus* event handler:

```
function onGotFocus
   this.keyboard( "{Home}" )
   // set timer:
   this.ModTimer.enabled := true
return // onGotFocus event

function onLostFocus
   // turn timer off:
   this.modTimer.enabled := false
return
```

Add this code before the *endclass* statement:

```
function isModified
   // called from an object that doesn't understand form references:
   oForm = this.parent.form
   oThis = this.parent

   // set custom property of form:
   if type( "oForm.modified" ) # "L"
      oForm.modified = false
   endif

   // set the "new" value to value currently in entryfield
   // control, so that ultimately we can save it out to
   // the field ...
   oThis.newValue := oThis.value
   // if it's read-only we don't want to
   // do anything to the colors:
   if oThis.ReadOnly
      return
   endif
   // change the color of the control if the value
   // is different than the original:
   if oThis.oldValue # oThis.newValue
      // change the color
      oThis.colorNormal    := "Blue/Window"
      oThis.colorHighlight := "Blue/0x80ffff"
      // set modified property:
      oThis.modified := true
      // set form's property:
      oForm.modified := true
   else
      oThis.colorNormal    := "WindowText/Window"
      oThis.colorHighlight := "WindowText/0x80ffff"
      oThis.Modified       := false
   endif // this.oldValue ...
return // isModified event
```

Save and exit the Source Code Editor. It is time to go back to the custom form, and work on that initialization routine.

Back to the Custom Form

In the code that we will need to call from Init(), we need:

- ... to be able to find the query for each control that is "linked" to a field in a table.
- ... to set the *value* property of the control to match the data.

As you might imagine, this code can be a little complicated. I spent quite a bit of time working with this, and with a lot of assistance from several folk in the newsgroups, came up with the following. The code is written in such a way that it can be called not only when the form first opens, but also when navigating through a table:

In the *init* method, add this line *(before the* return *statement)*:

```
class::LoadData()
```

You then need to create the method *LoadData*. This method will do the following:

- Check to see if the array *aSQLControls (created by our custom controls)* exists. If not, it will return an error and stop ...
- Loop through the array, first calling another method: *FindQuery*, which will look for the query objects based on the custom control property *tableName*.
- Assuming the query object is found, we then try to find the field, using the custom control property *fieldname*.
- Assuming that is found, we assign the value of the field to the *value* property of the control.

This code looks like the following:

```
Function LoadData
    local nControls, nFields, cTable, oQuery, bOK

    // if the array is undefined, there is nothing
    // for us to do:
    if type( "form.aSQLControls" ) == "U"
        msgbox( "Cannot load data, form is missing aSQLControls array.",;
            "LoadData Error", 16 )
        return
    endif

    // Need to loop through the array:
    for nControls = 1 to form.aSQLControls.size
        // We need to look at the first control to see what
        // the tableName is:
        cTable = form.aSQLControls[ nControls ].tableName
        // if the developer has made an error, rather than
        // crashing the software, move on to the next
        // control:
        if empty( cTable ) or ;
            empty( form.aSQLControls[ nControls ].fieldName )
            loop
        endif

        // call FindQuery method with the name of the table
        oQuery = class::FindQuery( cTable )
```

```
      if oQuery == null
          return // dealt with errors in FindQuery method
      endif

      // if we found this, we have the table/query, let's try
      // to find the field
      bOK = false
      for nFields = 1 to oQuery.rowset.fields.size

          if oQuery.rowset.fields[nFields].fieldName.toUpperCase()== ;
              form.aSQLControls[nControls].fieldName.toUpperCase()

              // found it:
              bOK := true

              // load the value property from the table:
              form.aSQLControls[ nControls ].value := ;
                      oQuery.rowset.fields[ nFields ].value
          endif // attempt to find field

          // not found, assign null value
          if not bOK
              form.aSQLControls[ nControls ].value := null
          endif

          // set some custom properties:
          form.aSQLControls[ nControls ].newValue := null
          form.aSQLControls[ nControls ].oldValue := ;
              form.aSQLControls[ nControls ].value
          form.aSQLControls[ nControls ].modified := false
          form.aSQLControls[ nControls ].error    := false
          // set colors:
          form.aSQLControls[ nControls ].colorNormal := ;
                                  "WindowText/Window"
          form.aSQLControls[ nControls ].colorHighlight :=;
                                  "WindowText/0x80ffff"
      next // nFields
  next // nControls
return
```

The FindQuery method also checks for errors, and helps get things going:

- It needs to see if the Data Module's *aROQuery* array is available – if not it will return an error (which is checked for in the *LoadData* method)
- Loop through the array of *ADOQuery* object references, looking at the *name* property and comparing to the UI object's *tableName* property which was passed *to* the method as a parameter
- If not found we return an error
- If found, we return the object reference for the query object, which is then used in the LoadData method.

The method looks like the following:

```
function FindQuery( cTable )
    // if the data module does not have the custom
    // array needed, we also can't do anything:
    if type( "form.DataLayerDataModule1.aROQuery" ) # "A"
        msgbox( "Cannot load data, Data Module is missing "+;
```

```
            aROQuery array.",;
            "FindQuery Error", 16 )
      return false
   endif

   private aQueries, qQuery
   qQuery = null

   // check array to see if tablename matches
   // the name property of the query:
   aQueries = form.DataLayerDataModule1.aROQuery
   for nQuery = 1 to aQueries.size
      if aQueries[ nQuery ].name.toUpperCase() ==;
            cTable.rightTrim().toUpperCase()
         qQuery = aQueries[ nQuery ]
      endif
   next

   if qQuery == null
      msgbox( "Table '"+cTable+"': No query "+;
            "found using this tablename ...", ;
            "FindQuery Error", 16 )
   endif

   // We have what we need, return it to the calling point:
return qQuery
```

Having this code in the custom form means that when you create the actual forms that will be used to work with the data, you don't need to reproduce it in each form – you can call it as needed.

Next we will start building the interface itself.

The Customer Form

This is an invoicing application, why are we not starting with the invoice? The invoice form itself is probably the most complex form in the application, so I chose to start with a simpler form.

The Customer form is designed to work *only* with the customer table. As with any form that interacts with data, the form should be able to do the following:

- Search for a record
- Navigate through the data
- View data
- Edit data
- Add new records
- Delete records

Most of the data forms I create have two pages – one to search for a record (using a "Seeker" control), and the main page that displays the data itself.

We will start with viewing and editing data, but we will be adding quite a bit of functionality.

First let's create the form. In the Navigator, click the "Forms" tab, and then double-click the icon labeled "[New Form]". Before you do anything else, it is best to tell dBASE you want this based on our Custom form. To do that, click "File", and in the menu select "Set Custom Form Class". A small dialog will appear:

Figure 5-3

Click the "Pencil" button and select the file "UILayer.cfm". You will see the dialog change:

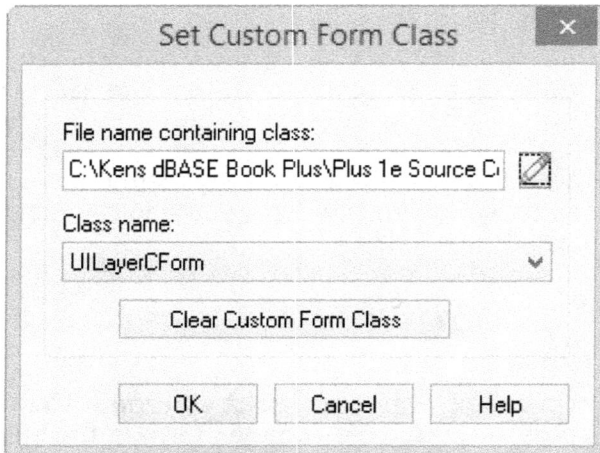

Figure 5-4

The path for the file of course will match how your code is set up. Click "OK" and the form will change. Press Ctrl+S to save the form, and name it "Customers" *(without the quotes)*.

We will start, as noted, with some small changes. The first deals with the text that will appear on the *titlebar* of the form, and then the text in the *TitleText* control. In the Inspector, find the *text* property, and type: "Customers" (again without the quotes). Then click the Title Text once to select it, then click again *(this is not the same as double-click)* to put into edit mode. Change the text again to say "Customers", and click off the form. Press Ctrl+S to save your work.

To start everything off, we need to set up controls to interact with the data, but because I really try to use Custom classes for nearly everything, we're going to create a custom TextLabel control. To do that, for the moment, close the Form Designer, and open the file SQLFormControls.cc in the Source Code Editor.

Add the following above the SQLEntryfield class definition:

```
class SQLTextLabel( oParent ) of TextLabel( oParent ) custom
   with (this)
      alignHorizontal := 2 // Right
      alignVertical   := 1 // Middle
      fontBold        := true
      fontName        := "WindowText"
      metric          := 6 // Pixels
      text            := "SQLTextLabel:"
   endwith
endclass
```

For now, save and close the custom class file. In the Command Window, type:

```
set procedure to SQLFormControls.cc
```

Then open the Customers form in the Form Designer (right click the icon, and select "Design Form").

The Component Palette should now display a "Custom" tab. Click that, and you should see your custom controls.

Select the SQLTextLabel control and drag it to the design surface, and in the Inspector change the *text* property to: "Customer Number:" (without the quotes). Change the *name* property to "CustNumLabel" without the quotes *(be sure to press the Enter key after typing this)*.

Drag a SQLEntryfield control to the surface, and place it next to the label, and change the *name* property to "CustNumEF".

> **NOTE**
> The Customer Number is a Primary Key field in the table. There are coders who believe you should never reveal these to the user, and they should be something stored completely behind the scenes *(not appearing anywhere in the UI)*. I disagree, and find that having multiple identifiers is silly. The biggest concern is that the value should *never* be modified by the user. We will avoid that when we get to some code for the form later … *Have no fear, this has been planned for.* One could argue cases where perhaps an employee ID might require extra characters that aren't part of an autoincrement (or other primary key) field value, but for most cases I have no problem with showing the primary key to the user.

Repeat the creation of TextLabel and Entryfield controls using the custom classes on the Component Palette for the following fields:

- BusinessName
- Address1
- Address2
- City
- State
- PostalCode
- EmailAddress

The names of the controls should be similar to the fieldnames, but use EF for Entryfield and "Label" for the TextLabel controls. Lay these out in a "pleasing" fashion. When done, you should have a form that looks similar to:

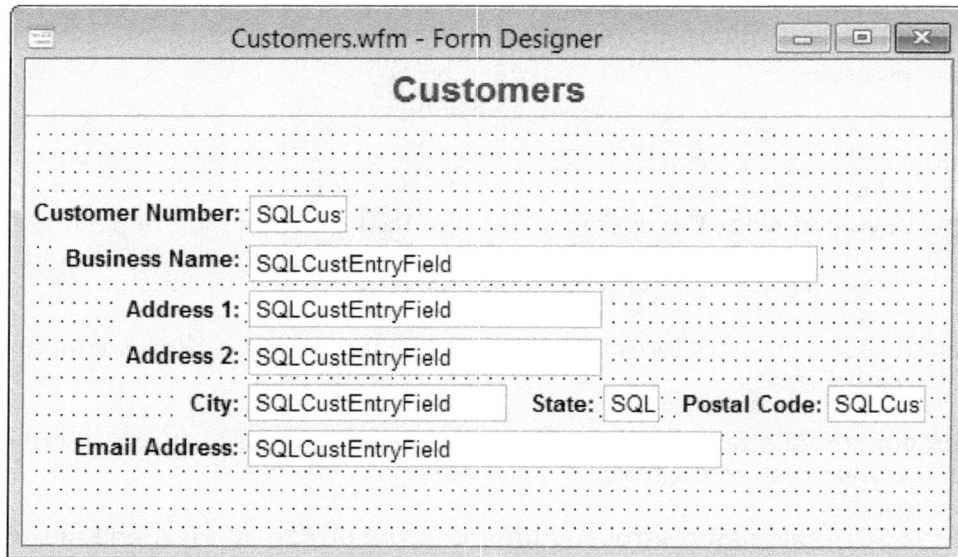

Figure 5-5

You could, if it helps you visualize what is happening, set the *value* properties for each control so they mean something when editing the form *(it is a little confusing to see the name of the control there, but one can get used to anything ...).*

I have intentionally left some room at the top of the form and at the bottom, and I resized the form as needed to get the controls to fit. I also eye-balled (guessed) the widths of the *entryfield* controls. When you start actually testing the form, you can tinker with the widths so that everything appears the way you need it to.

There are a few things we can do here before getting into code for the form. Click on the State Entryfield (whatever you called it), we know that the standard State Codes in the United States are two characters, so we can limit the input to two characters, and we can force it to upper case. In the Inspector, click the *picture* property and type two exclamation points (!!). For the Postal Code entryfield, we know the user is going to enter numbers, and we're going to assume they need the full 9 digit postal code, which includes a dash in it. Find the *picture* property there, and type: "99999-9999" *(without the quotes)*. You may find you need to widen the *entryfield*, which may mean readjusting the form width.

Some Code

At this point you are going to need to start working with code for this form. We need to do something similar to what we have done before – we're going to overwrite the startup code for the form, and call a specific routine to set the properties of the controls.

Click on the form, and in the Inspector click the "Methods" tab. Click on *open* and then the button to the right. You will see a dialog that asks "form.form. is linked to a method outside of the form; do you want to overwrite that?". Click "Yes". Enter the code needed to fill this in:

```
function form_open()
   class::Local_Init()
return CUSTOMERSFORM::open()
```

Repeat for the *readModal* method:

```
function form_readModal()
   class::Local_Init()
return CUSTOMERSFORM::readModal()
```

And create a new method:

```
function Local_Init
   class::SetupControls()
   UILAYERCFORM::Init()
return
```

We are not naming the custom method "init" as we did in the custom form, to avoid any confusion with method names, instead we use "Local_Init" to indicate that this is an initialization routine in *this* form. The code is in the order given so that the controls are given values for the properties that are needed, and then the code in the custom form should fire, which will actually select the information needed and apply it to the controls.

The SetupControls method of the form needs to contain references to each control, with specific properties. Each one requires the *tableName* and *fieldName* properties, and if you wish you can use some of the other ones we set up, such as *readOnly*, which is a good idea for the Customer Number field.

```
function SetupControls
    // method required to set custom properties of the controls,
    // defaultValue is important when appending, and maxLength
    // is important for character fields, so user cannot
    // enter more data than the width of the field in the table:
    form.CustNumEF.tableName      := "Customers"
    form.CustNumEF.fieldName      := "CustomerNumber"
    form.CustNumEF.readOnly       := true
    form.CustNumEF.includeInQuery := false
    form.BusNameEF.tableName      := "Customers"
    form.BusNameEF.fieldName      := "BusinessName"
    form.BusNameEF.defaultValue   := ""
    form.BusNameEF.maxLength      := 3C
    // we can use this to force focus on a specific control
    form.firstControl             = form.BusNameEF
    form.Address1EF.tableName     := "Customers"
    form.Address1EF.fieldName     := "Address1"
    form.Address1EF.defaultValue  := ""
    form.Address1EF.maxLength     := 25
    form.Address2EF.tableName     := "Customers"
    form.Address2EF.fieldName     := "Address2"
    form.Address2EF.defaultValue  := ""
    form.Address2EF.maxLength     := 25
    form.CityEF.tableName         := "Customers"
    form.CityEF.fieldName         := "City"
    form.CityEF.defaultValue      := ""
    form.CityEF.maxLength         := 30
```

```
form.StateEF.tableName          := "Customers"
form.StateEF.fieldName          := "State"
form.StateEF.defaultValue       := ""
form.StateEF.maxLength          := 2
form.PostalCodeEF.tableName     := "Customers"
form.PostalCodeEF.fieldName     := "PostalCode"
form.PostalCodeEF.defaultValue  := ""
form.PostalCodeEF.maxLength     := 10
form.EmailAddrEF.tableName      := "Customers"
form.EmailAddrEF.fieldName      := "EmailAddress"
form.EmailAddrEF.defaultValue   := ""
form.EmailAddrEF.maxLength      := 60
   return
```

Save and close your changes. Try running the form – if all works, the first record in the Customers Table should appear in the controls, as if they were *dataLinked* the "old" way.

The one issue that occurs (while testing this), is that the CustNumEF control has focus, because it is the first control on the form that can gain focus. The difficulty is that a) it does not appear as if it is read-only although the user cannot change anything, and b) it does not take on the color it should. One way around this is to add one more overridden bit of code – the *onOpen* event handler.

Open the form in the Form Designer, and click the "Events" tab of the Inspector. Find the *onOpen* event, click it, and click the button on the right side of the inspector. In the Source Code Editor, make these changes:

```
function form_onOpen()
   form.BusNameEF.setFocus()
return
```

As you might expect, there will need to be more that is done with this form to make it as functional as we would like, but this is our starting point.

Navigate through the Entryfields, make a change in one of the values *(since this is the read-only query, you can't effect any changes to the actual data)*. Notice that the control should change color, indicating a change – as defined in the custom class!

Navigating the Table

One of the important abilities of any data form is to navigate in the table, or to move from record to record. For a single-table form such as the Customers form, this is not *too* complicated. However, we are going to work with a combination of new custom controls (pushbuttons), the custom form, and more. In a later chapter of this book we will enhance the appearance of the pushbuttons.

It is useful is to set a sort sequence for the table being used, otherwise while navigating, the user will see the data in the order it was added to the table – which makes it difficult to find specific records. Since we are working with customers we should probably sort the table on the BusinessName field. We will add a method to the Customers form that sets the sequence, and then we need to modify some code we worked with earlier.

Open the Customers form in the Source Code Editor, and add this method *before* the *endclass* statement:

```
function SetSequence
    // set the form's rowset property, because we can
    // work with it for some of the controls ...
    form.rowset := form.DataLayerDataModule1.Customers.rowset

    // load the data again (from custom form):
    UILAYERCFORM::LoadData()
return
```

Note the call to the method of the custom form's method *LoadData* at the end – this ensures that the record displayed is the first record in the current sequence.

It might be necessary after setting the *active* property to *true*, to add one more statement to requery the data:

```
form.DataLayerDataModule1.Customers.requery()
```

But in this current form, it does not seem to be necessary.

We then need to move back up to the *LocalInit()* method, and add a call to this method:

```
function Local_Init
    // call our own code:
    class::SetupControls()
    // call the overwritten code, so it executes as well!
    UILAYERCFORM::Init()
    // call the SetSequence method:
    class::SetSequence()
return
```

This ensures that the sequence is set properly.

Custom Pushbuttons

In order to facilitate navigation through the data, we will create some custom pushbuttons. To do this, in the Command Window type:

```
create file ADOCustomButtons.cc
```

We're going to work off "standard" custom class concepts here *(discussed in many places in* The dBASE Book*)*, and create a base pushbutton class that the other buttons are "based" on. This allows you to set some common properties for all these pushbuttons:

```
class BaseButton( oParent ) of Pushbutton( oParent )
    with( this )
        text       := "Base Class"
        metric     := 6 // Pixels
        width      := 64
        height     := 24
        speedBar   := true // can't get focus
    endwith
endclass
```

The buttons that are subclassed from the BaseButton above for now will look like:

```
class TopButton( oParent ) of BaseButton( oParent ) custom
   with( this )
       text := "First"
   endwith
endclass

class PreviousButton( oParent ) of BaseButton( oParent ) custom
   with( this )
       text := "Previous"
   endwith
endclass

class NextButton( oParent ) of BaseButton( oParent ) custom
   with( this )
       text := "Next"
   endwith
endclass

class BottomButton( oParent ) of BaseButton( oParent ) custom
   with( this )
       text := "Last"
   endwith
endclass
```

Now that you have the buttons themselves, let's place them on the custom form. In the Command Window type:

```
set procedure to SQLCustomButtons.cc
```

Open the form UILayer.cfm in the Form Designer. Click on the Component Palette's "Custom" tab, and notice you have your buttons. Drag one each of the main buttons (TopButton through BottomButton – four in all) to the design surface, and arrange them so you have something like the following:

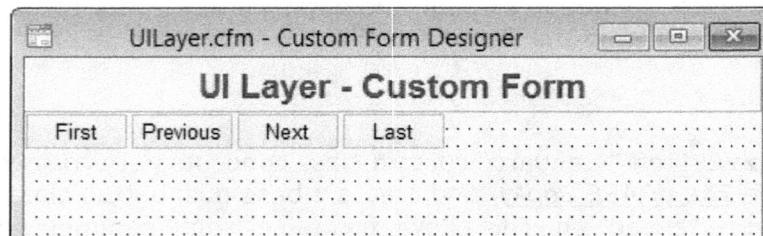

Figure 5-6

From here we need to determine the code to navigate through the tables.

In order to help, we are going to add some code to the BaseButton that can be called as needed to ensure we have a rowset object to work with. This does require that the form's rowset property be set *(as shown above in the SetSequence method of the Customers form)*.

Before the *endclass* statement for the BaseButton class, add the following:

```
function getRowset()
   local rRowToActOn
   rRowToActOn = null // default
   // check to see if rowset property has been set:
   if this.rowset # null
      rRowToActOn = this.rowset
     // ok, this.rowset has not been set, check to see
     // if the parent has a rowset that's valid
     // (the parent will be "NavigateButtons", a container,
     // or the form):
   elseif type( "this.parent.rowset" ) == "O" and;
          this.parent.rowset # null
      rRowToActOn = this.parent.rowset
   // otherwise we check for the form's rowset:
   elseif form.rowset # null
      rRowToActOn = form.rowset
   endif // this.rowset # null
   return rRowToActOn
```

The first button is the "TopButton" – this goes to the top of the rowset. The code shown is based *(loosely)* on code in the dUFLP's *"CustButt.cc"* custom class file. I have simplified it in places. It should be noted that this code does not take into account if you have made any changes to the data.

Add the following code for the pushbutton's *onClick* event hander (be sure to add it *before* the *endclass* statement):

```
function onClick
   local rRowToActOn, nState, nAnswer
   rRowToActOn = null

   // check to see if rowset property has been set:
   rRowToActOn = super::GetRowset()

   // is there a valid rowset?
   if rRowToActOn == null
      msgbox( "Cannot Navigate with no rowset!",;
            "Can't do it!", 16 )
      return
   else
      // form.modified property should be being set
      // when a control loses focus if you are using
      // the SQLFormControls classes:
      if type( "form.modified" ) # "L"
         form.modified = false
      endif
      if form.modified
         if msgbox( "Save changes before leaving record?", ;
                   "Data has changed",32+4) == 6 // Yes
               form.SaveRecord()
         endif // msgbox()
      endif // form.modified
      // navigate to first record
      rRowToActOn.first()
   endif
return
```

At this point we are referencing code that does not exist yet, which belongs in the UILayer.cfm file. We should get that set up before moving to the next pushbutton.

Add More Code to Custom Form

In addition, note the reference to a custom property of the form called *modified* – it appears that while the *ADORowset* object has a *modified* property we cannot change it *(attempts to do so while working on this code did not return an error, but the value was not changed when it was checked for)*. Hence, we are creating our own custom property of the form. This is there specifically to notify us if the current row has been modified. You can leave the current custom class file open, but now you need to open the UILayer.cfm file in the Source Code Editor. Find the method "LoadData", go to the bottom of it, just before the *return* statement, and add:

```
// done loading the data, set custom form properties
// to false, if they haven't been created yet, this will
// create them:
form.append   = false
form.modified = false
```

We need to another method to the custom form that will handle gathering the information necessary to save the current record and passing it to the Data Module's code.

In the Data Module (DataLayer.dmd) we have a method to save changes to a row called *UpdateRow*, but we need to consider if the individual who clicked a navigation button was adding a new row – there is a method for this called *AddRow* in the Data Module as well. In order to attempt to cover these two very different situations, we are going to need to add yet another custom property to the form, called *append (see above)*. We can check to see if it exists (if not, we're obviously not appending a row), and if the property is set to *true* we need to call the Data Module's *AddRow* method, otherwise we call the *UpdateRow* method.

We're going to use different method names from the ones used in the Data Module, to avoid any issues or concerns. The first method is the one to Save the Record:

```
function SaveRecord
   if type( "form.append" ) == "U"
      form.append = false
   endif
   // need an array (and other variables) for this:
   private aSave, nSave, nControls, cTable, oQuery
   local cPrimary, nPrimary
   aSave = new array(1,2)
   nSave = 0
   // if we are appending:
   if form.append
      // Before we load the array, we need to ensure that
      // we have the primary key information ... and we
      // will need it to return to this row once saved:
      nSave = 1
      // Primary Key should always be first field in table:
```

```
      cPrimary = form.rowset.fields[1].fieldName
      aSave[ 1, 1] = cPrimary
         cSeq = form.rowset.Sequence
      aSave[ 1, 2 ] = GetNextKey( cSeq )
      nPrimary = aSave[ 1, 2 ]
      // need table name:
      cTable = form.aSQLControls[ 1 ].tableName
      // load array from form.aSQLControls array:
      for nControls = 1 to form.aSQLControls.size
          // don't process this one
          if not form.aSQLControls[ nControls ].includeInQuery
             loop
          endif
          nSave++
          aSave.grow( 1 ) // add row to array
          // add to array:
          aSave[nSave,1]= form.aSQLControls[ nControls ].fieldName
          aSave[nSave,2]= form.aSQLControls[ nControls ].value
      next // nControls
      // call code to actually save this row
      form.DataLayerDataModule1.AddRow( cTable, aSave )
   else // saving a changed record:
      // get name of table
      cTable   = form.aSQLControls[ 1 ].tableName
      // load array from form.aSQLControls array:
      for nControls = 1 to form.aSQLControls.size
          if not form.aSQLControls[ nControls ].includeInQuery
             loop
          endif
          // Add only fields that have been modified (which should
          // avoid the primary key)
          if form.aSQLControls[ nControls ].modified
             nSave++
             if nSave > 1
                aSave.grow( 1 ) // add row to array
             endif // nSave > 1
             aSave[nSave, 1]=form.aSQLControls[ nControls ].fieldName
             aSave[nSave, 2]=form.aSQLControls[ nControls ].value
          endif // readOnly
      next // nControls
      // deal with empty array:
      if aSave.size/2 == 1
         if aSave[1,1] == false
            form.modified := false
            return
         endif
      endif
      // we also need the primary key name and value:
      cPrimary = form.rowset.fields[1].fieldName
      nPrimary = form.rowset.fields[1].value
      // and pass the data to the Data Module:
      form.DataLayerDataModule1.UpdateRow( cTable, cPrimary, ;
                                       nPrimary, aSave )
endif // form.append
// refresh the query display updated version
// of record in form.
oQuery = class::FindQuery( cTable )
oQuery.requery()
```

```
    // navigate to the row just edited/appended:
    cFind = cPrimary+"="+nPrimary
    try
       oQuery.rowset.applyLocate( cFind )
    catch( ADOexception e )
       ? e.code, e.message
       // Navigate to first row
       oQuery.rowset.first()
    endtry
    // load the data, and away we go
    class::LoadData()
    class::ResetControls()
return
```

The code above, in the "form.append" section, calls a function called
GetNextKey(). This function needs to be *after* the *endClass* statement for the
custom form:

```
function GetNextKey( cGenName )
    // This function accepts the name of a
    // Sequence (or Generator), increments
    // the value, and returns it, so that
    // you can use it when saving a new
    // record, also reference the value
    // as needed. Original code by
    // Mervyn Bick, 2015
    private dGen, qGen, nVal, cCmd
    dGen = new ADODatabase()
    dGen.databaseName := "BookSample_ADO_RO"
    dGen.loginString  := "SYSDBA/masterkey"
    dGen.active       := true

    qGen = new ADOQuery()
    qGen.database     := dGen
    cCmd = "Select Gen_ID("+cGenName+",1) from MyGen"
    qGen.sql          = cCmd
    qGen.requestLive := false
    qGen.active      := true
    qGen.rowset.first()

    // next key value:
    nVal = qGen.rowset.fields[1].value

    // deactivate:
    qGen.active := false
    dGen.active := false
return nVal
```

We need to add a method to the form called "ResetControls", as mentioned
above – the purpose is to set properties and values back to their default status.
This should be before the *endclass* statement:

```
function ResetControls
    // we need to loop through the controls
    // and reset specific properties:
    for nControls = 1 to form.aSQLControls.size
       if not form.aSQLControls[ nControls ].readOnly
```

```
        form.aSQLControls[ nControls ].modified := false
        form.aSQLControls[ nControls ].error     := false
        form.aSQLControls[ nControls ].newValue := ;
            form.aSQLControls[ nControls ].value
        form.aSQLControls[ nControls ].oldValue := ;
            form.aSQLControls[ nControls ].value
        // set colors:
        form.aSQLControls[ nControls ].colorNormal := ;
            "WindowText/Window"
        form.aSQLControls[ nControls ].colorHighlight :=;
            "WindowText/0x80ffff"
      endif // not readonly
    next // nControls
  return
```

There will be (at least) two more methods added to the custom form class, but we will get to that in a bit.

Save and close the UILayer.cfm file in the Source Code Editor, and go back to the SQLCustomButtons.cc class file.

More Pushbuttons

The PreviousButton requires a bit more checking – we do not wish to navigate *beyond* the beginning of the data – that would cause errors:

```
function onClick
   local rRowToActOn, nState, nAnswer
   rRowToActOn = null
   // check to see if rowset property has been set:
   rRowToActOn = super::GetRowset()

   // is there a valid rowset?
   if rRowToActOn == null
      msgbox( "Cannot Navigate with no rowset!",;
            "Can't do it!", 16 )
      return
   else
      // form.modified property should be being set
      // when a control loses focus if you are using
      // the SQLFormControls classes:
      if type( "form.modified" ) # "L"
         form.modified = false
      endif
      if form.modified
         if msgbox( "Save changes before leaving record?", ;
                  "Data has changed",32+4) == 6 // Yes
               form.SaveRecord()
         endif // msgbox()
      endif // form.modified
      // attempt to navigate:
      if ( not rRowToActOn.next(-1) )
         msgbox( "At first row in rowset", ;
               "Can't Navigate!", 64 )
         rRowToActOn.next() // back off end of rowset marker
      endif // navigate
   endif // rRowToActOn
return
```

The NextButton performs nearly identical code, but rather than using "-1" as a parameter to the *next* method, we leave it out completely, which will navigate the other direction – for this and the "Bottom" button I am not snowing *all* the code, just the navigation part, which is what is different between them *(if building the code yourself, copy and paste, and then modify the navigation portion of the code)*:

```
if ( not rRowToActOn.next() )
   msgbox( "At last row in rowset", ;
            "Can't Navigate!", 64 )
   rRowToActOn.next(-1) // back off end of rowset marker
endif
```

And finally, the BottomButton goes to the end of the data, and the code is similar to the TopButton:

```
// navigate to the last row:
rRowToActOn.last()
```

And Back to the Custom Form

Save and close the custom class file, and then open the UILayer.cfm file in the Form Designer. We are going to use the form's *onNavigate* event handler which automatically fires when you navigate in a row that is assigned to the form's *rowset* property.

In the Inspector, click the "Events" tab, find the *onNavigate* event, click on it, then click the button. In the Source Code Editor, enter the following:

```
function form_onNavigate(nWorkArea)
   class::LoadData()
return
```

This will reload the controls with the data for the current row! Save and exit the Form Designer.

Testing the Form

To test all this, double-click the Customers form and click on the buttons, try navigating back and forth *(there should only be six records, so it will not take too long)*.

Your form should look something like this:

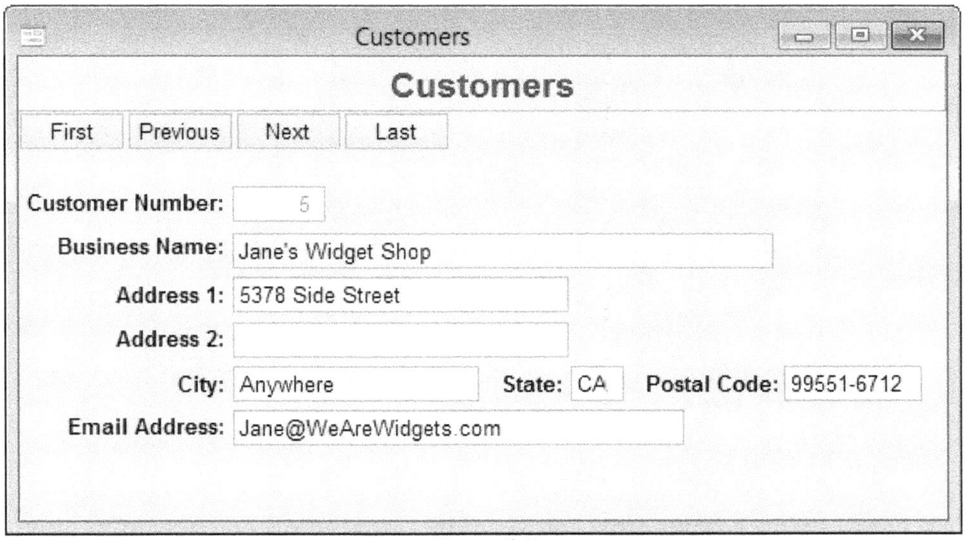

Figure 5-7

Editing the Data

For the moment the form is in pretty good shape, but we need to add some more buttons. The first one will add a new row to the table, the second will save changes to an existing row, the next will abandon changes to the existing row *(reload the data from the table into the controls)*, and the last will delete the existing record.

We actually have most of the program code necessary, but we need to create the custom pushbuttons, add the appropriate *onClick* event handlers, as well as add some more code to the Custom Form.

The Save Button

The Save Button is designed to save changes to the data, back to the table. However, the actual method for saving the data is not contained in the button's code, it is contained in the Custom Form and the Data Module:

```
class SaveButton( oParent ) of BaseButton( oParent ) custom
   with( this )
      text := "Save"
   endwith

   function onClick
      local rRowToActOn, nState, nAnswer
      rRowToActOn = null

      // check to see if rowset property has been set:
      rRowToActOn = super::GetRowset()

      // is there a valid rowset?
      if rRowToActOn == null
         msgbox( "Cannot Save with no rowset!",;
                 "Can't do it!", 16 )
         return
      else
         // form.modified property should be being set
         // by the controls …
```

```
            if type( "form.modified" ) # "L"
               form.modified = false
               return // nothing to save
            endif
            // call SaveRecord() method
            if form.modified
               form.SaveRecord()
            endif // form.modified
         endif
      return
   endclass
```

The most important part of this is the code that calls the form's *SaveRecord*
event handler, which we have discussed previously.

The Abandon Button

It is often a good idea to just be able to abandon the contents of the current row
– if your user makes a truly odd edit, or is just having a bad time of it, the option
to abandon changes is good. The code for this basically re-loads the information
for this record back into the controls, and re-sets any properties that have been
modified.

This would look like:

```
   class AbandonButton( oParent ) of BaseButton( oParent ) custom
      with( this )
         text := "Abandon"
      endwith

      function onClick
         local rRowToActOn, nState, nAnswer
         rRowToActOn = null

         // check to see if rowset property has been set:
         rRowToActOn = super::GetRowset()

         // is there a valid rowset?
         if rRowToActOn == null
            msgbox( "Cannot Abandon with no rowset!",;
                    "Can't do it!", 16 )
            return
         else
            if type( "form.modified" ) # "L"
               form.modified = false
               return // nothing to save
            endif
            // call AbandonRecord() method
            if form.modified
               form.AbandonRecord()
            endif // form.modified
         endif
      return
   endclass
```

For this to work, we need a new method in the Custom Form file UILayer.cfm – if
it is not open in the Source Code Editor, you should open it, and add the
following code before the *endClass* statement:

```
function AbandonRecord
   if type( "form.append" ) == "U"
      form.append = false
   endif

   if form.append
      if not form.rowset.next(-1) // previous record -- if we error
         form.rowset.first()       // first record
         return // form's onNavigate will load the data
      endif // navigate
   else
      // If here, user was not appending, but editing:
      class::LoadData()
   endif // form.append

   // reset appearance of controls and some of the
   // custom properties:
   class::ResetControls()
return
```

This was surprisingly the easiest of the code to put together, because there isn't that much that really needs to be done.

The Append Button

You need the ability to set the form into Append Mode, as it were, which basically means clearing out the controls, creating a new record buffer. This will mean resetting properties to their defaults, setting the *value* property to a default value of some sort for an empty field, etc.

The pushbutton looks like this:

```
class AppendButton( oParent ) of BaseButton( oParent ) custom
   with( this )
      text := "Append"
   endwith

   function onClick
      local rRowToActOn, nState, nAnswer
      rRowToActOn = null

      // check to see if rowset property has been set:
      rRowToActOn = super::GetRowset()

      // is there a valid rowset?
      if rRowToActOn == null
         msgbox( "Cannot Append with no rowset!",;
                 "Can't do it!", 16 )
         return
      else
         if type( "form.modified" ) # "L"
            form.modified = false
         endif
         // as the AppendRecord method clears out the controls,
         // check to see if the user wants to save any changes:
         if form.modified
            if msgbox( "Save changes before leaving record?", ;
```

```
                              "Data has changed",32+4) == 6 // Yes
                        form.SaveRecord()
                  endif // msgbox()
             endif // form.modified
             // call AppendRecord() method
             form.AppendRecord()
          endif
      return
   endclass
```

For this to work, we need yet another method in the Custom Form Class, so in the Source Code Editor for that class, before the *endClass* statement, add the following:

```
function AppendRecord
    if type( "form.aSQLControls" ) == "U"
       msgbox( "Cannot check data types, form is missing "+;
                "aSQLControls array.",;
                "AppendRecord Error", 16 )
       return
    endif

    private nControls
    for nControls = 1 to form.aSQLControls.size
        // assign properties
        form.aSQLControls[ nControls ].value    := ;
            form.aSQLControls[ nControls ].defaultValue
        form.aSQLControls[ nControls ].oldValue := ;
            form.aSQLControls[ nControls ].defaultValue
        form.aSQLControls[ nControls ].newValue := null
        form.aSQLControls[ nControls ].modified := false
        form.aSQLControls[ nControls ].error    := false
        // set colors:
        form.aSQLControls[nControls].colorNormal := "WindowText/Window"
        form.aSQLControls[nControls].colorHighlight := ;
                                          "WindowText/0x80ffff"
    next // nControls
    // set the form's append property
    form.append    := true
    // reset the form's modified property (just to be sure)
    form.modified := false
return
```

It should be noted that this code does not take into account a variety of field types, such as BLOBs and such – it really deals with the basics.

The Delete Button

The Delete button is special – it requires some extra custom properties, which are then passed on to the DeleteRecord method, and so on. These are only used when you have a parent/child relationship and you need to delete matching child rows for the parent table (a *cascade delete*).

The code for the Delete Button looks like the following:

```
class DeleteButton( oParent ) of BaseButton( oParent ) custom
   with( this )
      text := "Delete"
   endwith
   this.cascade        = false
   this.childTable     = null
   this.foreignKeyField = null

   function onClick
      local rRowToActOn, nState, nAnswer
      rRowToActOn = null

      // check to see if rowset property has been set:
      rRowToActOn = super::GetRowset()

      // is there a valid rowset?
      if rRowToActOn == null
         msgbox( "Cannot Delete with no rowset!",;
                 "Can't do it!", 16 )
         return
      else
         // ask if they really want to delete the record:
         if msgbox( "Are you sure you wish to delete this record?",;
                    "Delete Record?", 32+4 ) == 6 // Yes
            // call DeleteRecord() method
            form.DeleteRecord( this.cascade, this.childTable, ;
                    this.foreignKeyField )
         endif // msgbox()
      endif // row
   return
endclass
```

This will, as with the other buttons, require code in the Custom Form class that looks like:

```
function DeleteRecord( bCascade, cChildTable, cForeignField )
   local cTable, cPrimary, nPrimary
   // we must assume that the first field in the
   // table is the primary key -- it makes it easier ...
   cTable   = form.aSQLControls[ 1 ].tableName
   cPrimary = form.aSQLControls[ 1 ].fieldName
   nPrimary = form.aSQLControls[ 1 ].value

   // get primary key for row we want to display AFTER the delete
   // normally we back up one row, so if we were on the fifth row
   // we would, after deleting, display the fourth. But if we're
   // deleting the FIRST row ... or the table is empty ...
   private oQuery, nNewPrimary
   oQuery = class::FindQuery( cTable )
   if oQuery.rowset.atFirst() // at first row
      oQuery.rowset.next() // go to row AFTER current one
   else
      oQuery.rowset.next( -1 ) // otherwise go to row BEFORE this one
   endif
   nNewPrimary = oQuery.rowset.fields[ 1 ].value

   // and pass the data to the Data Module:
```

```
         if not bCascade
            form.DataLayerDataModule1.DeleteRow( cTable, cPrimary, nPrimary )
         else
            if empty( cChildTable ) or empty( cForeignField )
               msgbox( "Cannot perform cascade delete, check values "+;
                       "of parameters.",;
                       "DeleteRecord Error", 16 )
               return
            else
               form.DataLayerDataModule1.DeleteRow( cTable, cPrimary,;
                       nPrimary, bCascade, cChildTable, cForeignField )
            endif // empty( ... )
         endif // not bCascade

         // need to refresh the query, and deal with which row
         // to display ...
         oQuery.requery()
         if oQuery.rowset.count() > 0
            cFind = cPrimary+"="+nNewPrimary
            try
               oQuery.rowset.applyLocate( cFind )
            catch( ADOexception e )
               e.code, e.message
            endtry
            // load the data, and away we go
            class::LoadData()
         endif
         class::ResetControls()
      return
```

As noted in several places, for a more complex database, this would probably need to be expanded to deal with cascading deletes processed through an array of necessary values, and so on.

The Close Form Button

The Close Form button needs to deal with closing the form – seems pretty straightforward, but … what if the user was editing a record? We need to ask if they wish to save before closing the form, and if so, call the form's *SaveRecord* method. The code for this button is:

```
   class CloseButton( oParent ) of BaseButton( oParent ) custom
      with( this )
         text := "Close "
      endwith

      function onClick
         local rRowToActOn
         rRowToActOn = null

         // check to see if rowset property has been set:
         rRowToActOn = super::GetRowset()

         // is there a valid rowset?
         if rRowToActOn == null
            // if not, then just close the form
            form.close()
         endif
```

```
      if form.modified
         if msgbox( "Save changes before closing form?", ;
                    "Data has changed",32+4) == 6 // Yes
            form.SaveRecord()
         endif // msgbox()
      endif // form.modified
      // close the form:
      form.close()
   return
endclass
```

Whew! After all that, we need to add these buttons to the form, so save and close everything in the Source Code Editor, and add these buttons. You should type the following in the Command Window:

```
set procedure to SQLCustomButtons.cc
```

Open the UILayer Custom Form in the Form Designer, add the buttons, so you get something that looks like *(this may require widening the form)*:

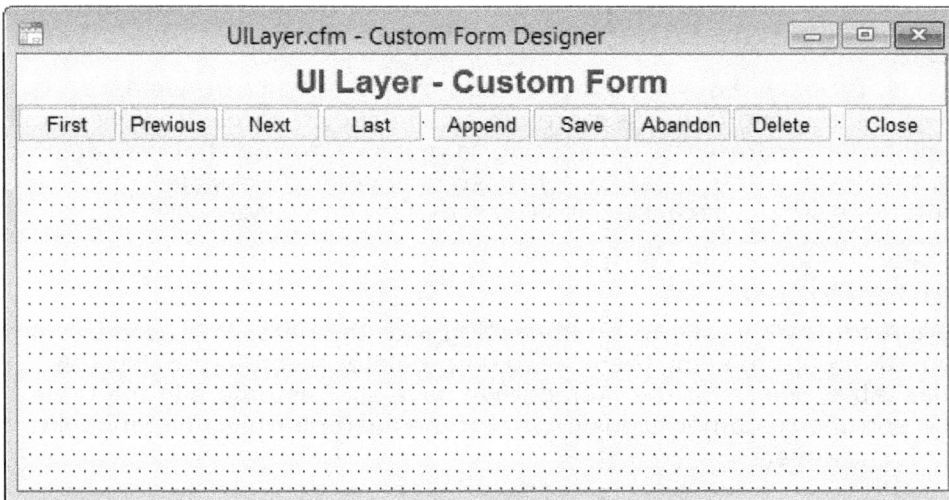

Figure 5-8

Save and close the custom form (Ctrl+W).

You may need to open the Customer form in the Form Designer and change the width so that you can see all the buttons. Once adjusted, save and exit the designer and run the form:

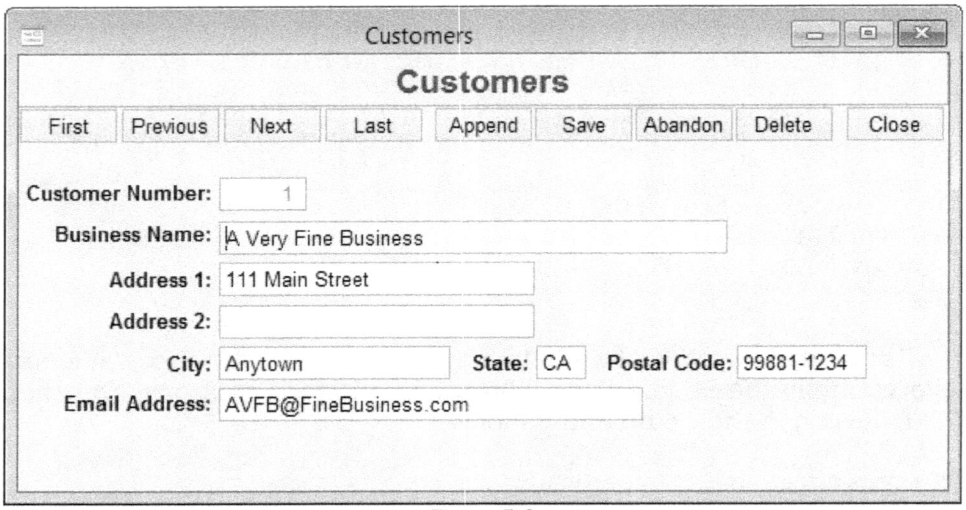

Figure 5-9

You may want to experiment a bit – use the pushbuttons, see how they work with the form, fix any typos in the code, etc. Once done, we'll move on.

> **📝 NOTE**
> This code, for a system with a lot of users, would need to be enhanced to deal with requerying the data more often than shown here. Otherwise your user might find themselves attempting to modify a record that was deleted by another user, etc. I chose to not try to deal with all possible permutations simply because this is already fairly involved.

Finding a Record
Finding a record is a vital part of interacting with the data. It is used to simply look something up, to allow the user to edit, delete, records, etc. For this particular table, where for the moment we have six Customers in the table, finding a specific customer is easy. What if the customer base expands into the thousands, however?

With our controls not being dataLinked this can be a bit more complicated, but it can work. Some time ago Tom Gleaton (a user in the dBASE newsgroups) took a version of the Seeker class that comes with dBASE (mSeeker.cc, worked on by Marc Van den Berghen, Roland Wingerter, Rich Assaf) to make it work with the dBASE ADO Data objects. Included in the sample code (this will be added in the latest versions of the dUFLP as well), the class is mSeekerADO.cc.

I am not including the class definition in this chapter as it is fairly lengthy – if you want to use this, it is in the sample code *(and the dUFLP as well)*.

In the Command Window:

```
set procedure to SQLFormControls.cc
set procedure to mSeekerADO.cc
```

And then open the Custom Form (UILayer.cfm) in the Form Designer. By doing this in the Custom Form, as with the pushbuttons we created earlier, the forms subclassed from the Custom Form do not need to have everything added.

Before we work with the seeker object, we are going to work with the second page of the form, by using a Tabbox control.

In the toolbar in dBASE, find the "Next Form Page" button (a page with a blue right arrow) and click it. The form will appear to be empty, except for the Title control (if you set the *pageNo* property to 0 earlier).

Setting Tabbox Control on Form

On the Component Palette (on the "Standard" tab), find the *Tabbox* control. Drag it to the form's surface.

Click on the *dataSource* property and then the button on the right.

- This will open the "Datasource Property Builder" window
- Click the "Pencil" button
- In the dialog "Build Array", click "Delete" to remove the default text
- In the entryfield on the left under "String", type: "Detail" *(without the quotes)* and click "Add"
- In the same entryfield type: "Find Record" and click "Add"
- Click "OK" (close the Build Array dialog)
- Click "OK" (close the Data Source Property Builder dialog)

You should see there are now two tabs.

Change the following properties:

- *colorNormal*: Blue
- *colorHighlight:* Blue/BtnFace

Click the "Events" tab in the Inspector, find the *onSelChange* event – this is where clicking on the tabs changes the page of the form – however you have to tell dBASE what to do. Click the event, click the button, and in the event handler code, add:

```
function TABBOX1_onSelChange()
   // Tabbox changes the page number on the form:
   form.pageNo := this.curSel
return
```

In the form's *Init* method, add this code:

```
// make sure Tabbox is on the correct
// page:
form.pageNo         := 1
form.Tabbox1.curSel := 1
```

We will come back to the Tabbox control in a bit.

Using a Seeker Control

On the Component Palette, click the "Custom" tab, and find "SQLTextLabel" and drag that to the design surface, move it under the title, to the left, and change the text to the following (without the quotes): "Search for XXX:" (the idea is for each form you would change the "XXX" to the name of the field ...).

If necessary, in the Command Window, type:

```
set procedure to mSeekerADO.cc
```

On the Component Palette *(still on the "Custom" tab)*, select "mSeekerADO" and place a copy on the form. Place it to the right of the *textLabel* control, and adjust size, position, etc.

There is code that will be necessary in a form's startup code, but we will deal with that in the Customer form in a bit.

Setting up the Grid

In order to see the navigation occur, we are going to use a grid – the tricky thing with grids is setting up the dataLinks and all that. Since the Data Module is instantiated in such a way that it is not available in the designer, we will have to do this the hard way – in code. This again will be completed in the individual forms you are using, not in the custom form. Here we can only do a few things.

In the Component Palette, click the "Standard" tab, and find the standard grid control. Change the *name* property to "SeekerGrid" (without the quotes), so that if you use a different grid control on your forms, it won't be confused with this one. Set the following properties:

- *rowSelect*: true
- *colorRowSelect*: WindowText/0x80ffff
- *bgColor*: White
- *vScrollBar*: true
- *allowAddRows*: false
- *allowColumnMoving*: false
- *allowColumnSizing*: false
- *allowEditing*: false
- *allowRowSizing*: false

Adjust the size of the grid control so it fills most of the screen surface under the controls at the top and above the Tabbox control at the bottom. Save and close the form in the Form Designer.

The difficulty here is that the custom form does not have any tables associated with it, so we cannot define the columns for the grid as we might like. There are many ways to work with setting up a grid. The most obvious: tinkering with the code, running the form, testing it, returning to the code and modifying properties, etc., to be very frustrating. So, we will do something different.

The following steps are *only* for the purpose of obtaining the information we need to set up the grid in the form we are going to actually use – once done, the form we are about to create can be deleted.

In the Navigator double-click the [New Form] button. If the form designer creates a form based on the custom form, then go to the "File" menu, click "Set Custom Form Class", click "Clear Custom Form Class", and then "OK". Click on the Navigator, go to the "Tables" tab, in the combobox select "BookSample_ADO_RO", and log in if needed (SysDBA, masterkey).

Move the form around, so that you can see the tables, drag the "Customers" table to the form. Set the form's *metric* property to 6 (Pixels). Then drag a grid component to the form.

Set the following properties:

- *datalink*: Customers1 *(what will appear in the Inspector is form.customers1.rowset)*
- *columns*: Click on this property and click the first button on the left – in the "Columns Property Builder" dialog, select the fields:
    - BusinessName
    - Address1
    - Address2
    - City
    - State
    - Click "OK"
- Adjust the width of the columns by working with the headers, so you get something like Figure 5-10 (below).

We're going to adjust the names of the columns so they are not all caps, and clean up the text a little. This means working on each column one by one. Click on the "BusinessName" column, and notice that the Inspector shows that column.

Click the "Heading" control, and the "I" (Inspect) button. You will see the properties of the heading control. Change the *value* property to: Business Name *(mixed case and add a space between the two words)*.

Repeat for each of the columns. Save the form as "CustomerGridDetails".

In the Command Window:

```
close databases
```

If you need to readjust anything on this form, you will need to open the database again (and login) before opening the form in the Designer.

Then open the new form in the Source Code Editor. We need to pull details from here so that we can set up the grid in the Customers form. Also open the custom form UILayer.cfm in the Source Code Editor.

In the custom form, in the *Local_Init* method add the following before the *return* statement:

```
// Set up Seeker Grid Control:
class::SetUpSeekerGrid()
```

We need to add code to define the details of the grid. What I have done is to simplify some of the code (not putting default values in, and so on), using the information from the CustomerGridDetails form. Note that I decided to not use the Address2 field in the grid. Add this code before the *endclass* statement of the (custom) form:

```
function SetUpSeekerGrid
    // Necessary to manually set up the grid here:
    with( form.SeekerGrid )
        width = 514
        left = 40
        dataLink = form.rowset
```

```
              // first column
              columns["Column1"] = new GRIDCOLUMN(form.SeekerGrid)
              columns["Column1"].dataLink=form.rowset.fields["businessname"]
              columns["Column1"].width     = 155
              columns["Column1"].headingControl.value = "Business Name"
              // second column
              columns["Column2"] = new GRIDCOLUMN(form.SeekerGrid)
              columns["Column2"].dataLink = form.rowset.fields["address1"]
              columns["Column2"].width     = 136
              columns["Column2"].headingControl.value = "Address 1"
              // next column
              columns["Column3"] = new GRIDCOLUMN(form.SeekerGrid)
              columns["Column3"].dataLink = form.rowset.fields["city"]
              columns["Column3"].width     = 125
              columns["Column3"].headingControl.value = "City"
              // next column
              columns["Column4"] = new GRIDCOLUMN(form.SeekerGrid)
              columns["Column4"].dataLink = form.rowset.fields["state"]
              columns["Column4"].width     = 50
              columns["Column4"].headingControl.value = "State"
        endwith
    return
```

While you are in the code, we need to add a single line of code for the seeker control to use. The *mSeekerADO* control needs to use the rowset's *sort* property, so it can sequence the data correctly. This property uses the field we are searching on.

In the method *SetSequence*, add this code before the call to the custom form's *LoadData* method:

```
        // for the seeker control (in the Custom Form) we need
        // to use the sort property:
        form.rowset.sort := "BusinessName"

        // for the seeker we need to force the rowset:
        form.mSeekerADO1.rowset := form.rowset
```

Save and close the code in the Source Code Editor.

Open the form in the Form Designer, click on the "Next Form Page" button in the toolbar, click on the *textLabel* next to the *mSeekerADO* control. In the inspector, change the text to:

```
    Search for Business Name:
```

You will need to widen the control, and possibly readjust the controls on the form a bit. Close the Form Designer.

When you run the form, if all is working properly, click the "Find Record" tab of the *tabbox* control, it should look like this:

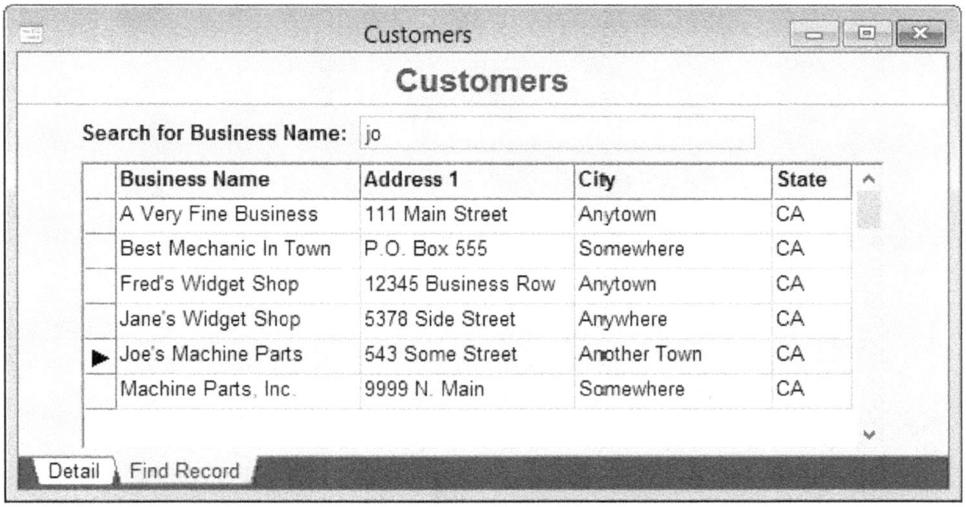

Figure 5-10

In the example screen capture (Figure 5-10), I started typing "jo" to find the first row with those two letters. Note that there is a vertical scroll bar, because we never know if we'll need one.

To make sure the *mSeekerADO* control gets focus when we change tabs, you can modify code in the custom form UILayer.cfm (open in the Source Code Editor), and go to the *TABBOX1_onSelChange* method and modify it appropriately:

```
// Tabbox changes the page number on the form:
form.pageNo := this.curSel
if this.curSel == 1
    if type( "form.FirstControl" ) == "O" // object
        form.FirstControl.setFocus()
    endif
else
    form.rowset.first()
    form.MSeekerADO1.setFocus()
endif
```

Whew! At this point, we are *mostly* done with the Customers form. We may need to do a bit more in the next chapter, but for now we can call it complete.

The Inventory Form

At this point, the Inventory form will follow the same pattern as the Customers form, however, it will be much easier to create – the process of creating the Customers form was more difficult because we also were creating many features of the custom form UILayer.cfm, and we were creating the controls we need.

- Create a new form as derived from the UILayer.cfm (see page 93)
- Make changes to the text of the title, and the form's *text* property as well.
- Save it as "Inventory".
- Add controls – *textLabel* and *entryfield* controls (use the custom ones – see page 95):
  - ○ ItemNumber
    - ▪ ItemNumLabel (for textlabel)
    - ▪ *text*: Item Number:
    - ▪ ItemNumEF (for entryfield)

- o ItemDescription
  - ItemDescLabel (for textlabel)
  - *text*: Description:
  - ItemDescEF (for entryfield)
- o CostPerItem
  - CostLabel (for textlabel)
  - *text*: Cost per Item:
  - CostEF (for enryfield)
  - *picture*: 999.99 *(set picture property)*
- Adjust sizes and appearances of controls …
- Set startup code (see page 99).
  - o *Open* and *ReadModal* methods: be sure to copy the same code we used for the Customers form (you might want to open that form in the Source Code Editor and copy and paste …).
- Set code for the SetSequence method this way (page 118):

```
function SetSequence
    // set the form's rowset property, because we can
    // work with it for some of the controls ...
    form.rowset := form.DataLayerDataModule1.Inventory.rowset

    // for the seeker control (in the Custom Form) we need
    // to use the sort property:
    form.rowset.sort := "ItemDescription"

    // for the seeker we need to force the rowset:
    form.mSeekerADO1.rowset := form.rowset

    // load the data again (from custom form):
    UILAYERCFORM::LoadData()
return
```

- Set code for the SetupControls method this way (page 97):

```
function SetupControls
    // method required to set custom properties of the controls,
    // defaultValue is important when appending, and maxLength
    // is important for character fields, so user cannot
    // enter more data than the field contains:
    form.ItemNumEF.tableName     := "Inventory"
    form.ItemNumEF.fieldName      := "ItemNumber"
    form.ItemNumEF.readOnly       := true
    form.ItemNumEF.includeInQuery := false
    form.ItemDescEF.tableName     := "Inventory"
    form.ItemDescEF.fieldName     := "ItemDescription"
    form.ItemDescEF.defaultValue := ""
    form.ItemDescEF.maxLength      := 100
    // we can use this to force focus on a specific control
    form.firstControl             = form.ItemDescEF
    form.CostEF.tableName         := "Inventory"
    form.CostEF.fieldName         := "CostPerItem"
    form.CostEF.defaultValue       := 0
return
```

- Set code for the grid by using the same procedure we did on page 116. You should have something *similar* to the following:

```
function SetUpSeekerGrid
    // Necessary to manually set up the grid here:
```

```
with( form.SeekerGrid )
   width = 526
   left = 30
   dataLink = form.rowset
   // first column
   columns["Column1"] = new GRIDCOLUMN(form.SeekerGrid)
   columns["Column1"].dataLink= form.rowset.fields["itemnumber"]
   columns["Column1"].width     = 100
   columns["Column1"].headingControl.value = "Item Number"
   // second column
   columns["Column2"] = new GRIDCOLUMN(form.SeekerGrid)
 columns["Column2"].dataLink=form.rowset.fields["itemdescription"]
   columns["Column2"].width     = 271
   columns["Column2"].headingControl.value = "Description"
   // next column
   columns["Column3"] = new GRIDCOLUMN(form.SeekerGrid)
   columns["Column3"].dataLink = form.rowset.fields["costperitem"]
   columns["Column3"].width     = 110
   columns["Column3"].headingControl.value = "Cost Per Item"
endwith
```

- Set an event handler for the *onOpen* event for the form (page 98):

```
function form_onOpen()
   // force focus on the Item Description Entryfield:
   form.ItemDescEF.setFocus()
return
```

- On the second page, in the Form Designer, change the label for the textLabel control next to the seeker to:
  - Search for Description

Save the form, and close the Form Designer. That was a bit of work, but it was easier than the Customers form. If you run the form you should see (Figure 5-11):

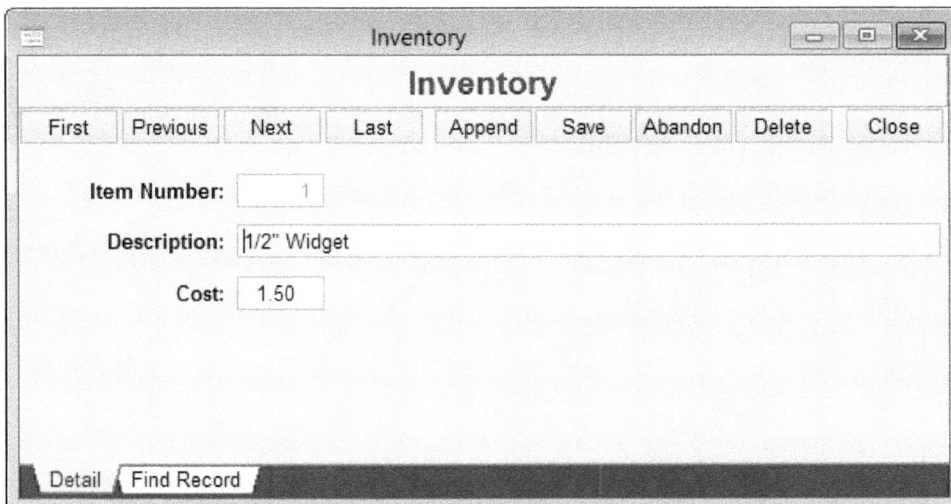

Figure 5-11

And if you click the "Find Record" tab, you should see:

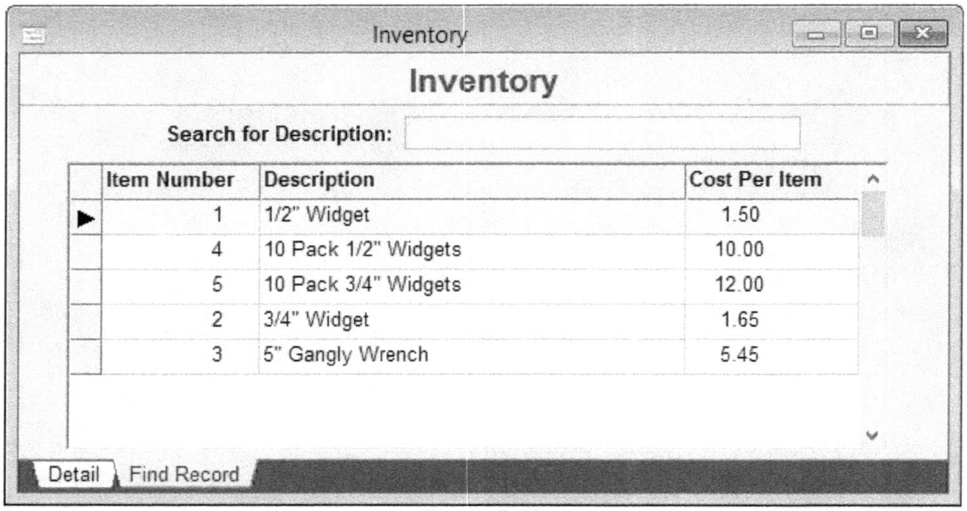

Figure 5-12

Other Forms

For any application there are likely to be many forms. This is a relatively simple application, and as such, the two forms we have created here are the foundation for other work we need to do. You may note this chapter is fairly lengthy … the other two forms we will be working on for this application need to work with multiple tables on the same form. As such, they will be in the next chapter, rather than making this one any longer than it already is.

Of course part of the reason this chapter is so long is that we built a lot of code that can be used for other single-table forms. The code we have built can also be used for multi-table forms, which we will see in Chapter 6, but sometimes we need to modify how it works.

Sample Code for This Chapter

The following is a listing of the sample code in the "Chapter 05" folder, if you downloaded it from my website. You may use the code contained in these forms for your own applications if you desire, with the caveat that credit be given appropriately.

- **BusinessLayer.cc** – The BusinessLayer class for the sample application.
- **CreateDatabase.prg** – Program to create the tables and set up the sequences, add some data, and more. This is the table design for the sample application.
- **CustomerGridDetails.wfm** – A form used to lay out the grid on the Customers form.
- **Customers.wfm** – The User-Interface form for the Customers table.
- **DataLayer.dmd** – The DataLayer for the sample application.
- **Inventory.wfm** – The User-Interface form for the Inventory table.
- **InventoryGridDetails.wfm** – A form used to lay out the grid on the Inventory form.
- **MSeekerADO.cc** – Seeker class designed to work with ADO tables.
- **SQLCustomFormButtons.cc** – Custom class file containing buttons to be used with the sample application.
- **SQLFormControls.cc** – Custom class file containing the form controls used in the sample application.

Summary

We have two more forms to create (the Invoices form), I am putting them in a new chapter simply because this chapter is already pretty lengthy, and I am feeling like I need to split things up. The Line Items and Invoices forms will, of a necessity be a bit more complex – they will work with multiple tables, and in some cases call other forms to complete what needs to be done.

All of this is, of a necessity, a bit complicated as the goal is to create code that is as "generic" as possible that can be used as a basis for your own applications. With just a little work, for example, you can copy the DataLayer.dmd and UILayer.cfm files, and make them work for you, either with ADO Databases (using the ADO Data objects), SQL Server Databases that use the BDE/ODBC (and hence the OODML data objects), or even with local (.DBF) tables.

Chapter 6: Using ADO Database Classes in an Application, Part 3

In this chapter we will be continuing the simple *application* using ADO Database objects that we started in Chapter 4. The plan is to finish everything in this chapter.

In Chapter 5 we spent a huge amount of time on the UI Layer, and a lot of code that is meant to be "generic" – meaning it is not specific to this application, and can be used in other applications as a foundation.

We will continue with multi-table forms in this chapter, and then we will revisit the Business Layer briefly.

Multi-Table Forms

Multi-Table forms, by definition, are a bit more complicated. We really need two for this application, one to handle the Line-Items table *(which also uses the Inventory table)*, and the other to put the invoices together, using all four of the tables in the application *(not counting the "MyGen" table)*.

We will start with the Line Items form, although this form would not normally be used on its own. The Line Item details typically are part of the Invoice itself, where you might use the Inventory table for other purposes, or you might use the Customers table for other purposes.

The Line Items Form
The LineItems form is a tricky one, in that you would want to display the descriptions from the Inventory table on the LineItems *form*, and also copy the cost per item over when you are appending a row *(but only then, allowing the user to edit the cost if necessary)*.

Typically this form would only *ever* be displayed when called from the main Invoice form, the idea being to allow the user to add/edit/remove Line Items on the invoice. In order to get data from the Inventory, it will be necessary to open the Inventory form *from* the Line Items form.

To start, some of this will be the same as the other forms we have worked on:
- Create a new form as derived from the UILayer.cfm (see page 93)
- Make changes to the text of the title, and the form's *text* property as well.
- Save it as "LineItems".
- Add controls for now – same as before for each field – *textLabel* and *entryfield* controls (use the custom ones – see page 95):
    - InvoiceNumber
        - InvNumLabel (for textlabel)
        - *text*: Invoice Number:
        - InvoiceNumEF (for entryfield)
    - ItemNumber
        - ItemNumLabel (for textlabel)

- - *text*: Item Number:
  - ItemNumEF (for entryfield)
  - *when*: {; return false}
  (change the event handler in the Inspector)
  - *colorNormal*: "Gray/Window"
  (change this property)
  - Quantity
    - QtyLabel: (for textlabel)
    - *text*: Quantity Ordered:
    - QtyEF: (for entryfield)
    - *picture*: 999
    (set picture property)
  - CostPerItem
    - CostLabel (for textlabel)
    - *text*: Cost Per Item:
    - CostEF (for enryfield)
    - *picture*: 999.99
    (set picture property)
- Adjust sizes and appearances of controls ...
- Set startup code (see page 99).
  - *Open* and *ReadModal* methods as well as the *Local_Init* method: be sure to copy the same code we used for the Customers form (you might want to open that form in the Source Code Editor and copy and paste ...).
  - Remove the line:
    ```
    class::SetUpSeekerGrid()
    ```
    from both of these two methods.
- Set code for the SetSequence method this way (page 118):

```
function SetSequence
    // set the form's rowset property, because we can
    // work with it for some of the controls ...
    form.rowset := form.DataLayerDataModule1.LineItems.rowset

    // use the sort property:
    form.rowset.sort := "InvoiceNumber"

    // if we have a new invoice, set a custom property
    // of the form:
    form.NewInvoice = false
    if form.rowset.count() == 0
        form.NewInvoice := true
    endif

    // load the data (from custom form):
    UILAYERCFORM::LoadData()
return
```

- Set code for the SetupControls method this way (page 97):

```
function SetupControls
    // method required to set custom properties of the controls,
    // defaultValue is important when appending, and maxLength
    // is important for character fields, so user cannot
    // enter more data than the field contains:
    if type( "form.InvoiceNum" ) # "N"
        form.InvoiceNum = 3
```

```
endif
form.InvNumEF.tableName        := "LineItems"
form.InvNumEF.fieldName        := "InvoiceNumber"
form.InvNumEF.value            := form.InvoiceNum
form.InvNumEF.defaultValue     := form.InvoiceNum
form.InvNumEF.readOnly         := true
form.ItemNumEF.tableName       := "LineItems"
form.ItemNumEF.fieldName       := "ItemNumber"
form.ItemNumEF.defaultValue    := 1
form.QtyEF.tableName           := "LineItems"
form.QtyEF.fieldName           := "Quantity"
form.QtyEF.defaultValue        := 1
// we can use this to force focus on a specific control
form.firstControl               = form.QtyEF
form.CostEF.tableName          := "LineItems"
form.CostEF.fieldName          := "CostPerItem"
form.CostEF.defaultValue       := 0.00
// ensure there is no attempt to write this to the
// table:
form.ItemDescEF.includeInQuery := false
return
```

- We will not be using the second page of the form, so select the tabbox control at the bottom of the form, and change:
  - *visible*: false
- Set an event handler for the *onOpen* event for the form (page 98):

```
function form_onOpen()
    // force focus on the Item Description Entryfield:
    form.ItemQtyEF.setFocus()
return
```

Save and close the form in the Form Designer, and then try running it. You should see:

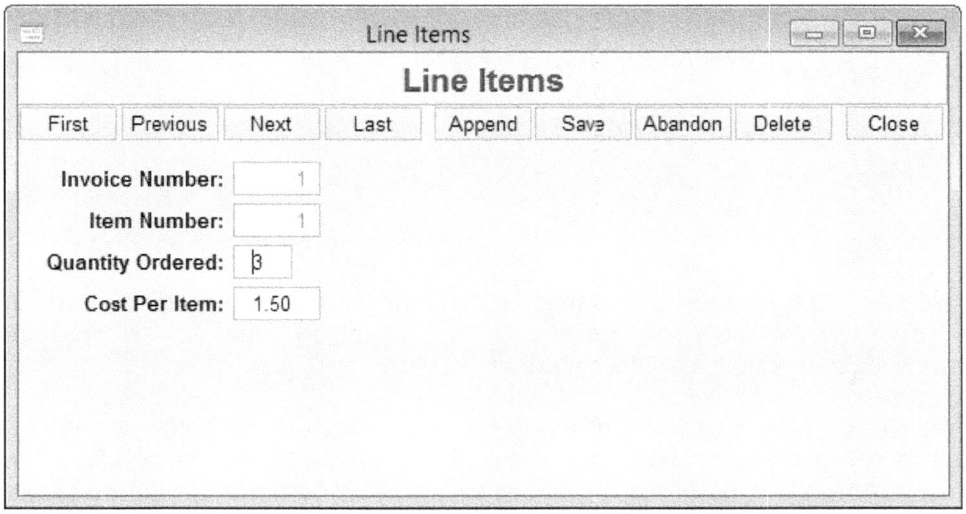

Figure 6-1

Notice that the Item Number *entryfield* is disabled. This is because we want the user to select an item from Inventory in a different way. We will deal with that later in this chapter.

Display the Item Description

In order to show the user the name of the product the customer is purchasing, we need to add a couple more controls on the form, and move some around. My recommendation is *(in the Form Designer)* to move the Quantity Ordered and Cost Per Item objects down and leave room for more controls. Then add the following (from the Custom tab of the Component Palette) and set properties as shown:

- SQLTextLabel
    - *name*: ItemDescLabel
    - *text*: Item Description:
- SQLEntryfield
    - *name:* ItemDescEF
    - *when*: {; return false}
    (change the event handler in the Inspector)
    - *colorNormal*: "Gray/Window"
    (change this property)

You should make the ItemDescEF entryfield fairly large *(the field in the Inventory table is 100 characters, after all)*. Note that the entryfield is *also* set to be disabled *(colorNormal property and when event handler)*.

At this point, if you save the form, close the Form Designer, and run it, the form should look like:

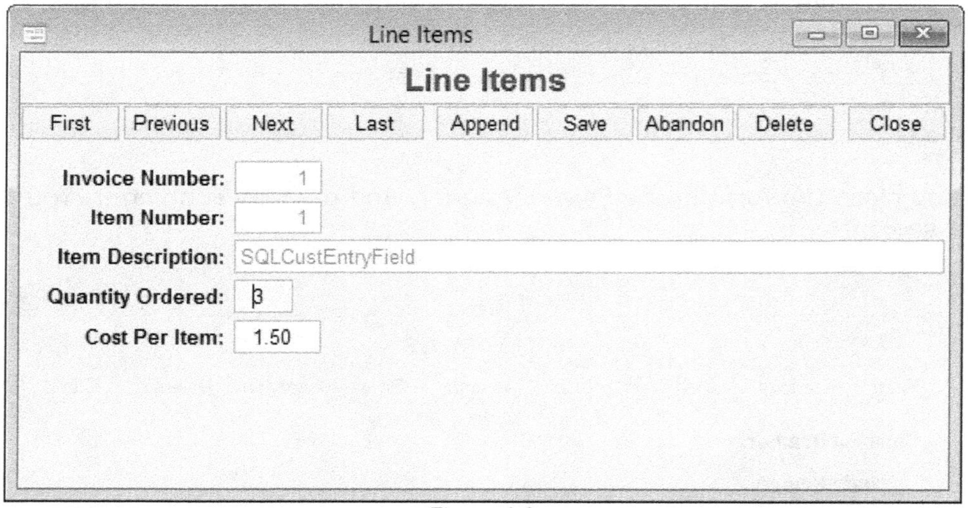

Figure 6-2

What we need is a method of looking up the Item Number, and displaying the Item Description. When we add a new record (append), we will also need to bring the *Cost Per Item* value over to this form.

We need to add a new method of the form that looks up the value of the Item Number in the Inventory table, and returns the information required. All things considered this is not really that difficult a task. The complexity will be making sure it is called when it is needed.

Open the form in the Source Code Editor, and add the following before the *endClass* statement:

```
function FindItem
    /*
       Method to find the Item Description from the
       Item Number ...:
    */
    local nFind, rInventory
    nFind = form.ItemNumEF.value // the value currently
                                 // in the ItemNum Entryfield
    // create shortcut to Inventory rowset:
    rInventory = form.DataLayerDataModule1.Inventory.rowset
    // make sure we're sorting correctly:
    rInventory.sort = "ItemNumber"
    rInventory.applyLocate( [ItemNumber = ]+nFind )
    if not rInventory.endOfSet
       form.ItemDescEF.value := ;
          rInventory.fields["ItemDescription"].value
    else
       form.ItemDescEF.value := "** Not Found **"
    endif
 return
```

Of course one hopes that the item will always be found, but that's an issue for you to handle *(and may be a data integrity issue – if a user deletes an inventory item it can cause some serious problems!)*. To ensure that the generic code in the custom form class does not attempt to write the value of this *entryfield* to the table (since there is no ItemDescription field in the LineItems table), find the *SetupControls* method, and add the following (before the *return* statement):

```
    form.ItemDescEF.includeInQuery := false
```

At this point, we need to be able to call the *FindItem* method in appropriate parts of the code. The first place would be to add this to the end of the *SetSequence* method (before the *return* statement):

```
    // make sure we load the Item Description:
    class::FindItem()
```

Save the form in the Source Code Editor, and open it in the Form Designer. In the Inspector, click the "Events" tab, find the *onNavigate* event handler (for the form), click it, then click the button that appears. When asked about overwriting the method, click "Yes". Add the following code:

```
function form_onNavigate(nWorkArea)
    // call code in custom form:
    UILayerCForm::form_onNavigate()
    // make sure we load the Item Description:
    class::FindItem()
 return
```

It is important that we call the original code in the custom form, and then when done we call the code to the new *FindItem* method. To test this, run the form, and try navigating through a few rows. Your form should look something like:

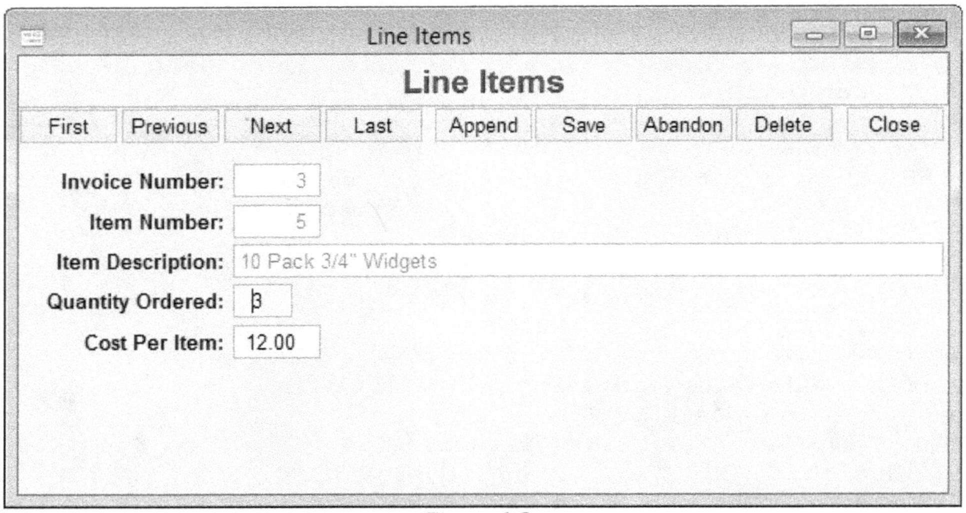

Figure 6-3

We will come back to how we allow the user to change the item in the form. We have some more work to do.

Add a Grid

For any invoice, a customer may order more than one item. The difficulty then becomes displaying all the items, and navigating through the data. For the other two forms in this application we used the grid on the second page of the form. For the Line Items form, it is useful to see everything in one place. We'll add a grid under the other controls, but we need to hook up the Item Description as well. For this to work, we're going to place two new *ADOQuery* objects on the form (and for those to work, we need an *ADODatabase* object). Close the form if it is open.

Open the form in the Source Code Editor, and go to the *SetSequence* method. Add the following after the statement "form.rowset.sort ...":

```
// for the lookup for the ItemNumber in the LineItems Grid:
form.LineItemsForGrid.rowset.fields["ItemNumber"].lookupRowset:=;
    form.InventoryForGrid.rowset
```

Save and close changes in the Source Code Editor.

Open the form back in the Form Designer. Drag an *ADODatabase* object to the form surface. Change the following properties:

- *name*: DatabaseForGrid
- *databaseName*: BOOKSAMPLE_ADO_RO
- *active*: true

Drag two *ADOQuery* objects to the form (click the "ADO Access" tab on the Component Palette first), and set these properties for the first query:

- *name*: LineItemsForGrid
- *database*: DatabaseForGrid *(select from list)*
- *sql*: select * from LineItems
- *active*: true

For the second query change these properties:

- *name*: InventoryForGrid
- *database*: DatabaseForGrid
- *sql*: select ItemNumber, ItemDescription from Inventory
- *active*: true

We'll have to make a change to the SQL statement for the LineItems query later, but one thing at a time.

Click the "Standard" tab on the Component Palette, and bring a grid object over, under the other controls. Set the following properties:

- *name*: LineItemGrid
- *datalink*: LineItemsForGrid
  (dBASE will change this to: form.lineitemsforgrid.rowset)
- *rowSelect*: true
- *colorRowSelect*: WindowText/0x80ffff
- *vScrollBar*: 1 (On)

The rest of the work for the grid is going to need to be done the same way we set up the grid for the other forms – we're going to have to create a form that will allow us to design the grid, and then copy just the information we need over.

Before closing the form, note the width of the form (on my screen it is 596 pixels wide) – we will want this to design the width of the grid based on *this* form.

Designing the Grid
In the Navigator window, double click the [New Form] icon, turn off the custom form settings (File | Set Custom Form Class | Clear Custom Form Class), and don't save changes.

With the new form, set the *metric* property to 6, resize the form appropriately, setting the *width* property to the width of your LineItems form.

Open the BookSample_ADO_RO database in the Navigator and log in if needed. Drag the LineItems and Inventory tables to the design surface. Set the following properties for the Inventory table:

- *active*: false
- *sql*: select ItemNumber, ItemDescription from inventory
- *active*: true

Click on the LineItems table, and in the Inspector:

- Click on *rowset*, click the "I" button ("I" for Inspect)
- Click on *fields*, click the "I" button
- Click on *ItemNumber*, click the "I" button
- Find the *lookupRowset* property, and select "INVENTORY1" – dBASE will change this to: form.inventory1.rowset

Drag a *grid* control from the Component Palette to the design surface, and make the following changes:

- *datalink*: LineItems (dBASE will change this to):
  form.lineitems1.rowset
- *columns:* Click on this in the Inspector, select the first button, which will open the Columns Property Builder, and select:

- o LINEITEMS1.ITEMNUMBER
  - o LINEITEMS1.COSTPERITEM

Click "OK"

Adjust the column widths, there are only two, so just work with this. The ItemNumber is showing the ItemDescription value from the Inventory table, because that is what the *lookupRowset* property of the field does.

Back to the LineItems Form

Save and close the form, and using the values from that form (open it in the Source Code Editor), we need to add a new method to the LineItems form that will help us display information for the user *(which means having both forms open in the Source Code Editor, using the tabs at the top to switch back and forth …)*:

```
function SetUpLIGrid
   // Necessary to manually set up the grid here:
   with( form.LineItemsGrid )
      width = 580
      left = 7
      dataLink = form.rowset
      // first column
      columns["Column1"] = new GRIDCOLUMN(form.LineItemsGrid)
      columns["Column1"].dataLink=form.rowset.fields["itemnumber"]
      columns["Column1"].width     = 425
      columns["Column1"].headingControl.value="Item Description"
      // second column
      columns["Column2"] = new GRIDCOLUMN(form.LineItemsGrid)
      columns["Column2"].dataLink=form.rowset.fields["costperitem"]
      columns["Column2"].width     = 110
      columns["Column2"].headingControl.value = "Cost Per Item"
   endwith
return
```

Then, in the *open* and *readModal* methods, before the *return* statement, add the following:

```
class::SetUpLIGrid()
```

Save and exit the Source Code Editor. At this time, if you were to run the form, the grid will show all Line Items in the table because we are not filtering things down to a specific invoice.

Navigation in Form

One difficulty that will rapidly become apparent is that navigating in the form does not update the grid, and navigating in the grid does not update the form. This is because we are using different *rowsets* to display the same information. While there are advantages to this, there are obviously disadvantages as well.

The code we're going to use gets a little strange here, because of the way the event handlers work in dBASE forms.

We need to open the LineItems form back in the Form Designer again. When you it is open, on the Inspector, click the "Events" tab, and find the form's *onNavigate* event handler. Click it, and then click the button to the right of it. Add the following before the *return* statement:

```
// Update LineItems Grid:
class::UpdateLIGrid()
```

Next, back on the form, click the *LineItemsForGrid* ADOQuery object on the form. On the "Properties" tab of the inspector, find the *rowset* property and click it, then click the "I" button. Click the "Events" tab, find the *onNavigate* event handler, click it, and click the button on the right *(when entering the code, be sure to read the comments, they explain a lot)*. In the Source Code Editor, enter:

```
function rowset_onNavigate(type, nRows)
    // when we navigate here, we need to ensure we navigate
    // properly on the main form.

    // To avoid a loop in the form's code, we must
    // disable the form's onNavigate event handler:
    form.onNavigate := null
    // Find the matching item in the form's rowset:
    local nItem
    nItem = form.LineItemsForGrid.rowset.fields["LineItemNumber"].value
    form.rowset.applyLocate( [LineItemNumber=]+nItem )
    if form.rowset.endOfSet
        ? "Not Found"
    endif

    // call the code normally
    // in the onNavigate event handler:
    UILayerCForm::LoadData()
    // make sure we load the Item Description:
    class::FindItem()

    // hook the form's onNavigate event handler back up:
    form.onNavigate := class::FORM_ONNAVIGATE
return
```

If you examine the code, you will see that we had to set the form's *onNavigate* event handler to null – disabling the "normal" code. The reason for that is the code here does a search in the rowset associated with the form, which causes navigation. When that occurs, the form's *onNavigate* event handler fires, which then causes the rowset associated with the grid (the one that caused *this* event to fire) to navigate, which puts us into a loop. By disabling the form's *onNavigate* event handler, we avoid the loop. But we also need to fire most of the code in that event handler, which is why the two method calls are made. Then we re-connect the form's *onNavigate* event handler so that if you navigate in the main part of the form, everything still works properly. It took a bit of work to make this happen and avoid an infinite loop *(and some hair-pulling in the process …)*.

If you save all your work, close the Source Code Editor, and run the form, you should see:

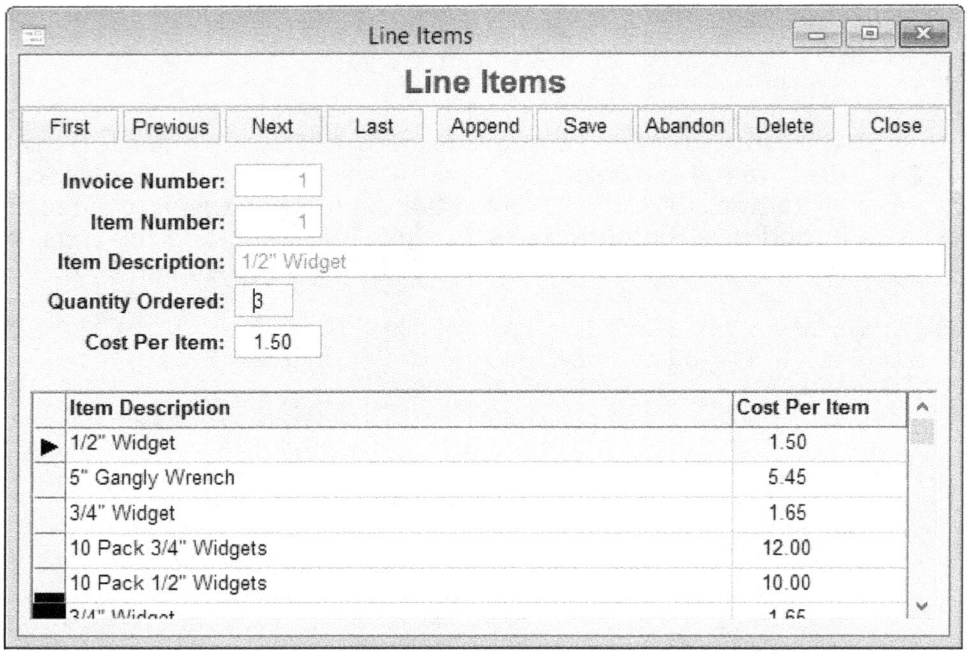

Figure 6-4

Set Form for a Single Invoice

By definition, this form really should only be called from the Invoice form, so that you can see/edit/add/remove Line Items for that invoice. This will require some changes in the code. We will have to rely on a custom property of the form called "InvoiceNum", which we can use to filter the data.

So that while testing the form by itself we can see it working correctly, we need to modify the code that is used to open the form. We are going to ensure that this custom property exists and set a default value if it doesn't. Open the Line Items form in the Source Code Editor, find the *SetSequence* method and add this code at the top (right after the *function* statement):

```
if type( "form.InvoiceNum" ) # "N"
   form.InvoiceNum = 3 // has four line items
endif
```

We now need to modify the *sql* statement for the rowset, so that it limits the data to just the Invoice Number that we need. Add this code directly below the code you just added:

```
// modify the sql statement for the LineItems query:
form.DataLayerDataModule1.LineItems.active := false
form.DataLayerDataModule1.LineItems.sql    := ;
   "select * from LineItems where InvoiceNumber="+form.InvoiceNum
form.DataLayerDataModule1.LineItems.active := true
```

This limits the main part of the form to this invoice number, but what about the query used for the grid? This is tricky because there is currently a bug in dBASE with a query attached to a grid that you have defined the columns for that causes a Memory Access Violation (MAV).

Mervyn Bick points out that you can use parameters with the query used for the *LineItemsForGrid* query. This will take a couple of steps. First, close the Source Code Editor, and open the form in the Form Designer.

One issue I discovered is when you navigate through the LineItems using the pushbuttons, if you hit the endOfSet you can run into an error. Add the following to the code in the method *UpdateLIGrid* right after the *function* statement:

```
if form.rowset.endOfSet
   return
endif
```

Save and close the form in the Source Code Editor. Open the form in the Form Designer. Click on the ADOQuery "LineItemsForGrid", in the Inspector:

- *active*: false
- *sql*: select * from LineItems where InvoiceNumber=:InvNum
- Click on *parameters* and click the "I" button
- Click on *InvNum* and the "I" button
- *type*: Integer
- *value*: 3
- Use the "back" button at the top of the Inspector twice
- *active*: true

You will actually see the grid show just the four Line Items for this invoice! However, it seems the Form Designer does not stream this out *(a new bug)*. If you actually save and run the form, the grid will be empty. This is a way to test the parameter though. We need to now go back to the Source Code Editor, so close the form and open it in the Editor.

In the *SetSequence* method, after the code we added earlier, insert this code:

```
// using a parameter in the sql statement, the following
// sets the display correctly:
form.LineItemsForGrid.params[ "InvNum" ] := form.InvoiceNum
form.LineItemsForGrid.requery()
```

If you now run the form, you will see the data in the grid matches Invoice 3, and everything is great. Keep in mind that ultimately when this is called from the Invoice form, we will set the form's custom property "InvoiceNum" to whatever Invoice number we need.

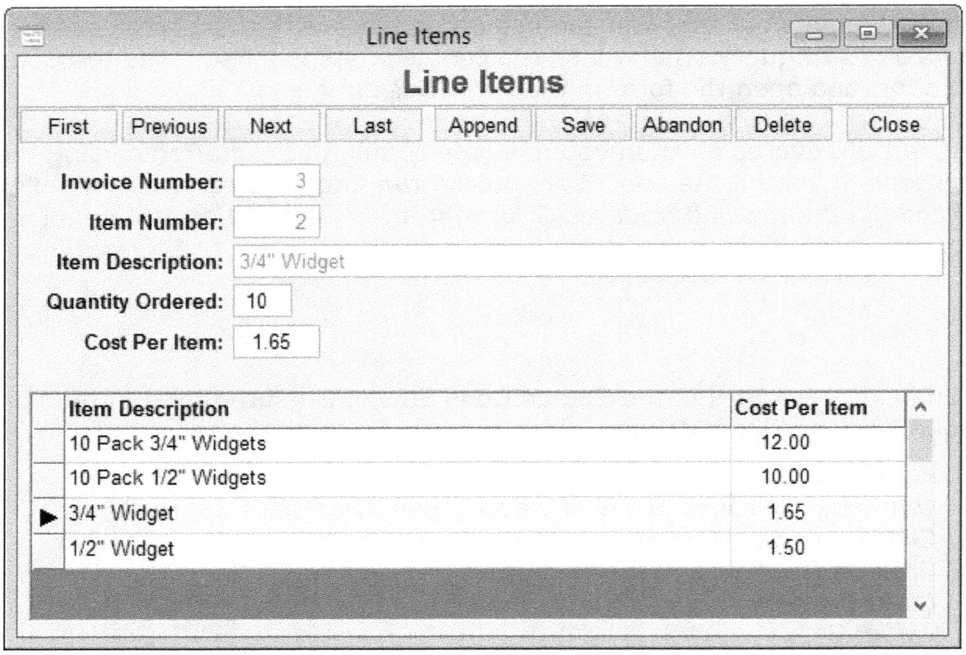

Figure 6-5

At this point there are only a couple more things that need to be done.

Edit Line Items

If your customer goofed and ordered the wrong item, *or* someone added the wrong item to the invoice, you could delete it, or you could change the item. The difficulty at the moment is that the Item Number and Item Description entryfields are disabled.

The reason they are set the way they are is that if you rely on the person using the form to enter a correct value, they will invariably get something wrong. What we need to do is to allow the user to change the current item. All the data in your Inventory table *should* be correct, so we will call the Inventory form. To do that we will need to use a pushbutton.

Open the LineItems form in the Form Designer. On the Component Palette select the Pushbutton and place one on the form above the Item Description entryfield, to the right side of the form. Change these properties:

- *name*: ChangeItemBtn
- *text:* Change Item
- *speedBar*: true
- Modify the size/position so it looks good to you
- In the Inspector click "Events"
- *onClick*: click this and then the first button

In the Source Code Editor for the *onClick* event handler, add the following code:

```
function CHANGEITEMBTN_onClick
   /*
      Code to call the Inventory form, allow user to
      select an item, when form is closed we return that
      information here.
   */
   private fInv, nItem, cItem, nCost
   set procedure to Inventory.wfm
   fInv = new InventoryForm()
   fInv.mdi := false
   fInv.autoCenter := true
   fInv.readModal() // user must close the form
   nItem = fInv.rowset.fields["ItemNumber"].value
   cItem =fInv.rowset.fields["ItemDescription"].value.rightTrim()
   nCost = fInv.rowset.fields["CostPerItem"].value

   // check to see if values are different -- if they are,
   // ask if user wants to change the current item to this:
   if form.ItemNumEF.value # nItem
      if msgbox( "Do you wish to change this Line Item to "+chr(13)+;
         "Item "+nItem+": "+cItem+"?",;
         "Change Item?", 32+4 ) == 6
         // user said "Yes", we will change it:
         form.ItemNumEF.value    := nItem
         form.ItemNumEF.newValue := nItem
         form.ItemNumEF.modified := true
         form.ItemDescEF.value   := cItem
         form.CostEF.value       := nCost
         form.CostEF.newValue    := nCost
         form.CostEF.modified    := true
         form.modified           := true
      endif // msgbox
   endif // form.ItemNumEF ...

   // cleanup:
   fInv.release()
   fInv := null
   close procedure Inventory.wfm
return
```

If you examine the code, you will see we are forcing the controls to set *modified* properties and such to be sure that when we save the changes they are properly saved.

When this form is called from the Invoice form, we need to create a "dummy" first record for the Line Items table – this is due to some issue *(possibly a bug, but it is hard to determine)* where the *lookupRowset* we are using to display the Description of the Line Item disappears and I have not found a way to force it to return. Hence, we need to add the following code in the form's onOpen event handler:

```
function form_onOpen()
   // force focus on the Item Description Entryfield:
   form.ItemQtyEF.setFocus()
   // need user to select correct first item
   // for new invoice
   if type( "form.NewInvoice" ) # "L"
      form.NewInvoice = false
   endif
   if form.NewInvoice
      class::ChangeItemBtn_onClick()
   endif
return
```

The custom form property "NewInvoice" should be being set in the Invoice form's code for adding a new invoice (which we will create later in this chapter). We have a check for it here just in case.

Add Line Items

Adding a new item requires we look up something in the Inventory form. This code will appear very similar to what we're doing when we use the Change Item button from above. However, in this case we need to overwrite the code for the AppendButton. Open the form in the Form Designer, if it is not open already.

Click the Append button, and in the Inspector, click the "Events" tab, find *onClick*, click this, and then click the button to the right. When asked about overwriting the code, click "Yes", and enter the following:

```
function APPENDBUTTON1_onClick()
   // we need to call original code:
   AppendButton::OnClick()
   // now we need to select an item from
   // the inventory:
   private fInv, nItem, cItem, nCost
   set procedure to Inventory.wfm
   fInv = new InventoryForm()
   fInv.mdi := false
   fInv.autoCenter := true
   fInv.readModal() // user must close the form
   nItem = fInv.rowset.fields["ItemNumber"].value
   cItem =fInv.rowset.fields["ItemDescription"].value.rightTrim()
   nCost = fInv.rowset.fields["CostPerItem"].value
   // insert item into form:
   form.ItemNumEF.value    := nItem
   form.ItemNumEF.newValue := nItem
   form.ItemNumEF.modified := true
   form.ItemDescEF.value   := cItem
   form.CostEF.value       := nCost
   form.CostEF.newValue    := nCost
   form.CostEF.modified    := true
   form.append             := true
   // cleanup:
   fInv.release()
   fInv := null
   close procedure Inventory.wfm
return
```

Refresh ALL Data

There's only one problem now. When the changes are saved, or when they are deleted, the query used for the grid is not refreshed properly, and changes do not appear. We need to overwrite the save and delete button's code.

Open the form in the Form Designer if is not already open.

Click the *Save* button, click the "Events" tab, find *onClick*, click this, and then click the button to the right. When asked about overwriting the code, click "Yes", and enter the following:

```
function SAVEBUTTON1_onClick()
    // overwritten button code, call original:
    SaveButton::OnClick()
    // no matter what, requery the rowset used for the grid:
    form.LineItemsForGrid.requery()
    if form.NewInvoice // we started with no LineItems
       form.NewInvoice = false // only do this for first row
    endif
    // ensure grid is updated
    class::UpdateLIGrid()
return
```

We will do the same for the Delete button, but with the following code:

```
function DELETEBUTTON1_onClick()
    // overwritten button code, call original:
    DeleteButton::OnClick()
    // The reason we did this is because everything
    // else has been updated, but the LineItemsForGrid
    // rowset has not ...
    form.LineItemsForGrid.requery()
    class::UpdateLIGrid()
return
```

And there we have it! At this point, everything in your form should work correctly, the display will update properly, and so on. Try running the form, navigating, adding, editing, deleting Line Items …

The Invoices Form

The Invoices form is the culmination of everything for this application. It is the place where the users will enter invoices. As with everything else in this application, this is a relatively simple invoicing form, it doesn't take into account all the functionality that many businesses have to work with (how paid, sales tax, shipping costs, etc.).

The Invoices form will need to allow the user to create a new invoice, edit an existing invoice, and possibly delete one. We will take a look at each of these, as not surprisingly, the code for the pushbuttons will need to be overwritten to allow specific processing.

Start a new form (in the Navigator, double-click the [New Form] icon), and if necessary, set the custom form class to the UILayer.cfm file. Save the form as "Invoices".

Change the TitleText control's *text* property and the form's *text* property to "Invoices" (without the quotes).

We need to set up controls for information about the Invoice itself – drag appropriate SQLTextLabel and SQLEntryfield controls to the design surface, and set the following properties:

- InvoiceNumber
    - *name*: InvNumLabel (for textlabel)
    - *text*: Invoice Number:
    - *name*: InvNumEF (for entryfield)
- InvoiceDate
    - *name*: InvDateLabel (for textlabel)
    - *text*: Date:
    - *name*: InvDateEF (for entryfield)
    - *type*: Date (in the Inspector, find *type*, click "T" button …)
- CustomerNumber
    - *name*: CustNumLabel (for textlabel)
    - *text*: Customer Number:
    - *name*: CustNumEF (for entryfield)

Notice that we are using the Customer Number for the *Invoice* here, not from the Customers table. We are going to need to work with the Customers table, but we'll get to that.

Before we get into working with the other tables we need, let's get the basic code set up that we're going to need for the form, following the same structure as other forms we've worked with.

- Set startup code (see page 99).
    - *Open* and *ReadModal* and *Local_Init* methods: be sure to copy the same code we used for the Customers form (you might want to open that form in the Source Code Editor and copy and paste …).
- Set code for the SetSequence method this way (page 118):

```
function SetSequence
    // set the form's rowset property, because we can
    // work with it for some of the controls ...
    form.rowset := form.DataLayerDataModule1.Invoices.rowset

    // for the seeker control (in the Custom Form) we need
    // to use the sort property:
    form.rowset.sort := "InvoiceNumber"

    // for the seeker we need to force the rowset:
    form.mSeekerADO1.rowset := form.rowset

    // load the data again (from custom form):
    UILAYERCFORM::LoadData()
return
```

- Set code for the SetupControls method this way (page 97):

```
function SetupControls
    // method required to set custom properties of the controls,
    // defaultValue is important when appending, and maxLength
    // is important for character fields, so user cannot
    // enter more data than the field contains:
```

```
form.InvNumEF.tableName        := "Invoices"
form.InvNumEF.fieldName        := "InvoiceNumber"
form.InvNumEF.readOnly         := true
form.InvNumEF.includeInQuery   := false
form.InvDateEF.tableName       := "Invoices"
form.InvDateEF.fieldName       := "InvoiceDate"
form.InvDateEF.defaultValue    := date()
// we can use this to force focus on a specific control
form.firstControl               = form.InvDateEF
form.CustNumEF.tableName       := "Invoices"
form.CustNumEF.fieldName       := "CustomerNumber"
form.CustNumEF.readOnly        := true
return
```

- Set code for the grid by using the same procedure we did on page 116. Note that we actually will come back to this – it is going to take some work, but we need the method in the form's source code:

```
function SetUpSeekerGrid
    // Necessary to manually set up the grid here:
// code left blank for now - we will return to it
    return
```

- Set an event handler for the *onOpen* event for the form (page 98):

```
function form_onOpen()
    // force focus on the Item Description Entryfield:
    form.InvDateEF.setFocus()
return
```

- On the second page, in the Form Designer, change the label for the textLabel control next to the seeker to:
    - Search for Invoice:

We will come back to the grid, but before we do, we need to set up code similar to the Line Items form that looks for the customer information. We will start by adding controls to the form that display *(but do not allow editing of)* the Customer data. All of these controls will need to be read-only, and will be done similar to what we did with the Line Items Description field. Add items to the form as below:

- BusinessName
    - *name*: BusNameLabel (for textlabel)
    - *text*: Business Name:
    - *name*: BusNameEF (for entryfield)
    - *when*: {; return false}
      (change the event handler in the Inspector)
    - *colorNormal*: "Gray/Window"
      (change this property)
- Address1
    - *name*: Address1Label (for textlabel)
    - *text*: Address:
    - *name*: Address1EF (for entryfield)
    - *when*: {; return false}
      (change the event handler in the Inspector)
    - *colorNormal*: "Gray/Window"
      (change this property)
- Address2
    - *No textlabel necessary*

- o *name*: Address2EF (for entryfield)
- o *when*: {; return false}
  (change the event handler in the Inspector)
- o *colorNormal*: "Gray/Window"
  (change this property)
- City
  - o *name*: CityLabel (for textlabel)
  - o *text*: City:
  - o *name*: CityEF (for entryfield)
  - o *when*: {; return false}
    (change the event handler in the Inspector)
  - o *colorNormal*: "Gray/Window"
    (change this property)
- State
  - o *name*: StateLabel (for textlabel)
  - o *text*: State:
  - o *name*: StateEF (for entryfield)
  - o *when*: {; return false}
    (change the event handler in the Inspector)
  - o *colorNormal*: "Gray/Window"
    (change this property)
- PostalCode
  - o *name*: PostalCodeLabel (for textlabel)
  - o *text*: Postal Code:
  - o *name*: PostalCodeEF (for entryfield)
  - o *when*: {; return false}
    (change the event handler in the Inspector)
  - o *colorNormal*: "Gray/Window"
    (change this property)
- EmailAddress
  - o *name*: EmailLabel (for textlabel)
  - o *text*: Email Address:
  - o *name*: EmailEF (for entryfield)
  - o *when*: {; return false}
    (change the event handler in the Inspector)
  - o *colorNormal*: "Gray/Window"
    (change this property)

One could argue that it is not necessary to include all the fields for the Customer on the form, but sometimes when interacting with the customer it is easier to just verify the data here, rather than opening the Customer form to see all their information.

When the form opens, and when the Invoice table is navigated, we need to update the customer information on the form. Since we're not displaying this in a grid, the issue of navigation in one table interfering with navigation in the other goes away, but we do need to add code to update the form.

Save the form and open it in the Source Code Editor.

In the *SetupControls* method, add the following before the *return* statement:

```
// The Customers section of the data -- we need to
// set the entryfields so that they are ignored
// when changes get made ...:
form.BusNameEF.includeInQuery    := false
form.BusNameEF.readOnly          := true
form.Address1EF.includeInQuery   := false
form.Address1EF.readOnly         := true
form.Address2EF.includeInQuery   := false
form.Address2EF.readOnly         := true
form.CityEF.includeInQuery       := false
form.CityEF.readOnly             := true
form.StateEF.includeInQuery      := false
form.StateEF.readOnly            := true
form.PostalCodeEF.includeInQuery := false
form.PostalCodeEF.readOnly       := true
form.EMailEF.includeInQuery      := false
form.EMailEF.readOnly            := true
```

Before the *endClass* statement, add the following code:

```
function FindCustomer
    local nFind, rCustomers
    nFind = form.CustNumEF.value // the value currently
                                 // in the CustNum Entryfield
    // create shortcut to Customers rowset:
    rCustomers = form.DataLayerDataModule1.Customers.rowset
    // make sure we're sorting correctly:
    rCustomers.sort = "CustomerNumber"
    rCustomers.applyLocate( [CustomerNumber = ]+nFind )
    if not rCustomers.endOfSet
        // load the controls:
        form.BusNameEF.value    := ;
            rCustomers.fields["BusinessName"].value
        form.Address1EF.value   := ;
            rCustomers.fields["Address1"].value
        form.Address2EF.value   := ;
            rCustomers.fields["Address2"].value
        form.CityEF.value       := ;
            rCustomers.fields["City"].value
        form.StateEF.value      := ;
            rCustomers.fields["State"].value
        form.PostalCodeEF.value := ;
            rCustomers.fields["PostalCode"].value
        form.EmailEF.value      := ;
            rCustomers.fields["EmailAddress"].value
    else
        form.BusNameEF.value    := "** Not Found **"
        form.Address1EF.value   := ""
        form.Address2EF.value   := ""
        form.CityEF.value       := ""
        form.StateEF.value      := ""
        form.PostalCodeEF.value := ""
        form.EmailEF.value      := ""
    endif
return
```

At this point, we need to be able to call the *FindCustomer* method in appropriate parts of the code. The first place would be to add this to the end of the *SetSequence* method (before the *return* statement):

```
// make sure we load the Customer Data:
class::FindCustomer()
```

The next will require that we save the form in the Source Code Editor, and open it in the Form Designer. In the Inspector, click the "Events" tab, find the *onNavigate* event handler, click it, then click the button that appears. When asked about overwriting the method, click "Yes". Add the following code:

```
function form_onNavigate(nWorkArea)
    // call code in custom form:
    UILayerCForm::form_onNavigate()
    // make sure we load the Customer Data:
    class::FindCustomer()
return
```

It is important that we call the original code in the custom form, and then when done we call the code to the new *FindCustomer* method. To test this, run the form, and try navigating through a few rows. Your form should look something like:

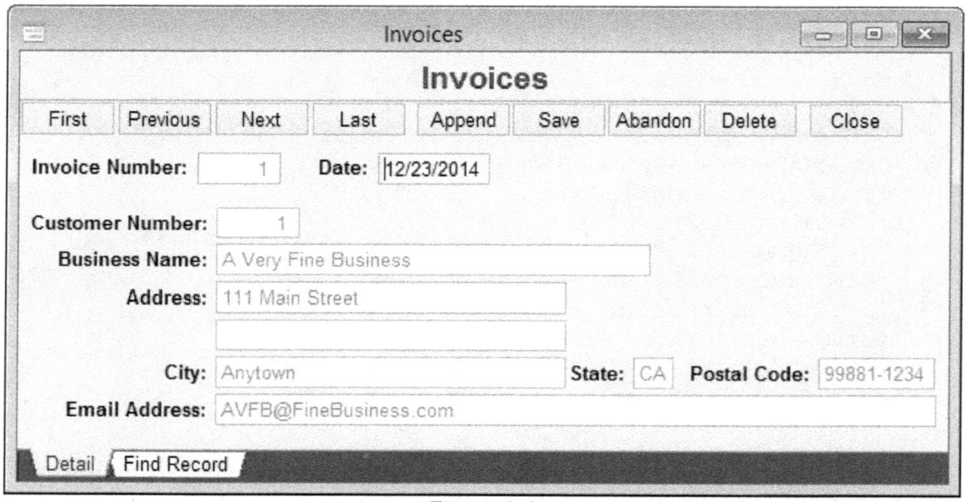

Figure 6-6

As you navigate you will see the Customer information should update appropriately.

You may want to use a *rectangle*, or *line* objects, to put around the customer data as a way to visually separate this information from the rest.

Below this, you will need to display the Line Item data. This will be a lot more complicated. Before we get to the Line Item data, let's deal with the seeker grid on the second page of the form. For this to work we will need to do the same type of thing we have done in the past, in this case for the Line Item table. We want to display, rather than the Customer Number, the Customer Name.

Find Record Page of Form
This will require a different method of working with the seeker grid and control this time.

For this (and the Line Items part of the form) to work, we need to add an *ADODatabase* object. Open the form in the Form Designer, on the Component Palette tab, select "ADO Access" and drag an *ADODatabase* object to the form. Set the following properties:

- *name*: BookSampleForGrids
- *database*: BOOKSAMPLE_ADO_RO
- *loginString*: SYSDBA/masterkey
- *active*: true

Next, we need two *ADOQuery* objects, set the following properties:

- *name*: InvoicesForSeeker
- *databaseName*: form.booksampleforgrids *(this should be the default)*
- *sql*: select * from Invoices
- *active*: true

For the second query:

- *name*: CustomersForSeeker
- *databaseName*: form.booksampleforgrids *(this should be the default)*
- *sql*: select CustomerNumber, BusinessName from Customers
- *active*: true

Save and close the form.

You will need to set up a form to get the grid columns you want as we have done in the past. This will require a similar setup as above on that form, so you have the Business Name appearing in the grid.

Once you have this, we need to create the code for the "SetupSeekerGrid" method of the Invoices form. It should look *similar* to:

```
function SetUpSeekerGrid
   // Necessary to manually set up the grid here:
   with( form.SeekerGrid )
      width = 562
      left = 30
      dataLink = form.InvoicesForSeeker.rowset
      // first column
      columns["Column1"] = new GRIDCOLUMN(form.SeekerGrid)
      columns["Column1"].dataLink= ;
         form.InvoicesForSeeker.rowset.fields["InvoiceNumber"]
      columns["Column1"].width     = 119
      columns["Column1"].headingControl.value = "Invoice Number"
      // second column
      columns["Column2"] = new GRIDCOLUMN(form.SeekerGrid)
      columns["Column2"].dataLink=;
         form.InvoicesForSeeker.rowset.fields["InvoiceDate"]
      columns["Column2"].width     = 96
      columns["Column2"].headingControl.value = "Date"
      // next column
      columns["Column3"] = new GRIDCOLUMN(form.SeekerGrid)
      columns["Column3"].dataLink = ;
```

```
      form.InvoicesForSeeker.rowset.fields["customernumber"]
    columns["Column3"].width      = 300
    columns["Column3"].headingControl.value = "Business Name"
  endwith
return
```

If the grid is set up to search by Invoice Numbers, we have a problem. The difficulty is that the mSeekerADO class can only search for character values. In addition, this code does not recognize the *lookupSQL* property of the Company Number field, so we need to set that.

Go to the *SetSequence* method. We need to add/modify some code – make appropriate changes based on the information below::

```
// for the form we need to use the sort property:
form.rowset.sort := "InvoiceNumber"
// for the seeker, we need a different rowset's sort:
form.InvoicesForSeeker.rowset.sort := "InvoiceNumber"
// for the seeker we need to force the rowset:
form.mSeekerADO1.rowset := form.InvoicesForSeeker.rowset
// for the lookup for the CustomerNumber in the Seeker Grid:
form.InvoicesForSeeker.rowset.fields["CustomerNumber"].lookupRowset:=;
    form.CustomersForSeeker.rowset
```

The seeker object is going to be a problem here … however there is a relatively simple solution. In the mSeekerADO class, I have added a new class that is subclassed from the mSeekerADO class, overwriting a couple of methods. The class is named mNumSeekerADO, and appears to work properly with numeric values, as long as the rowset's *sort* property is set to the correct field.

To use this new seeker class, we will have to hide the standard *mSeekerADO* class, and put this new object on the form in place of it. Open the form in the Form designer, go to the second page. Click on the mSeekerADO1 object, and set the *visible* property to *false*, click the "Custom" tab, and select the *mNumSeekerADO* class, and place an instance of that on the form.

There are some issues – this control does not automatically receive focus when the Tabbox changes, and navigation in this table does not automatically navigate in the main form.

To deal with the first issue, in the Form Designer, we can overwrite the Tabbox control's *onSelChange* event handler. Click the Tabbox, in the Inspector, on the "Events" tab, find *onSelChange*, click it, and click the button on the right. When asked about overwriting the code, click "Yes". Change the code to:

```
function TABBOX1_onSelChange()
   // Tabbox changes the page number on the form:
   form.pageNo := this.curSel
   if this.curSel == 1
      if type( "form.FirstControl" ) == "O" // object
         form.FirstControl.setFocus()
      endif
   else
      form.rowset.first()
      form.mNumSeekerADO1.setFocus()
   endif
return
```

The big change is the statement in bold above setting focus on the correct seeker control.

The other thing we need to do is to navigate on the main form when we navigate in this rowset, so that when the user clicks on the "Detail" tab, they will see the record selected on the "Find Record" tab.

Open the form in the Form Designer, click on the "InvoicesForSeeker" query object. On the Inspector click the *rowset* and the "I" button, select the "Events" tab, find *onNavigate* and click it, then click the button on the right. Add the following code:

```
function rowset_onNavigate(type, nRows)
   // InvoicesForSeeker rowset, we need to handle
   // navigation on the primary form to match:
   local nFind, oForm
   oForm = this.parent.parent // parent1=ADOQuery,parent2=form
   nFind = this.fields["InvoiceNumber"].value
   // find it in the rowset:
   oForm.rowset.applyLocate( [InvoiceNumber=]+nFind )
return
```

Because the form's *onNavigate* event handler is set to update the controls of the form, the use of *applyLocate* will navigate and the form will update. Save and close your work.

Line Items

The display of the Line Items for the Invoice form is obviously an important part of what needs to occur. Recall that the Line Items table relies on the Inventory table for the Item Descriptions, so we will have to do something similar for this table to what we did for the Customers table above.

Because we have an unknown quantity of items to be displayed, using a grid makes a lot of sense. On the Line Items form we did something similar to what we need here, but it would be useful to have a line total – a total for each line item ordered. We know the cost, we know the number of items ordered – we really need to be able to have a total – which can then be used for a grand total for the invoice.

Start by creating a form just to lay everything out, which we will then use later for the Invoice form. In the Navigator, double-click the "[New Form]" icon, set the *metric* property to 6, and then add the follow ng:

ADODatabase

- *name*: ForLineItems
- *databaseName*: BOOKSAMPLE_ADO_RO
- *loginString*: SYSDBA/masterkey
- *active*: true

ADOQuery #1 (note the calculated field)

- *name*: LineItems
- *sql*: select LineItems.*, Quantity*CostPerItem as LineTotal from LineItems
- *active*: true

ADOQuery #2

- *name*: Inventory
- *sql*: select ItemNumber, ItemDescription from Inventory
- *active* := true

Select a *grid* from the "Standard" tab of the Component Palette and drag it to the design surface. Save the form as "LineItemsForInvoice" *(to avoid overwriting the other form created to design the grid for the Line Items form …)*.

Set the lookup for the Item Description:

- click on the *LineItems* query
- select *rowset*, and the "I" button
- select *fields* and the "I" button
- find the *ItemNumber* field and click the "I" button
- find *lookupRowset*, select "Inventory

For the grid:

- *dataLink*: LineItems (the Inspector will change this to "form.lineitems.rowset")
- *columns*: click the first button, and add these fields:
    - INVENTORY.ITEMNUMBER
    - LINEITEMS.ITEMNUMBER
    - LINEITEMS.QUANTITY
    - LINEITEMS.COSTPERITEM
    - LINEITEMS.LINETOTAL
- Adjust the column widths

Save the form and exit the form designer.

Open the Invoices form in the Form Designer, and add two ADOQuery objects to the form *(we already have an active ADODatabase object pointing to the correct database)*. Set the following properties (these will be the same as above):

ADOQuery #1 (note the calculated field)

- *name*: LineItems
- *sql*: select LineItems.*, Quantity*CostPerItem as LineTotal from LineItems
- *active*: true

ADOQuery #2

- *name*: Inventory
- *sql*: select ItemNumber, ItemDescription from Inventory
- *active*: true

Here's the tricky part – the *lookupSQL* property we set on the form above actually may cause problems due to the way the Form Designer streams out the constructor code. So we must set this up in the *SetSequence* method of the form. Save and close the form, and then open it in the Source Code Editor. Find the *SetSequence* method, and add this code *(I suggest adding it after the other lookupRowset code)*:

```
// for the lookup for the ItemDescription in the Line Items table:
form.LineItems.rowset.fields["ItemNumber"].lookupRowset := ;
   form.Inventory.rowset
```

Save and close your work in the Source Code Editor *(we will have to come back and add some more in a bit)*.

Open the form in the Form Designer. We need to add a grid to the bottom of the form, so change the height of the form (make it taller), and add a grid. Then set the following properties:

- *name*: LineItemGrid
- *allowAddRows*: false
- *allowColumnMoving*: false
- *allowColumnSizing*: false
- *allowEditing*: false
- *allowRowSizing*: false
- *rowSelect*: true
- *bgColor*: White
- *colorRowSelect*: WindowText/0x80ffff
- *vScrollBar*: 1

Save the form, and close the form in the Form Designer. We need to add code to set up this grid, and then set up details to handle navigation.

In the *Local_Init* method add the following after the other code:

```
// Set up LineItem Grid Control:
class::SetUpLineItemGrid()
```

Add the *SetupLineItemGrid* method (before the *endclass* statement) – yours should look similar to this based on the test form you created:

```
function SetupLineItemGrid
   // Necessary to manually set up the grid here:
   with( form.LineItemGrid )
      width = 514
      left = 50
      dataLink = form.LineItems.rowset
      // first column
      columns["Column1"] = new GRIDCOLUMN(form.LineItemGrid)
      columns["Column1"].dataLink = ;
         form.LineItems.rowset.fields["itemnumber"]
      columns["Column1"].width    = 204
```

```
      columns["Column1"].headingControl.value = ;
         "Item Description"
      // next column
      columns["Column2"] = new GRIDCOLUMN(form.LineItemGrid)
      columns["Column2"].dataLink = ;
         form.LineItems.rowset.fields["quantity"]
      columns["Column2"].width     = 91
      columns["Column2"].headingControl.value = "Qty Ordered"
      // next column
      columns["Column3"] = new GRIDCOLUMN(form.LineItemGrid)
      columns["Column3"].dataLink = ;
         form.LineItems.rowset.fields["costperitem"]
      columns["Column3"].width     = 97
      columns["Column3"].headingControl.value = "Cost Per Item"
      // next column
      columns["Column4"] = new GRIDCOLUMN(form.LineItemGrid)
      columns["Column4"].dataLink = ;
         form.LineItems.rowset.fields["linetotal"]
      columns["Column4"].width     = 76
      columns["Column4"].headingControl.value = "Total"
   endwith
return
```

The tricky part is setting the Line Items display for *just* this invoice. You may recall from the LineItems form that we had to use a parameter to filter the data – we are going to do the same thing here. In the *SetSequence* method of the form, add the following (after the "form.rowset …" statement):

```
   // we need to limit the LineItems displayed in the LineItem
   // grid:
   form.LineItems.active := false
   form.LineItems.sql := ;
      "select LineItems.*, Quantity*CostPerItem as LineTotal "+;
         "from LineItems where InvoiceNumber = :InvNum"
   nInvoice = form.rowset.fields["InvoiceNumber"].value
   form.LineItems.params[ "InvNum" ] := nInvoice
   form.LineItems.active := true
   form.LineItems.requery()
```

This does the initial setup, but if you navigate in the Invoices table, the Line Items are not updated. So we need to add some code to the form's *onNavigate* event handler (before the *return* statement).

```
   // Update the LineItems to display just the ones
   // for the current invoice:
   local nInvoice
   nInvoice = form.rowset.fields["InvoiceNumber"].value
   form.LineItems.params[ "InvNum" ] := nInvoice
   form.LineItems.requery()
```

You may want to add a TextLabel control above the grid that notes this is the Line Items portion of the form.

If you run the form and navigate ("Next") a couple of times, you should see something like the following:

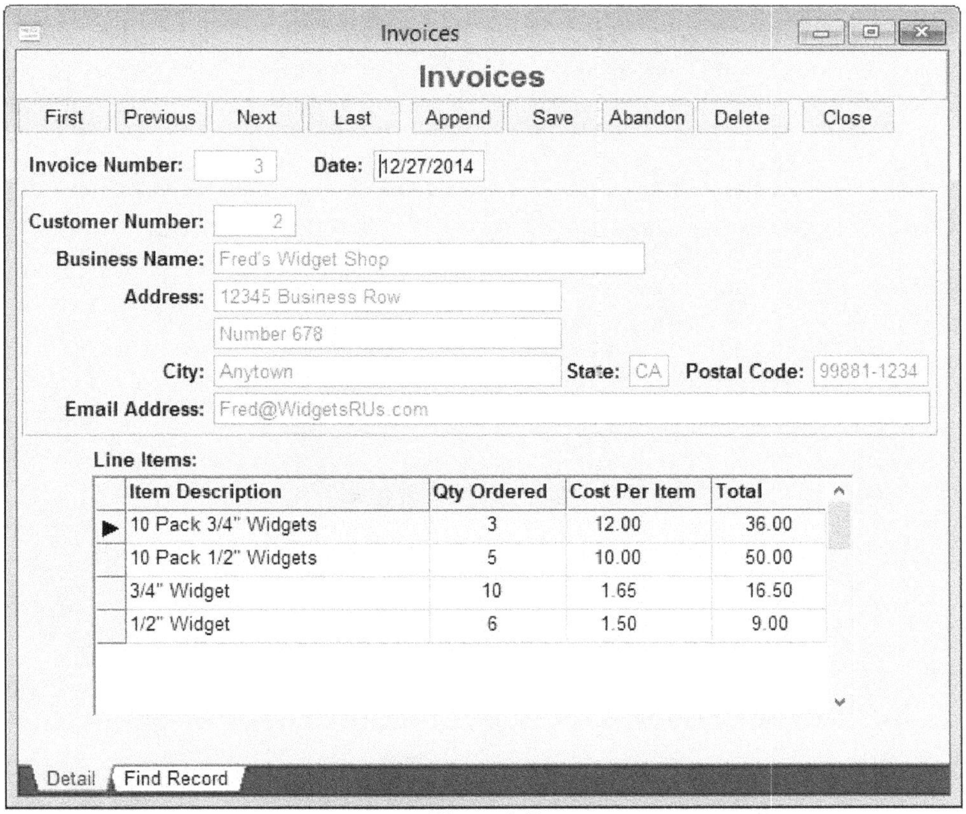

Figure 6-7

Most of the controls on this form are not editable! The only one the user should be able to directly edit is the date. This enforces data integrity, because (shortly) we will require the use of lookup forms to edit/change the customer, and add/edit/remove items from the Line Items.

Invoice Total

Before we get to all that, we're going to add one more item that is useful for any invoice – a grand total. We'll place this under the grid, and try to line it up at least *close* to the Total column for the line items.

Open the form in the Form Designer (which may mean closing it first). In the designer, drag a *SQLTextLabel* and a *SQLEntryfield* to the design surface. Make these changes:

- *name*: InvTotalLabel (textabel control)
- *text*: Invoice Total:
- *name*: InvTotalEF (entryfield control)
- *picture*: 9,999.99
- *when*: {; return false}
  (change the event handler in the Inspector)
- *colorNormal*: "Gray/Window"
  (change this property)

Line the controls up, put the entryfield to the bottom right of the grid, but not under the scrollbar. You can tinker with the appearance of this later to get it *just right* ...

Close the form designer, and open the form in the Source Code Editor. In the *form_onNavigate* event handler, add the following before the *return* statement:

```
class::UpdateLineItems()
```

And before the form's *endClass* statement add the following code:

```
function UpdateLineItems
   local nInvoice, nGrandTotal
   nInvoice = form.rowset.fields["InvoiceNumber"].value
   form.LineItems.params[ "InvNum" ] := nInvoice
   form.LineItems.requery()
   // we need to total the LineItems
   nGrandTotal = 0
   // loop through the items, get a total
   do while not form.LineItems.rowset.endOfSet
      nGrandTotal+=form.LineItems.rowset.fields["LineTotal"].value
      form.LineItems.rowset.next()
   enddo
   // go back to the top of the rowset
   form.LineItems.rowset.first()
   // change value in Entryfield:
   form.InvTotalEF.value := nGrandTotal
return
```

And one more modification, add the following in the *form_onOpen* event handler, again before the *return* statement:

```
// call navigate code to get grand total:
class::UpdateLineItems()
```

If you run the form, and navigate to the third invoice, you should see a form very similar to this:

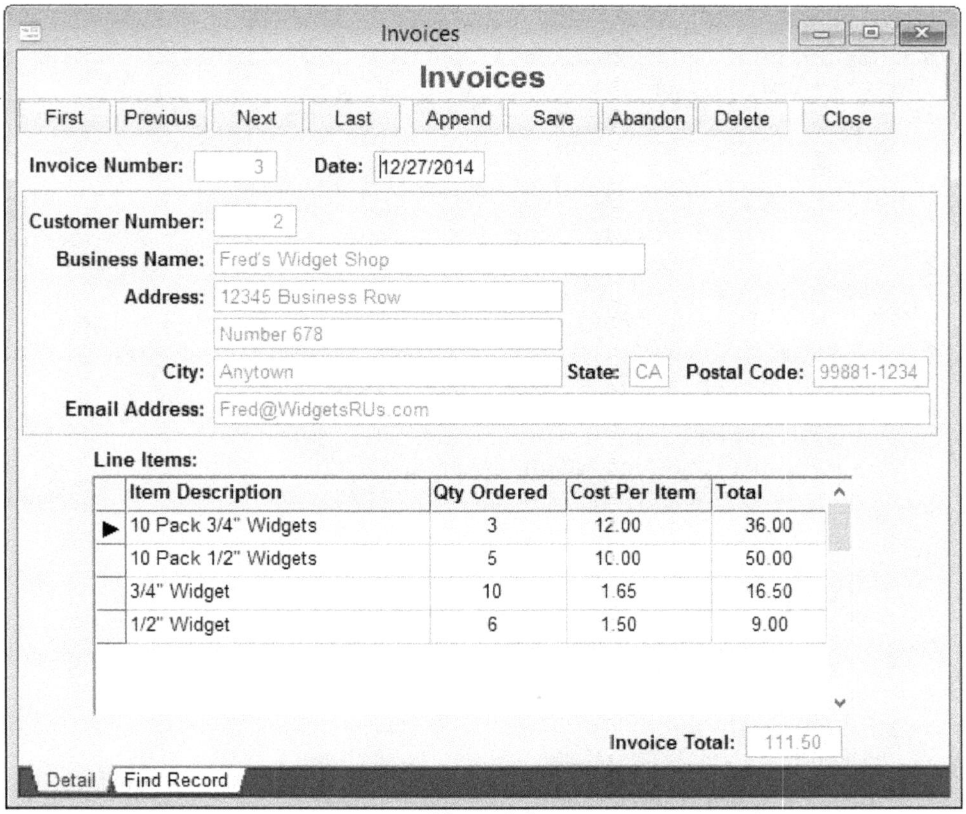

Figure 6-8

Now we have a pretty good layout, and a working form. Again, this does not take into account things like sales tax, and other issues that a real Invoice system would require, I will leave that to the developer.

Edit Customer

Up until now we've been getting everything else laid out for the form, but a form where all you can do is view the data, and not change anything *(except the Invoice Date)* is not the most useful …

What if the person who created the original invoice selected the wrong customer? The basics for this will be very similar to what we did with the Line Items form, where we called an existing form allowing the user to find the correct item, and when the form is closed, replace the item in the original form.

For this we obviously want to work with Customers. Following the same concept, with the form in the Form Designer, add a new Pushbutton control to the surface of the form, near the customer data. Change the following properties:

- *name*: EditCustBtn
- *text*: Edit Customer
- *speedBar*: true

Click the "Events" tab of the Inspector, click on the *onClick* event, and click the first button. Enter the following code for the event handler:

```
Function EDITCUSTBTN_onClick()
   local fCust, nCustNum, cBusName
   set procedure to Customers.wfm
   fCust = new CustomersForm()
   fCust.mdi        := false
   fCust.autoCenter := true
   // Open the form:
   fCust.readModal()
   // When the user closes the form, we
   // need to get the current Customer
   // Number:
   nCustNum = fCust.rowset.fields["CustomerNumber"].value
   cBusName=fCust.rowset.fields["BusinessName"].value.rightTrim()
   // check to see if it's the same:
   if form.CustNumEF.value # nCustNum // not the same
      // ask if they want to change:
      if msgbox( "Do you wish to change this Customer to "+;
               chr(13)+ cBusName+"?",;
               "Change Customer?", 32+4 ) == 6
         // user said "Yes", we will change it:
         form.CustNumEF.value    := nCustNum
         form.CustNumEF.newValue := nCustNum
         form.CustNumEF.modified := true
         form.modified           := true
      endif // msgbox
   endif // form.CustNumEF
   // cleanup:
   fCust.release()
   fCust := null
   close procedure Customers.wfm
   // redisplay customer data:
   class::FindCustomer()
return
```

Once you have this, save the form, run it, and try changing the customer for one of the invoices. This works rather well.

Edit Line Items

The interesting thing with this one, is that we have already got the Line Items form pretty much ready to go. When we designed and tested it, we planned for the form being called from the Invoice form, and so there isn't a lot we need to do. We do have to provide the Invoice Number before the form gets opened using a custom property. Otherwise the code here is, if anything, simpler than the code above.

Open the form in the Form Designer, add a pushbutton to the surface near (above) the grid for the LineItems. Change the following properties:

- *name*: EditLIBtn
- *text*: Edit Line Items
- *speedBar*: true

Click the "Events" tab of the Inspector, click on the *onClick* event, and click the first button. Enter the following code for the event handler:

```
function EDITLIBTN_onClick()
   local fLI
   set procedure to LineItems.wfm
   fLI = new LineItemsForm()
   fLI.mdi         := false
   fLI.autoCenter := true
   // VERY IMPORTANT -- set the InvoiceNum
   // custom property:
   fLI.InvoiceNum = form.InvNumEF.value
   // ALSO very important
   if form.Append // if we are adding a new invoice
      fLI.NewInvoice = true
   else
      fLI.NewInvoice = false
   endif
   // Open the form:
   fLI.readModal()
   // when we return, any changes to the Line Items
   // will have been made.
   // cleanup:
   fLI.release()
   fLI := null
   close procedure LineItems.wfm
   // but we DO need to redisplay them. This
   // will ensure not only the results of a
   // requery, but that the grand total is
   // udpated ...
   class::UpdateLineItems()
return
```

I have not added any sort of error trapping here to deal with removing *all* Line Items from an Invoice. This is obviously something that *could* happen, although it shouldn't. If a user wises to delete the Invoice itself they should do so from the Invoice.

We do have some code set to ensure that when the List Items form is called, it knows that we are adding a new invoice (the custom property *NewInvoice*).

Save and run the form, try using the new Edit Line Item button. Your form should look something like:

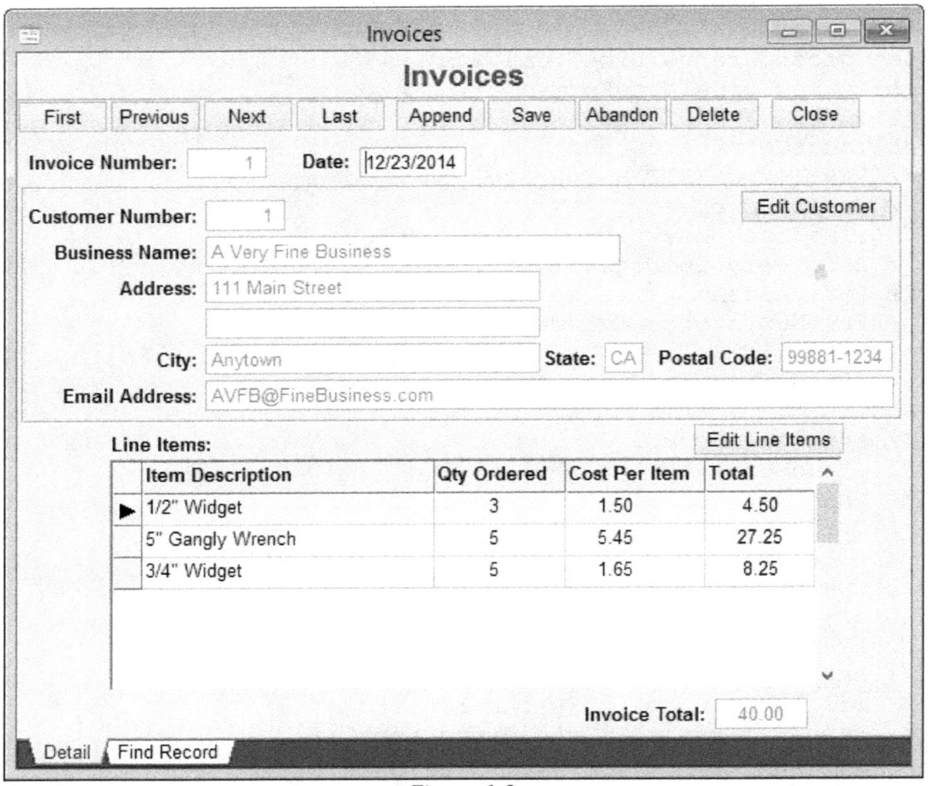

Figure 6-9

Add New Invoice

Creating a new invoice is a bit different from working with a single table form. The invoice consists of two primary parts: The Invoice data (Invoice Number, Invoice Date, and a link to the Customer data), and the Line Items.

The difficulty is that to work with the Line Items, you have to have the Invoice Number, as that is the field that links the data to the Invoice – and you cannot get the Invoice Number until you save the Invoice data.

On the flip side, what if, part way through creation of the Invoice, the customer backs out (cancels the order, whatever)? We will deal with that in the "Abandon" code later in the chapter.

So the way this is going to work is that when the user clicks the "Append" button:

- The form's custom property *append* is set
- A default value for date is set (using the *date* function)
- User is required to select a customer from the Customers form (or add a new customer)
- The **code** will issue a save on the current data – this is not a call to the standard Save button's *onClick* event handler, it allows us to retrieve the Invoice Number and use it for the Line Items form.
- Due to an oddity in the way the code in the LineItems form works, we have to add ONE Line Item as a "dummy" record, and set a custom property of the LineItems form …

- The Line Items form will be opened, and a call to the Inventory form will be made to force the user to select the first Line Item
- We leave the form's custom *append* property set, because the user (or customer) may decide to abandon ...

This last bullet item allows the customer to back out of the Invoice. If the user clicks the Abandon button, the Invoice itself is deleted (and if there were Line Items, they are deleted), *then* the form's *append* property is turned off.

With the form in the Form Designer, click the "Append" button, in the Inspector click the "Events" tab, click on *onClick*, click the button, and when asked about overwriting the code, click "Yes". Enter the following:

```
function APPENDBUTTON1_onClick()
    // Overwritten code for the Append Button:
    form.append = true // set the custom property
    // set values
    form.InvNumEF.value      := null
    form.InvDateEF.value     := form.InvDateEF.defaultValue
    form.CustNumEF.value     := null
    form.BusNameEF.value     := ""
    form.Address1EF.value    := ""
    form.Address2EF.value    := ""
    form.CityEF.value        := ""
    form.StateEF.value       := ""
    form.PostalCodeEF.value  := ""
    form.EmailEF.value       := ""
    // get the customer data:
    class::EditCustBtn_onClick()
    // save the changes:
    private aSave
    aSave = new array( 3, 2 ) // 3 rows, 2 columns
    aSave[ 1, 1 ] = "InvoiceNumber"
    aSave[ 1, 2 ] = GetNextKey( "InvNum_Seq" )
    aSave[ 2, 1 ] = "InvoiceDate"
    aSave[ 2, 2 ] = form.InvDateEF.value
    aSave[ 3, 1 ] = "CustomerNumber"
    aSave[ 3, 2 ] = form.CustNumEF.value
    form.DataLayerDataModule1.AddRow( "Invoices", aSave )
    form.rowset.parent.requery()
    form.rowset.applyLocate( "InvoiceNumber="+aSave[1,2] )
    UILayerCForm::LoadData()
    UILayerCForm::ResetControls()
    // reset the form's append property,
    // because in the custom form the methods
    // above set this property to false:
    form.append := true
    // Here's the tricky thing ... we need to have
    // a default Line Item, because the form for
    // Line Items gets weird without there being
    // at least one record:
    aSave = new array( 5, 2 ) // 5 rows, 2 columns
    aSave[ 1, 1 ] = "LineItemNumber"
    aSave[ 1, 2 ] = GetNextKey( "LINum_Seq" )
    aSave[ 2, 1 ] = "InvoiceNumber"
    aSave[ 2, 2 ] = form.InvNumEF.value
    aSave[ 3, 1 ] = "ItemNumber"
```

```
        aSave[ 3, 2 ] = 1
        aSave[ 4, 1 ] = "Quantity"
        aSave[ 4, 2 ] = 1
        aSave[ 5, 1 ] = "CostPerItem"
        aSave[ 5, 2 ] = 0.00
        form.DataLayerDataModule1.AddRow( "LineItems", aSave )
        // deal with LineItems:
        class::EditLIBtn_onClick()
    return
```

It is also necessary to ensure that the form's *append* property is preserved throughout all the processing that occurs, so note that we have add a small amount of code in the EditLIButton's *onClick* event handler, before the release of the *fLI* form *(the comment references "cleanup")*:

```
    if fLI.NewInvoice
        // ensure that the form.append
        // property is still set:
        form.append := true
    endif
```

Save Changes to Invoice

Oddly enough, no changes need to be made for the Save button to fire exactly as required. The Invoice itself only has three fields, the user can only edit one of them directly, but if they change the Customer, that value is handled properly as well.

Abandon Changes to Invoice

Abandoning changes to an invoice, the way we have this working, is a difficult proposition. If the user has added a new Invoice they *may* still wish to abandon it. At that point, we really need to delete the current invoice. If they wish to abandon other changes, what other changes are there? The Invoice Date, and the Customer are the only parts of this form that allow modification. The Line Items are automatically saved. There's no simple way to abandon those once the user has closed the Line Items form.

With the form in the Form Designer, click the "Abandon" button, in the Inspector click the "Events" tab, click on *onClick*, click the button, and when asked about overwriting the code, click "Yes". Enter the following:

```
    function ABANDONBUTTON1_onClick()
        // Overwritten Abandon button code
        if form.append
            // Ask the user if they really want to delete the
            // new Invoice:
            if msgbox( "Do you wish to delete the new "+chr(13)+;
                        "invoice you are working on?",;
                        "Abandon Changes", 32+4 ) == 6 // Yes
                // we need to deal with a cascade delete,
                // but only if there are LineItems ...
                // we need THIS row first ... so we can
                // navigate to it after the following:
                nCurrent = form.rowset.fields["InvoiceNumber"].value
                // before we delete, we need to figure out where
                // we will navigate to after deleting and requerying
                // the data:
```

```
      if form.rowset.atFirst() // first row
         form.rowset.next() // navigate to next row
      else
         form.rowset.next(-1) // otherwise navigate back one
      endif
      nFind = form.rowset.fields[ "InvoiceNumber" ].value
      // back to row we need to delete:
      form.rowset.applyLocate( [InvoiceNumber=]+nCurrent )
      if form.LineItems.rowset.count() == 0 // no Line Items
         // delete the invoice:
         UILayerCForm::DeleteRecord( false )
      else // we have line items, we need to cascade delete them:
         UILayerCForm::DeleteRecord(true,"LineItems","InvoiceNumber")
      endif
      // reset this custom property
      form.append := false
      // redisplay ...
      form.rowset.parent.requery()
      form.rowset.applyLocate( [InvoiceNumber=]+nFind )
      // form's onNavigate should do the rest
   endif // msgbox()
else // not appending:
   // try just calling the standard Abandon button:
   AbandonButton::onClick()
   // update customer if necessary
   class::FindCustomer()
endif // form.append
return
```

The tricky part as always is to leave the form displaying valid data, which is why the issue with finding a primary key value to navigate to in the code shown above.

Delete Invoice

The tricky part of deleting an invoice is the cascade delete – do you want to leave the Line Items left as orphaned records? On the flip side, while we have a relationship with the Customers table, we don't want to delete any customers when we delete an Invoice.

The way the code for deleting records is set up in the UILayer *(custom form)*, this is actually relatively easy. As a matter of fact, everything that is needed is set up – we just need to add a (or modify) some custom properties of the Delete button itself. This can be done in the form's setup code.

Open the Invoice Form in the Source Code Editor, go to the *SetupControls* method, and add the following before the *return* statement:

```
   // Set custom properties for the Delete button:
   form.DeleteButton1.cascade         := true
   form.DeleteButton1.childTable      := "LineItems"
   form.DeleteButton1.foreignKeyField := "InvoiceNumber"
```

When the user clicks the Delete button, they will be asked about deleting like normal, and because of these custom properties, the code we set up in the definition of this custom button class and in the UILayer custom form will ensure that a proper cascade occurs.

Print Invoice

The last thing that any Invoicing app *must* have is the ability to print an invoice.

For the purpose of the book I am not going to walk the reader through the process of building an Invoice report *(shameless plug: see The dBASE Reports Book)*, but the sample application does have one, you can review the source code to see how I put it together, etc. To use it, the best place to call the report is from the Invoice form, as you are viewing it at this time.

To do this, I am going to add a Print button to the form, and attach some code that will (assuming you have an invoice report) render the report to the screen in a default reportViewer object.

For this, add a Pushbutton and set properties as with the other buttons (*name*, *text*, *speedbar*), and for the *onClick* event handler:

```
function PRINTBTN_onClick()
   /*
      Code to print an invoice:
   */
   local rInv, nInvNum
   nInvNum = form.InvNumEF.value
   // set up report
   set procedure to Invoice.rep
   rInv = new InvoiceReport()
   rInv.InvoiceNum = nInvNum
   rInv.render()
return
```

If you wanted to get fancy and set this up to work with the dUFLP's Preview form you would need to modify the code a bit, and modify the overwritten *render* method of the report.

Duplicate Records?

I am afraid I am going to cop out here. Duplicate records are a database administrator's nightmare, and most of the time they are generated completely by accident. However, testing for duplicates can be tricky.

I do want to point out a suggestion made by Jan Hoelterling in the newsgroups, however, if you are concerned with duplicate records in a database (which can happen obviously):

> "Why not compare the content of the record buffer to the content of the controls before determining what to save? That would be the safest, as it would also help you handle instances correctly where the user changed something, but changed it back. No need to save in that case ..."

I will leave the coding of this to the reader, if you need to do it. Honestly it wouldn't be that hard, and would really only need changing the Custom Form class, the *SaveRecord* method. BUT, I need to move on.

Back to the Business Layer

There are many ways one could implement validation, which is at least a part of the Business Layer for your application. I have put a lot of thought into this, and consulted with folk in the newsgroups for dBASE, trying to come up with "the best" idea, and am not sure I have a single "best" that I can present. The code I am presenting here will do for now, but I leave anything beyond this to you, the reader.

What I have done is to create a custom class for the Customers table contained in the file BusinessLayer.cc. I have set the code to work with form-level validation, meaning that when the user attempts to save the record the validation will be performed. The example below is for the Customers form. You can add the rest as needed.

To use this, we will need to modify the Customers form by overwriting the code for the Save button.

> **NOTE**
> While working on this part of the application, I found a bug in dBASE that wiped out *all* the controls on my form in the Form Designer. This was disconcerting, to say the least. Luckily I had a backup copy of the form. **Here's the point:** It is a good idea to back up your work before you start doing some things. I suggest doing so right now ... create a folder and copy all the forms (at the least) into that folder. That way, if something happens, you can recover with minimal hair-pulling.

Open the Customers form in the Form Designer. Click the "Save" button, in the Inspector, click the "Events" tab, find *onClick* and click it, then click the button to the right. In the Source Code Editor, add:

```
function SAVEBUTTON1_onClick()
   // form level validation:
   set procedure to BusinessLayer.cc
   oValid = new CustValidate( form.aSQLControls )
   bOK = oValid.FormLevel()
   release object oValid
   oValid = null
   close procedure BusinessLayer.cc
   if not bOK
      return
   endif
   // call overwritten code:
   SaveButton::onClick()
return
```

There is an issue here – if you use the navigation buttons, this code will not be called. You could overwrite that code as well, and add something similar, it would take a bit more work (ask if the user wants to save, etc.). I will leave this to the reader to work out.

Open or create a file: BusinessLayer.cc. In that file, add the following:

```
#DEFINE HIGHLIGHT       "WindowText/0x80ffff" // yellow background
#DEFINE NORMAL          "WindowText/Window"
#DEFINE ERRORCOLOR      "WHITE/RED"
class CustValidate // Customer Validation
   function FormLevel
      parameters aControls
```

```
// These errors should only ever be seen by the developer
// while testing ...:
if pCount() < 1
   msgbox( "Validation requires a reference to "+chr(13)+;
           "the form's aSQLControls array.",;
           "CustValidate Error", 16 )
   return
endif
if type( "aControls" ) # "A"
   msgbox( "Parameter for validation requires a "+chr(13)+;
      "reference to the form's aSQLControls array.",;
      "CustValidate Error", 16 )
   return
endif
// make reference a custom property of the class:
this.Controls = aControls
// return value, set to assume all is okay:
local bCtrlValid, bFormValid
bFormValid = true
// call individual methods as needed:
// 1: Customer Number -- no validation required
// 2: Business Name:
bCtrlValid = class::BusNameValid( this.Controls[ 2 ].value)
class::SetErrorColors( this.Controls[ 2 ], bCtrlValid )
if not bCtrlValid
   this.Controls[ 2 ].error := true
   bFormValid := false
else
   this.Controls[ 2 ].error := false
endif
// 3: Address 1
bCtrlValid = class::Address1Valid( this.Controls[3].value)
class::SetErrorColors( this.Controls[ 3 ], bCtrlValid )
if not bCtrlValid
   this.Controls[ 3 ].error := true
   bFormValid := false
else
   this.Controls[ 3 ].error := false
endif
```

** CODE SNIPPED HERE ** See source code for full version

```
return bFormValid
// End of method: FormLevel

function BusNameValid
   // validate the Business Name field
   // Only requirement is that it not be empty
   parameters cBusName
   local bOK
   bOK = true
   if empty( cBusName )
      bOK = false
   endif
return bOK
```

** CODE SNIPPED HERE ** See source code for full version

```
   function SetErrorColors
      // Set control colors
      parameter oControl, bOK
      if bOK
         // reset colors:
         oControl.colorNormal    := NORMAL
         oControl.colorHighlight := HIGHLIGHT
      else
         // set error color:
         oControl.colorNormal    := ERRORCOLOR
         oControl.colorHighlight := ERRORCOLOR
      endif
   return
endclass
```

The code above has a couple of statements that state "** CODE SNIPPED HERE" in there – this is because this is fairly lengthy, and the goal is to give you an idea. You can read all the code in the source for this chapter. Note that the email address validation uses code from the dUFLP, it has been inserted into the BusinessLayer.cc file, to simplify things for readers not using the dUFLP for their code development.

On advantage to this code over my initial goal (quickly looping through the controls) is that each validation method can be called separately for specific purposes (for example, you might want to check the validation of the email address while working on some other part of the application).

I have given a framework to try to build your application with. For a more robust application you will need to add your own touches, functionality, features, etc.

Adding to this, the file *SQLFormControls.cc* has more than just the *SQLTextLabel* and *SQLEntryfield* controls in it. A developer might need or want to use a *spinbox* control for a numeric or date field, or a *combobox* for another field. I have added similar code as with the *SQLEntryfield* control (using the same custom properties, and methods where appropriate) to a set of controls that might be useful, and done some minimal testing to make sure they *can* work, but not the full testing that has been done with this application and the *SQLEntryfield*. I have hopes that at some point someone will have the time to expand these out and make them more useful.

Making a Full Application

In the Source Code for this chapter you will see several items that have not been discussed in these pages – this is part of my "standard" framework for setting up an application for use in dBASE. To run this application as a full dBASE application (inside dBASE), in the Command Window, with the source code laid out properly:

```
   do start
```

The application will run with a menu, and so on … All of this code is discussed more fully in <u>The dBASE Book</u>, and will not be discussed here.

Again, this is not a fully functional application, but it has enough to actually run, and when we get to the deployment parts of this book, it should be enough to build a functioning executable that we can set up as an example for deployment.

163

Sample Code for This Chapter

The following is a listing of the sample code in the "Chapter 06" folder, if you downloaded it from my website. You may use the code contained in these forms for your own applications if you desire, with the caveat that credit be given appropriately.

- **About.ico** – an icon file (from IconExperience) used on the About form.
- **About.wfm** – "About this application" form, called from the menu.
- **BusinessLayer.cc** – The BusinessLayer class for the sample application.
- **Cleanup.bat** – Simple DOS batch file I use to erase backup files, compiled files, etc.
- **CreateDatabase.prg** – Program to create the tables and set up the sequences, add some data, and more. This is the table design for the sample application.
- **Customers.wfm** – The User-Interface form for the Customers table.
- **DataLayer.dmd** – The DataLayer for the sample application.
- **Gear.png** – Image (from IconExperience) used on at least one form …
- **Inventory.wfm** – The User-Interface form for the Inventory table.
- **Invoice.ini** – INI file used with a compiled version of the sample application.
- **InvoiceGridDetails** – Form used to lay out the grid on the Invoice form.
- **Invoices.wfm** – The Invoice form.
- **LineItems.wfm** – The Line Items form.
- **LinteItemsForInvoice.wfm** – Form used to get relationships and sample grid working for the Invoice form.
- **LineItemsGridDetail.wfm** – Form used to lay out the grid on the LineItems form.
- **MSeekerADO.cc** – Seeker class designed to work with ADO tables.
- **Node.png** – Image (from IconExperience) used on at least one form.
- **SaveEnv.cc** – Save the basic dBASE environment when starting an application, it saves details to the .INI file, so they can be restored when the application closes.
- **Setup.prg** – Setup program for the application.
- **SQLCustomFormButtons.cc** – Custom class file containing buttons to be used with the sample application.
- **SQLFormControls.cc** – Custom class file containing the form controls used in the sample application.
- **Start.prg** – Program to actually start the application.
- **UILayer.cfm** – Custom form for the application.

Summary

Whew! There are of course other parts to a full application, these three chapters have focused mostly on the User Interface, because in order to get everything to work there was a LOT to do. All that code that was created was meant to make it easier to build future applications without as much effort. And most applications will be more involved. You might need, for example, to see all Invoices for a specific Customer, and of course there is a lot of other functionality not set up here. Some of these wouldn't be too difficult to put together, but for now, I need to move on to other parts of this tome.

In order to build this application for your edification, I went through a huge learning curve myself. Several concepts were very difficult for me to grasp, mostly because of my own stubbornness, I fear.

In the process, I also discovered several bugs which have been reported to the R&D team through the dBASE newsgroups. By the time this book is published it is possible some of them will have been fixed.

I have to thank various people from the dBASE newsgroups, all of these folk pointed out errors in my own logic, ways to work through issues, had a huge amount of patience with me, and were just generally good sounding boards for getting me through all of this:

- Mervyn Bick
- Andre Knappstein
- Ronnie MacGregor
- Bruce Beacham
- Heinz Kesting
- John Noble

If I forgot anyone here, it is not intentional …

NOTES:

Part III: New Features and Functionality

When dBASE 8 was released by the developers at dBASE, LLC, they gave us quite a bit of new functionality, and have been expanding on it since. In the last few chapters we looked at the ADO classes in dBASE, and using them to build an application that does not use the Borland Database Engine.

In the next few chapters we will take a look at some of the other new features that have been added since dBASE Plus 2.8 was released.

Chapter 7: New Graphics Engine and New Images

When dBASE Plus 8 was released, we (the developers) found a new User Interface (see Chapter 1), and a new graphics engine. Along with the graphics engine, the good people at dBASE, LLC forged an alliance with a graphics company called **glyFX** (you can visit their website at: http://www.glyfx.com/). In addition, in the same folders as the glyFX images, there are some texture images that can be used either with Web applications, or for the backgrounds of your forms.

The Graphics Engine

The new Graphics libraries now built-in to dBASE *(FreeImage libraries, details can be found at: http://freeimage.sourceforge.net/features.html, Marty Kay at dBASE notes you can find out "more than you want to know" from this website ...)* allow for better handling of .JPG and .PNG images.

File Formats
dBASE applications, pushbuttons, toolbars, etc., can now work with .JPG, .PNG and other image formats that used to be a bit problematic. There was some specific effort to work with the .PNG alpha channel.

Large Icon Format
One relief is that when you build an application with a .ICO file that was designed for Windows 7 *(and later)* your application will not crash. This occurred in earlier versions of dBASE because the newer .ICO files have more images contained in them (different sizes), and dBASE did not know what to do when you tried to use them, causing a crash.

Editing Images
In dBASE Plus 8 *(and later versions)* right-clicking an image gives you the option "Design Image". This opens whatever editing software is hooked up on your computer through Windows' file associations to edit images (for example, when I installed Corel's PaintShop Pro™ it became the default image editor on my computer).

dBASE Plus 10 adds a tie-in to the software FotoGrafix© *(installed WITH dBASE)*, which can be used to edit images. FotoGrafix is freeware (free software) that can be downloaded and installed with your own applications:

```
http://lmadhavan.com/fotografix/
```

To use this in dBASE's IDE, select an image in the Navigator, right-click it, and select "Edit in FotoGrafix". When you do this, your image will come up in FotoGrafix. This software has a lot of standard image editing abilities of more complex *(and expensive)* software, including changing colors, transformation options, rotating an image, and a lot more.

New Images by glyFX

When dBASE Plus is installed you will see (if you watch the screen during the process) that it takes some time to install the images. This is because they are being installed with several file formats (.bmp, .gif, .png and .ico (Icons)) at several different sizes for all (but the .ico files) – 16x16, 24x24, 32x32, 48x48, 64x64, and 256x256 (for the "Aero" version – Windows 7 and later) – all measured in pixels. The .bmp files all have the standard dBASE transparent color for the background, but if you look at the .gif and .png files, the transparency is built-in.

So where are all these files stored?

When dBASE installs the files, for dBASE Plus release 8 or 9 (change the folder path appropriately) it puts them in the standard folder structure:

    C:\Program Data\dBASE\Plus8\Media\Images\glyfx\

For dBASE Plus 10 (or later) the images are stored here:

    C:\Users\Public\Documents\dBASE\Plus10\Media\Images\glyfx

And from there you can view images designed either for Windows XP or for "Aero" – which is Windows 7 and later versions of Windows. I am not sure if there will be updates for Windows 8 or Windows 10 …

According to the glyFX website, the folder structure under "AERO" (which is Windows 7 or later) is:

CE: Complete Edition
LE: Large Edition
SE: Small Edition

I recommend using the images from the CE folders, because this is the most complete set of images provided. There three different variations of an image. If you just look at the first image in the folder *(I am showing the 256x256 size version)* you will see:

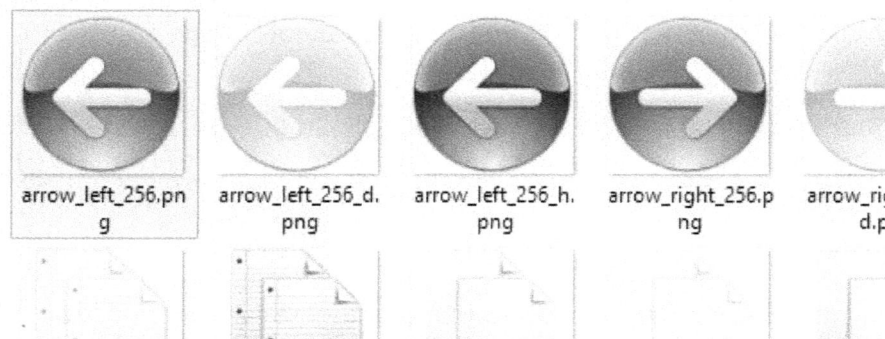

Figure 7-1

Note that the first is the "standard" button, the second is the "down" or "disabled" button, and the third is the "hot" button – meaning if on a toolbar *(or a pushbutton if you use certain abilities)* the mouse is over the button.

The images can be accessed using the Source Code Alias:

```
:Glyfx:
```

but you would need to add a folder path after that. For example:

```
:Glyfx:\Aero\CE\dBASE Aero\PNG\256x256\arrow_left_256.png
```

This is a bit unwieldy. I recommend instead that you find the images you wish to use, copy them to a folder of their own, and create your own Source Code Alias.

For the purpose of this example, I copied the 24x24 bit images to a folder called "24", and set a Source Code Alias to point to them named *MyGlyfx24*. A simple example form is shown below using this. It uses all three states for the pushbutton image. There are actually four buttons, the first three just use the three different images for the buttons to show them, the fourth one is designed to be interactive – if you run the sample form from the Source Code Folder for this chapter, move the mouse over the fourth button and see the change of the image …:

Figure 7-2

For these buttons to use a 24x24 bit image, the *height* of the button is actually set to 32 pixels. The fourth button "Try Me", is set with code for the *onMouseOver* and *onMouseOut* event handlers to change the *upBitmap* property to point to the "hot" image when the mouse is over the button, and when the mouse exits the button to change it back.

For a full application you could set images on pushbuttons instead of text *(effectively creating your own toolbar)*, you can use these images on toolbars, etc. If you have The dBASE Book, you have examples of these *(using different images)*.

Other Images

In addition, start with dBASE Plus 10, Michael Rozlig (CEO of dBASE) has followed through with a promise to provide more images that can be easily deployed with an application, using DLL files. These include images from the Google Material Interface collection, and images from the Geotag Icon Project by Yusuke Kamiyamane, all of which are open source. Michael has noted that it is quite possible in future builds that we will see more DLL files with more image options.

The resource DLL files that have been provided, including the one that has been shipping with dBASE for years called "resource.dll" are in the folder:

```
C:\Users\Public\Documents\dBASE\Plus10\Media\Resources
```

These are referenced by the Source Code Alias:

```
:resources:
```

So to use the standard "resource.dll" file:

```
:resources:Resource.dll
```

The constructor code for a pushbutton might look like:

```
Upbitmap = "resource #20 :resources:resource.dll"
```

When deploying applications that use the resource files, you need to be sure to include the DLL files that you are actually using in your deployment. This will be discussed again in a later chapter of this book.

Resource Files

The list of new Resource Files is quite large. As noted above, there is a specific folder containing them all. The following is a list of the individual .DLLs containing images that you can use. When you build and deploy your application(s), if you choose to use these, you need to be sure to deploy the appropriate .DLLs.

The.DLLs have a matching .PDF file that lists all the images.

The difficulty with the .PDF files is that the image display for small images are pixelated – they are displayed as an image object but not at their original size, so they are stretched to fit, causing pixilation. The Fugue images are very difficult to see because of this. In addition, the transparent background is often displayed in the PDF files as black, so black on black is hard to see *(as you might imagine)*. I have provided tools for you to use (see later in this chapter), so you can see the images and determine which ones you might want to use in your applications.

It should be noted that in dBASE Plus 10.0 (the first releases), the Resource Chooser dialog cannot handle .PNG files stored in a .DLL. Selecting one of the files above will take you back to the Resource.dll file, because of it. However, I have been promised that this is a high priority item to be fixed in a point release, probably by the time this is published.

Google Material Interface Images

The Google Material Interface images:

```
https://www.google.com/design/icons/
```

come in a range of image sizes:

- 18x18 pixels
- 24x24 pixels
- 36x36 pixels
- 54x54 pixels
- 72x72 pixels
- 96x96 pixels
- 108x108 pixels
- 144x144 pixels
- 192x192 pixels

In addition, most of these images come in standard colors of:

- Black
- Grey600
- White

Some of them come with other colors as well. The PDF files that are in the same folder as the DLL files give you a good idea what is available. These images use a standard naming practice:

```
ic_imagename_color_size
```

(**color** and **size** are from the lists given above). The image name is sometimes more than one word, if so, an underscore is used. To use an image on a pushbutton from one of the DLL files in the resources folder, the syntax is a little different:

```
upBitmap = "RESOURCE png/ic_add_black_24x24 :resources:dContent.dll"
```

Note that you must start (after "RESOURCE") with "png/" – this tells dBASE the file is a png image. You could put the full path to the resource file, but that would get unwieldy quickly. It is easier to use the source code alias.

All of these images have a transparent background, which means that if you use either a pushbutton with the *systemTheme* property set to *false* and a *colorNormal* property set, or an image object, the color of the pushbutton's background is what will come through.

Fugue

These images are by Yusuke Kamiyamane, provided under the Creative Commons Attribution 3.0 License, and are part of a Geotag Icon Project. These came from this website:

```
http://p.yusukekamiyamane.com/
```

They are free to use, as long as they are properly attributed *(if you have a resource editor you can see that these have the appropriate attributions in each file)*. These work similar to the images from the Google Material Interface, except that the .DLL files are split into specific sizes.

These are full color, but come in limited sizes – 16x16, 24x24 and 32x32. The 16x16 pixel images are the most complete set, requiring four .DLL files to contain them all, the other two DLL files contain a subset of the 16x16 images in the larger sizes.

Tools

I created a couple of forms that may be useful to you as a developer. The first is a simple form using the GMI images to show some of the more "standard" pushbuttons my forms tend to have on them. It was an interesting exercise trying to find appropriate images to do what I needed.

To assist, there is a second form that allows you to search through the various .DLL files to find what you need. It uses a table ("ResourceImages.dbf") in the same folder as the forms.

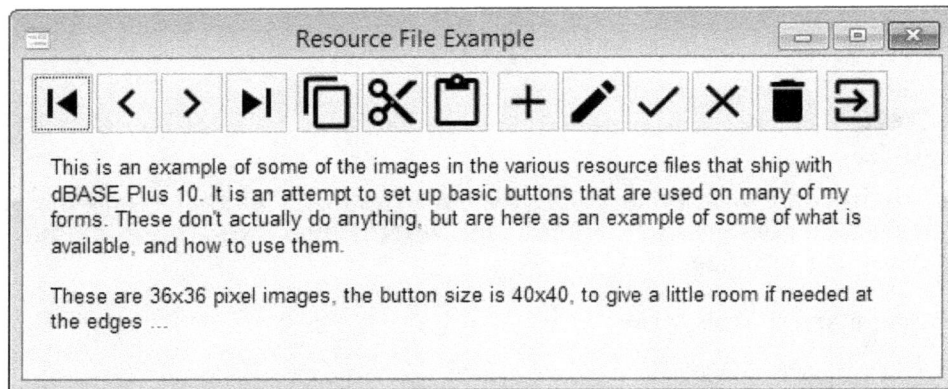

Figure 7-3

In addition, I threw together another form (see Figure 7-3) that might be useful for a developer – it lists all the new Resource .dll files in the :resources: source code alias, and all the images, and shows them on pushbuttons. If you click the buttons, the *upBitmap* property's text is copied to the clipboard, so you can paste it into your own form.

There may be a version of this in the dBASE Samples *(possibly modified by the support staff)*, this is my original version. I will be placing this in the dBASE Users' Function Library Project (dUFLP) as well.

Figure 7-4

Textures

Installed with dBASE, starting in dBASE Plus 8, are a set of texture images that can be used in the background of a form, or for a web application. These images are set for a variety of screen resolutions, and are designed to be tiled *(for a web page that means it is repeated as necessary)*.

These can be found in this folder:

```
C:\ProgramData\dBASE\Plus9\Media\Images\Texture
```

(If you are using dBASE Plus 8, change the "9" to "8" in the path above, if using dBASE Plus 10, see note below ...)

There is a source code alias for the textures folder, however in dBASE Plus 9 *(which I am using for a good portion of this book, except where features are specific to dBASE Plus 10)*, the alias has an incorrect path in it. You can easily fix it by going to the Desktop Properties of dBASE (Properties menu, "Desktop Properties"), clicking on "Source Aliases", select "Textures", and change the path from:

```
C:\ProgramData\dBASE\Plus9\Media\Images\Textures
```

to *(remove the trailing "s")*:

```
C:\ProgramData\dBASE\Plus9\Media\Images\Texture
```

It should also be noted that the path will be *very* different in dBASE Plus 10:

```
C:\Users\Public\Documents\dBASE\Plus10\Media\Images\Textures
```

When you select a texture for a form (set the *background*) property, dBASE should automatically insert the Source Code Alias "Textures" into the path. For example:

```
background = ;
    "filename :Textures:lt_blue_brushed_Metal_1-33_1600x1200.jpg"
```

This would allow you to create a form that looked like:

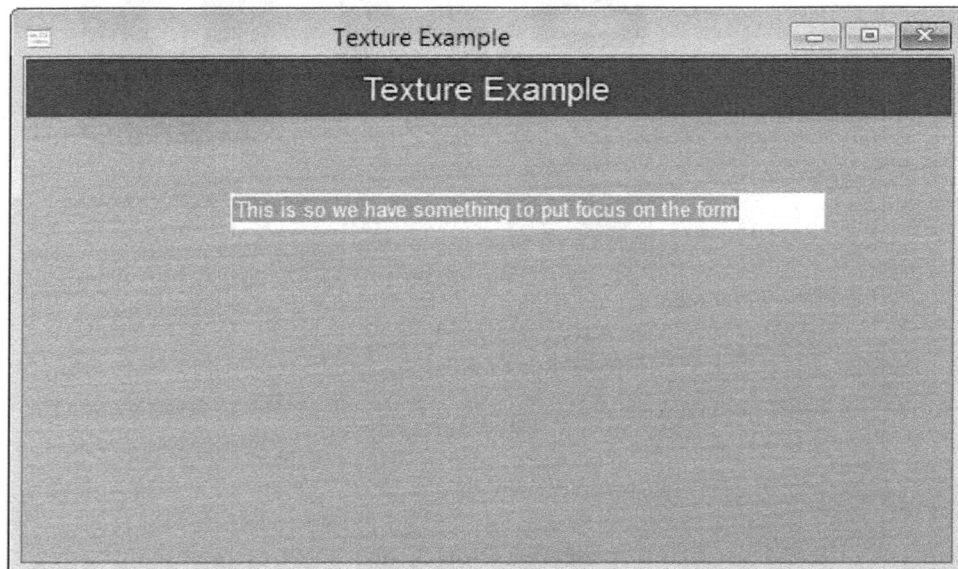

Figure 7-5

DoubleBufferred

The form object in dBASE has a new property: *doubleBufferred* – the purpose of which is to work with transparent containers (a container object with the *transparent* property set to *true*) and objects better. There is a warning in the help that using this property can slow down the loading of a form.

In older versions of dBASE, if a container's *transparent* property was set to *true* and it was on a form with anything under the container (an image, for example), the container would not show the item under the container. However, it will show the background *color* of the form. If the form's *doubleBuffered* property is set to *true*, you can see the image under the container properly.

In theory, this should work for a Notebook control as well, but the Notebook does not currently have a *transparent* property.

176

This property was designed to work with all controls on a form. A simple example is shown below using a couple of images, a container, and so on.

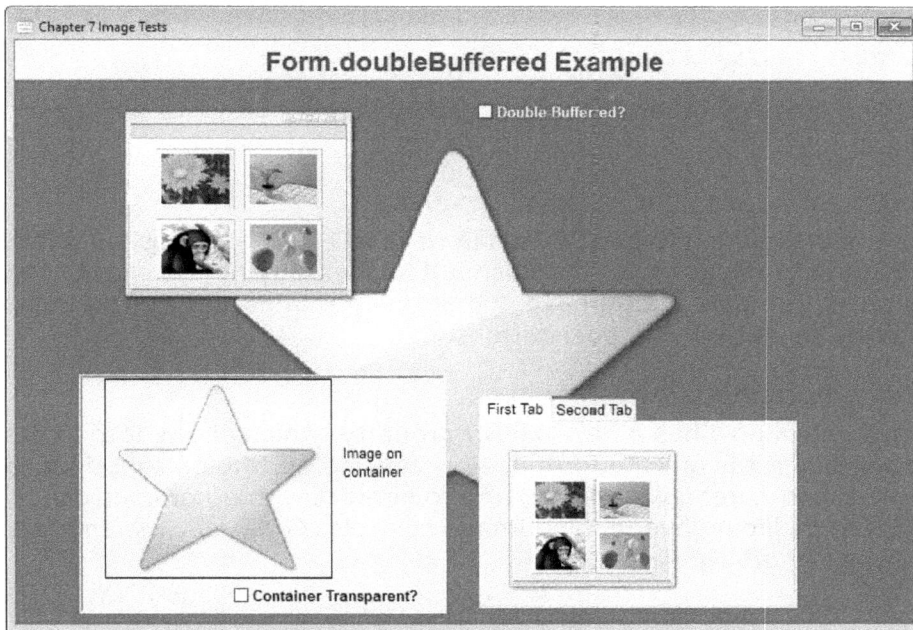

Figure 7-6

If you check the "Container Transparent?" checkbox, you will see that you get the background color of the form, and you can see the images below it. Clicking "Double Buffered?" doesn't seem to make much difference for this form:

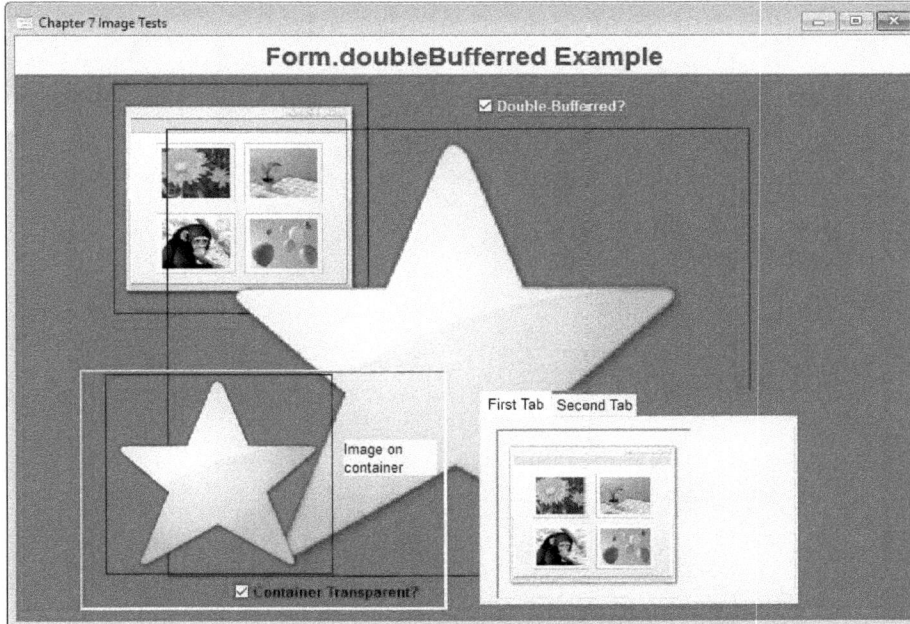

Figure 7-7

There are some developers who have forms with hundreds of objects, images, and more, and they state that the *doubleBufferred* property does make a difference for how the controls are displayed.

It has been pointed out that this property can slow down a large application – so should only be used if needed, perhaps on a form-by-form basis.

Miscellaneous

The following lists any other changes in dBASE Plus for graphics not mentioned above.

Pushbutton – *scaleBitmaps* Property

This property was added to dBASE Plus in release 10. The purpose is to allow dBASE to "force" images to fit on a Pushbutton that may not be exactly the size that you need. The only issue I have is that this pixelates some of the images when resizing them to fit the pushbuttons.

Image – *transparent* Property

The image control now has a *transparent* property, which allows it to interact with the container it is on (the form itself is considered to be a container, but also the container and notebook objects), and to interact with other controls appropriately, including overlapping image controls. *(This was implemented in a hot-fix release of dBASE Plus 10.)*

Sample Code for This Chapter

The following is a listing of the sample code in the "Chapter 07" folder, if you downloaded it from my website. You may use the code contained in these forms for your own applications if you desire, with the caveat that credit be given appropriately.

- **Arrow_left_24.png** – Image (from Icon Experience) used as part of the doubleBufferred example form.
- **doubleBufferredExample.wfm** – Form used to show some of what the form's new doubleBuffered property can do for you.
- **Favourites_256.png** – Image (from Icon Experience) used as part of the doubleBufferred example form.
- **GlyFXImageExample.wfm** – Example form showing some basics of the use of the GlyFX button images.
- **Resource File Example.wfm** – Example of using the Resource Files that ship with dBASE Plus 10 on pushbuttons.
- **ResourceImages.dbf** – Table containing data used in the ShowResources form.
- **ShowResources.wfm** – Form designed to show the contents of the resource files that ship with dBASE Plus 10 (and later). It uses the table "ResourceImages.dbf", and if the developers at dBASE update the resources, the table needs to be modified to reflect those changes.
- **TextureExample.wfm** – Example of the use of one of the texture files that ships with dBASE.
- **View_256.png** – Image (from Icon Experience) used as part of the doubleBufferred example form.

Summary

As you can see, there has been a lot of work done with dBASE to enhance the graphics abilities, including quite a few new options of more modern graphics *(something dBASE has been sorely lacking for a long time)*. Hopefully more work will be done to provide even more graphics for users.

Of course, if you have read or used <u>The dBASE Book</u> *(3rd Edition)*, you know that I use images from Icon Experience (http://www.iconexperience.com/) for many of my own applications. The toolbars in dBASE Plus (starting with 8 and moving forward) are using images from Axialis Software™ (some of which are free -- http://www.axialis.com/). Axialis has a software package for editing icons and images called Axialis IconWorkshop, as well.

Each of us will tend to migrate to what works for us. I am not endorsing any particular company, just pointing out that there are a lot of options out there.

Chapter 8: The Grid Controls

This chapter started out just being about the new GridEx control (see below), but as I was digging into the documentation on dBASE Plus release 10, I found mention of some enhancements to the *existing* grid, so I will be discussing those as well.

Grid Enhancements

The original grid in dBASE is an excellent control, but like most controls, people are always asking for more. The folk at dBASE, LLC have been listening, and have enhanced the existing grid, while working on implementing the new one (see the rest of this chapter).

For the existing grid, a new property has been added:

cellFocusBorderStyle

The purpose of this property is to allow the user to have a visual confirmation which cell has focus by changing the borderStyle of the individual cell.

The default setting for this is 4 (Single) – a complete listing of styles is in the table below:

Border Style	Description
0	Default
1	Raised
2	Lowered
3	None
4	Single *(default)*
5	Double
6	Drop shadow
7	Client
8	Modal
9	Etched in
10	Etched out

These are the standard border styles used throughout dBASE. The example below shows this, using the standard Fish table in the Samples folder:

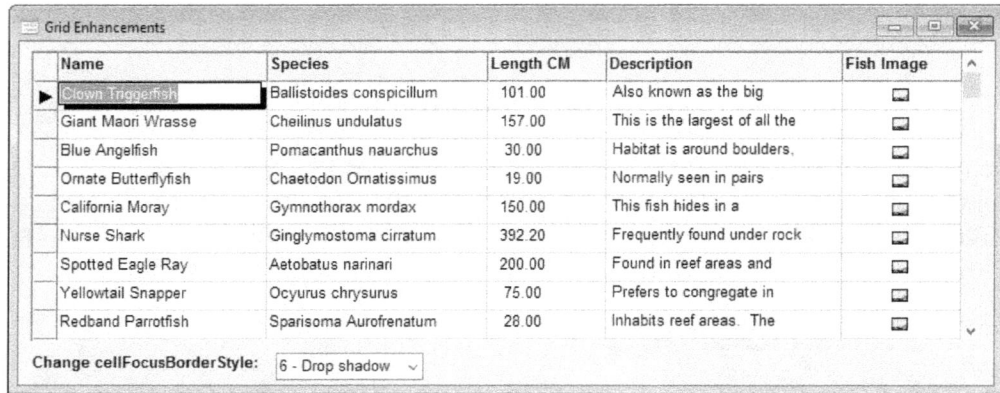

Figure 8-1

This is set to use the style 6 (Drop shadow), and you can see the current cell shows the drop shadow. I changed the *cellHeight* property of the grid a bit to allow for room for the drop shadow effect, otherwise the text will be truncated at the bottom.

At the time I am writing this, this new property seems to be the only enhancement to the current grid control.

The New GridEx Control

This is the promised "New Grid" for dBASE. The developers at dBASE promise that after the release of dBASE Plus 10, it will be enhanced and more functionality added *(for a point release, most likely)*.

The GridEx control is based on "Ultimate Grid", a freeware grid. Details can be found at:

```
http://www.codeproject.com/Articles/20183/The-Ultimate-Grid-Home-Page
```

This is from a library of code designed to work with the Microsoft Foundation Classes.

Ultimate Grid has been implemented *in* dBASE as *GridEx*. The developers have been working on hooking up the functionality to the Inspector, the Form Designer, and so on. The first release of dBASE Plus 10 does not have all the functionality included. Examining the web page, you can see that a lot of functionality is available, including individual cell colors, focus rectangles, and a lot more. Hopefully over time we will see more of these abilities.

Unfortunately at the time dBASE Plus 10 was released, there was no information in the online help, so all of the following is based on my own experimentation with the control. This new control is only partially implemented, although we have been promised that in a release somewhere down the road (possibly, but don't quote me, 10.5?) we will see more functionality.

GridEx and Components

The following is a breakdown of the properties, events and methods specific to the GridEx object. There will be a couple of example forms showing the use of this new control later. The grid is a container for column objects, so we need to break this down.

The GridEx Control

This is the main control itself. It can be used without specifying the columns (using the *columnLens* property – see below), or you can gain more control over the grid by specifying the column.

Properties

The properties listed here are the ones specific to this control.

columnLens: This allows the developer to control the columns of the grid. This works quite a bit differently from the standard Grid in dBASE, examples will be given later in this chapter.

hasColumnHeadings: Does the grid have columnHeadings? The default for this is *true*.

hasRowHeadings: Does the grid have *rowHeadings*? The default for this is *true*. The row headings may be misleading, as they are simply numbers, similar to an Excel spreadsheet – they might confuse a user if you are displaying a key field, and of course if a record is deleted or a record is added into the table displayed, the *rowHeading* number will not remain static or attached to a specific record. In otherwords, if looking at a grid and your user deletes the record associated with the *rowHeading* numbered 40, the *rowHeading* number remains 40, and the record *after* the one deleted is now associated with that number. Use this feature with caution or your users will be terribly confused.

Events

In the first release of this grid, there are no events specific to this control.

Methods

In the first release of this grid, there are no methods specific to this control.

columnLens Control

This is very similar to the columns array of the standard Grid control – it is a container for the columns in your grid, no editable properties, has no events, and two methods, one to add a new column, one to delete an existing column.

GridExColumn Control

The GridEx column object must be instantiated as part of the grid's columnLens:

```
columnLens.add(new GRIDEXCOLUMN(form.GRIDEX1))
```

From here you can work with each column. You would need to add the columns as you needed. The following is copied out of the Source Code for the first example in this chapter:

```
columnLens.add(new GRIDEXCOLUMN(form.GRIDEX1))
with (columnLens[1])
    title = "Name"
    field = "Name"
endwith

columnLens.add(new GRIDEXCOLUMN(form.GRIDEX1))
with (columnLens[2])
    title = "Species"
    field = "Species"
endwith
```

Properties

There are a variety of properties *(most of which have no effect in the first release)*. The following are for the *Normal* column type.

field: This is effectively the datalink – it links this column to a specific field – Simply enter the name of the field.

headingFontx: There are several headingFont properties, which are only available if the *headingFontOverride* property is *true* (?). These allow you to override the GridEx's properties for the heading.

colorNormal: Standard foreground/background colors.

ellipsis: This defaults to *false*. If you set this to true and run the form containing the grid, it will display part of the text in a field, followed by an ellipsis (…) showing there is more text. The column width may dramatically change (to the width of the *title* text).

headingColorNormal: The color of the heading control.

headingFontOverride: Allows the font properties for the heading to change? Defaults to *false*.

multiline: Allows text in a column to display across multiple lines (changing the row height?). The default setting is *false*.

title: The text that displays in the heading for the column. This does not have to be the name of the field, it can be whatever you need it to be.

widthInitial: The starting width of the column when the grid is first displayed.

Events

Currently blank in the Column Property Builder dialog.

Methods

Currently blank in the Column Property Builder dialog.

Building a Grid

This control is pretty flexible, but if you are used to working with the standard Grid that has been in dBASE for many years, you may find yourself confused. So I felt that in this chapter the first thing I needed to do was walk you through the process of using this control. If you follow along you will get a feel for how to work with it, and then can start going from there on your own.

Any grid used to work with a table must first have a table to work with. We'll use the standard "Fish" table in the dBASE Samples for our first example.

Example 1 – The Fish Table

To start, create a new form in the Form Designer, using the Navigator (also in the Form Designer) find the "Tables" tab, and then using the "Look In:" combobox, select the "dBASE Samples" database alias. Drag the "Fish" table to the design surface (which will also create a database object pointing to the alias). If the "Fish" query does not have focus, click it, and in the Inspector find the *sql* property, and change it to (adding the bold text):

```
Select * from FISH.DBF order by name
```

Set the form's *metric* property to "6 – Pixels", and then save it as "GridEx Example 1".

In the Component Palette find "GridEx", and drag this to the surface and resize it so it fills a good part of the form. When you do this the form will not look like it has a grid, just a white rectangle.

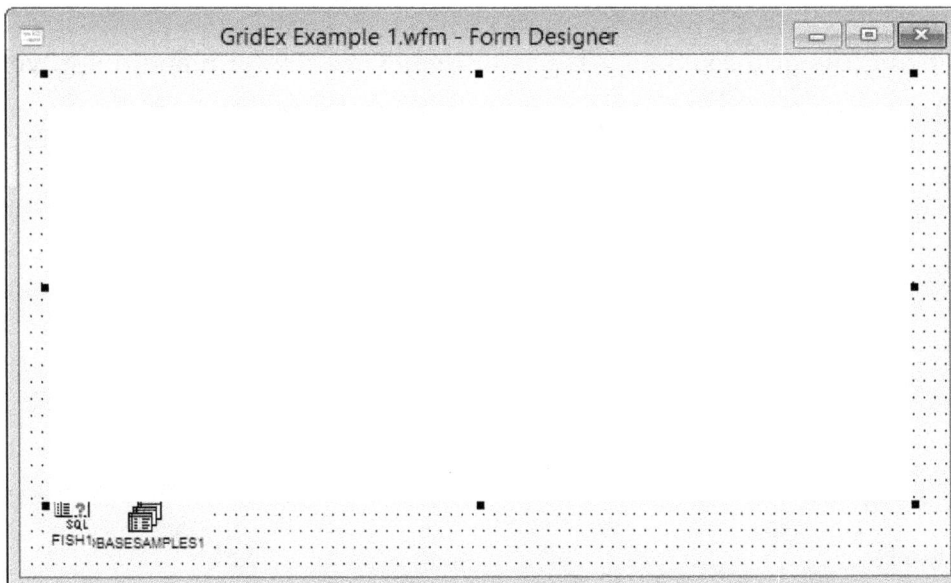

Figure 8-2

Note that at the top of the grid (see the sizing handles?) is a gray section as well – that is the column heading region, which we will work with.

So, like most controls in dBASE, you need to set the GridEx's *dataLink* property, so it knows what data to use. Doing that will cause an immediate change in the grid:

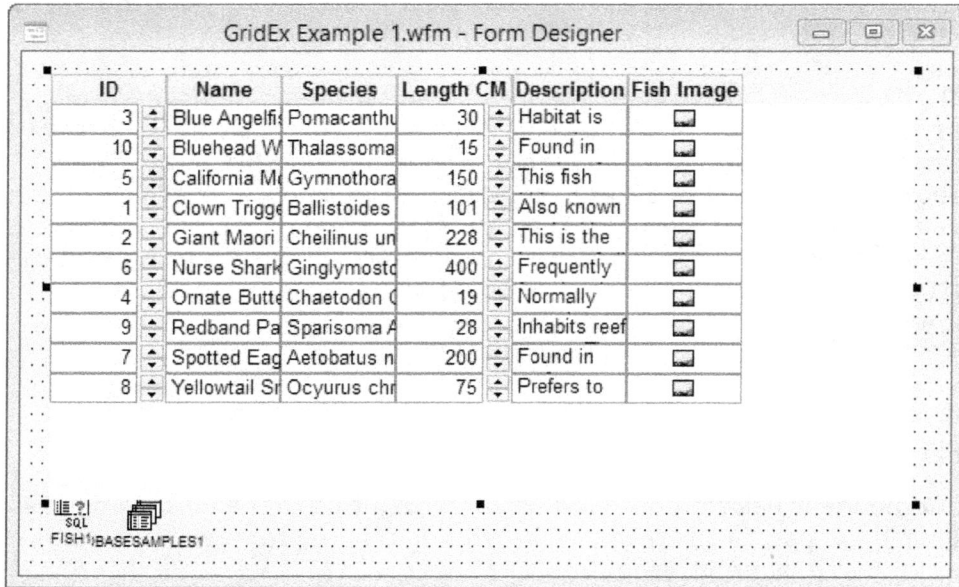

Figure 8-3

At this point, the grid could be just used. If you save the form and run it, you will see:

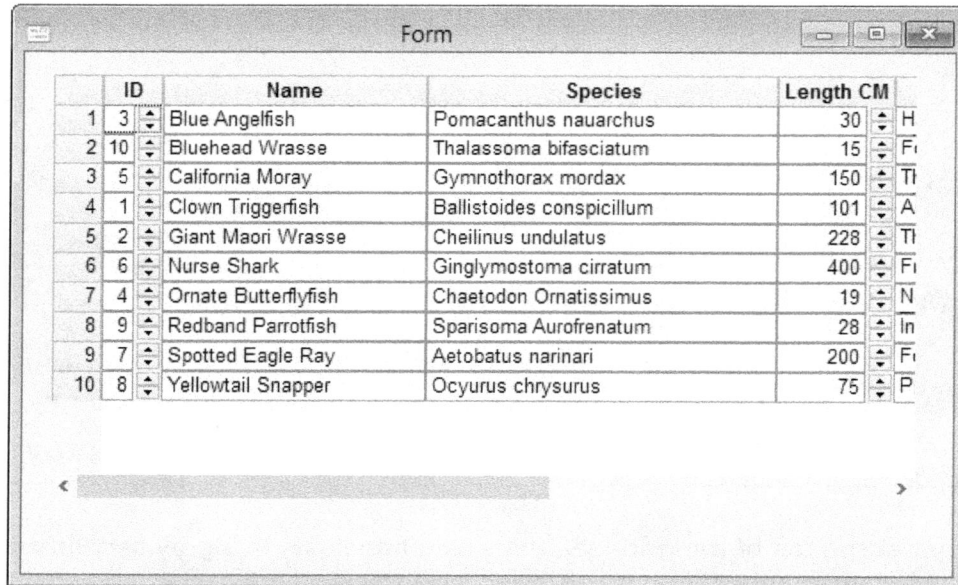

Figure 8-4

Interestingly, this looks a little different from what you saw in the designer. First, notice that there is a row-heading column on the left. This is something you can turn on or off, by changing the control's *hasRowHeadings* property to *false*. Also note that the column widths are different. The GridEx control apparently attempts to determine a good width for each column based on the contents of the fields.

Setting Columns

Typically most developers want to set the columns that are displayed, so we need to take a look at this.

Bring the form back into the Form Designer if you ran the form, and click on the GridEx control to give it focus. Notice that in the Inspector, right above the *dataLink* property is a *columnLens* property. This is how we bring up the Column Builder, which as noted earlier, is quite different from what we are used to seeing in dBASE for the standard Grid.

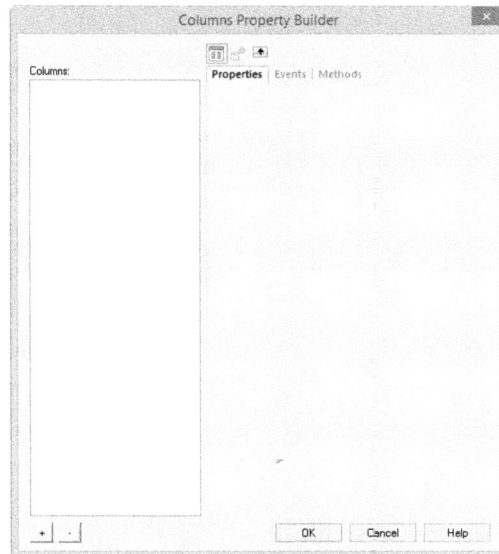

Figure 8-5

Since no columns have been specifically set, this is a *very* empty and plain looking dialog. The first thing to note is under the "Columns" listing is a pair of buttons, one with a "+" on it, the other a "-". If you think about it, they make sense, one adds a new column, the other deletes an existing column from the list.

Click the plus button ("+"), and you will see:

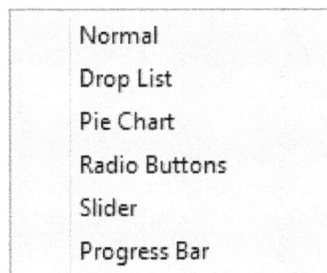

Normal

Drop List

Pie Chart

Radio Buttons

Slider

Progress Bar

Figure 8-6

We're going to work with normal columns. The other options do not really work right now, or not well. For now, click "Normal", and you will see:

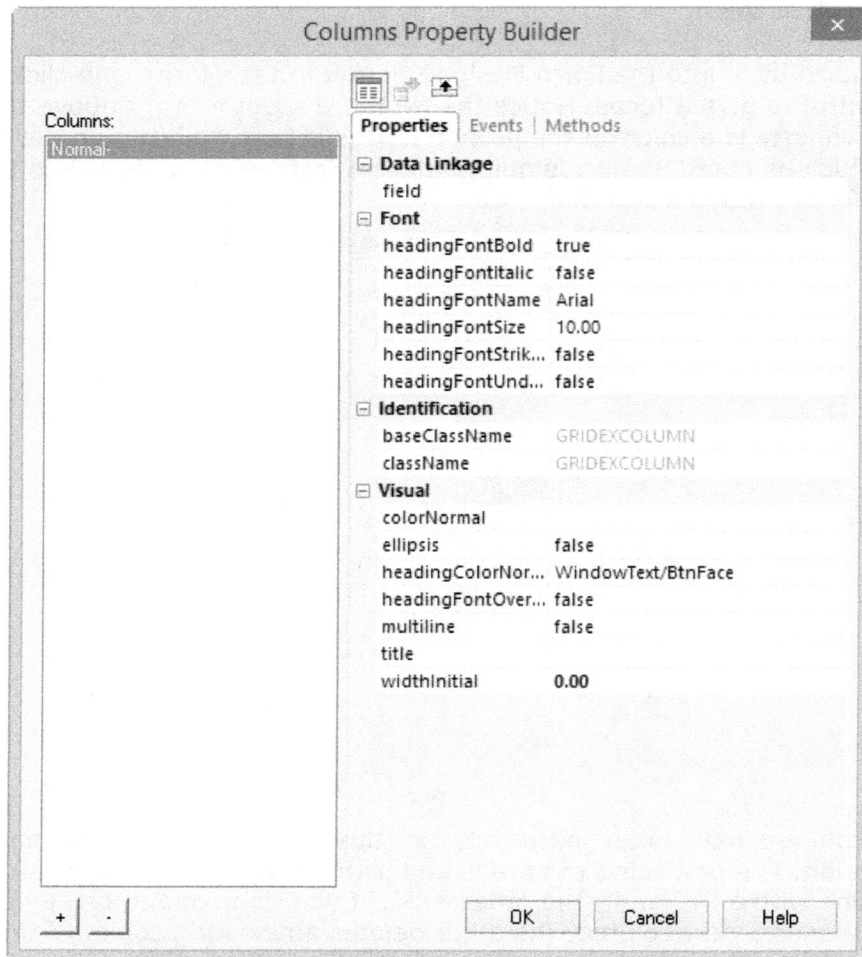

Figure 8-7

The developers at dBASE have embedded the standard dBASE inspector into this dialog, which is kind of cool. We can work with the individual columns from here, setting properties as needed. For each field you would need a datalink – in this dialog you have to specify the field name. At the time I am writing this, clicking on *field*, and the button to the right, brings up a string builder dialog. You can just type the name of the field in the inspector. So if I wanted to display the "Name" field first, I would type "Name" (without the quotes). This dialog is not as interactive as one might like – changes are not apparent until you close the dialog. Before we do, the heading text (defined by the *title* property) is not set, so you should probably put the name of the field there as well. Click on the *title* property and type "Name" (without the quotes).

If you click "OK", the Form Designer now shows:

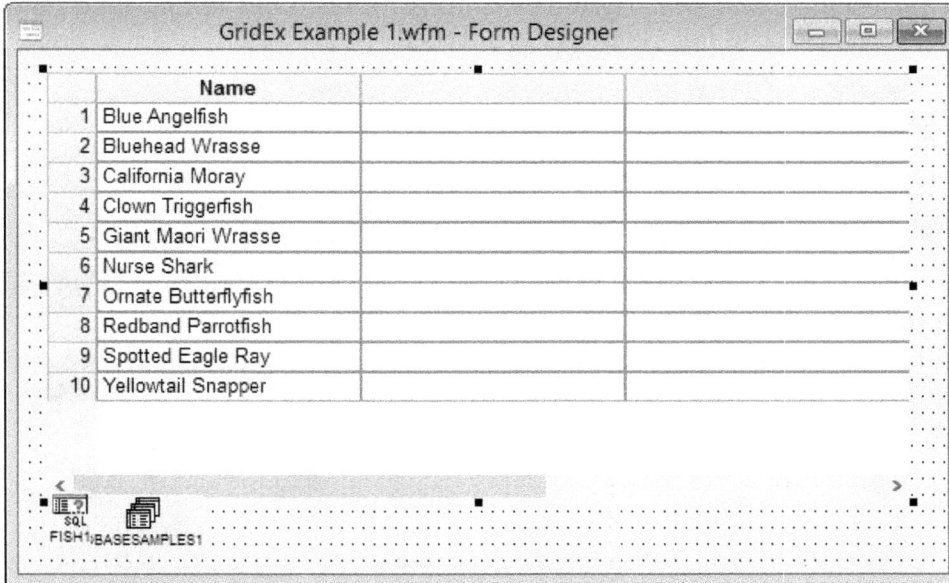

Figure 8-8

If you run the form, you should see:

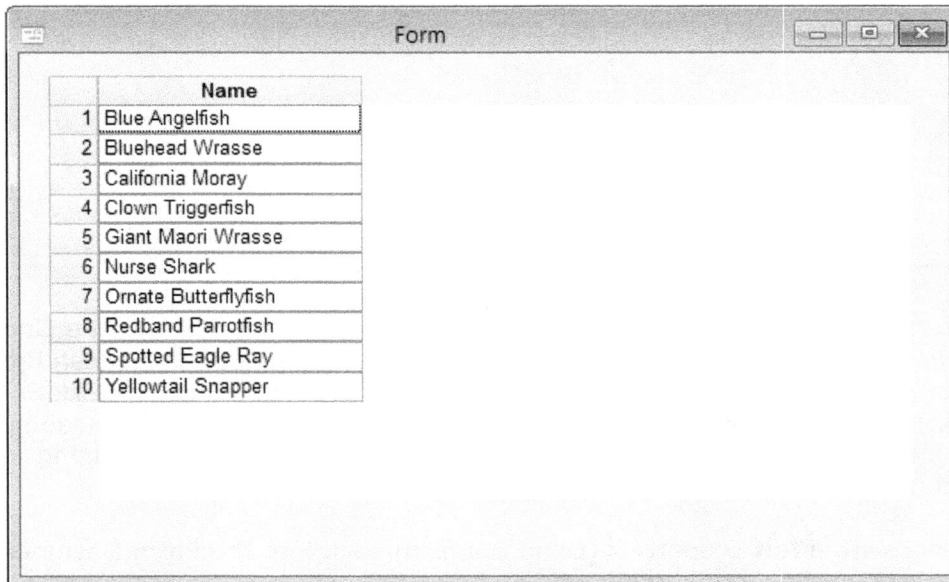

Figure 8-9

189

Obviously you are going to want other columns, so you should bring this back to the Form Designer, and add "Normal" columns for each of the following fields – be sure to set both the *field* and *title* properties:

- Species
- Length CM
- Description
- Fish Image

Note that you can use spaces, and do not need quotes in the *field* property.

When I did this *(remember that I am working with the first release of dBASE Plus 10)* the form did not display the new columns until I ran the form:

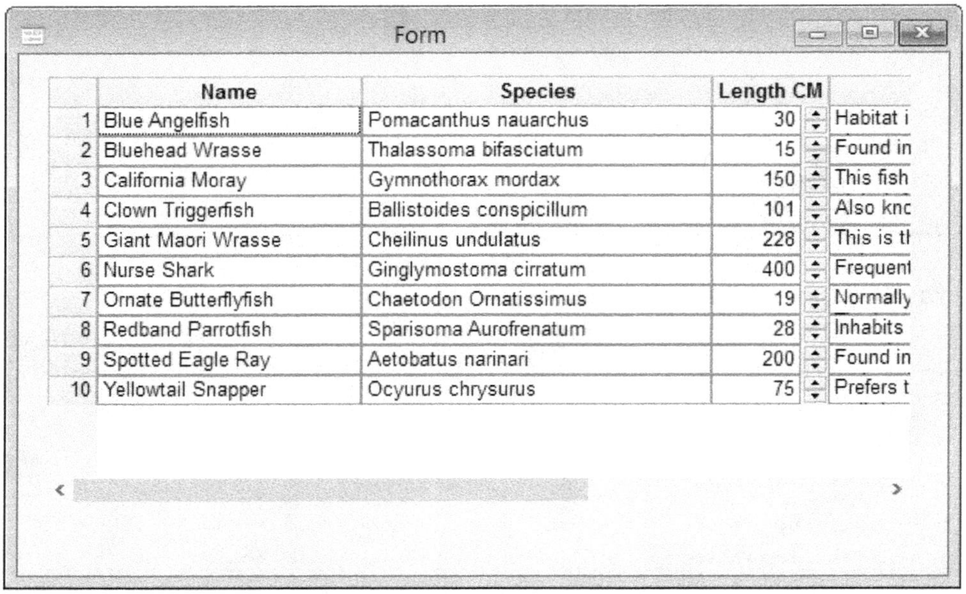

	Name	Species	Length CM	
1	Blue Angelfish	Pomacanthus nauarchus	30	Habitat i
2	Bluehead Wrasse	Thalassoma bifasciatum	15	Found in
3	California Moray	Gymnothorax mordax	150	This fish
4	Clown Triggerfish	Ballistoides conspicillum	101	Also knc
5	Giant Maori Wrasse	Cheilinus undulatus	228	This is tl
6	Nurse Shark	Ginglymostoma cirratum	400	Frequent
7	Ornate Butterflyfish	Chaetodon Ornatissimus	19	Normally
8	Redband Parrotfish	Sparisoma Aurofrenatum	28	Inhabits
9	Spotted Eagle Ray	Aetobatus narinari	200	Found in
10	Yellowtail Snapper	Ocyurus chrysurus	75	Prefers t

Figure 8-10

Note that this is actually very close to the same as when we first set the GridEx's *dataLink* property. We are only missing the ID column, which for the Fish table the user does not need to see. The column widths are defined by the GridEx control, but we might want to define those. In addition, does the rowHeading really need to be there? Showing the row numbers can be a bit misleading (indeed, if the ID column were displayed these would not match).

Let's work with a few properties (bring the form back into the Form Designer if it is not). First on the GridEx itself:

Set the *hasRowHeadings* property to *false*. These will immediately disappear, because we are not in the *columnLens*.

Set the *colorHighlight* property to "HighLightText/Yellow" (without the quotes).

Next to modify the columns, you will need to work with the *columnLens* instead of directly modifying individual columns (as you may have done with the standard Grid in dBASE).

Click the *columnLens* property and then the button and then the first button in the Inspector (the other button, with the "I" will inspect the *columnLens*, which doesn't have a lot you can work with).

Select the fourth column "Normal-Description" if it is not already selected, and change the following:

- *multiline* – set this to *true*

Save the form and run it.

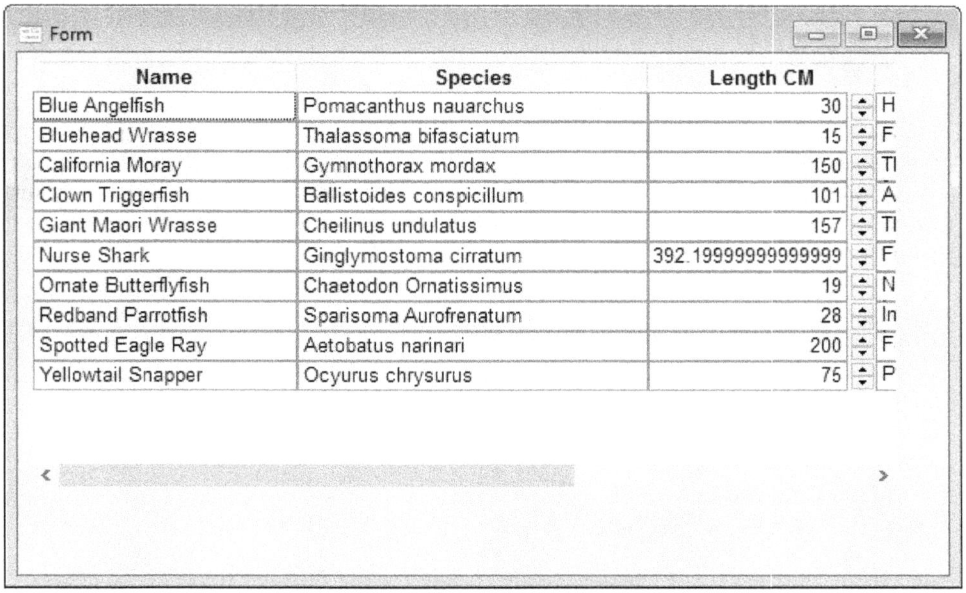

Name	Species	Length CM	
Blue Angelfish	Pomacanthus nauarchus	30	H
Bluehead Wrasse	Thalassoma bifasciatum	15	F
California Moray	Gymnothorax mordax	150	Tl
Clown Triggerfish	Ballistoides conspicillum	101	A
Giant Maori Wrasse	Cheilinus undulatus	157	Tl
Nurse Shark	Ginglymostoma cirratum	392.19999999999999	F
Ornate Butterflyfish	Chaetodon Ornatissimus	19	N
Redband Parrotfish	Sparisoma Aurofrenatum	28	In
Spotted Eagle Ray	Aetobatus narinari	200	F
Yellowtail Snapper	Ocyurus chrysurus	75	P

Figure 5-11

This does not look a *lot* different. The color did not come through, nor does the *multiline* property seem to do anything (at this time).

As noted earlier, the developers are prioritizing how and what they want to surface next and get to work with this control. By the time you purchase it, some of the functionality may already be implemented.

Sample Code for This Chapter

The following is a listing of the sample code in the "Chapter 08" folder, if you downloaded it from my website. You may use the code contained in these forms for your own applications if you desire, with the caveat that credit be given appropriately.

- **GridEnhancement.wfm** – Form used to show the new *cellFocusBorderStyle* property of the standard grid.
- **GridExExample.wfm** – A form to show the basics of the GridEx control.

Summary

The GridEx control has a lot of potential, and we have been promised that more of this will be surfaced over time. The developers at dBASE will have put out a survey asking developers what they would like to see, and should be working on it. By the time this book is published some of this new functionality may be available.

I think you will find the next chapter of some interest with the new ListView control.

Chapter 9: The ListView Control

This takes me back to the days when I worked at Borland. When Randy Solton and his team started to work on Visual dBASE 7, one of the new controls was a ListView object. They had taken on a huge project however, and after a lot of work, this particular item was commented out of the base code and never released to the public.

Over the years, this object has been mostly ignored in the base code for dBASE, until now. It appears that this new control is actually based on one in the Microsoft Foundation Classes, so perhaps some of the issues with the original have been resolved this way. Either way, you now have the ability to use this control in your own applications.

What Is It?

The first question that you are most likely to ask is "What is this thing?" or "What is a ListView Object?"

A ListView object or control is a way of showing information on a form in a visual manner with quite a variety of options. An example of a ListView object you most likely are familiar with is the display in "Windows Explorer" (or if you are using Windows 8 or later, "File Explorer". If you open this to display the contents of any folder, you might see something like the display in Figure 9-1:

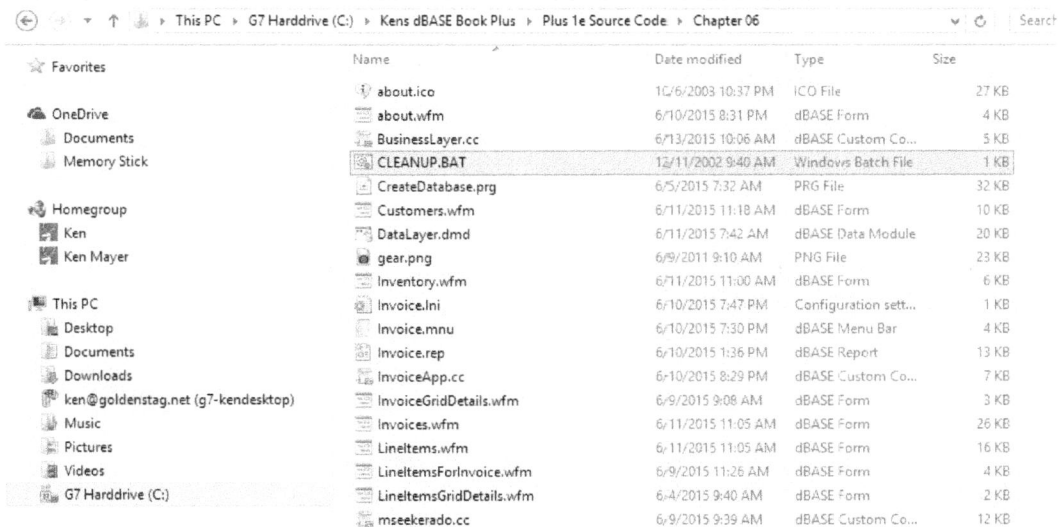

Name	Date modified	Type	Size
about.ico	10/6/2003 10:37 PM	ICO File	27 KB
about.wfm	6/10/2015 8:31 PM	dBASE Form	4 KB
BusinessLayer.cc	6/13/2015 10:06 AM	dBASE Custom Co...	5 KB
CLEANUP.BAT	12/11/2002 9:40 AM	Windows Batch File	1 KB
CreateDatabase.prg	6/5/2015 7:32 AM	PRG File	32 KB
Customers.wfm	6/11/2015 11:18 AM	dBASE Form	10 KB
DataLayer.dmd	6/11/2015 7:42 AM	dBASE Data Module	20 KB
gear.png	6/9/2011 9:10 AM	PNG File	23 KB
Inventory.wfm	6/11/2015 11:00 AM	dBASE Form	6 KB
Invoice.Ini	6/10/2015 7:47 PM	Configuration sett...	1 KB
Invoice.mnu	6/10/2015 7:30 PM	dBASE Menu Bar	4 KB
Invoice.rep	6/10/2015 1:36 PM	dBASE Report	13 KB
InvoiceApp.cc	6/10/2015 8:29 PM	dBASE Custom Co...	7 KB
InvoiceGridDetails.wfm	6/9/2015 9:08 AM	dBASE Form	3 KB
Invoices.wfm	6/11/2015 11:05 AM	dBASE Form	26 KB
LineItems.wfm	6/11/2015 11:05 AM	dBASE Form	16 KB
LineItemsForInvoice.wfm	6/9/2015 11:26 AM	dBASE Form	4 KB
LineItemsGridDetails.wfm	6/4/2015 9:40 AM	dBASE Form	2 KB
mseekerado.cc	6/9/2015 9:39 AM	dBASE Custom Co...	12 KB

Figure 9-1

This is part of the window (cropped), the information in the display on the right side of the window is a ListView *(on the left we might have either a ListView or a TreeView, I honestly don't know)*.

You have some options for the display in the ListView on the right – you can show large icons, you can show details (as here), and other variations.

The ListView control in dBASE appears to have quite a bit of functionality attached to it. Before we start trying to work with one, let's break it down a bit – look at the properties, events and methods.

The ListView Object

From a programmer's point of view, the ListView object is a container for some other objects, but the main ListView itself is the primary control. You need to get a feel for that as well as the other controls. The controls that are contained by the ListView are *columns*, *groups*, and *items*.

Properties

As with all controls in dBASE, there are some common properties, we will examine the ones that are specific to the ListView control itself.

The Inspector has two groups that we will examine for properties specific to this control:

Controls

columnCount: This allows you to define how many columns you want. Using the File Explorer as an example (see Figure 9-1), we see four columns.

columns: This is an object reference to an array containing each column. We will examine this as a separate object shortly.

groupCount: As with *columnCount* above, this allows the developer to determine the number of groups.

groups: This is an object reference to an array containing each group. We will examine this as a separate entity shortly.

itemCount: The number of items in the ListView object.

items: This is an object reference to an array containing each group. We will examine this as a separate entity shortly.

Miscellaneous

allowEditLabels: Determines if the user can change the text displayed for each item. The default value for this is *true*.

allowMoveItems: Determines if the user can move items around in the list. The default value for this is *true*. Note: Your users can only move items around when the mode is 0 (Large Icon), 1 (Small Icon), or 4 (Tile), and your ListView is not set to use groups (meaning there are no groups, and the *items* do not have groups assigned to them). It should also be noted that if a user moves the items on the ListView, their place in the array is not changed, and even if you tried streaming them out to a new array, they would be in the same order they were in when loaded to the ListView.

header: Determines if the ListView displays headers for the columns. The default value for this is *true*.

largeIconSize and *largeIconWidth*: sizes for the icons when the ListView's *mode* property is set to 0 (Large Icon).

mode: Determine which mode (from the list below) to display the ListView in. The default value for this is "0 – Large Icon".

Mode	Meaning
0 – Large Icon	Ignores the *details* array, shows the text for each item, and the "large" icon. This respects groups if the *showGroups* property is set. This is the default.
1 – Small Icon	Ignores the *details* array, shows the text for each item, and the "small" icon. This respects groups if the *showGroups* property is set.
2 – List	Ignores the *details* array, shows the items in a list in order. This also ignores groups, even if the *showGroups* property is *true*.
3 – Details	If *header* is true, this will lay out the ListView with headings. Whether or not the *header* property is *true*, the *text* for each *item* will be in column 1, and the *details* array for each item will be in subsequent columns.
4 - Tile	Lays out the items showing the "large" icon in a tile pattern, keeps them in groups if the *showGroups* property is set.

showGroups: Determines if groups should be shown. The default value for this is *false*.

tileAutoSize: set size of icon automatically to fit the most items on the screen, when the *mode* property is set to 5 (Tile). The default for this property is *true*. Affects *tileWidth* and *tileHeight* properties.

tileWidth: If the *tileAutoSize* property is *false*, this allows the developer to determine how wide to make the icon. If the *tileAutoSize* property is *true*, this property is ignored. The default size is 50 (pixels).

tileHeight: If the *tileAutoSize* property is *false*, this allows the developer to determine how tall to make the icon. If the *tileAutoSize* property is *true*, this property is ignored. The default for this property is 70 (pixels).

tileMaxLines: The maximum number of lines an icon can take when in tile mode. The default setting is 3.

Events

As with other controls there are a lot of common events, the following are ones that are specific to this control that you should be aware of. As always if the event handler name starts with *can* it fires before the event occurs (editLabel, selChange) and *must* return a logical value of either *true* or *false*, and if it starts with *on* the event handler fires after the event occurs.

canEditLabel: can be used by a developer to set a condition whether or not the user can change the text of a label.

onEditLabel: once a user has changed the text, you can execute specific code. (An example might be if your ListView contained a list of filenames, if you allow the user to edit the label, you might want to rename the file itself so it matches the change in the ListView control).

canSelChange: can the user change the selection?

onSelChange: when the user changes the selection, do you want some specific action to occur?

Methods
There are a small number of methods for this control, these two are very specific to the control.

addItemsFromArray: allows you to define an array of items, and load the information into the ListView control from the array. At this time you can load an array of items, assign an image, and a group:

```
form.ListView1.addItemsFromArray( aItems, "FILENAME MyIcon.ico",;
                                form.ListView1.groups[1] )
```

The icon and group references are optional, but if used will assign the same values to each item in the array of items. The first parameter, the array needs to be a single column array with the names of the items to be loaded.

getSelectedCount: returns a numeric value of the number of items currently selected (a user can select multiple items by using standard Windows keystrokes combined with the mouse, such as Shift+Click, or Ctrl+Click).

selected: returns an array of all items currently selected. A simple example of use would be:

```
a = form.ListView1.selected()
if a.size == 0
   ? "Nothing selected"
else
   // you could also loop through a list of
   // selected items if more than one:
   ? a[1].text
endif
```

The ListView Columns Objects
The columns objects are two separate items – the first is just the array of the columns, the second are the columns themselves. To work with columns, you must set the number of columns in the Inspector using the *ListView* object's *columnCount* property. If, for example, you set it to 4, then in the inspector you click on *columns* you will see in the inspector that there are four, with default names of "column1", "column2", etc.

To reference a column in code you would need to use something like:

```
? form.ListView1.columns["column1"].text
```

Columns Array
The Columns array has no editable properties, no events, and only two methods:

add: allows you to add a column to the ListView programmatically. This requires an object reference for a new *listcolumn* as a parameter. This would be done something like:

```
oColumn = new ListColumn( form.MyListView )
oColumn.text   := "My New Column"
oColumn.width := 150
form.MyListView.columns.add( oColumn )
```

delete: allows you to remove a column *from* the ListView programmatically. This requires a numeric value – the column number – as a parameter. This would work in a fashion similar to the following:

```
form.MyListView.columns.delete( 3 )
```

It should be noted that if you delete a column and there are columns *after* that (let us say you had a ListView with 5 columns, and you deleted number 3), the columns would be internally renumbered, so that column 4 becomes 3, and so on.

Columns

The columns themselves have two properties you can modify, and one each event and method. The *baseClassName* for this control is: *listcolumn*.

text: this is the text that would appear in the heading, if you have the *header* property set to *true* for the main *ListView* object.

width: the width of the column. At this time you cannot change the width property by dragging the column headers around in the Form Designer, so you would need to set a specific width.

The event and method have to deal with releasing the column. You have a *beforeRelease* event handler, and the *release* method.

Groups Array

As with columns, the groups array is just a container for the groups themselves. The idea is that you can "group" the information in the ListView control. The groups array has the same events and methods of the columns array.

Groups

The group object, is a way to group the items in the ListView control. If you choose to use groups, you must assign each item to the group you wish it to display in. Groups are collapsible, meaning that the user can choose to ignore the contents of a group by collapsing it. We will examine this once we have some example forms later in the chapter.

The *group* object has four properties that you can work with:

alignHorizontal: the alignment of the text for the group. The default is "0 – Left", you can have "1 – Center", or "2 – Right"

footer: this is optional, it will display at the bottom of the group, it is most likely to be useful if you have multiple groups in a ListView.

footerAlignment: alignment of the footer. The default is "0 – Left".

text: The text for the group heading.

Items Array
The items array is again much like the other two arrays, an object reference for an array of the different items in the ListView.

Items
The items themselves have several properties of interest.

group: allows you to define which group an item is part of.

details: this is an array of information, which should match the other columns, if you choose to use multiple columns. As an example, if you were creating a list of files, the array might contain the Date Modified, Type, and File Size information to be displayed.

focus: This allows you to specify if the *item* has focus when the form opens. Default is *false*. Focus puts a dotted border around the outside of the control. You can set multiple *items* to have the *focus* property set to *true*.

image: lets you specify an image (using an Icon file) to display with the specific item.

selected: This allows you to specify if the *item* is selected when the form opens, or to query in code to see which item (or items) has been selected. The default is *false*. You can set multiple *items* to have the *selected* property set to *true* when the form opens.

text: the text that will display for the item. Again, if you were doing a list of files, it would be the filename. For a ListView with multiple columns (using the *details* array noted above) this is what is in the first column, anything in the *details* array would be listed in the other columns (2 through whatever).

ListView Examples

In order to see this control in action, I created a few examples for you to look at. If you have the source code for this book, you should be able to run these and see how they work. Keep in mind that the sample forms will only work in dBASE Plus 10.0 or later.

A Small List of Movies
This first example is really meant to show the basics of what many of the options can do for a ListView control.

I manually entered all the items, assigned icon images to them, etc. I created the groups, set the columns, and so on. I don't recommend this, as it is time-consuming – particularly if you have a large amount of data. The ListView's addFromArray method will be very handy. It should also be noted that the icon files in the folder are ones that I have permission to use and to distribute *(they are from a collection I purchased)*, but you do not have a license to use them in your own application(s).

The form lists some movies (from my own collection), with some basic information about them. There are some controls at the bottom to allow you to change some ListView properties and see the difference in how the information is displayed. I will show a few screen shots below, but you can use this to experiment a bit.

Figure 9-2

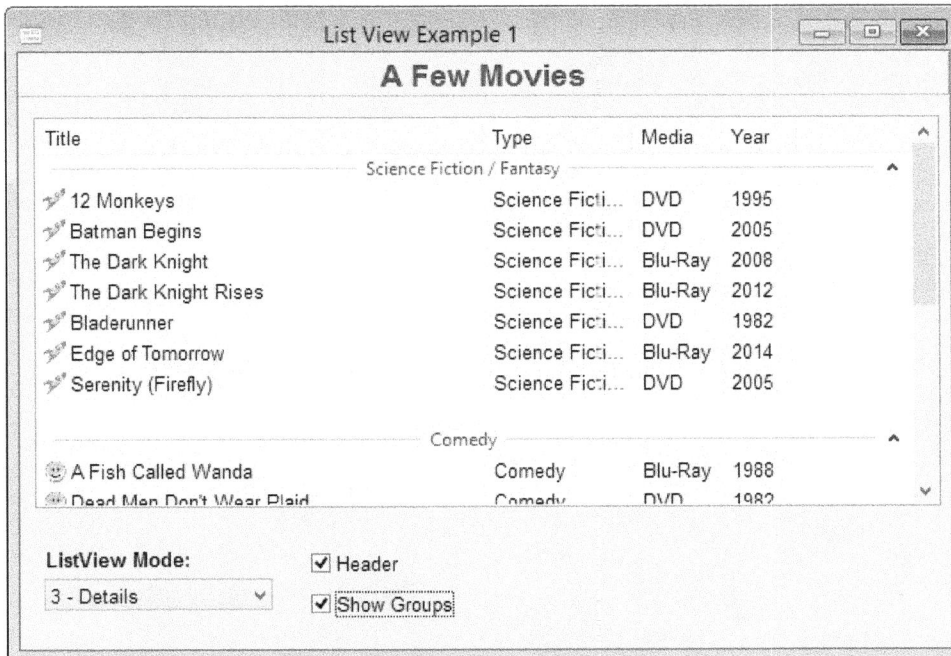

Figure 9-3

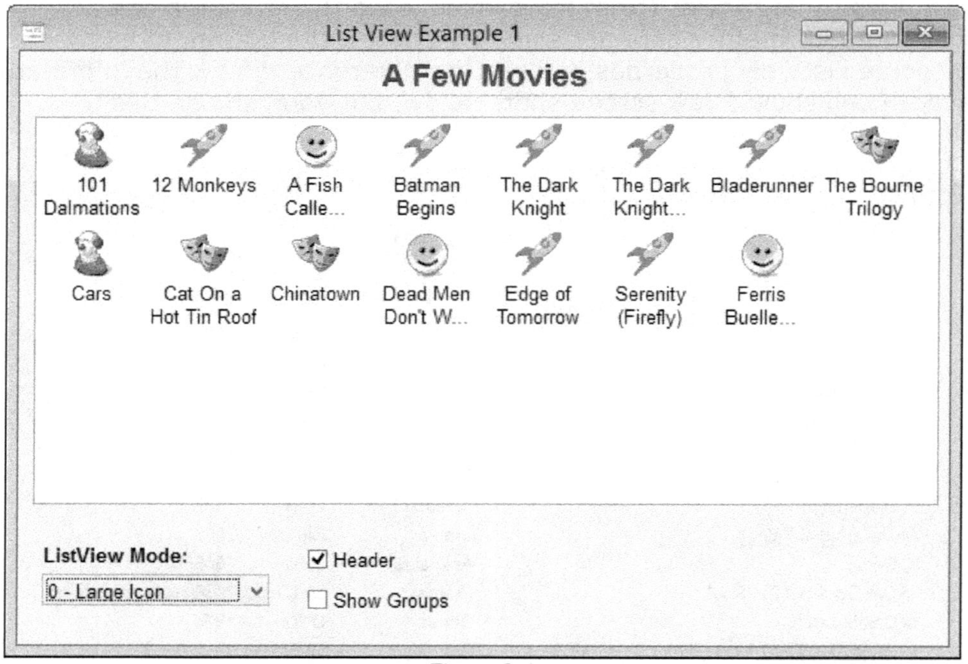

Figure 9-4

As you can see, this is a pretty flexible control. The various options can give you many different ways to display information for your users.

A File List

Emulating the Windows / File Explorer is something we could attempt to do using a ListView control. This requires using programming techniques to get the information needed, so that it can be displayed properly. Obviously it would be a bit more involved.

For this to work, you need to get a list of the files in the folder that you are pointing to. When setting up the form, the ListView control only has a few things set in the Form Designer:

- *name*: SampleListView
- *mode*: 3
- *columnCount*: 3

The names of each column have been changed and width set.

I decided to use a method that already exists and has been used for a variety of purposes over the years, the *array* object's *dir*() method. The form (see image below) has an entryfield used to display the current path. The code to get the file list is:

```
function LoadFileList
   // Get a list of files:
   local aFiles, cPath
   cPath = form.FolderEF.value.rightTrim()
   aFiles = new array()
   aFiles.dir( cPath+"\*.*" )
   // we use a custom property
   // of the form so we don't
```

```
        // have to deal with passing
        // parameters:
        form.aFiles = aFiles
    return
```

Once I have the list of files (and some other information), the code gets more complicated, as you need to read information out of the array, and add *items* to the ListView control, assigning properties.

```
function LoadList
    // Load the ListView with the files
    // to be displayed.
    if type( "form.aFiles" ) # "A"
        msgbox( "Need custom property object reference "+chr(13)+;
                "for array of files to display (form.aFiles).",;
                "LoadList Error", 16 )
        return
    endif
    // sort file list:
    try
        form.aFiles.sort(1) // ascending, first column
    catch( exception e )
        // empty array:
        msgbox( "No files in this folder ...",;
                "LoadList Error", 32 )
        form.SampleListView.itemCount := 0 // empty it out
        return
    endtry
    // loop through array and build items list
    // for ListView:
    local i, oList, cName, nCount, aDetail
    oList = form.SampleListView
    oList.itemCount = 0
    for i = 1 to ( form.aFiles.size / 5 ) // five columns
        // don't add "backup" files:
        if "backup" $ lower( form.aFiles[ i, 1 ] )
            loop
        endif
        // add an Item to the List:
        oList.itemCount++
        nCount = oList.itemCount
        // name of item:
        cName = "item"+nCount
        // assign file name:
        oList.items[ cName ].text := form.aFiles[ i, 1 ]
        // set up literaly array for details:
        aDetail = "{'"+;
                form.aFiles[ i, 3 ]+;
                "','"+;
                int( round((form.aFiles[i,2]/1024), 0 ) )+"K"+;
                "'}"
        // assign to details array of item:
        oList.items[ cName ].details = "ARRAY "+aDetail
        cFile = lower( form.aFiles[ i, 1 ] )
        do case
            case ".wfm" $ cFile or ".cfm" $ cFile or;
                ".wfo" $ cFile or ".cfo" $ cFile
```

```
                   oList.items[cName].image = "filename form_blue.ico"
         case ".prg" $ cFile or ".pro" $ cfile
                   oList.items[ cName ].image = "filename gears.ico"
         case ".bmp" $ cFile or ".ico" $ cFile or;
              ".png" $ cFile or ".jpg" $ cFile
                   oList.items[ cName ].image = "filename palette.ico"
         case ".rep" $ cFile or ".reo" $ cfile
                oList.items[cName].image="filename orientation_portrait.ico"
         otherwise // anything else
                   oList.items[ cName ].image = "filename unknown.ico"
         endcase
      next // i
   return
```

There is other code, the form's startup deals with obtaining the current folder, there is a pushbutton which allows the user to change folders, and more.

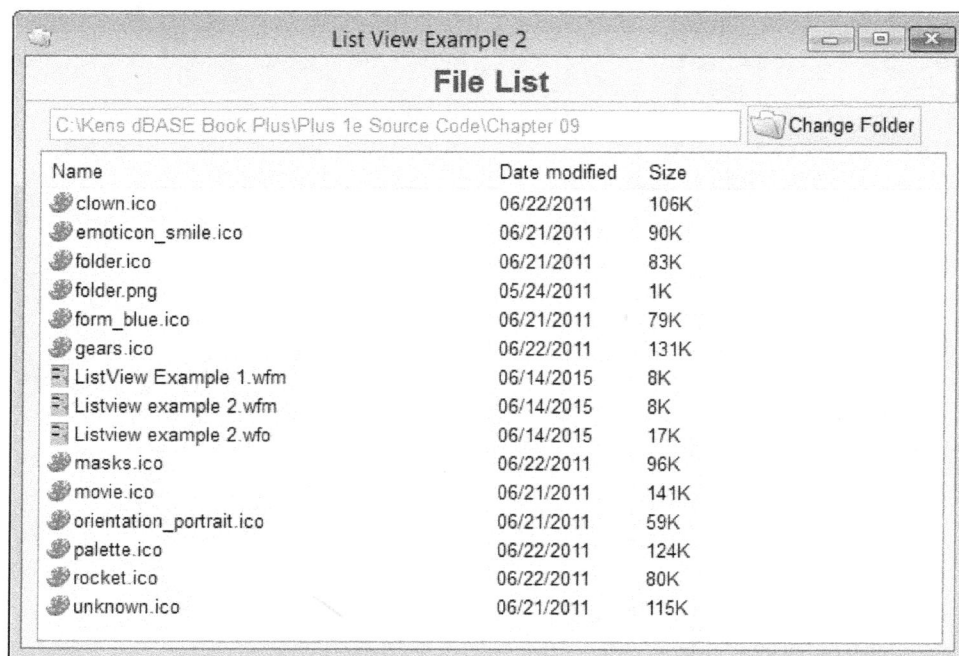

Figure 9-5

For this to be more robust, the ListView form needs some enhancements, the code to load the files would need to be able to handle more file types than I programmed for the example. Perhaps even an array that listed each possible file extension, the icon (and path to the icon file), and more. One could add the ability to delete items, drag files over using drag and drop, and a lot more. I will leave that to the reader.

Work With a Table

It is possible to use a ListView control with a table, but there is no "datalink" or other property to connect the contents of a table to this object.

To make this work you will need to assume that the table is read-only (although if you *really* wanted to, you could probably add code to write information back to the table, I don't believe this control is the best way to do that).

The form opens and reads the content of the table, loading the information as needed, using a method to loop through the data. For this example we are using the Fish table in the DBASESAMPLES database (which is installed with dBASE). The ListView has already got the columns set up, and the *mode* is set to 3 (Details). The *allowEditLabels* property is set to *false*.

This is the code called when the form is run:

```
function Init
    // get data:
    local oRow, oList
    private aDetails
    // shortcuts:
    oRow = form.rowset
    oList = form.samplelistview
    // empty the list
    oList.itemCount := 0
    // first row of rowset
    oRow.first()
    do while not oRow.endOfSet
        // add one to item counter:
        oList.itemCount++
        // add name as text for this item:
        oList.items[ oList.itemCount ].text := ;
            oRow.fields[ "Name" ].value.rightTrim()
        // add Species and Length CM fields as
        // description array:
        aDetails = new array()
        aDetails.add( oRow.fields[ "Species" ].value.rightTrim() )
        aDetails.add( oRow.fields[ "Length CM" ].value )
        oList.items[ oList.itemCount ].details = "ARRAY aDetails"
        // next row
        oRow.next()
    enddo
    // set first item as selected:
    oList.items[ 1 ].selected := true
return
```

The form's *onOpen* event handler needs to be called, because the controls will not have actually be instantiated in the *Init* method above:

```
function form_onOpen()
    // once form is open (and everything
    // is instantiated):
    class::Navigate()
return
```

You will note this calls the navigation routine which ensures that the editor and image objects are loaded with the correct information:

```
function Navigate
    // this requires that we actually navigate through
    // the table to land on the item the user
    // has selected by clicking on it:
    local oRow, cText, a
    a = form.SampleListView.selected()
```

```
if a.size == 0 // assume first row
   cText = form.SampleListView.items[1].text
else
   cText = a[1].text
endif
oRow = form.rowset

// find the current item:
oRow.locateOptions := 3 // Match partial length and ignore case
// find it:
oRow.applyLocate( [Name=']+cText+['] )
return
```

And the last thing we need is code that executes when the ListItem's selection is changed, using the *onSelChange* event handler for the *ListItem* control:

```
function SAMPLELISTVIEW_onSelChange()
   class::Navigate()
return
```

After all that, the reason for the Navigation code is because in order to display the Description and Fish Image fields of the table, we are using Editor and Image controls that are appropriately linked to these fields of the table. Hence, we need to navigate in the table to display these.

What you get when you run the form, is the following:

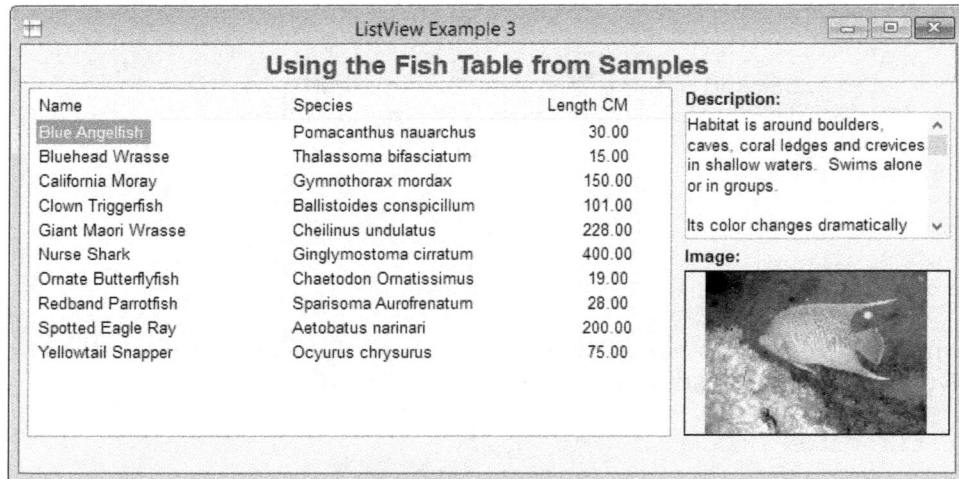

Figure 9-6

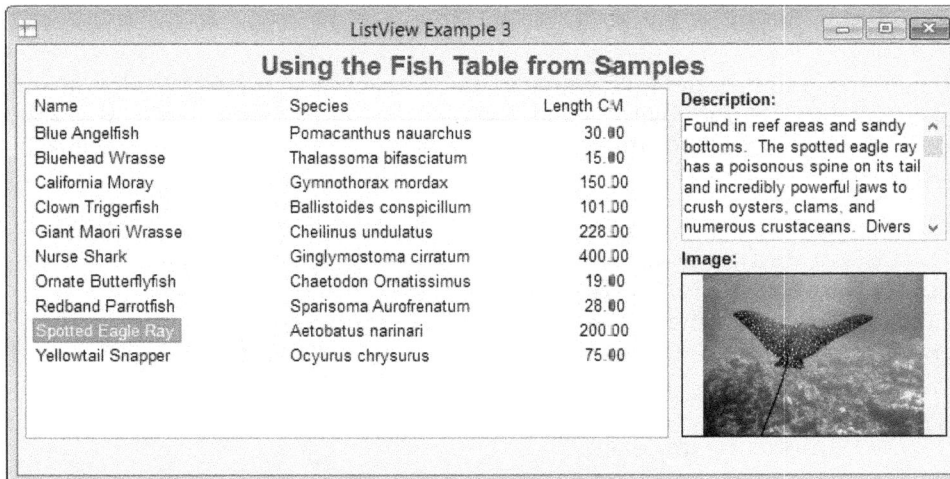

Figure 9-7

As you "navigate" by clicking on the names, the contents of the editor and image controls update to match the current selection.

Keep in mind that the ListView control is not truly meant to be used with tables, I was mostly intrigued with the idea of doing it, and thought this would make an interesting third example for the book. I don't really suggest this as a standard control for working with tables, though.

Other Examples

In addition to the examples in this chapter of the book, in the:

```
C:\ProgramData\dBASE\Plus10\Samples
```

folder you will see that there are a couple of ListView examples provided by Kathy K. at dBASE, which will display the contents of a folder showing specific dBASE files (.PRG, etc.), allowing you to open them in the Source Code Editor, run them, etc. These examples provide different code techniques from mine, but the ideas are similar, and may provide some functionality that you would find useful in your own applications. These are named:

- dBASE File Groups.wfm
- dBASE File List.wfm

The first uses groups, the second does not.

Sample Code for This Chapter

The following is a listing of the sample code in the "Chapter 09" folder, if you downloaded it from my website. You may use the code contained in these forms for your own applications if you desire, with the caveat that credit be given appropriately.

- **ListView Example 1.wfm** – A sample form used with this chapter.
- **ListView Example 2.wfm** – A sample form used with this chapter.
- **ListView Example 3.wfm** – A sample form used with this chapter.
- **Icons** used with these forms – all from IconExperience (don't use in your own applications – there are license issues – I own the license, you do not ...):
  - Clown.ico
  - Emoticon_smile.ico
  - Folder.ico
  - Folder.png
  - Form_blue.ico
  - Gears.ico
  - Masks.ico
  - Movie.ico
  - Orientation_portrait.ico
  - Palette.ico
  - Rocket.ico
  - Table_row.ico
  - Unknown.ico

Summary

Working with a new control can be fun, it can be kind of exciting, the most intriguing thing is figuring out how you might want to use this control in your own application.

I hope this chapter gives you some ideas, and maybe will help you get started creating your own ListView controls in dBASE.

I have to thank Kathy Kolosky for coming to my rescue when I was working on this, providing some details and code for me to look at, so I could try to document how the new control works. Bruce Beacham also gave me a couple of enhancements for the first example ...

Chapter 10: The SQL Builder

In The dBASE Book, all three editions, I have basically stated that the SQL Builder was ... okay, but it wasn't all that useful. Heck, I just tried to run it in dBASE Plus 2.8, and it crashed dBASE. I am sure there's something going on there, but still ...

Released with dBASE Plus 8, there is a new SQL Builder – this one is uses a drag and drop interface, but is much more useful to a programmer.

This chapter will walk you through some simple work with the SQL Builder, using the DBASESAMPLES database, which has *(oddly enough)* a set of tables used for an Invoice system. *(This data was created independent of my work in earlier chapters of the book, and I did not look at it for any of what I wrote in those chapters.)*

A Simple SQL Query

Like anything, let's start with a simple query, and then we'll move up to working with related tables.

If you start the SQL Builder in dBASE (in the Navigator, click the "SQL" tab, then double-click [New SQL]), you will see something like:

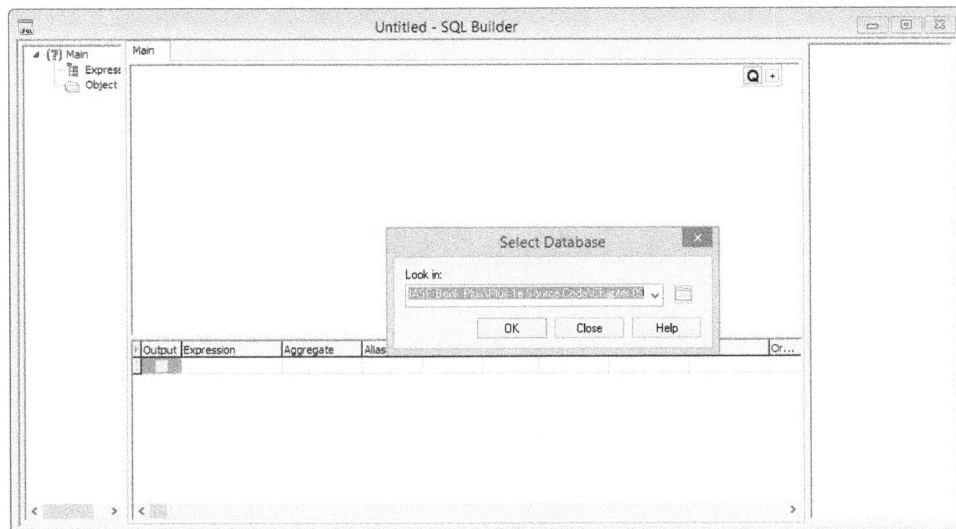

Figure 10-1

You need to select the database to work with. If you close this, you will have the design screen, but there is not a lot you can work with. For the example here, select DBASESAMPLES from the list and click "OK".

Note the list of tables is now on the right:

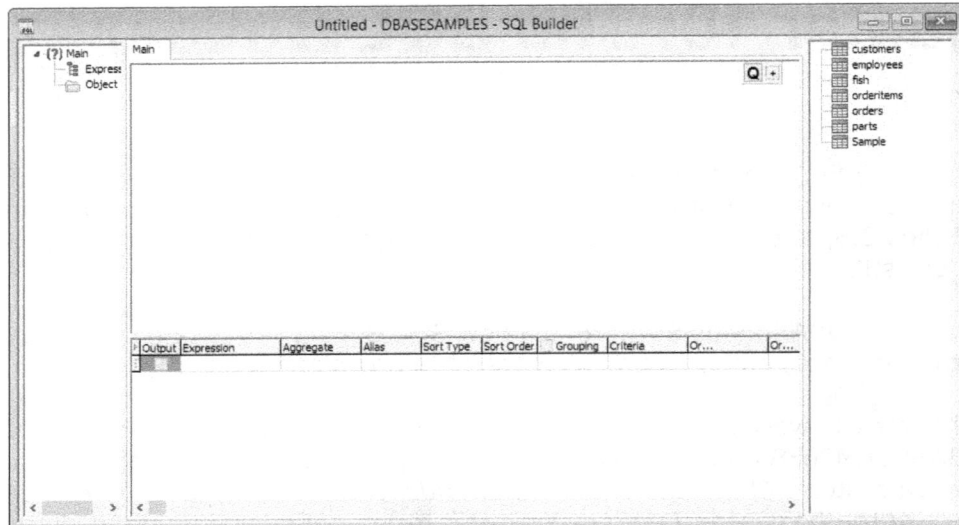

Figure 10-2

We want to work with the Customers table, so double-click that table from the list.

You should now get a floating window inside the main work area that contains all the fields in the table, with checkboxes. If you widen the pane on the left, you will see that it shows the name of the table there:

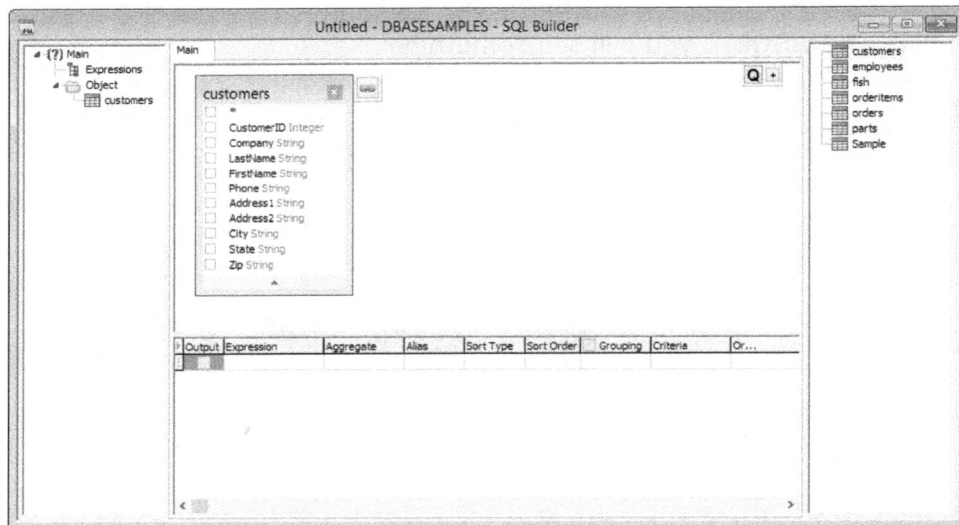

Figure 10-3

From here you should select the fields you wish to work with. For now, select all fields by clicking next to the asterisk (*).

This changes the display, both in the bottom and left panes:

208

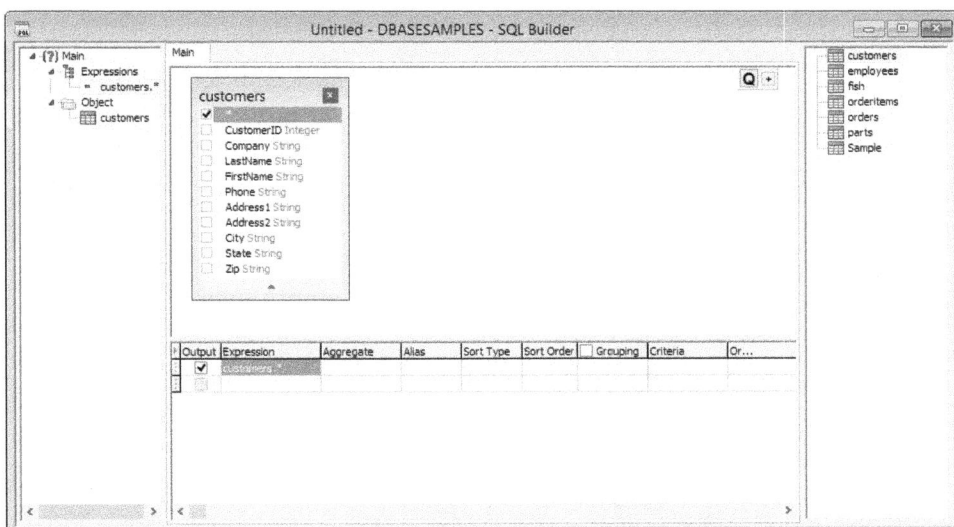
Figure 10-4

The difficulty is that if you want to do anything, such as sorting the data on a specific field (or fields), you cannot easily do that from here. If you uncheck the "*" and select all fields individually, you actually have more control:

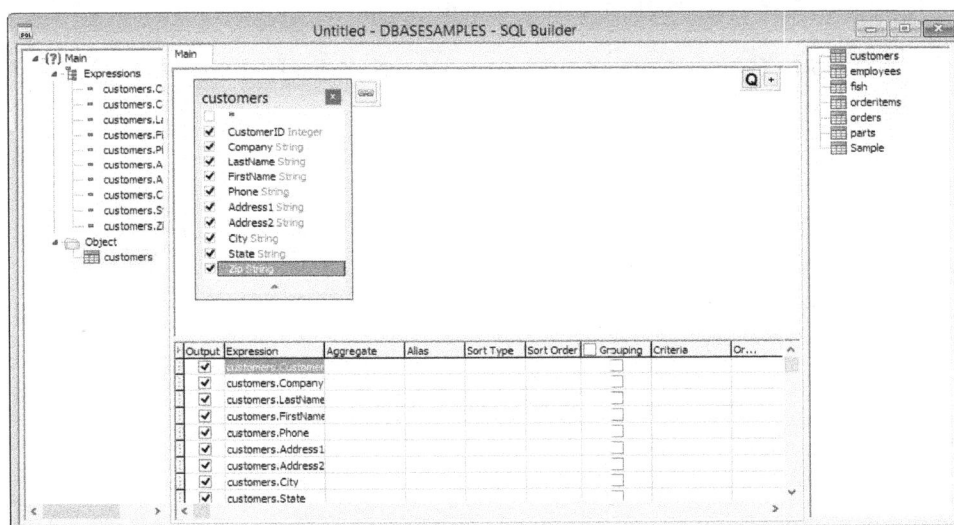
Figure 10-5

Once again, you might want to readjust the left pane's width a bit, so you can see more detail. You can also adjust the width of the "Expression" column in the grid in the bottom pane of this window.

Now if you wanted to sort on fields, you can select the specific field (use Company Name), the Sort Type, and set it to "Ascending". The screen will change again:

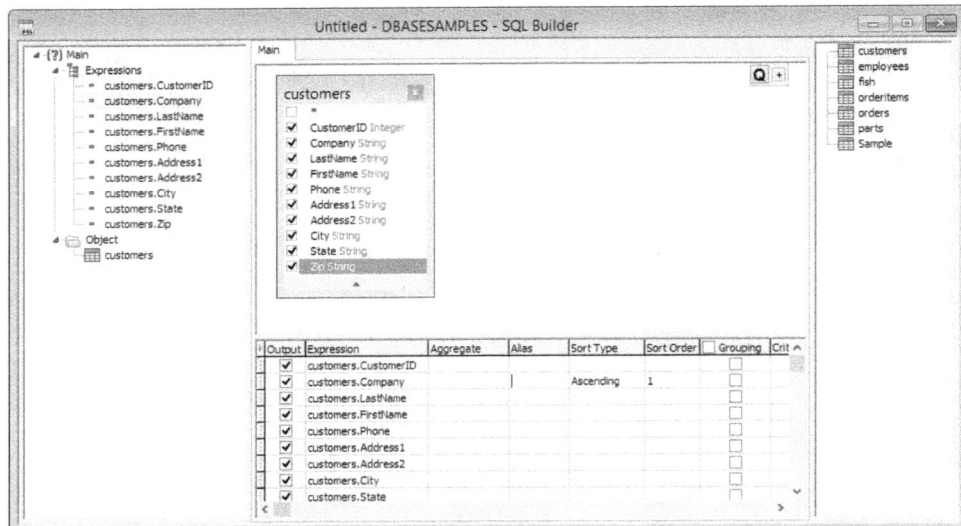

Figure 10-6

If you wanted to, you could select other fields to sort on, but for now we're keeping this simple. Save this (Ctrl+S) and name it "Customers". Close the SQL Builder and open the new SQL file in the Source Code Editor (right-click it ...).

In the Source Code Editor, you should see code that looks like:

```
--Database:DBASESAMPLES
Select customers.CustomerID,
  customers.Company,
  customers.LastName,
  customers.FirstName,
  customers.Phone,
  customers.Address1,
  customers.Address2,
  customers.City,
  customers.State,
  customers.Zip
From customers
Order By customers.Company
```

If you close the source code editor without making any changes, and then in the Navigator double-click the SQL file, you should see your data appear in a grid, sorted by the Company field:

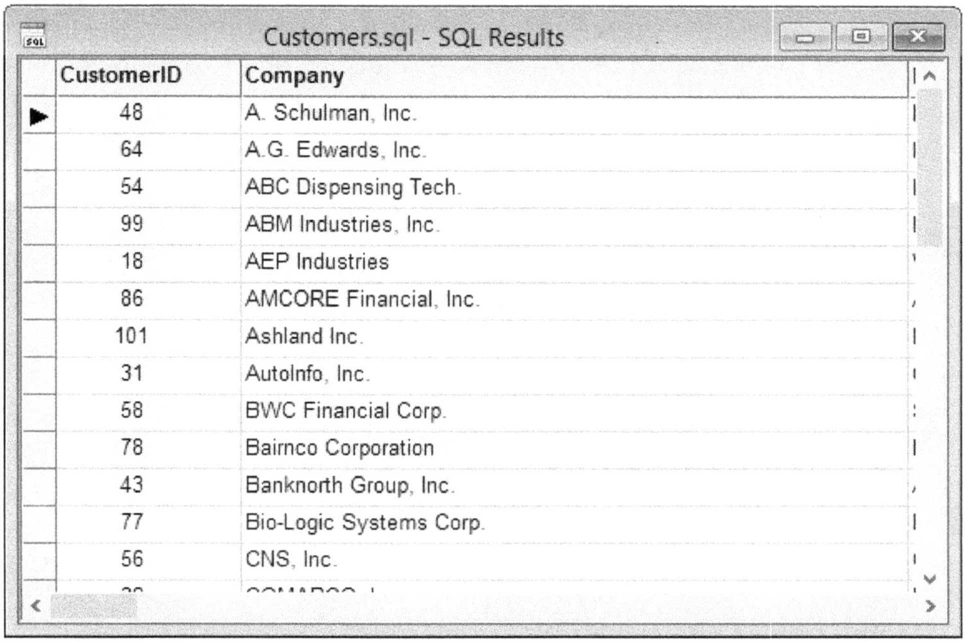

CustomerID	Company
48	A. Schulman, Inc.
64	A.G. Edwards, Inc.
54	ABC Dispensing Tech.
99	ABM Industries, Inc.
18	AEP Industries
86	AMCORE Financial, Inc.
101	Ashland Inc.
31	AutoInfo, Inc.
58	BWC Financial Corp.
78	Bairnco Corporation
43	Banknorth Group, Inc.
77	Bio-Logic Systems Corp.
56	CNS, Inc.

Figure 10-7

This is pretty simple. How would you use it beyond the actual SQL file?

> **NOTE**
> The form object has a *view* property, but apparently the format of the code streamed by the SQL Builder is not something that can be understood by the form in dBASE.

Using the SQL Generated in a Form

To use this in a form, examine the source code streamed out by the SQL Builder.

What exactly do you need here? If you wish to limit the fields, you can list the specific fields, although in this example we used all of them. Since we're only using one table in the SQL statement, we can remove the name of the table from the fieldnames. So what you end up with is:

```
select * from Customers order by Company
```

We will use that for the Query in a moment.

Create a new form in the Form Designer. Place a Database object on the design surface, set these properties:

- *name*: DBASESAMPLES
- *databaseName*: DBASESAMPLES
- *active*: true

Then place a Query object on the design surface and set these properties:

- *name:* CUSTOMERS
- *database*: DBASESAMPLES
  The Form Designer will change this to "form.dbasesamples"
- *sql*: select * from Customers order by Company
- *active*: true

Place a grid on the form, set the *dataLink* property to "Customers". At this point you could then specify the columns to display and more. But just looking at the simple form you will see that the customers are displayed in sorted sequence:

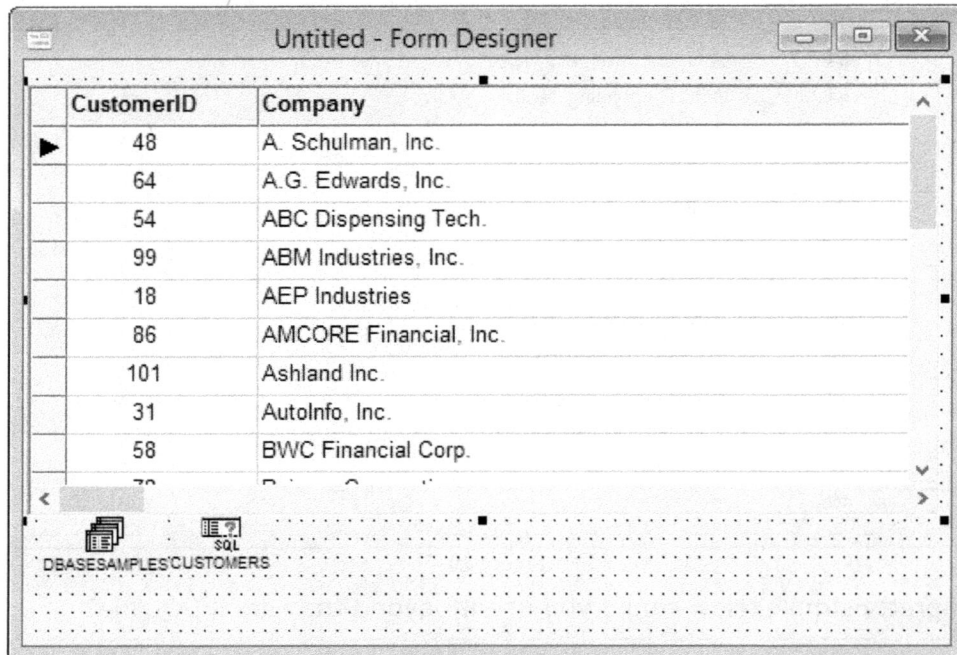

Figure 10-8

Obviously if you are using .DBF files, and have indexes, you might want to use the index instead, but this is just a starting point.

More Complex – Multiple Tables

The SQL designer is more useful when you need to get data from multiple tables. Using the same database as an example, if you wanted to get some information from one table to display with another, such as the OrderItems table, which has a link to the Parts table – which among other things has the name of the part, you could set up a query that showed the Description from the Parts table for the items in the OrderItems table.

Start a New SQL object in the Navigator the same way we did before, selecign the DBASESAMPLES database. Place the OrderItems table on the design surface (double-click from list of tables), and then place the Parts table on the design surface.

Select from the OrderItems table the fields "ItemNo", "PartID", "Quantity", and "Price".

Then drag the PartID over to the "PartsID" field in the "Parts" table. You should see a line appear showing the link.

In the grid below, click on the "orderitems.PartsID" field, click the down-arrow for the combobox, and select "parts.Description". Save and run the SQL. The grid that displays will show the Description instead of the Part ID. It may look at first like there is an error, but if you scroll down the data far enough, you should see that the PartID changes to a new item (and if you examined the data in the OrderItems table, this would be correct).

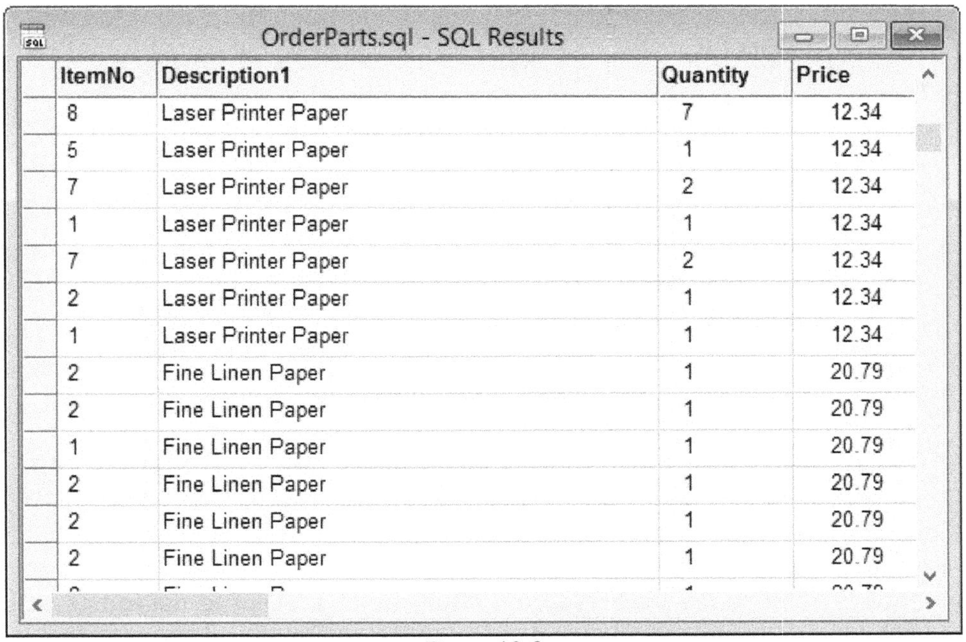

ItemNo	Description1	Quantity	Price
8	Laser Printer Paper	7	12.34
5	Laser Printer Paper	1	12.34
7	Laser Printer Paper	2	12.34
1	Laser Printer Paper	1	12.34
7	Laser Printer Paper	2	12.34
2	Laser Printer Paper	1	12.34
1	Laser Printer Paper	1	12.34
2	Fine Linen Paper	1	20.79
2	Fine Linen Paper	1	20.79
1	Fine Linen Paper	1	20.79
2	Fine Linen Paper	1	20.79
2	Fine Linen Paper	1	20.79
2	Fine Linen Paper	1	20.79

Figure 10-9

If you open the SQL file in the Source Code Editor, you will see the code:

```
--Database:DBASESAMPLES
Select orderitems.ItemNo,
  parts.Description As Description1,
  orderitems.Quantity,
  orderitems.Price
From orderitems
  Inner Join parts On orderitems.PartID = parts.PartID
```

This is where the SQL Builder becomes more useful to a developer – you can build the commands and determine how things like the joins work without having to try to visualize them on your own.

To use this in a form, you could use the SQL statement pretty much as shown. Since this query uses two tables, the table names become important for at least some of the fieldnames:

```
Select ItemNo, parts.Description as Description1, Quantity, Price
from OrderItems inner join parts on orderitems.partid =
parts.partid
```

The above is one statement.

Again, you can create a form, add a Database as shown previously. Then add a query object as shown. Set the *sql* property to the statement shown above, and then set the *active* property to *true*.

Set a grid on the form, set the *dataLink* property, readjust the grid a bit, and you should see something like:

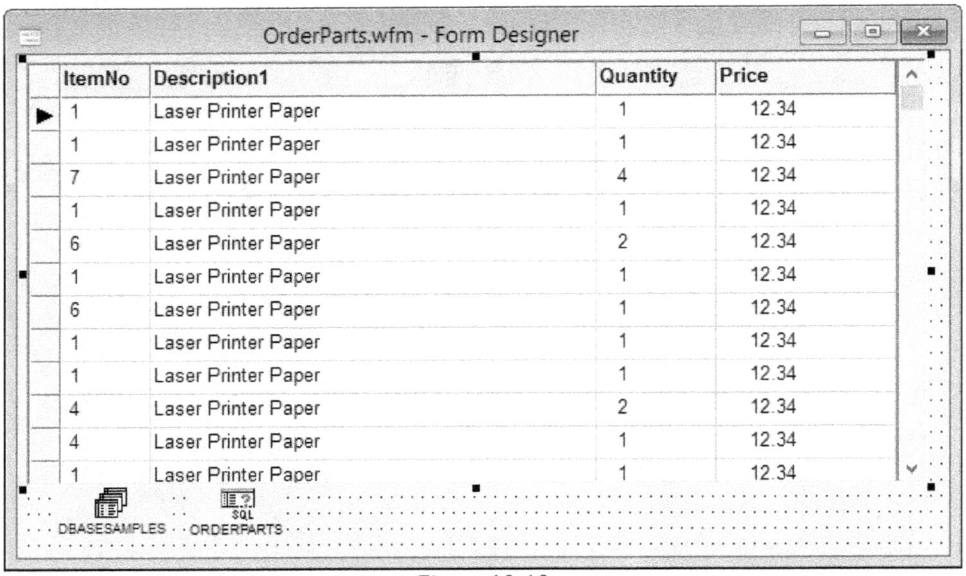

Figure 10-10

If you wanted to get really involved, you could build a SQL file using the SQL Builder that joined the tables necessary to create an invoice, then use that code elsewhere, such as in a Data Module, or a Report, or …

Be aware that the more complex the SQL statement, the less likely the data will be writeable. If you need to link tables in such a way that you can edit them, or use complex sort sequences, you should find other methods of doing so.

That said, the SQL Builder is a useful learning tool, if nothing else. It can help you get a better understanding of SQL.

Sample Code for This Chapter

The following is a listing of the sample code in the "Chapter 10" folder, if you downloaded it from my website. You may use the code contained in these forms for your own applications if you desire, with the caveat that credit be given appropriately.

- **Customers.sql** – SQL File created with SQL Builder as example in this chapter.
- **Customers.wfm** – Form using the SQL statement generated from the SQL file above.
- **OrderParts.sql** – SQL File created with SQL Builder as example in this chapter.
- **OrderParts.wfm** – Form using the SQL statement generated from the SQL file above.

Summary

This is a relatively short chapter, but it is meant to be a kind of overview on using the SQL Builder. This is not a tool I use much for my own applications, however there are developers who use this a lot. There are many ways to get to where you need to go, and this is just one tool in your toolbox to help you get there.

Chapter 11: The Data Module Designer

When dBASE Plus 2.8 was released the Data Module Designer was dQuery *(it was created quite some time earlier than dBASE Plus 2.8, but that was the version my previous books stopped at)*. Some people liked it, others didn't, but it did what was needed. It was a fairly complex tool, with many features built in, including import of data from external sources, export to external files, and more. However, it became a bit unwieldy and had bugs that made it difficult for some developers to use properly.

When dBASE Plus 8 was released, the developers removed dQuery from the product, and put in a more simple Data Module Designer. This is what is available in dBASE Plus releases 8 through 10.

Rumor has it that in a later version of dBASE, there will be a new and revised version of dQuery.

The Data Module Designer

The Data Module designer is available to create re-usable code that you can use in more than one form, report, etc. The resulting file is a Data Module. You can work with Custom Data Modules, and can subclass a Data Module from the Custom Data Module.

The concept of Custom Data Modules is the same as Custom Forms or Custom Reports, and these have been discussed in The dBASE Book in all three editions. For the purpose of just learning a bit about this tool, we will use a standard Data Module.

A Simple Data Module

To create a new Data Module, click on the "Data Modules" tab of the Navigator, and double-click "[New Data Module]". You will see a *very* simple design surface:

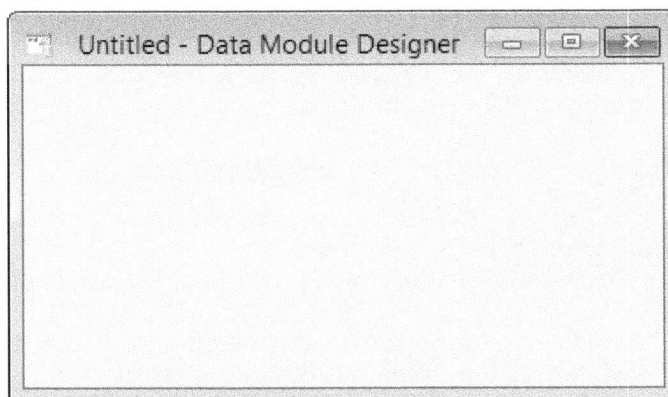

Figure 11-1

The Data Module Designer can work with Drag and Drop (drag tables from the Navigator to the surface), or you can add data objects from the Component Palette.

This first Data Module will use a single table. From the Component Palette drag a Database object to the surface, and set the following properties:

- *name*: DBASESAMPLES
- *database*: DBASESAMPLES
- *active*: true

Then drag a query object to the design surface and set these properties:

- *name*: Customers
- *database*: DBASESAMPLES
  The designer will change this to: form.dbasesamples
- *sql*: select * from customers
- *active*: true

To use the Company index (so the data is sorted by Company name), click the *rowset* object, the first button that appears, and find the *indexName* property. Select "Company" from the list.

You should see:

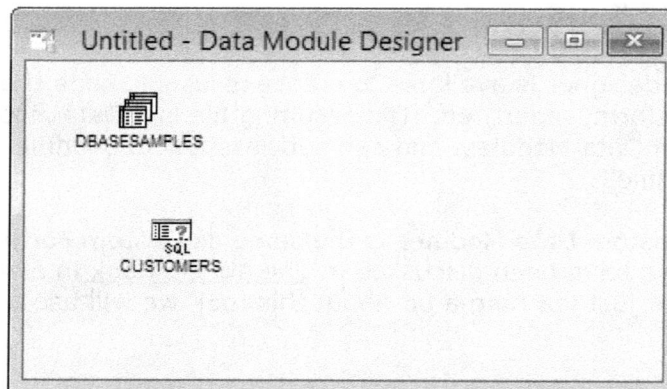

Figure 11-2

Save the Data Module as "Customers" and close the Data Module Designer.

Using a Data Module

Unlike a SQL file, you cannot "run" a Data Module. If you double-click a Data Module in the Navigator, it will open in the designer.

To use the Data Module with a form, you have three options:

1. Use the form's *dataModRef* property, which makes it more difficult to work with (the object references are unwieldy),
2. You can drag a Data Module onto the form's design surface (which we will do), or
3. Open the Data Module in the form's code and access the data that way. This option, while flexible, makes it difficult to work with in the Form Designer, because the Designer does not execute the form's startup code, so it does not know about the Data Module. You can see this in the application created in Chapters 4-6 of this book, if you are interested.

We will use the second option here.

Create a form, set any properties you might wish (such as the *metric* property), and then with the form open, click on the Navigator. Drag the Customers Data Module to the design surface:

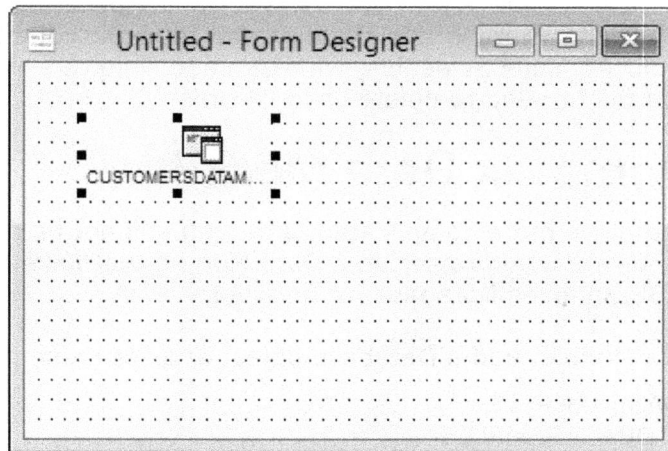

Figure 11-3

If you click on the form, and examine the Inspector, scroll to find the *rowset* property. You should see:

```
form.customersdatamodule1.customers.rowset
```

You can now add controls, such as a grid or entryfields (and of course other form controls), *dataLink* them to fields of the table referenced by the form's *rowset* property, and you are set.

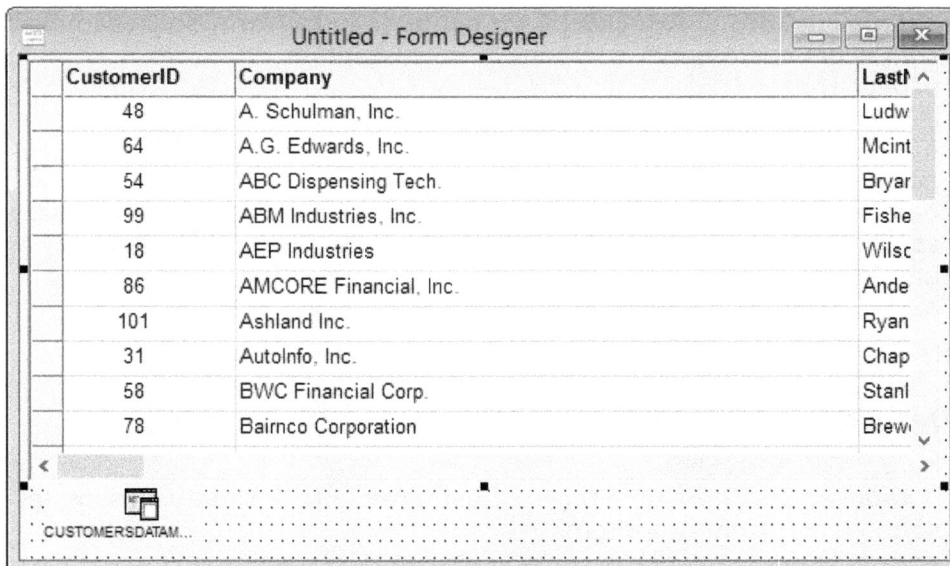

Figure 11-4

This is however awfully simple, and you could have done this without a Data Module, it would actually be easier to just place the Database and Query objects directly on the form. We have done nothing here that would be difficult to reproduce in different forms, etc.

The power of the Data Module is that you can set up complicated links between tables, and as noted elsewhere in this chapter, add reusable code that can be used in different places (such as dealing with Cascade Deletes – if you delete a parent record, you might need to delete child records ...).

A More Complex Data Module

The following example is more complicated, although still not as complex as can be done. For this we are going to set up a Data Module that links together the tables in the dBASE Samples Database for an invoice.

Create a new Data Module, add a Database object and set these properties:

- *name*: DBASESAMPLES
- *database*: DBASESAMPLES
- *active*: true

Add a Query object and set these properties:

- *name*: ORDERS
- *database*: DBASESAMPLES (if not set already to "form.dbasesamples")
- *sql*: select * from orders
- *active*: true

Add a Query object and set these properties:

- *name*: CUSTOMERS
- *database*: DBASESAMPLES (if not set already to "form.dbasesamples")
- *sql*: select customerid, company from customers
- *active*: true

Add a Query object and set these properties:

- *name*: EMPLOYEES
- *database*: DBASESAMPLES (if not set already to "form.dbasesamples")
- *sql*: select employeeid, firstname||" "||lastname as fullname from employees
- *active*: true

(Note we are creating a calculated field for the employee name ...)

Add a Query object and set these properties:

- *name*: ORDERITEMS
- *database*: DBASESAMPLES (if not set already to "form.dbasesamples")
- *sql*: select * from orderitems
- *active*: true

Add a Query object and set these properties:

- *name*: PARTS
- *database*: DBASESAMPLES (if not set already to "form.dbasesamples")
- *sql*: select * from parts
- *active*: true

We now have all the controls, the fun part will be setting the links between the tables. Unfortunately, the Data Module Designer does not have the ability to visually show the links, as the SQL Builder does (see previous chapter of this book).

We need to know which fields link to which fields in different tables. If you examine the Orders table you will see for example that we have a Customer Number field, as well as an Employee Number field.

If we want to link these to the appropriate tables, we will need to set indexes, and then other properties. Click on the Customers query and in the Inspector find the *rowset* property, click it, and click the button that appears. Set these properties:

- *indexName*: CUSTOMERID

We will repeat this for the Employees table with the following changes:

- *indexName*: EMPLOYEEID

Once we have done that, we need to set up lookups for the fields in the Order that match. Click on the Orders query, find the *rowset* and click the "I" button and:

- *fields*: Click the "I" button
  - *CustomerID*: click the "I" button
  - *lookupRowset*: CUSTOMERS
  - Back up to the fields list (use the back arrow button)
  - *EmployeeID*: click the "I" button
  - *lookupRowset*: EMPLOYEES

For the Parts query, we only need to do a little:

- *indexName*: PARTID

It gets a bit more complicated for the OrderItems table (or does it?):

- *indexName*: ORDERID
- *masterRowset*: ORDERS
  The form designer will change this to: form.orders.rowset
- *masterFields*: ORDERID
- *fields*: click this and click the "I" button
  - *partID*: click the "I" button
  - *lookupRowset*: "PARTS"

The purpose here is to set up the lookup for the Description of the part …

Save this as "Invoices". You should have something that looks like:

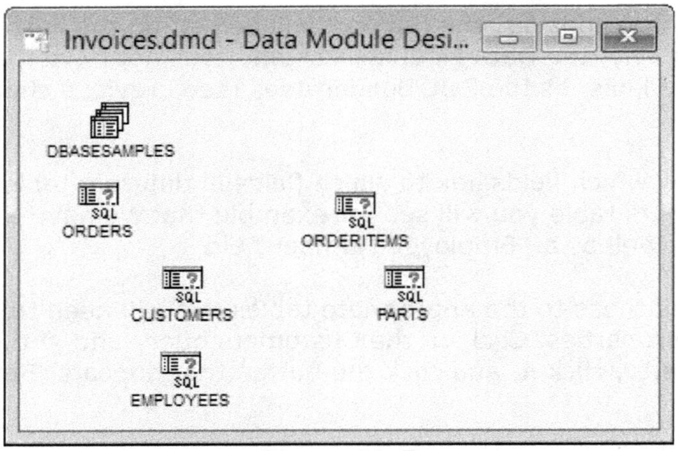

Figure 11-5

Using This Data Module

To use this on a form, there are many things we could do. For this example, a couple of grids are all that are necessary, although to make it truly useful you would really want to set things up with entryfields for some fields, and more.

Create a new form, set whatever properties you might wish (such as *metric*), and drag the Data Module "Invoices" to the design surface from the Navigator. Note that the form's *rowset* property should read:

```
form.invoicesdatamodule1.orders.rowset
```

If it does not, then change it by selecting the Orders table from the combobox.

Drag a grid to the surface, and set these properties:

- *datalink*: Orders
  The designer will change this to:
  form.invoicesdatamodule1.orders.rowset
- Resize the grid
- *columns*: click on this and click the first button (opens the Columns Property Builder dialog), and select the following fields:
  - ORDERS.OrderID
  - ORDERS.CustomerID
  - ORDERS.EmployeeID
  - ORDERS.OrderDate
  - ORDERS.ShipDate
  - Click "OK"
  - Change Column Widths, and if you feel the need, change the text on the columnHeadings (such as "fullname" should probably be "Employee")

Readjust column widths to make everything look good.

Add another grid to the form, and set these properties:

- *dataLink*: OrderItems
  The designer will change this to:
  form.invoicesdatamodule1.orderitems.rowset
- Resize the grid

- *columns*: click on this and click the first button (opens the Columns Property Builder dialog), and select the following fields:
    - ORDERITEMS.ItemNo
    - ORDERITEMS.PartID
    - ORDERITEMS.Quantity
    - ORDERITEMS.Price

Readjust column widths to make this look good, and after a bit of tinkering, you should see this in the Form Designer:

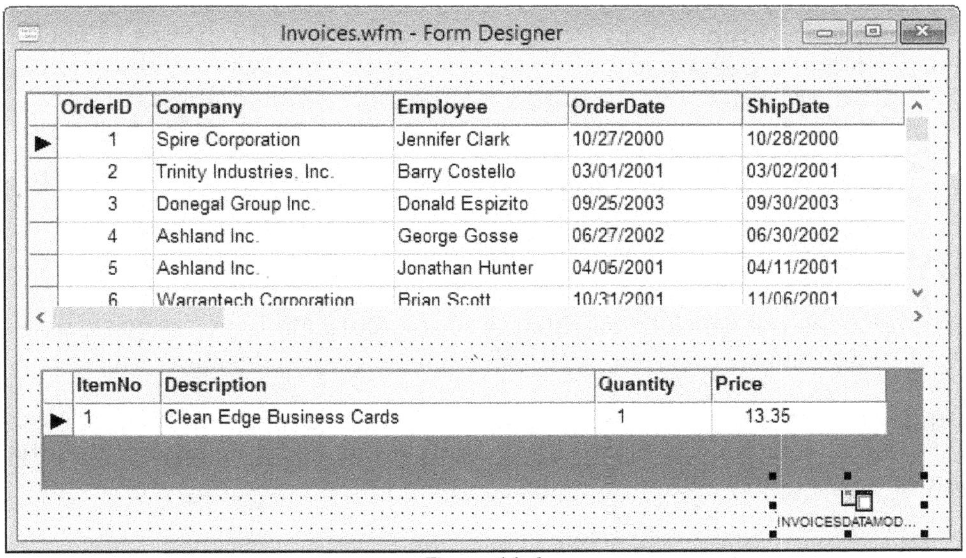

Figure 11-6

If you now run the form and click on various orders:

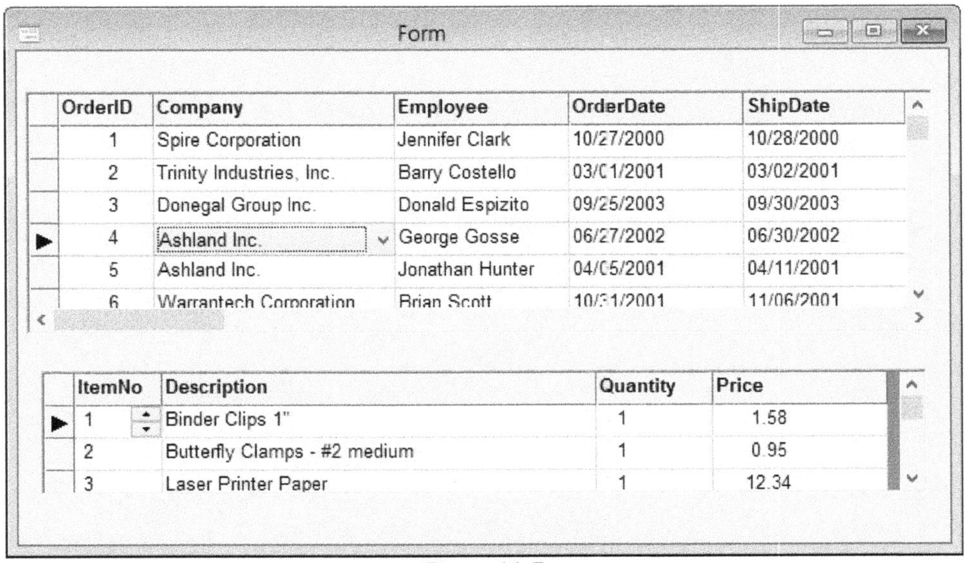

Figure 11-7

As a form, this is not the prettiest or the best designed, but it should help see how useful the Data Module is. With all the different links set up, you can do quite a bit. And again, if you added code (such as deleting an Order, you might want to delete the OrderItems associated with it – this is called a Cascade

Delete), the code could be used in multiple forms. You could use this same Data Module as it stands right now to create an invoice report.

Sample Code for This Chapter

The following is a listing of the sample code in the "Chapter 11" folder, if you downloaded it from my website. You may use the code contained in these forms for your own applications if you desire, with the caveat that credit be given appropriately.

- **Customers.dmd** – Data Module created to show the basics of using the Data Module Designer.
- **Customers.wfm** – Form used with the Data Module above.
- **Invoices.dmd** – Data Module created to show the basics of using the Data Module Designer.
- **Invoices.wfm** – Form used with the Data Module above.

Summary

This chapter does not get into all aspects of the Data Module Designer, and is meant as an overview.

You can get a better feel for a Data Module with lots of code in it, by going over Chapters 4-6 of this book, where a Data Module has code for adding/updating and deleting rows of tables.

Chapter 12: ActiveX Controls

The developers at dBASE, LLC have made huge improvements in how dBASE interacts with ActiveX controls, and have made arrangements to deploy some ActiveX controls with dBASE itself. Some of the improvements may not seem like much, but if you have struggled to work with ActiveX controls in dBASE you should find that over time the software is *better* at working with them.

While I won't go into huge detail for all of the new controls, I thought it might be useful to have an idea what we have, and the basics of using the ones that are installed with dBASE. It should be noted that you have the right to distribute these controls with your applications at no extra charge – that is both the dJv and Catalyst controls. I have provided examples for all of these controls, but they are not necessarily "fully functional", they are examples, designed to help you get started with them.

The dJv Controls (JEDI)

These are from an Open Source project (JEDI) that appears to have been stopped, and were included starting with dBASE Plus 8. They are made available to you for use on your forms. These include some interesting items, with a small amount of information below (I have included *some* sample forms in the Source Code folder for this chapter).

dJVClockX Control

This is a clock that can be placed on a form to show the current time, the date, even set an alarm. To use this, you need to create a form, in the Form Designer on the Component Palette, select this control and drag it to the form. You may want to widen it a bit so you can see the time.

Even in the form designer, the time is being updated without making any changes to the control:

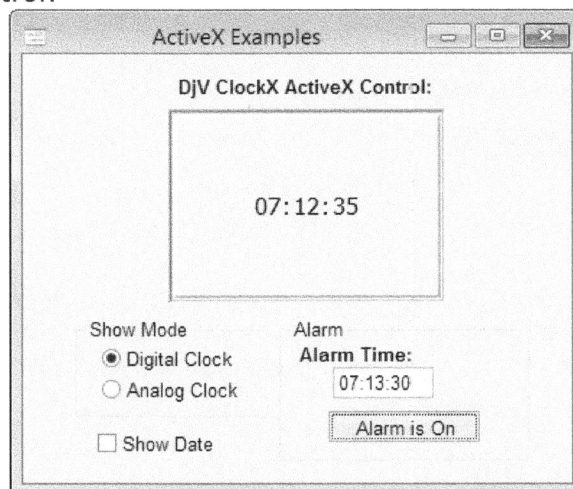

Figure 12-1

To really find out more about your options, in the Inspector, click on the *nativeObject* property, and the "I" button. Now you have access to the properties, events and methods of the control. A few basic things that you can do:

- *showDate*: defaults to false, set it to true, and you now see the date.
- *showMode*: defaults to 0 – digital, you can change it to 1 – analog, and get a standard clock with hour, minute and second hands … however this mode will not show the date, even if the *showDate* property is true.

Some of the features don't appear to do much, although you would want to tinker more. In the example form, setting the alarm will simply display a MsgBox. Using the PLAY SOUND command, or other techniques, you could do a lot more with it.

dJvDirectoryListboxX Control

This allows you to see the current folder structure, work through it, navigate around on a drive, and so on, simply by clicking – with no code required by the developer. It is remarkably easy to work with. Suggested setting:

- *scrollBars*: 2 – ssVertical

Using the event handler *onChange* you can have the form do something with the *directory* property. The example form displays the currently selected directory in an entryfield, but you could obviously use this to obtain files, and so on …

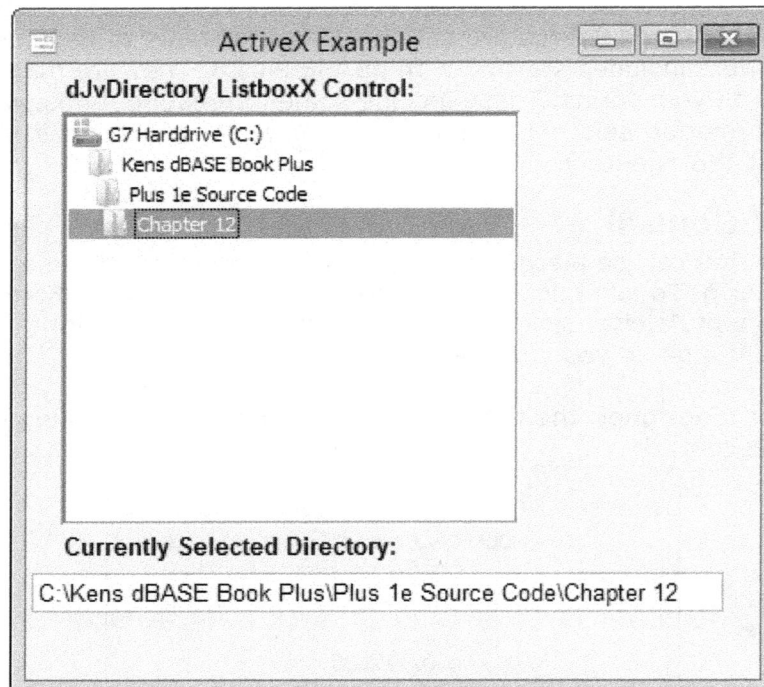

Figure 12-2

One caveat – this control will change the current active directory in dBASE *(or your application)*. If you want it to do that, great, if don't, you should save the current directory when the form opens, and restore the current directory when the form closes.

dJvDriveComboX Control

This is what it sounds like – a control to list the drives on your computer and to select the drive. You could probably use this in conjunction with the ListboxX control shown previously.

You can get the currently selected drive using the property *displayName* (from the *nativeObject* of the control).

Figure 12-3

dJvFileListBoxX Control

This again is what it sounds like – it gives a listing of the files in a specific folder. Properties that are useful right away (with little experimentation on my part):

- *Directory*: You can point to the folder you want to be looking in
- *Mask*: defaults to *.*, but you can use this to limit the files displayed
- *Filename*: Currently selected file – notice that this provides the full path

And the *onChange* event handler will let you determine what file was selected:

A quick example in the source code folder I am currently working with:

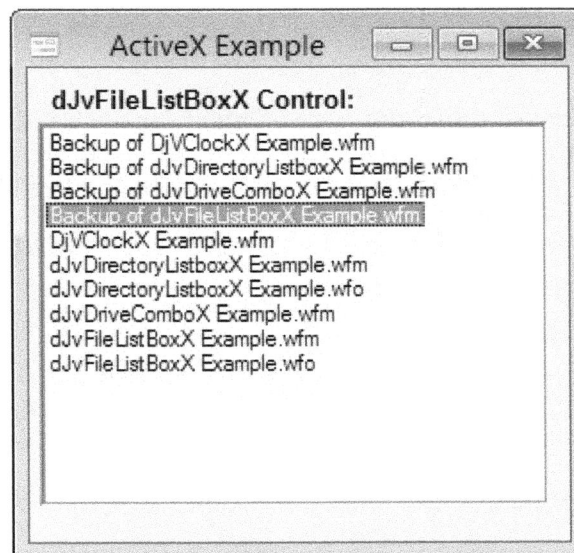

Figure 12-4

This next example uses all three of the controls that deal with the file structure in dBASE:

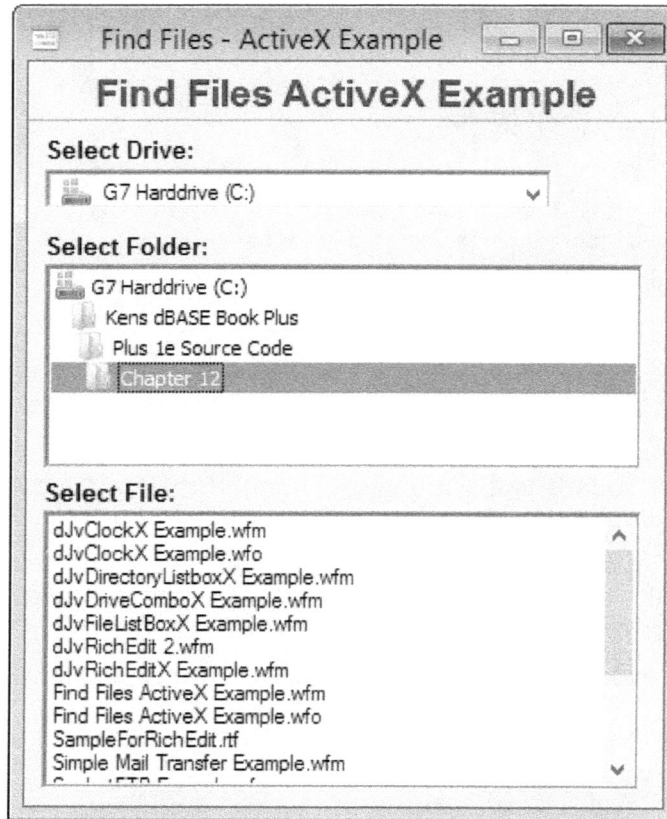

Figure 12-5

For this to work, we have to use the *nativeObject* for each of the first two controls using the *onChange* event handler to modify settings for the others, so selecting a drive will change the *directory* property of the directory control, and selecting a folder in that control will change the list of files displayed, and in this case, selecting a file will output the name of the file in the Output pane of the Command window.

dJvRichEditX Control

This is a Rich Text Format edit control, designed to read and write text in a Rich Text File (RTF) format. This is a fairly standardized file format, one that Windows "WordPad" understands, as does Word (and most word processors).

The *text* property is of course the most important, as it will contain the text to display/edit.

As an ActiveX control it does not have a *dataLink* property to link this to a field in a table. You could, during navigation on a form, update the text property of the control.

This is the only help I can find for this control:

```
http://wiki.delphi-jedi.org/wiki/JVCL_Help:TJvRichEdit
```

It's not exactly the most helpful, as the project appears to have been stopped by the developers who were working on it, and most of the "help" just leads to blank pages. There is limited help with dBASE for this control in the OLH.

The control does not come with a toolbar to handle formatting of text, so you have to build your own, as well as understanding some basics about how Rich Text Formatting works. Rich Text Format is not as easy to understand as HTML. While it is pretty powerful, it is very complicated. For example, any document (or field in a table, if you prefer) must begin with code that looks something like:

```
{\rtf1\ansi\deff0 {\fonttbl {\f0 Calibri; }}
```

And it must end with a curly brace (}). The tricky thing in the code above is the Font Table (fonttbl). You have to define at least one font, each font is separated by a semicolon from the others, so if you need multiple fonts it might look like:

```
{\fonttbl {\f0 Calibri; \f1 Times New Roman; }}
```

And so on. Fonts are referenced by the tag \fn where 'n' is a number. If you wanted your users to have access to different fonts, your code would have to be able to modify the font table *(and stream it back out)*. If you want to use colors for text, you have to define a color table, and again if you want your users to have access to the ability to select colors, your code would need to be able to modify *(and stream back out)* the color table.

Tagging text requires begin and end characters, so if you want to bold text:

```
\bBoldFaced Text\b0
```

and so on. This is based on creating an RTF file and then opening it in Windows Notepad, which shows all the tags. In addition, there is *no* documentation that shows how to change the formatting of text contained in the control and have it display properly. Just replacing "BoldFaced Text" with "\bBoldFaced Text\b0" does not display the text in bold, it shows it with the characters. Ivar B. Jessen has done some work with this control and posted it in the dBASE newsgroups, but it just seems like more work than it is worth.

What Ivar found was that this control requires the text be surrounded by the the font reference "\rtf1" and then "\b" to start the formatting, but rather than ending with the "\b0" tag, the whole set of text must be surrounded by curly braces. So the text would instead look like:

```
{\rtf1\bBoldFaced Text}
```

This is not really standard RTF, but I imagine that if you worked with it, it would display in most RTF enabled editors okay.

The form shown in the screen shot (Figure 12-6) is based heavily on work by Ivar, with some enhancements. Everything is in a container, so if you wanted to re-use it, you could pull the whole out into a .CC file, make sure you get the code for the button onClick event handlers, and then you could re-use this.

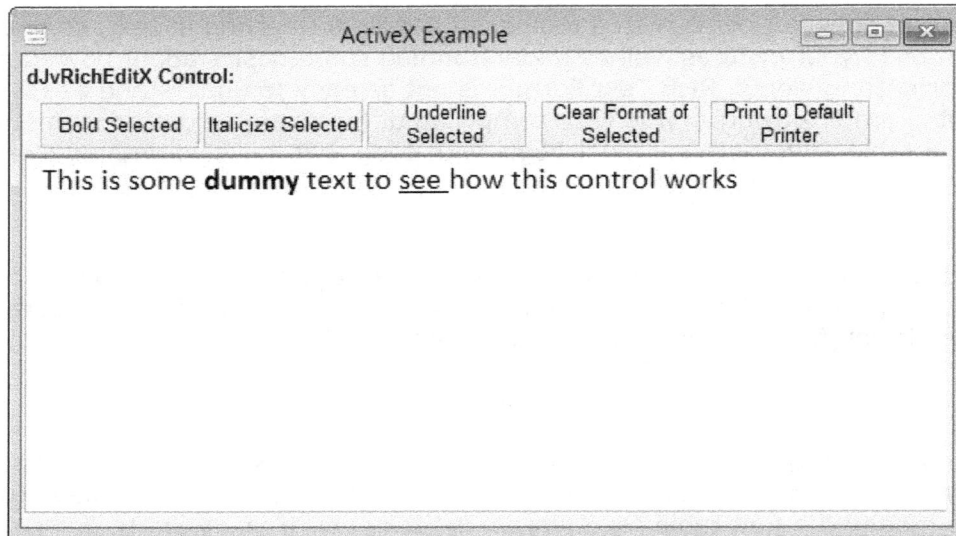

Figure 12-6

In the long run, if you need formatting abilities, you may want to either find a commercial RTF control, or use the built-in abilities of the Editor object in dBASE to work with HTML – it works, it's pretty easy to use, and most software understands HTML as well *(and frankly, RTF is kind of an outdated technology)*.

> ### 📝 NOTE
> There is a known issue with ActiveX controls that when placed on a report, what prints is not what is expected. This is an issue with reports and ActiveX controls, however, not this specific control. Do not rely on this ability with reports, at least for now. This ActiveX control has its own print method, but that is not useful in a report.

The Catalyst Controls

These were added in dBASE Plus 9, and are available for use with your applications. These controls allow you to perform actions such as FTP (File Transfer Protocol) – uploading and downloading files from a file server, managing the files; HTTP (HyperText Transfer Protocol) – uploading/downloading web pages and running web scripts; Post Office and Email; and "Windows Sockets" – the ability to plug in (as it were) to Windows and access features that are a bit more complicated …

Keep in mind that these controls are available for use "as is", and if you need more capabilities than what is provided, you may end up needing to purchase a license for a more robust version of some of them *(the SMTP control comes to mind, as while it works, .it is fairly limited in its functionality)*.

Documentation for these controls can be found online at:

```
http://sockettools.com/webhelp/activex/index.html
```

The example code is typically in Visual BASIC, but if you look at it you should be able to work out some details.

The controls themselves are non-visual controls – you can place them on a form and work with them, but you would typically use other controls to get information, display information, pass information back to the ActiveX control, and so on.

The samples that I have produced here are done using Forms, with the goal of obtaining the information interactively, and then calling the ActiveX controls as needed to do what they need to do.

You can access these controls programmatically in a fashion similar to:

```
// SMTP (Email):
oSMTP = new OleAutoClient("SocketTools.SmtpClient.8" )
// FTP:
oFTP = new OleAutoClient("SocketTools. FtpClient.8" )
```

Bernard Mouille provided a simple program (TestSocketWrench.prg) that I have included in the Source Code folder for this chapter that tests the various tools just to see which ones you have the ability to use. It will return "OK" or "No" for each. Once you have them instantiated (as above), then you can access properties, events and methods just as the samples shown here do. To inspect the oSMTP object and view its properties and such:

```
inspect( oSMTP )
```

The above command could be issued in a program *(although would not be useful in a running application)* or from the Command Window in dBASE.

SocketTools File Transfer Protocol Control 8.0:

For FTP Transfers to work, you need to know the address where you wish to upload files to or download them from; the username, the password and if the host uses a different FTP Port than the default, you would need to know the port number. This is so that you can connect to the server.

Once you connect to the server, you need the file, you need to know where on the server you are saving it to, and so on.

The control itself being nonvisual requires that you build the interface, and provide the information necessary. You can do some of this programmatically (and for some applications that might make the most sense). However, for some situations (such as this demonstration), you may want to provide an interface that asks for all the required information.

The example given here is based on a form by Bernard Mouille. I have worked with the interface a bit to make it easier to understand and use. However, Bernard spent a lot of his free time working out how to get this control to work properly, and I (with his permission) am using a lot of his code in this example form.

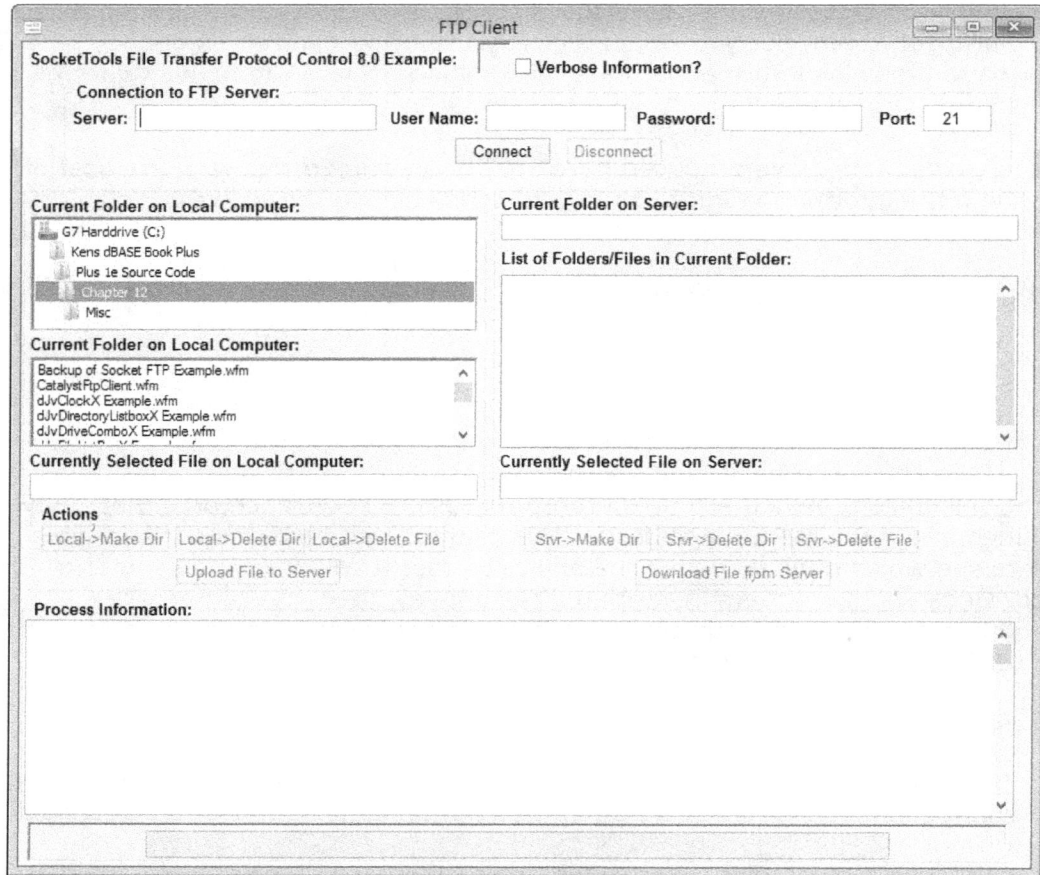

Figure 12-7

The little inset square by the title of the ActiveX is the actual control. The control itself is not interactive, but there is no *visible* property. I could have hidden it by placing it on another page of the form, or under some of the other controls. When in the Form Designer, you can just click the control, click on *nativeObject* and then the "I" button, and you will see all the properties, events and methods for the control.

One difficulty with this control is that the file path on the server has to be exact, matching case, etc. The problem is the error that comes back if you get it wrong is "Access Denied", which is a bit confusing.

You have options to download files, to get lists of files on the server, rename files on the server, delete files on the server, and more. This form does a LOT of these, but it doesn't handle multiple file uploads or downloads, it doesn't handle renaming anything on the server (or local computer).

See the comments at the beginning of the form in the Source Code Editor to note the use of various controls, including a Password Mask entryfield *(hides the password entered)*, and the dJv Folder and FileList controls, I copied the file INI.CC from the dUFLP, to handle saving the last server connected to ….

There is also a sample program "TestFTP.prg" that is extracted from an application of my own. It uploads a series of files to a server after generating them, updating a website. See comments in the code (I pulled the information needed to connect, etc. – to use this program you would need to fill in a few things which are commented in the code).

SocketTools Hypertext Transfer Protocol Control 8.0:

This control is designed to work with HTTP file transfers (upload/download), and Script Execution (running scripts on a web page). I spent a small amount of time on this one, because I feel that except for running scripts, you can do the rest with FTP. It might be useful if you do not have access to the FTP server, I suppose. The screen shot below is an example of the example form in action:

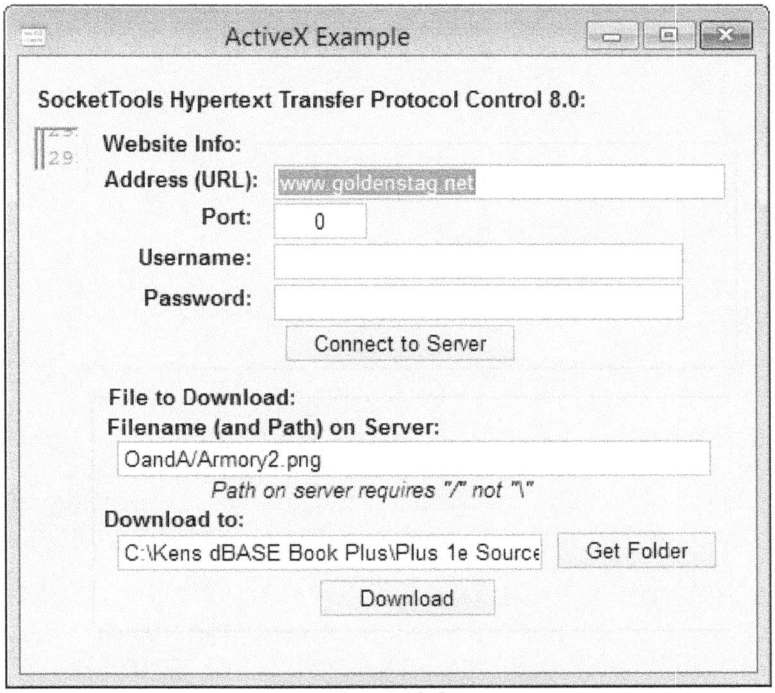

Figure 12-8

This downloaded just fine, but I should warn you *(and this is in the header documentation for the source code as well)* that I have not done thorough testing with this control – I did not try uploads, I did not deal with a server that required username and password, and I have not attempted to run web scripts. I will leave those exercises to you, gentle reader.

SocketTools Post Office Control 8.0:

This control gives you access to all the mail in a users' inbox, assuming you set everything up correctly. I spent the good part of one morning experimenting with this control, and have included in the Source Code folder for the chapter a form ("Post Office Example.wfm"). I used the online help to give me what I needed for this.

The examples require you fill in some information. This form retrieves the message headers for the user, and parses them. The form stores that information in a table called simply "Email", then loads the headers into a grid. It then allows you to *attempt* to view the contents of the message, but it appears the dBASE editor control is a bit limited and many of the emails I attempted to load did not display properly *(and threw an error, which I have trapped in the code ...)*. If you combined this with the SMTP control (described next), you could do a lot with email from within your own application!

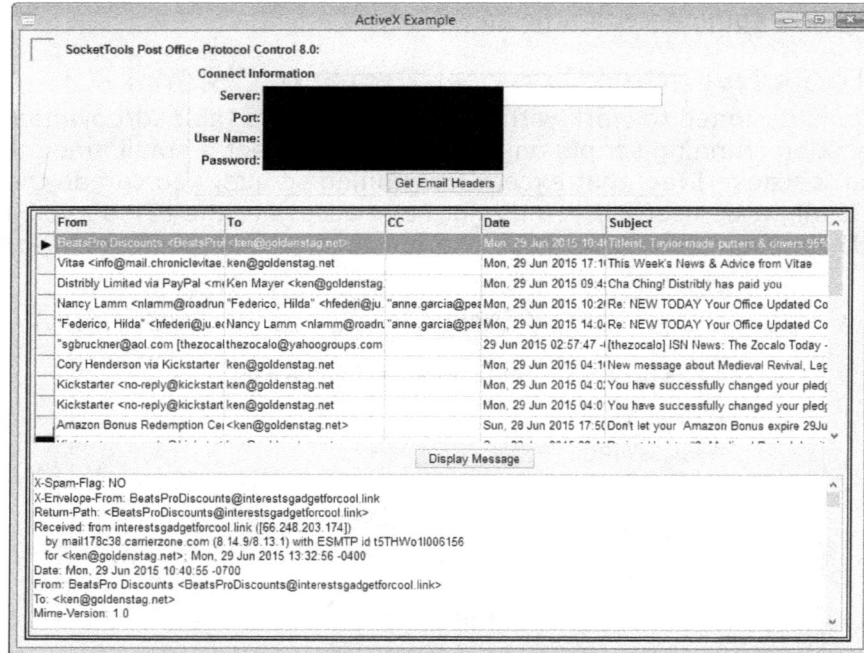

Figure 12-9

Note that I put a black block over the Connection information section on the screen shot, as this is my email server and I don't want to be giving that information away .... The data is sorted so that the most recent email is on top of the grid. The grid columns are sizable so you can drag them around ...

SocketTools Simple Mail Transfer Protocol Control 8.0:

Many developers ask in the newsgroups about sending email from dBASE, so I felt it was a good idea to give an example of using this control. While this control is limited, it can be used for some basic email services, such as setting up a simple form for a user to send bug-reports or feedback to the developer.

This is a bit complicated, as you need to know a lot about the different email protocols and which one is being used by the mail server you are connecting to. There are four main types:

- MIME (Multipurpose Internet Mail Extensions) – File attachments, HTML formatted messages, and others are covered by this standard. *(Catalyst has a control not included in the ones that come with dBASE called the "Mail Message Control", which handles more email options ...)*
- POP3 (Post Office Protocol v. 3) – used to retrieve messages from a users' mailbox on the server. *(Useful for the Post Office Control noted above.)*
- IMAP4 (Internet Message Access Protocol v.4) – used to manage information in the users' mailbox on the server. *(Useful for the Post Office Control ...)*
- SMTP (Simple Mail Transfer Protocol) used to deliver messages to one or more recipients.

The last is what this particular control is about. This control, according to the Catalyst documents implements standard and extended SMTP protocols.

To create an email message using these controls, you have to compose the message, if you are adding attachments, then do that, and finally you need to attempt to send the message.

Initial Setup

The initial setup is to establish the mail server, etc. You will need to know:

- **Host/Email Server Name**
- **Port** if server uses a port other than 25, which is the default. If the server requires authentication, it may use 587, but also may use 465. You should be sure ... Port 25 is often blocked to prevent spam.
- **User Name** – required to connect, a username and
- **Password**
- **Authentication** – You should also know if the server requires authentication

Compose the Header

The email must be plain text, and must include a header that is *very* specific – this is based on the MIME RFC 822 format. After a *huge* amount of trial and error, what I have determined appears to work is:

```
// MIME Header:
cOutput  = "" // empty string
cOutput += "From: "+ cFrom + EOL
cOutput += "To: "+ cTo + EOL
// Date is put into the header by the control ...
cOutput += "Subject: " + cSubject + EOL
cOutput += "Content-Type: text/plain; charset=us-ascii" + EOL
cOutput += "Content-Transfer-Encoding: 7bit" + EOL
cOutput += "MIME-Version: 1.0" + EOL
cOutPut += EOL
// End of MIME Header
```

The *cFrom* and *cTo* variables would be determined somewhere in earlier code. EOL is defined as a pre-processor directive, although it could simply be a variable, as Carriage Return + Line Feed (CRLF), or:

```
CHR(10)+CHR(13)
```

There must be a blank line after the MIME Header *(shown above)*.

Compose the Message

The message apparently really only works with plain text with this control, although the documentation makes it sound like you can do more, I have fumbled around with this for a while, and this is all I can get is plain text. A simple example of the body of a message might be:

```
// BODY
cOutput += "First line of text for message." + EOL
cOutput += "Second line of text for message." + EOL
cOutput += EOL
// END OF BODY
```

Note that each line again must end with the EOL character. If wanted a blank line between paragraphs, you would need to add that ... And note that the body must also end with a blank line.

Send the Message

There is a sendMessage() method of the oSMTL control, which requires the "From" and "To" email addresses, as well as the output or message text – which includes the full MIME header. When this works (my latest test does not seem to work and I have no idea why), it parses part of the MIME header, adds the appropriate date information, and a message ID.

Sample Code

In the source code for this chapter are a program (TestSMTP.prg) – this was my "testing ground", but you would need to insert values for variables; and a form (Simple Mail Transfer Example.wfm). It should be noted that at least one user wasn't able to get the sample code to work, receiving an error that read:

```
"This product is not licensed to perform this operation!"
```

Unfortunately, I honestly have no clue how to fix this.

This is an example of the form in the Source Code folder. I have been able to use this to successfully connect to, and send email through my domain hosted on Earthlink, which requires authentication to use, and so on:

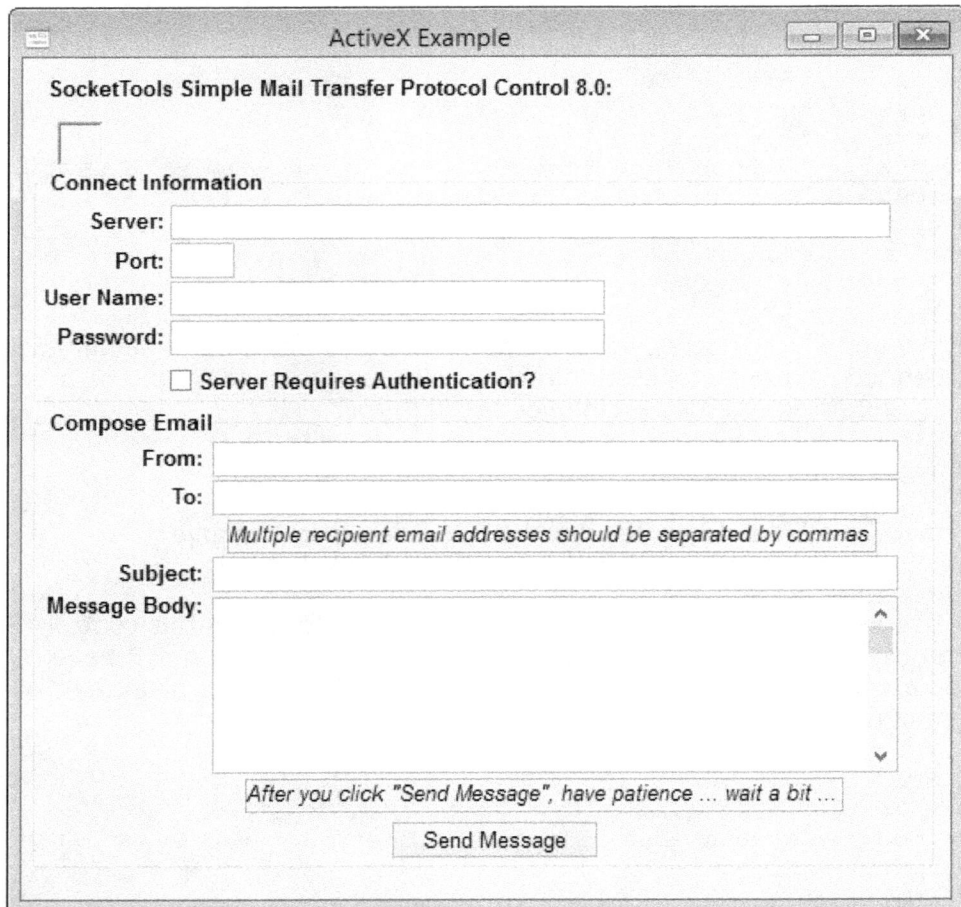

Figure 12-10

A bit of testing with formatting the Message Body, and I quickly discovered that the settings I am using for outgoing email end up not interpreting the HTML when it comes through. Plain text works perfectly fine, and pressing enter to start new paragraphs works *(the standard editor control in dBASE will insert the correct CR/LF for end of line)*, but sending HTML formatting ends up displaying the tags in the body of the message. There may be a way to change that, but I will leave that to you, the reader.

Need More?

Do you need to do more? For example, do you wish to send attachments? Then you would either need to purchase a full license to this control *(above and beyond the free license that comes with dBASE)*, or you can see what else is out there. Suggestions from users in the newsgroups:

- **Jmail** (written in Java): http://sourceforge.net/projects/javamailclient/
- **The Blat:** http://www.blat.net/
- **DiMac** w3JMail v 4.5:
  http://www.dimac.net/default2.asp?M=Products/MenuCOM.asp&P=Products/w3JMail/start.htm
- **Chilkat:** http://www.chilkatsoft.com/email-activex.asp
- **MarshallSoft**: https://www.marshallsoft.com/

SocketWrench Windows Sockets Control 8.0

This control was designed by Catalyst to assist developers in writing TCP/IP Client/Server applications.

> This works with Internet (and Intranet) protocols to communicate using SSL (Secure Sockets Layer) and TLS (Transport Layer Security) protocols. This avoids the need to use complex API calls. It can also assist a developer in avoiding some of the common problem-areas of this type of programming.
>
> Once set up, each instance of this control connects to a single socket, so if you need multiple sockets at one time you would need to have multiple instances of this ActiveX control running. This is most often used when the application acts as a server and has to handle multiple connections at once.

(The above is summarized from the overview for this control on the Catalyst website.)

Bernard Mouille in the dBASE newgroups and in private email worked with me to get an example to work, where you can pass information back and forth between two different computers on a network. Bernard showed huge patience and effort working with these controls, as the documentation is not very clear *(I believe they assume a certain level of knowledge)*. Here are screen shots of two forms, one Server, one Client, passing information back and forth:

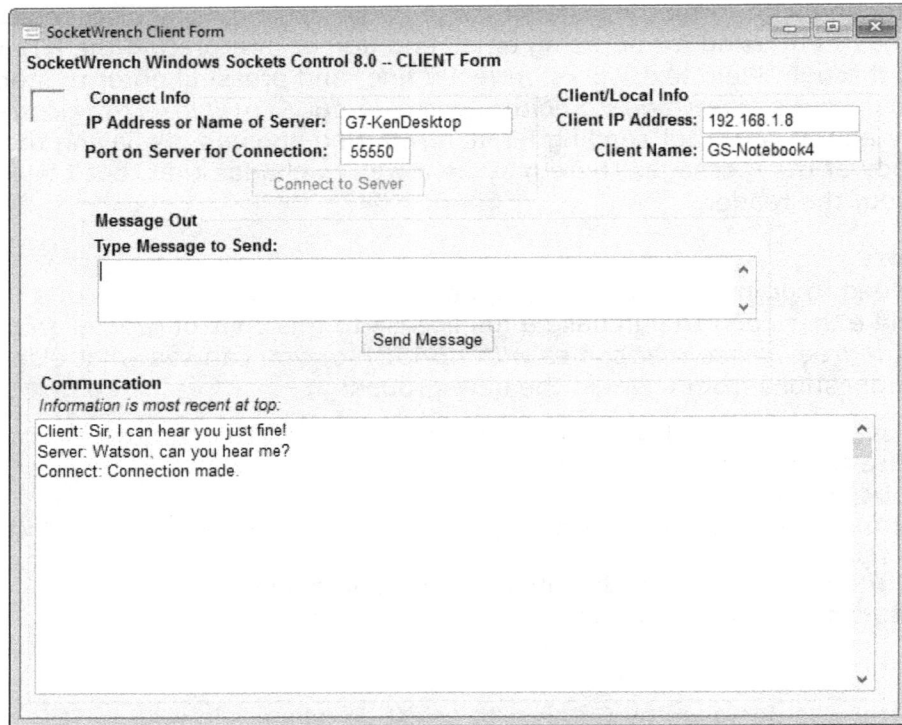

Figure 12-11

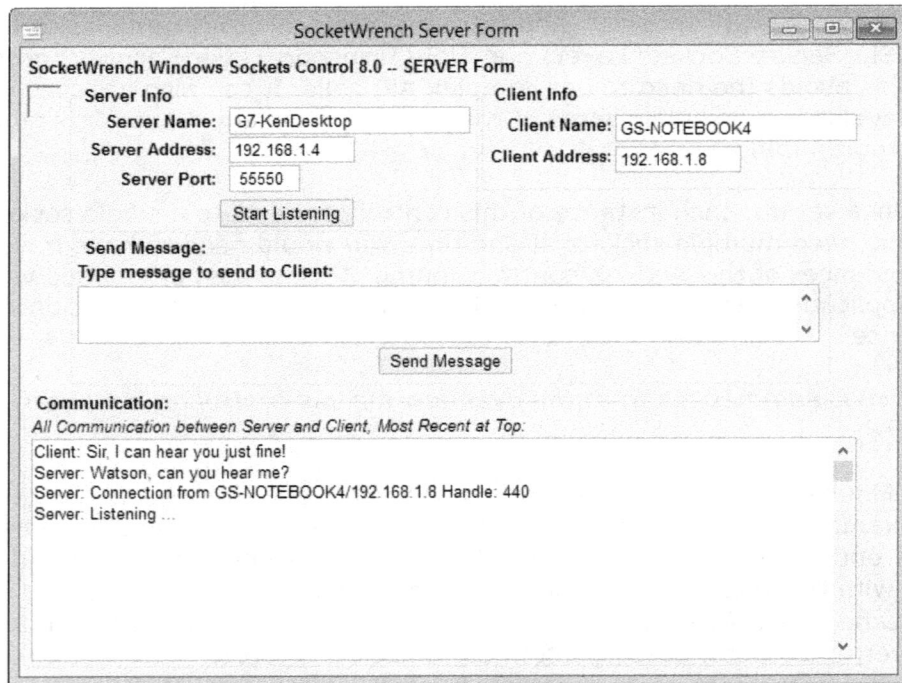

Figure 12-12

I tried tinkering with colors, but the dBASE editor control started to get a little strange *(I am sure it was some combination of the paragraph tags, and so on ...)*. Anyway, these forms are available like the others, in the Source Code folder for you to peruse and see if you can use them for anything.

Sample Code for This Chapter

The following is a listing of the sample code in the "Chapter 12" folder, if you downloaded it from my website. You may use the code contained in these forms for your own applications if you desire, with the caveat that credit be given appropriately.

- **dJvClockX Example.wfm** – Example form for this ActiveX Control
- **dJvDirectoryListboxX Example.wfm** – Example form for this ActiveX Control
- **dJvDriveComboX Example.wfm** – Example form for this ActiveX Control
- **dJvFileListBoxX Example.wfm** – Example form for this ActiveX Control
- **dJvRichEditX Example.wfm** – Example form for this ActiveX Control
- **Find Files ActiveX Example.wfm** – Example form for a combination of the dJVDriveComboX, dJvDirectoryListboxX, and dJvFileListBoxX ActiveX Controls
- **FTPMessage.wfm** – Used with TestFTP.prg
- **INI.cc** – Used with Socket FTP Example form, copied from the dUFLP
- **PasswordMaskEF.cc** – Password Mask Entryfield used with several of the Socket examples ...
- **Socket FTP Example.wfm** – Example form for this ActiveX Control
- **Socket HTTP Example.wfm** – Example form for this ActiveX Control
- **Socket Post Office Example.wfm** – Example form for this ActiveX Control
- **Socket SMTL Example.wfm** – Example form for this ActiveX Control
- **SocketWrench Client Example.wfm** – Example form for this ActiveX Control – Client form
- **SocketWrench Server Example.wfm** – Example form for this ActiveX Control – Server form
- **TestFTP.prg** – Example form for this ActiveX Control
- **TestSMTP.prg** – Example form for this ActiveX Control
- **TestSocketWrench.prg** – Program by Bernard Mouille to show what Catalyst ActiveX controls are installed and available
- **TimeFiel.cc** – used on the dJvClockX example form above.

Summary

As noted at the beginning of the chapter, with the licensing agreements that dBASE, LLC has with Catalyst, and the Jedi (dJv) controls being Open Source, you have the right to deploy these with your own applications. Deployment of applications will be discussed in a later chapter, and there will be a section on deploying ActiveX controls ...

The controls discussed in this chapter are the ones that are installed with dBASE. In <u>The dBASE Book</u> there is also a discussion on working with ActiveX controls. You might be surprised at what is installed on your computer and available for use. You can find free ActiveX controls on the web, you can purchase controls of course ... The use of these can enhance the abilities of the software immensely.

There are developers who have used Crystal Reports over the years, and in recent versions of dBASE ran into a lot of issues (with the ActiveX controls used by Crystal Reports), these were fixed with a hot-fix release of dBASE Plus 10, so if you have been working with Crystal Reports in your applications you should be able to do so with little or no trouble.

I need to make sure to thank here *(as well as in the body of the chapter)* both Bernard Mouille and Ivar B. Jessen for their patience and help getting this test code working ...

Chapter 13: Callbacks

Callbacks are a way to receive information back from interacting with a program outside of dBASE. This is related heavily to the W ndows API chapter in <u>The dBASE Book</u>, an area I am not all that comfortable working with, but ... The developers at dBASE introduced this functionality into the software with dBASE Plus 8.

The description of new Features in the online help for dBASE notes:

> CALLBACK allows you to write a function or method in dBL code and setup a pointer to it that can be passed to an external program - such as Windows or the BDE or some other 3rd party software that supports callbacks.

> Callbacks can be used to notify your program of specific events occurring with an external program OR to allow your program to modify what an external program is doing.

The online help for dBASE gives some syntax, but does not truly explain how these work.

The first thing you need is to know that the software supports Callbacks in the first place.

Callback Elements

From here there are three parts to the Callback functionality, defined below. Once we look at them, there will be some example code showing some basic functionality.

GETCALLADDRESS
This returns the memory location (address) of the Windows (or other program's) replacement function (see CALLBACK below), to be used in place of a standard dBASE function.

CALLBACK
The CALLBACK feature allows one to tell Windows to use a function in the dBASE program instead of one of its own internal functions.

RELEASE CALLBACK
Releases the references to the CALLBACK function(s) from memory – more importantly it releases the connection to the object that the function was attached to.

Sample Code

The developers at dBASE provided a sample form *(it will be in the Help for dBASE Plus 10, but should work fine in all versions of dBASE from 8 through to current, so it is in the folder of source code for this chapter)*, called MouseCallback.wfm *(not the original name – I renamed it because this is what is being shown)*. Not being a Windows API expert, I am using an explanation of the code provided by Mervyn Bick.

Every Windows window has attributes and the one we are interested in here is the method that processes messages.

```
#define GWL_WNDPROC (-4)
```

A constant that points GetWindowLong and SetWindowLong to the Windows window processor.

The following extern prototypes make Windows methods available to dBASE

```
extern CLONG GetWindowLong(CHANDLE, CINT) user32 from;
    "GetWindowLongA"
extern CLONG SetWindowLong(CHANDLE, CINT, CLONG) user32 ;
    from "SetWindowLongA"
```

Windows methods to get and set specific attributes of the window identified by the first parameter. There are methods for Unicode, eg GetWindowLongW, and ASCII, eg GetWindowLongA, in user32.dll. The prototypes ensure that we use the ASCII version.

```
extern CLONG CallWindowProc(CPTR, CHANDLE, CUINT, CUINT,;
    CUINT) user32 from "CallWindowProcA"
```

Windows method to execute a Windows procedure from within the dBASE program.

```
this.oldProc = GetWindowLong(this.hwnd, GWL_WNDPROC)
```

GetWindowLong has fetched the address of the form's internal window processor and saved it.

```
callback CLONG callWndProc(CHANDLE, CUINT, CUINT, CUINT);
    object this
```

This is a dBASE command telling Windows which function in the dBASE program is to be called from Windows. The function callWndProc in the program will now accept parameters from, and will be executed by, Windows.

```
this.newProc = GetCallAddress(this.callWndProc)
```

This is a dBASE function which gets the address in memory of the replacement function in dBASE and saves it for later use by SetWindowLong().

```
SetWindowLong(this.hwnd, GWL_WNDPROC, this.newProc)
```

This is telling Windows the address of the local function to use in place of its own function. Without the CALLBACK command, i.e. prior to dBASE 8, dBASE would not allow Windows to execute the local function.

```
? "hwnd:", this.hwnd, "oldProc:", this.oldProc,;
        "newProc:",this.newProc
```

The actual values don't mean much to a dBASE programmer as they will probably be different each time the form is run. They are displayed here just to show that the program has fetched the values.

The replacement function in the example simply lists ALL the Windows messages being passed to the form. The hWnd parameter isn't displayed as this would be rather pointless as the same value would appear in each line.

In real life one would monitor for specific messages and take appropriate action when they are seen.

```
function callWndProc(hWnd, uMsg, wParam, lParam)
   // ? [MSG:], uMsg, [WP:], wParam, [LP:], lParam
   ? [MSG:], itoh(uMsg), [WP:], itoh(wParam), [LP:], ;
           itoh(lParam)
   // It makes more sense to display the values in HEX as all
   // the constants representing messages,
   // listed as WM_cccccc in winuser.h, are given in HEX.
return CallWindowProc(this.oldProc, hwnd, uMsg, wParam, lParam)
```

The return from the local callWndProc function passes the intercepted parameters back to the internal Windows window processor and executes it.

The example given is absolutely "bare bones" to show how to use the CALLBACK feature. All it does is to show that it is possible to look "behind the scenes" to see what Windows is doing.

The Windows window processor for a form doesn't expect to receive keystrokes and so no keyboard input is displayed. It also doesn't receive mouseUp messages. If you choose to monitor, say, an entryfield which does accept keystrokes then these messages, including mouseUp messages, will also be displayed.

The example monitors all mouse messages to the form which leads to a gazillion 32 (0x20) messages. This message is WM_SETCURSOR and Windows generates this every time the mouse moves the cursor to a different pixel.

All of the explanation above is Mervyn's. I hope this makes sense to the coders who have been asking for this functionality!

Sample Code for This Chapter

The following is a listing of the sample code in the "Chapter 13" folder, if you downloaded it from my website. You may use the code contained in these forms for your own applications if you desire, with the caveat that credit be given appropriately.

- **MouseCallback.wfm** – A sample form created by Kathy Kolosky at dBASE to help show how Callbacks work.

Summary

As noted in all three editions of <u>The dBASE Book</u>, I am not very good at working with the Windows API, so I relied heavily on someone else. Jim Sare, who authored the chapter in the earlier books on working with the API has not been responding to emails for some years now, so instead, I have relied a lot on work that Mervyn Bick has been putting into this new feature.

This was a shorter chapter than some, because if you understand Windows API, then you should easily understand Callbacks, if you don't, then this chapter will be less useful in the first place.

Chapter 14: Miscellaneous Updates

dBASE, LLC has been constantly improving the software, there are some items that I didn't feel needed a whole chapter dedicated to them, but I wanted to make sure I at least discussed them. In this chapter we will take a look at:

- High Precision Math
- The Debugger
- Compiler, Symbol Space

High Precision Math

With dBASE Plus 8, we got a new math library added to dBASE. This is described below from the online help for dBASE:

> New High Precision Math (HPM) library, and wrapper has been added to the product. This new library implements the IEEE 754 Standard for Floating Point Arithmetic.
>
> dBASE wraps this standard around our number handling interface, which supports the following concepts:
>
> - Arithmetic formats: sets of binary and decimal floating-point data, which consist of finite numbers (including signed zeros and subnormal numbers), infinities, and special "not a number" values (NaNs)
> - Interchange formats: encodings (bit strings) that may be used to exchange floating-point data in an efficient and compact form
> - Rounding rules: properties to be satisfied when rounding numbers during arithmetic and conversions
> - Operations: arithmetic and other operations on arithmetic formats
> - Exception handling: indications of exceptional conditions (such as division by zero, overflow, etc.)
>
> When using a decimal floating point format the decimal representation will be preserved using:
>
> - 7 decimal digits for decimal32
> - 16 decimal digits for decimal64
> - 34 decimal digits for decimal128

So what does all this mean for you?

If you are using dBASE Plus 8, you will need to work with the number class (see later in this chapter), but in dBASE Plus 9 (and later), you don't need to do much, if anything, to work with High Precision values.

A lot depends on the type of math you have had to do in your applications. Some developers, over the years, have despaired over the fact that rounding in dBASE with very large or very small numbers lost information, causing coders to write specific functions, such as Ken Chan's *roundPrec()* function which was included in The dBASE Book, 3rd Edition, in Chapter 21.

Using the examples in The dBASE Book and dBASE Plus 9.51, the results are quite different – this was done in the Command Window:

```
set decimals to 18
x = 2.01
? x // result: 2.01 - in older versions of dBASE: 2.00999999999999787
x*= 100 // result: 201 - in older versions of dBASE: 200.99999999999971600
```

This, by itself, is quite an improvement. One of the examples Ken Chan gives is that a floating point number such as 9.825 is more accurately stored in the software as: 9.824999999999999999, meaning that there is no value 9.825. However, with the implementation of the higher precision capabilities in dBASE, 9.825 is exactly 9.825, and it is no longer necessary to use the function *roundPrec()*.

New Number Object

Created in dBASE Plus 8, the *Number* object is used for High Precision Math calculations. It allows for various properties and events to be used to help with very large numbers. This implements most of the specification for the IEEE 754 standard.

This is used in a couple of ways, but it may be obviated by the new SET HIGHPRECISION command in dBASE Plus 9 – meaning that if you are working with dBASE Plus 8 and need to work with high precision numbers, you may need this class, but in dBASE Plus 9 and later, you may not.

The number class works like other non-visual objects in dBASE, you must have an object reference and can set the value either at the time you instantiate the object, or you can set the *value* property at a later time:

```
oNum1 = new number( 1234567888.1232123 )
  // or:
oNum1 = new number()
oNum1.value := 1234567888.1232123
```

It is likely a good idea to work with the SET PRECISION command and the SET DECIMAL command to work with these numbers, so that values are not truncated or rounded.

The OLH for dBASE Plus shows this example:

```
SET PRECISION TO 34
SET DECIMAL TO 34
MYNUM1 = NEW NUMBER(24234321512514.2314134)
MYNUM2 = NEW NUMBER(234234234.7897070)
MYTOT = NEW NUMBER(MYNUM1 / MYNUM2)
? "Total is -> " + MYTOT.VALUE
```

And in the Command Window output pane:

```
Total is -> 103461.91082730304998757350859082 06
```

This class has a variety of properties that are described quite well in the OLH, no events, and some methods. The methods do not affect the *value* property, but return the results of calculations, such as the square root (*sqrt()* method) of the *value*. The Number class is in later versions of dBASE so that if you started using it in your dBASE Plus 8 applications, you do not have to rewrite any code.

SET HIGHPRECISION

Added in dBASE Plus 9, this setting works like *all* "SET" type commands. In this case it is either *ON* or *OFF*, the default in dBASE Plus 9 is *ON*. Using the exact same calculation given in the example shown above for the Number object, but with memory variables (not the *number* class):

```
x = 24234321512514.2314134
y = 234234234.7897070
nTot = x / y
? "Total is -> " + nTot
```

The results are:

```
Total is -> 103461.91082730304998757350859082O6
```

Exactly the same.

Except for the extra functionality that the Number object provides (the methods, and such – much of which is available in standard functions in dBASE, and/or the Math class), in dBASE Plus 9, you do not really need to be using the new *Number* object.

If for any reason you do *not* wish to use High Precision for math in your application, you can always turn this off:

```
SET HIGHPRECISION OFF
```

You can check the status of this setting:

```
? set ("highprecision")
```

Will return either ON or OFF ... and so on. You can also set this in the .INI file when deploying an application, the setting will be stored under this heading:

```
[OnOffCommandSettings]
HIGHPRECISION=ON // or OFF
```

Storing High Precision Numbers

Unfortunately, due to the nature of the Borland Database Engine (BDE) and local table numeric formats, it is not possible to store High Precision values in these tables (.DBF or .DB) except as character strings. You would then have to convert them back and forth working with data in tables.

Some SQL Server databases have field types that can handle higher precision values, you will need to check the documentation for those databases if you are using them.

Debugger

I have not, in <u>The dBASE Book</u>, spent much time on the Debugger in dBASE for specific reasons:

- When I learned to code, debuggers were not a part of the software, we just inserted output statements or *msgbox()* calls in areas we thought there were problems to see the content of variables, progress of a routine, etc.
- The debugger in dBASE has been problematic for many years, according to those who *do* use debuggers.

Because of these, I have never really done much with them. I have never felt comfortable working with debuggers. With the release of dBASE Plus 9, we get a debugger that works better, and the developers have been working to improve it. In dBASE Plus 10, the Debugger uses the Microsoft Foundation Classes more, and it looks more like part of the new versions of dBASE. There is documentation on the use of the Debugger in the OLH, although it is lacking in some areas.

Things that are useful:

- Breakpoints
- Watch
- Call Stack
- Trace

The term *breakpoint* refers to setting a point where the program will halt when run in the debugger. You then run the code, and when it reaches the breakpoint defined, it stops execution and you can examine it.

You can turn on various windows in the debugger, including the Watch window, which will allow you to specify variables to "watch". As a program progresses you can see the values … if you have breakpoints set then the value of the variable can be displayed at the breakpoint.

When you are running a program (or form, etc.) in dBASE and it halts due to an error, one of the options is to debug, which will open the program in the debugger.

As noted, I am not really all that comfortable with debuggers, but as a coder, having the software help you out is a good thing. You may want to spend some time working with the new and improved debugger and see if it will save you some frustration.

Another Debugging Tool

dBASE developers are quite inventive, and one of my friends in the community posted *(after I had been dealing with an issue)* a way to avoid debugging the way I was used to – with msgbox() function calls scattered throughout code. Jan Hoelterling pointed out two issues inherent with this particular method:

1) The message box can sometimes cause problems with the flow of code, particularly when working with the user-interface objects;
2) You have to click through each of those messages to see the program progress.

What Jan suggested was to download a program provided by Microsoft that can be used to help with debugging a program called "DebugView.exe". The program can be found here:

```
https://technet.microsoft.com/en-us/library/bb896647.aspx
```

I have downloaded it for you and it is in a .zip file in the Chapter 14 folder of the source code for this book.

The program (DebugView.exe) needs to be running before you start your testing *(the code here does not test to see if it is running or not)*, and then you can use the code shown below (Jan posted this in the beta newsgroups) – it needs to be in the folder the application is stored in, or you need to place it in your own custom library of code. If you do that, then you would need to use a source code alias:

```
set procedure to :MyCustomLibrary:OD
```

In your own code, where you might use a msgbox() function call to display the status of the code, you could instead use:

```
od( "The form's INIT method has been called" )
```

The text inside the parentheses will be displayed in DebugView's window, without interfering with the flow of your code.

```
Function OD
   parameter instring
   if type("OutputDebugString") # "FP"
      extern cVOID OutputDebugString( CPTR ) kernel32 ;
               from "OutputDebugStringA"
   endif
   OutputDebugString(ToUC(Instring))
return

Function ToUC
   parameter c
   LOCAL cTemp, x

   cTemp = Replicate(Chr(0), ((Len(c) - 1) / 2) + ;
                            ((Len(c) - 1) % 2))
   For x = 1 To Len(c)
      cTemp.SetByte(x - 1, Asc(SubStr(c, x)))
   EndFor
RETURN cTemp
```

The code in OD.prg in the source code folder is actually enhanced just a bit, allowing you to also write the same messages displayed in DebugView to an output log file.

Compiler, Symbol Space

Most users won't notice a lot, but the compiler is faster in dBASE Plus 10, due to expansion of the symbol tables and other internal tables. The goal is to make it easier to migrate to 64-bit executables *(someday …)*. Currently the symbol tables are at 32-bit, but can be expanded further as needed.

If your application is very large, with a huge number of variables, objects, and references, you will see less issues with running out of symbol space.

These images are based on images in the Help for dBASE Plus 10:

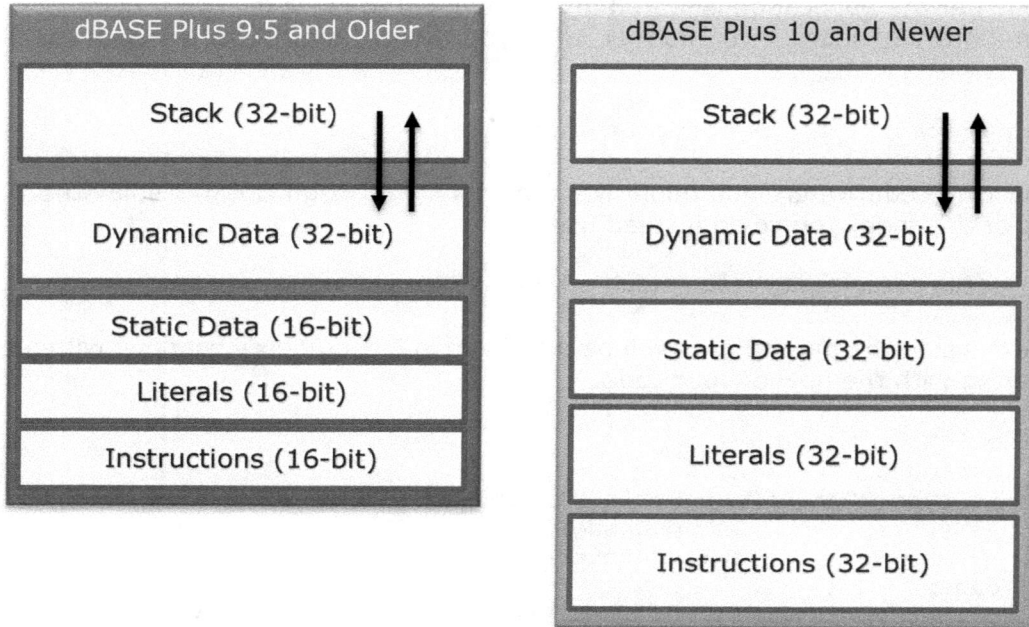

dBASE Plus 9.5 and Older
Stack (32-bit)
Dynamic Data (32-bit)
Static Data (16-bit)
Literals (16-bit)
Instructions (16-bit)

dBASE Plus 10 and Newer
Stack (32-bit)
Dynamic Data (32-bit)
Static Data (32-bit)
Literals (32-bit)
Instructions (32-bit)

Figure 14-1

dBASE should also understand references up to 256 characters in size (you can actually use references up to 4,000 characters long, but after 256 dBASE ignores them), where in earlier versions the longest variable (or reference) dBASE would recognize/work with was 32 characters.

This does mean that your code needs to be recompiled under dBASE Plus 10.

Sample Code for This Chapter

The following is a listing of the sample code in the "Chapter 14" folder, if you downloaded it from my website. You may use the code contained in these forms for your own applications if you desire, with the caveat that credit be given appropriately.

- **DebugView.zip** – the zip file from the Microsoft website containing the DebugView.exe and a couple of other files.
- **OD.prg** – Jan Hoelterling's code to assist debugging an application – uses DebugView.exe ...

Summary

This chapter was aimed at dealing with anything that didn't really fit into any of the other categories that have been covered throughout the book.

As you can see, the developers at dBASE, LLC are trying to improve the software across-the-board, and as the software continues to improve, so will your abilities to provide better applications to your end-users.

Thanks to Jan Hoelterling for his code (OD.prg and such), and to the dBASE, LLC team for all their assistance with this.

Part IV: Putting an Application Together

With advances in the software come changes in how you build your application, how you prepare it for delivery to your clients, and so on. The developers at dBASE have been listening to user requests over the years, and there have been some changes in how this works.

The chapter that follows is focused on *changes* in building and deploying your applications, so it will not go into everything that is in <u>The dBASE Book</u> *(3rd Edition)* which was fairly complete at that time. If you need to understand UAC concepts and such, you will need to look at that version of the book. I don't want to repeat more than necessary here.

Chapter 15: Building Your Application and Deploying It

This chapter may get a bit large – in <u>The dBASE Book</u> (3rd Ed.), the topics covered here were in separate chapters (25 through 28). My goal is to focus on differences between earlier versions of dBASE Plus and focus heavily on dBASE Plus 9.51 and dBASE Plus 10 – these two releases have had some changes, dBASE Plus 10 has the biggest.

New Application Properties

TabBar

In dBASE Plus *(starting with dBASE Plus 8)* with the new framework that is part of the IDE, is a property discussed back in the first chapters of this book:

```
_app.TabBar
```

This property determines if the tabbar displays in the IDE, but it is also available in your application. If you are using an MDI (multi-document interface) for your application, this is kind of a cool feature – individual tabs will appear for each form that is open, and the user can click on a tab to bring that form to the top and/or set focus on it … In your setup routines (or in your application class definition, again, see <u>The dBASE Book</u>, Chapter 25), you could add:

```
_app.TabBar := true
```

This is actually set to *true* by default. You also set the position (by default it is at the top of the frame, under the toolbar and menubar), but that would have to be done in your application's .INI file. Looking at the PLUS.INI file:

```
[MDITabs]
Show=1
Position=0
Style=0
```

The "Show" entry set to "1" (the default) says that they are on. You could set this to "0" and turn them off. The "Position" entry defaults to "0", which is "Top", setting this to "1" puts it on the bottom. Just because I thought I'd experiment, I tried setting the position to 2, and it left the tabs on the bottom, most likely the code in dBASE checks for any non-zero value – if it is zero it is on the top, anything else it is on the bottom.

The "Style" is interesting. The default is zero, and gives you tabs that look like:

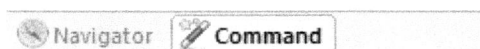
Figure 15-1

Changing this to a value of 1, the appearance changes rather dramatically:

Figure 15-2

And again just to experiment, I changed the value to 2 and it remained at this version, so the code is likely to be the same, any non-zero value will result in the second version of the tabs.

To summarize, these are the options for the TabBar properties in the .INI file:

Property	Setting/Meaning
Show	0 = Off
	1 = On
Position	0 = Top
	>0 = Bottom
Style	0 = "Standard" or "Square"
	>0 = "Slanted"

On the flip-side – if your application is SDI (Single-Document Interface), then you would probably want to just turn the TabBar off:

```
_app.TabBar := false
```

(Or in the .INI file, set the "Show" option to 0.)

Themes

Back in the first chapter we briefly looked at the themes. You can apply these themes in your own application in the application's .INI file:

```
[AppTheme]
Type=1
```

You would need to tinker with the number to find which number matches which theme, although I suspect from a little tinkering on my own that the themes match the menus with the first item in the list being 0:

Theme Type	Theme Name
0	System
1	Studio 1 *(default)*
2	Studio 2
3	Office 1 Flat
4	Office 2 Blue
5	Office 3 Luna
6	Office 3 Aqua
7	Office 3 Black
8	Office 3 Silver

Building Your Executable

Developers using dBASE have, over the years, requested many features when deploying an application, and the folk at dBASE, LLC have been listening. This part of the chapter will discuss some of the new options for building your executable dBASE Plus 10 *(and later)*. If you do not have The dBASE Book *(3rd Edition)*, you really need to get your hands on it – I will not be covering every detail for building an executable here, just the changes since the previous book. This material is covered in volume 2.

There are two main options for building your executable, the first is the most user-friendly – working with the Project Explorer, the other is to use the command line. We'll take a look at the new features using both.

dBASE Plus 8 and 9 did not do much in this area, but in dBASE Plus 10 we got a couple of new features that need to be looked at carefully. These are related to each other.

File Location Concerns

If you have built an application using dBASE Plus 8 or 9, and are now working in dBASE Plus 10, you may need to look at the file locations in the Project file for your application (if you are using one). See Chapter 1 for a detailed description of file locations for programs and custom classes stored in the Samples folders and so on.

Embed Runtime in Executable

This functionality has been requested by developers who don't want to deploy the runtime engine for dBASE as a separate install. This is particularly useful if you are also building an application that does not include the Borland Database Engine, but it can be handy anyway. Please note this is *only* available in dBASE Plus 10 (and later).

One caveat – if you build your executable this way, the appropriate runtime .DLL file(s) will need to be deployed – these contain the language strings and such that are used. When we get to deployment we'll come back to this concept.

Using the Project Explorer:

For this quick example I am going to use one of the Samples that ship with dBASE, the "Fish.prj" file *(note the path to the Samples folder, discussed back in Chapter 1)*. Opening this in dBASE, you should see something like:

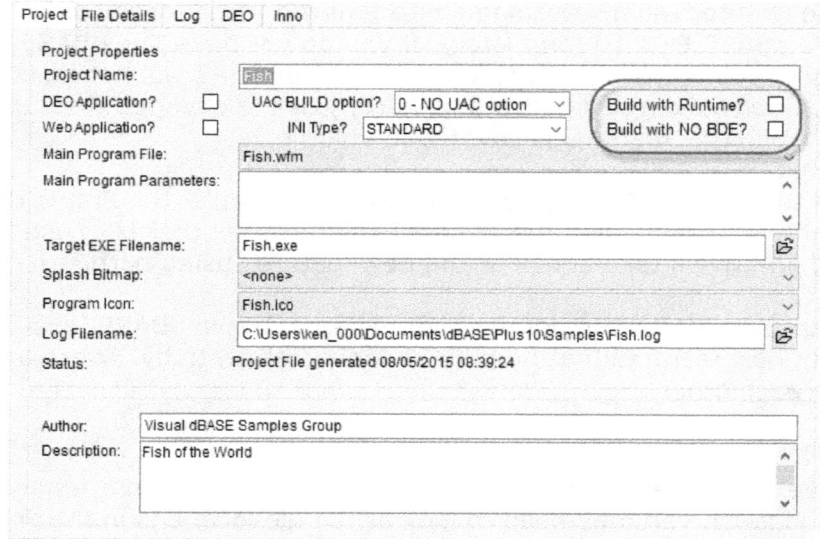

Figure 15-3

The part outlined in red on the right in the screen capture (Figure 15-3) shows two new options. We'll come back to the second one later. If you check the "Build with Runtime?" checkbox, when you tell dBASE to build the executable, it will include the runtime engine in the executable. This will of course make the executable quite a bit larger.

To give an idea, using the Fish.prj file, building the executable without the Runtime engine provides an executable of approx. 319KB in size. The executable with the Runtime engine will be approximately 19,113KB in size.

Checking the checkbox will first give a warning that you must deploy the language .DLL file(s) needed. The Project Explorer assumes you will be using it to deploy the application, so it then asks you to select the appropriate language .DLL you need – see table below as a reminder:

Language	DLL Name
English	PlusR_EN.dll
German	PlusR_DE.dll
Spanish	PlusR_ES.dll
French	PlusR_FR.dll
Italian	PlusR_IT.dll

The file you select will be added to your project. If your application is multi-lingual, you may want to select each that you need and add them to your project later.

NOTE: It is not a good idea to include this in the .EXE if you are trying to build everything else into your executable – dBASE seldom handles DLLs well if they are stored inside the program. I recommend just installing the file to the folder the .EXE is contained in.

Using the Command Line

The dBASE Plus BUILD command includes an optional parameter: RTEXE.

This could get fairly complex if not careful, but a Command Line to build an executable that embedded the Runtime engine in the .exe might look like:

```
BUILD filename,filename2,filename3 TO MyFile.exe RTEXE
```

Obviously this is fairly simple, and is not actually naming the files you would include. For details on all the options for the BUILD command, see the dBASE Plus HELP file (HELP BUILD).

If you prefer to use the BUILD command, you can use a Response file (.RSP). The important thing would be to include the RTEXE parameter on its own line, after some of the other options. Then using:

```
BUILD FROM MyRSP.RSP
```

Will cause dBASE to embed the runtime engine into the resulting executable.

Deployment Issue

If your application is not an ADO application, then you will still need to use the BDE. However, if you are embedding the runtime engine into the executable, this does not do anything about getting the BDE out to your user(s).

If you use the standard runtime installer to get the BDE, you are immediately invalidating the reason you embedded the runtime into the executable in the first place, because the runtime will be installed as well as the BDE. The folk at dBASE, LLC anticipated this, and have created a BDE-only installer, which will do as it sounds, only install the BDE.

Using the Project Explorer

With the Fish project as our example, if we use the Project Explorer to build the Inno Setup script for you, you will need to do a couple of things. First, click the "Inno" tab in the Project, and click on "Runtime". Your right side of the screen should look like this:

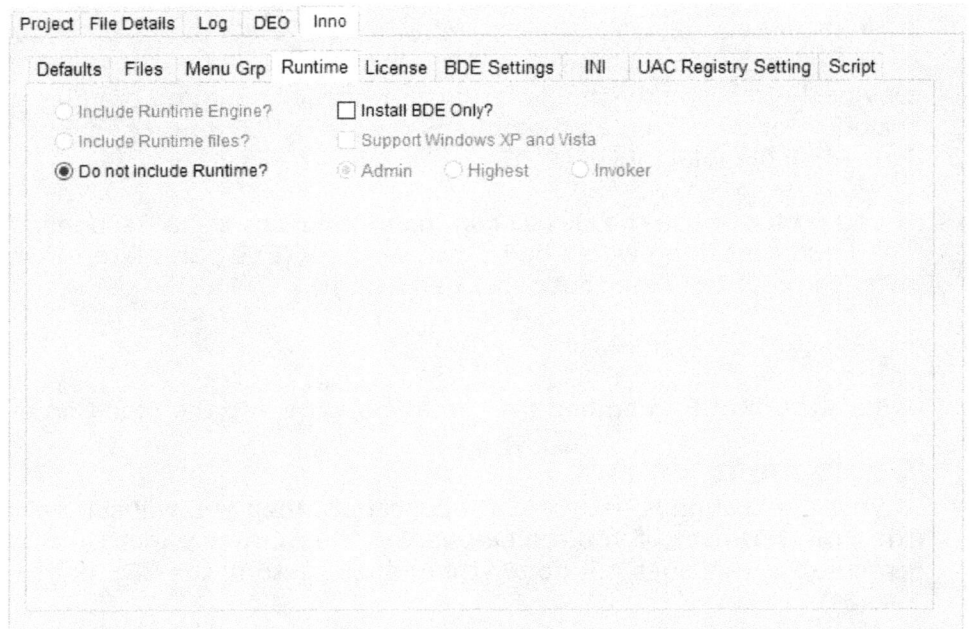

Figure 15-4

Click the "Install BDE Only?" checkbox. This will tell dBASE to find the BDE Only installer, and include it in the project, with appropriate instructions, when it builds the .ISS file for Inno Setup.

The BDE Alias for DBASESAMPLES is created as a User BDE Alias, meaning it is not stored in the BDE's IDAPI.CFG file.

For the "Fish" application (or any of the SAMPLES applications), the following needs to end up in the .INI file, although the path to the data will vary depending on where you install it to:

```
[UserBDEAliases]
0=dBASESamples
[dBASESamples]
Driver=dBASE
Options="PATH: C:\Users\UserName\Documents\dBASE\Plus10\Samples"
```

Save the Project after you create the .ISS file (on the "Inno" tab, click "Script", give a name for the ISS file – something like Fish.iss, and then click the "Generate script with settings" button).

For the .ISS script, you would need to add to the [INI] part (each of the following lines is a single statement for Inno Setup and should be on one line in the script, starting with "Filename:"; the last one uses three double-quotes on both sides of the string):

```
Filename: {localappdata} \Fish.ini; Section: UserBDEAliases;
Flags: UninsDeleteSection
Filename: {localappdata} \Fish.ini; Section: UserBDEAliases;
Key: dBASESamples; String: 0
Filename: {localappdata} \Fish.ini; Section: dBASESamples;
Flags: UninsDeleteSection
Filename: {localappdata} \Fish.ini; Section: dBASESamples;
Key: Driver; String: dBASE
Filename: {localappdata} \Fish.ini; Section: dBASESamples;
Key: Options; String: """PATH:
C:\Users\UserName\Documents\dBASE\Plus10\Samples"""
```

Discussed in several places – the Project Explorer will not remember the new items you added to the .ISS file, so you should save that information somewhere in case you need to change things.

Warning
The Project Explorer does not know that the Fish application uses the "resource.dll" file – if you choose to test this, you will want to add this file to the list of files in the Project before you build the .ISS script. Otherwise it will not be deployed with the application.

Manually Building the Inno Setup File
Without going into all the details of building a script for Inno Setup, you need to include all files that are to be deployed with your application in the [Files] section of the script.

In order to deploy this particular option (BDE Only) the most important thing to deal with here is that you need to deploy and run the BDE Installer. In the [Files] section of the Inno Setup script, add this (single line):

```
Source: "C:\Program Files (x86)\dBASE\Plus10\Runtime\BDE
Installer\BDE_Setup.exe"; DestDir: "{tmp}"; Flags:
ignoreversion deleteafterinstall
```

And then in the [Run] section (if there is none, add it after the [Files] section):

```
[RUN]
Filename: {tmp}\BDE_Setup.exe; Parameters: /S; StatusMsg:
"Installing dBASE Runtime and BDE..."; Flags:
runascurrentuser; WorkingDir: {tmp};
```

And as noted above (at the end of the "Project Explorer" description, you will need to add entries in the [INI] section of the script to define the User BDE Alias.

Build With No BDE
In versions of dBASE up to dBASE Plus 10, if your application did not use the Borland Database Engine (BDE), you were required to include in the executable's .INI file these lines:

```
[DataEngine]
DefaultEngine=None
```

Using the Project Explorer
In dBASE Plus 10 (and later) you can now check the checkbox on the first page of the Project Explorer for your Project, that says "Build With No BDE?". When you build the executable, information will be written into the executable that tells dBASE it does not need the BDE to perform data operations. This is only a good idea if your application either does not use tables, or if your application uses the ADO database controls *(and ONLY those)*.

Using the Command Line
The BUILD command also includes a parameter for this. The parameter is two words:

```
BDE OFF
```

And the .RSP file, if you chose to use that method of controlling the build, would include this on its own line.

It should be noted that this parameter is not required, you could *still* simply use the .INI settings shown above.

Suggestion:
If you choose to use this option, it is a good idea to either use the "Build with Runtime?" option (see above), or when you get to the Inno tab, and "Runtime", deploy only the runtime files. The dBASE Plus Runtime Installer automatically includes the BDE, so using that will put the BDE on your users' machines, even if your application does not need it.

Deploying the Application

Once your executable has been built, in whichever fashion you wish to build it, you need to be able to deploy the application. This section of the chapter again assumes you have access to <u>The dBASE Book</u> *(3rd Edition)* as a reference point, as again not all aspects of deployment will be included here. For this book, we will take a look at specific issues when deploying an application:

- ActiveX Controls
- Resource Files

- ADO Applications (without the BDE)
  - Deploying a SQL Server Database (server and data)
- Other Features/Enhancements to the Project Explorer

When discussing these different options, I will take a look at using the Project Explorer, as well as working directly with Inno Setup.

Deploying ActiveX Controls

In Chapter 12 examples were given for how to *use* the ActiveX controls that ship with dBASE. It's important to know how to actually deploy them.

Using the Project Manager

If you wish to deploy an ActiveX control *(or multiple ActiveX controls)* using the Project Manager, you need to make sure to start that these are in your project:

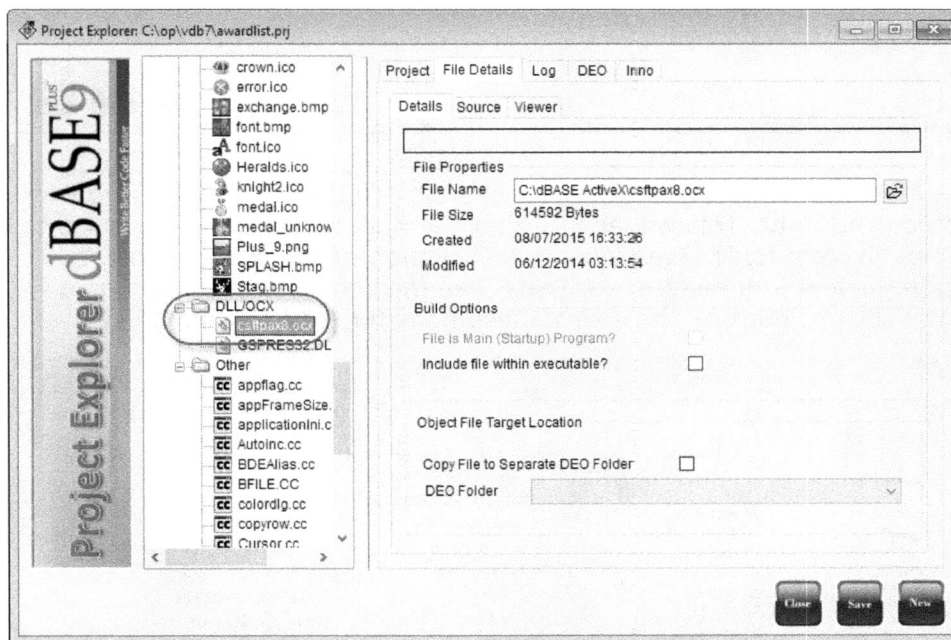

Figure 15-5

In Figure 15-14 above, note the DLL/OCX section. I have placed a red outline showing the Catalyst FTP ActiveX control.

When you click on the "Inno" tab, and then the "File" tab, find this particular item, and click it:

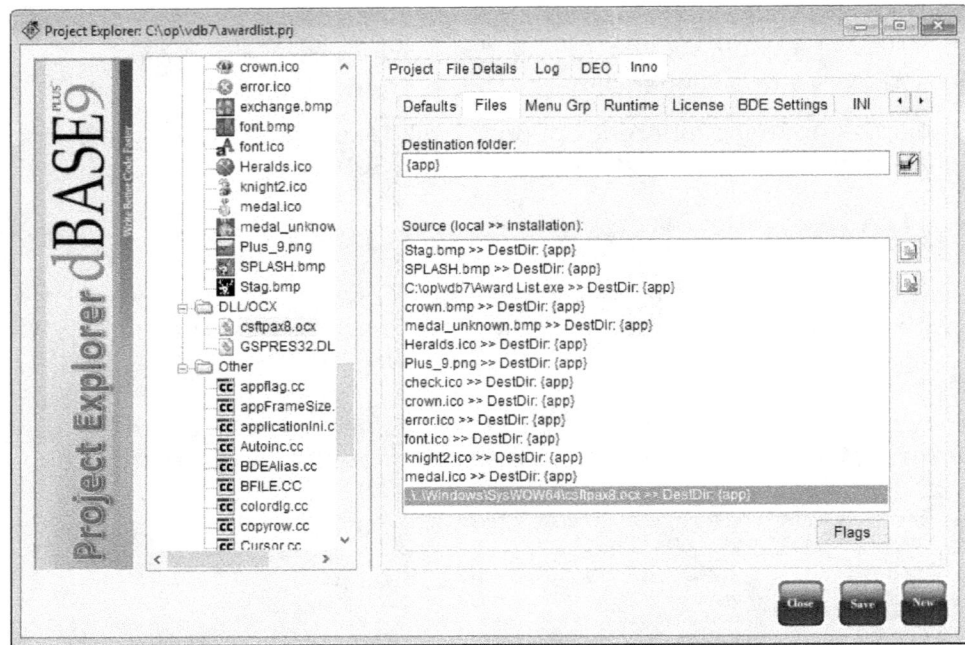

Figure 15-6

In the "Destination folder:" entryfield change "{app}" to "{sys}" and click the button on the right. This will ensure that the ActiveX control is installed to the Windows System folder *(see later in this section of the chapter on File Locations)*. Next you need to set flags *(see the Inno Setup section below)*, so click the "Flags" button, and select these flags for Inno Setup:

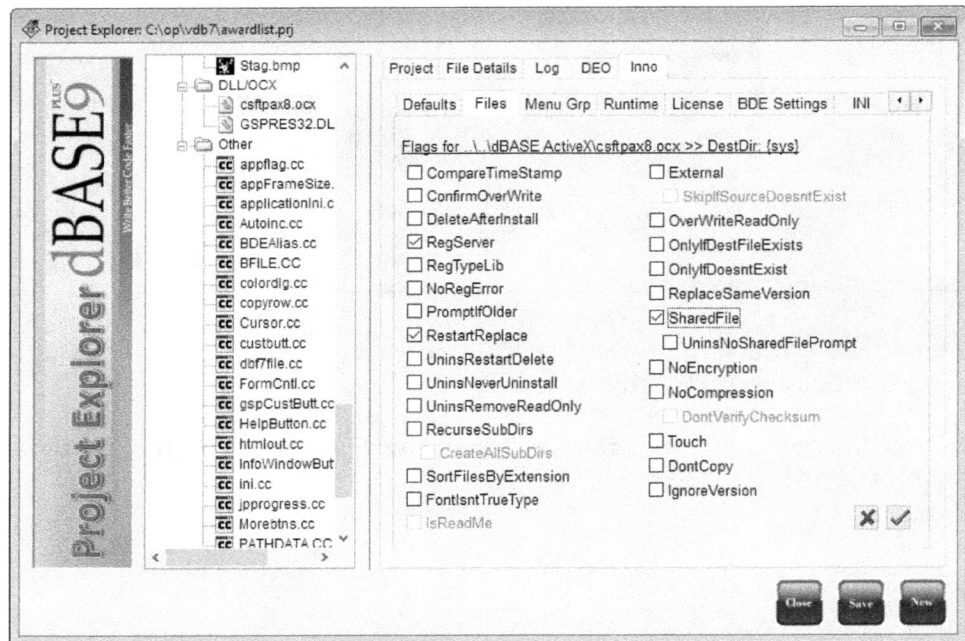

Figure 15-7

The items specifically checked are "RegServer", "RestartReplace", and "SharedFile". Click the green checkmark button, to save these flags. When you do, the entry in the Project Manager (on the Inno Setup main "Files" screen) will show the flags selected:

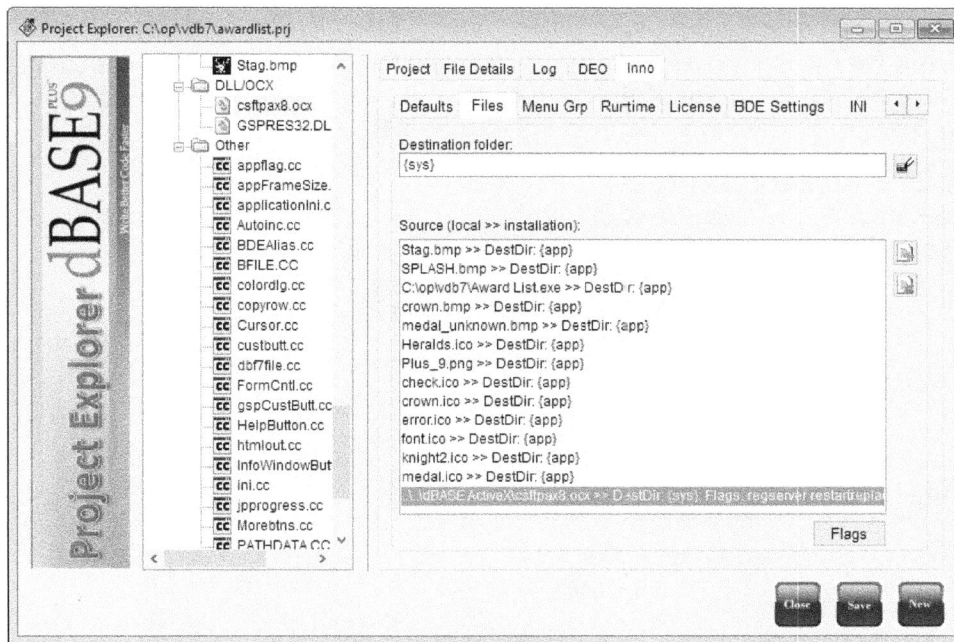
Figure 15-8

This will allow you to ensure the ActiveX control is installed properly.

Inno Setup

I had to do some digging on this one, because my inclination was to use the Windows RegSvr32.exe program to register an ActiveX with Windows, based on past information I had working with ActiveX controls.

I found that for some reason this doesn't work well in Inno Setup *(or from the Command Window in Windows …)*. Rick Miller from the dBASE newsgroups pointed out that there are some flags that can be used in Inno Setup, one of which executes the registration routines in Windows – the following statement would go in an Inno Setup script's Files section – as always with Inno Setup scripts the following is one statement (should not wrap in your script):

```
Source: "C:\dBASE ActiveX\csftpax8.ocx"; DestDir: "{sys}";
Flags: restartreplace regserver sharedfile
```

Below is a brief explanation of the flags, but you can look these up for more detail in the Inno Setup help:

restartreplace – The next time Windows is restarted, replace the ActiveX control with the current one. This avoids trying to overwrite it while it might be in use.

regserver – Registers the ActiveX control with Windows, bypassing the need to have a statement in the RUN section of your script.

sharedfile – This allows Windows to understand that this control might be being used by multiple applications – and if one application is uninstalled, to leave the control – don't uninstall it until or unless the last application that uses it is uninstalled.

File Locations

Realizing that it is kind of important when building an application that you have the ability to deploy the ActiveX controls, I did some searching to find the ActiveX files that are installed with dBASE Plus.

dJv (JEDI) ActiveX Controls:

These controls are all apparently stored in one .OCX file, in this folder (depending on the installation of dBASE):

```
C:\Program Files (x86)\dBASE\Plus9\Bin
```

(If using dBASE Plus 10, change the "9" to a "10" ...) The file is:

```
dBASE_Controls.ocx
```

This file contains all five of the dJv ActiveX controls discussed in Chapter 12.

Catalyst ActiveX Controls:

On my Windows 8, 64-bit computer, this is the location of the files:

```
C:\Windows\SysWOW64
```

If you are using a 32-bit version of Windows, check one of these folders, or simply search using Windows (or File) Explorer:

```
C:\Windows\System
C:\Windows\System32
```

Filename	Control
csftpax8.ocx	SocketTools File Transfer Protocol Client 8.0
cshtpax8.ocx	SocketTools Hypertext Transfer Protocol 8.0
csmtpax8.ocx	SocketTools Simple Mail Transfer Protocol 8.0
cspopax8.ocx	SocketTools Post Office Protocol 8.0
cswskax8.ocx	SocketWrench Windows Sockets Control 8.0

Store the Files Elsewhere

In discussing the issues of installing ActiveX controls with your applications, Rick Miller noted some possible concerns, and suggests copying these files to another location on your computer. The concerns are:

1) The file may be in use at the time you attempt to deploy it.
2) It may have been updated by another program that uses the control.
3) The file may have been changed for some other reason, the worst being a virus (the last thing you want to do is deploy a virus to your users' machines).

In order to avoid these particular issues you should consider copying them to another folder, such as:

```
C:\dBASE ActiveX
```

By doing that, when you deploy them you know what version you are deploying, and *(hopefully)* that the version being deployed has not been modified.

Rick also suggests that since at least the Catalyst controls were installed by dBASE to the Windows System folder, you should probably deploy to the same location. This is why, in the examples (both for the Project Explorer and for Inno Setup), I show changing the destination to the "{sys}" constant.

Deploying Resource Files

Deploying Resource files in dBASE is a lot easier than ActiveX controls – these are resources used by your application. They can include character strings, images, and more. If, for example, your application is multi-lingual, you might have multiple .DLL files you need to deploy for each language.

If you are using the new resource files that were included with dBASE Plus 10 for images on your forms, toolbars, etc., you will need to deploy the .DLL files with your application, and of course if you have created your own (which I have done in the past), you will need to deploy them.

An important aspect of the .DLL files is that they typically need to be installed in the same folder as your application (unless your code is set up to specifically use hard-coded paths). DEO (Dynamic External Objects) does not usually work well with resource files.

It is important to note where the resource files are. The new .DLL files that came with dBASE Plus 10 with all those images *(see Chapter 7)* are stored here:

```
C:\Users\Public\Documents\dBASE\Plus10\Media\Resources
```

Using the Project Explorer

When using the Project Explorer, you need to add each .DLL file you wish to deploy. If you are using the new resource files that ship with dBASE Plus 10 you need to navigate to the path containing these files when adding them to the Project (see above).

Using the sample folder for dBASE Plus 10, I will show adding one of these to a project:

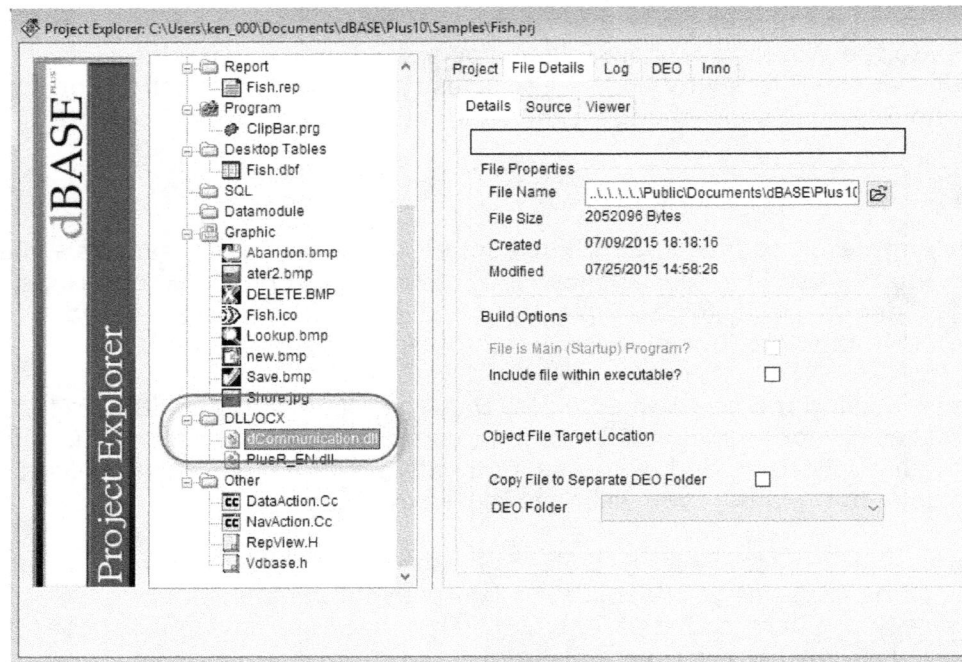

Figure 15-9

As long as this is listed here, when you go to deploy the application the file is automatically listed in the Inno Setup section (the "Inno" tab), under the "Files" tab. By default, dBASE will deploy this to the application folder ("{app}", and that is all you need to do, except to ensure that you include each resource file you need to deploy with your application.

Using Inno Setup

With Inno setup, you need to ensure that each .DLL file you wish to deploy is included in the [Files] section, with a line along the lines of:

```
; Deploy the dCommunication resource file:
Source:
"C:\Users\Public\Documents\dBASE\Plus10\Media\Resources\dCommu
nication.dll"; DestDir: "{app}"; Flags: ignoreversion
```

Once again keeping in mind that the above should be on one line of the Inno Setup file, starting with the "Source" keyword.

Deploying an ADO Application

The whole purpose behind building an ADO application for many developers is to get away from using the Borland Database Engine (BDE).

There are several areas you should be concerned with when dealing with this, I want to try to cover this fairly carefully. As such, for the purpose of demonstration, I will do as I did with the chapters on building an ADO application – create a step-by-step set of instructions. The first set will be done using the Project Explorer – the second set of instructions will be for Inno Setup only.

Once again, the sample code is available from my website, and the following assumes that you have this unzipped to an appropriate place on your computer.

It is usually a good idea to determine what you need to happen. So, what do we need the installer to do ultimately?

- Install the application and ancillary files.
- Install the data on the server.
- Install the Firebird (or other database) Server software.
- Install the Firebird ODBC Drivers.
- Set up the ODBC database connections.
- Modify the .INI file for the ADO Connection strings.

The big problem is that some of this cannot be easily automated. We will discuss this in more detail as we work through the details.

Server Installation vs. Client Installation?

Of course, there is one issue to consider here before starting – "Server Installation versus Client Installation?" What I mean by this, is that the end-user or client will probably not need to have either the SQL Server Database software installed, nor will they need to install the database itself. On the other hand, if you are installing the Server side, you would need to install everything – the server software, the database, etc.

One difficulty will be installing the database server and ODBC Drivers, as well as setting up the ODBC connections. I have not been able to find a way to automate these without user-intervention. Since there is not a good method of automating these, I recommend for you provide your customer with *very* detailed instructions, including a note that a simple typo in one of the dialog boxes will cause issues. If possible of course, setting up the server is something that you would do for your client. For new client computers *(new employee, replacing computers, etc.)* you would not want to have to come out to the customer's site every time.

An option – which we will use here – is to include PDF or Word documents that provide all of the details (screen captures, etc.), and a text document that can be displayed from the Inno Setup script at the end of the installation that points to the documents with the details. The text document will be named "AfterInstall.txt", and needs to be included in the install, as will the PDF documents. This option will be shown both with the Project Explorer and with manually creating the Inno Setup script.

Using the Project Explorer

The following set of instructions *(and screen captures)* will show setting up this deployment using the Project Explorer. One nice feature of dBASE Plus is that the PE has gotten more and more sophisticated over time, so a lot of what you need can be done through the PE. As noted above, this is going to be the full Server installation, for a Client installation, you should be able to copy the project file and remove the items you don't need.

Create the Project File

To start you need to double-click the "[New Project]" item in the dBASE Plus Navigator window to create a new project. (Once again this chapter is based on the idea that you have <u>The dBASE Book</u> (3rd Edition) available for reference.)

I saved this as "Invoice", and filled in a small amount of information as shown below (Figure 15-9):

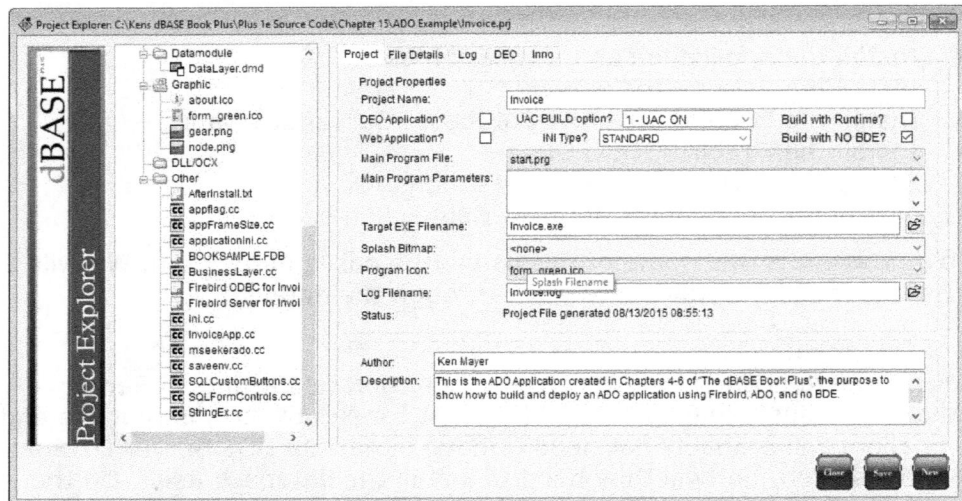

Figure 15-10

Note that I checked the "Build with NO BDE" checkbox, as mentioned earlier in this chapter. This app will be left as a non-DEO application (meaning all the source will be built into the .exe, although for a real-world application I would suggest actually using DEO for most cases), and I am setting it to use UAC (standard Windows file structure).

Next the files to be built into the executable and other files that you most likely will want to deploy need to be added to the project, and your start program needs to be determined, as well as any other basic settings you might want:

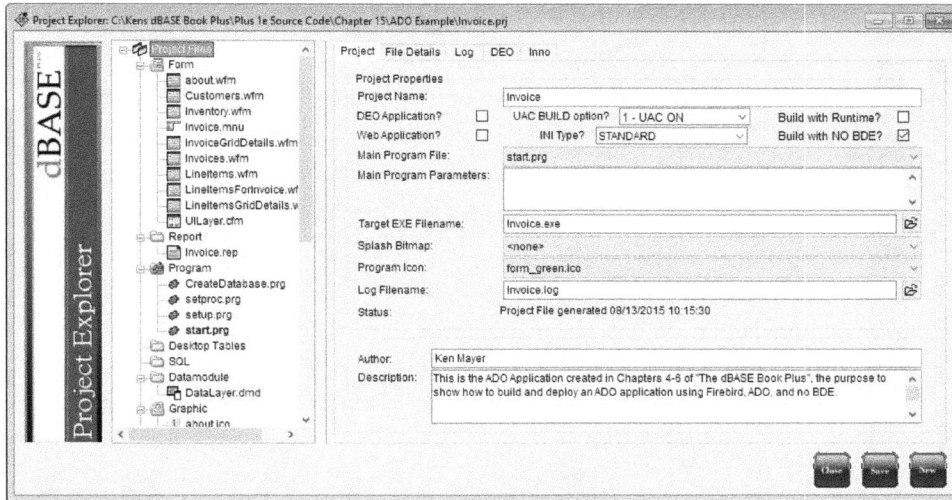

Figure 15-11

I included one more .ICO file from the Icon Experience set of images I've used in several locations in this book, to be used as the icon for the executable ("form_green.ico").

Add the Database and Other Files
It's a good idea to include the database when setting up the application on the network server. You should decide if you want the database installed to the same folder as the executable and other files.

We also need to deploy some documentation files (a couple of PDF files) in the "Documentation" folder.

Build the Executable
After selecting the files to be deployed and the source code to be built into the program, the next thing to do is to build the executable. If everything worked (and it should), then we need to get into the steps to prepare for deployment. *(I typically use the "Rebuild All" button when I build an executable – it ensures that any changes in the source code will be built properly.)*

Deployment Options
At this point we'll take a look at the features in the Project Explorer that help build the setup script used by Inno Setup. If you click the "Inno" tab, you will see something like:

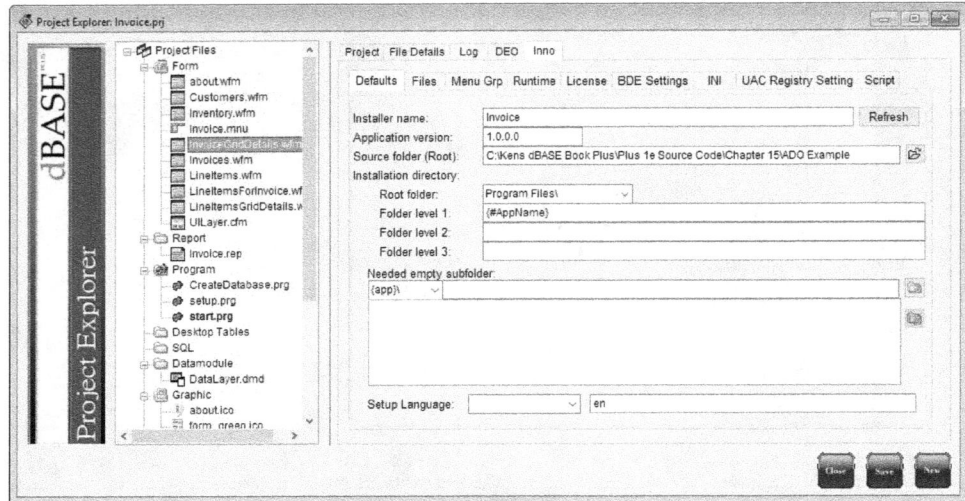

Figure 15-12

On the "Defaults" screen, if the database is going to be installed in another folder, you should set that up here. For example, you might simply want a "Data" folder under the application folder. In the "Needed empty subfolder" entryfield, type "Data", and click the button to the right. The screen will update to show *(the screen captures moving forward will show the notebook side of the screen, to make it easier to read)*:

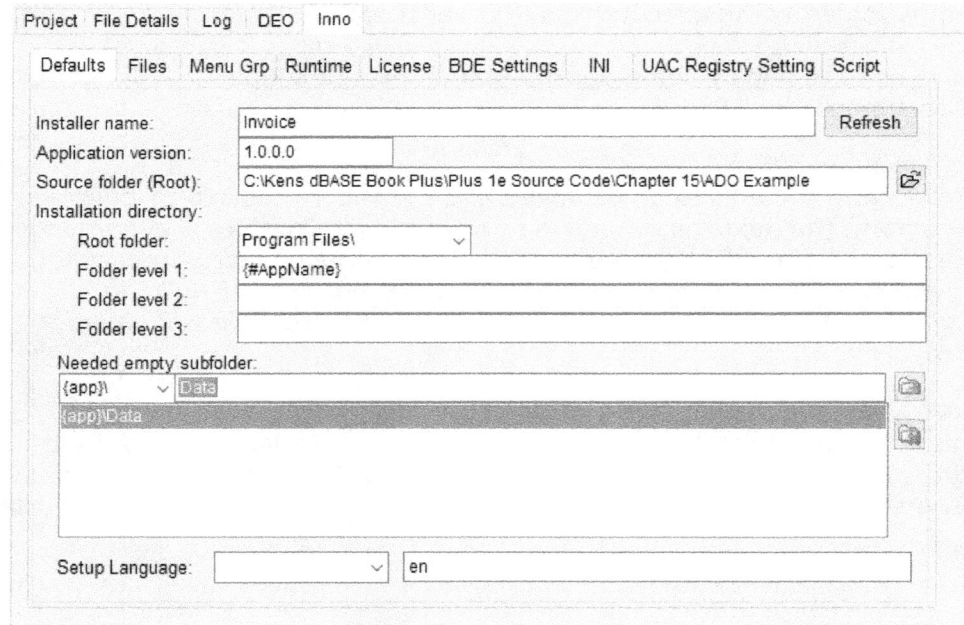

Figure 15-13

Repeat to include a "Documentation" folder. This will be used to deploy two documents that are referenced in the "AfterInstall" text document.

Click on "Files":

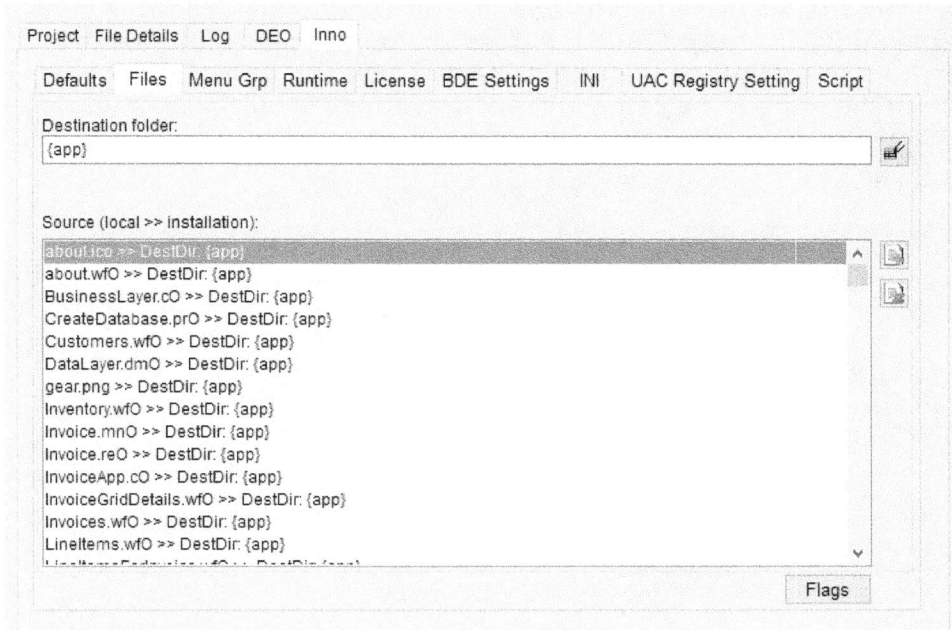

Figure 15-14

This lists each file in the project, and if you scroll down you will see the executable is also listed.

The idea is that dBASE will install all these files with your application. Interestingly, even though this is set as a non-DEO application, the project is including all of the object (compiled) versions of your source code. The individual files are being included in the .EXE, so you really do not need to deploy these as well. You can remove individual items by clicking on them, and using the "Remove a file entry" button on the right side, or you can Ctrl+Click on the items to select multiples and remove them all at once. Once you have cleaned this up:

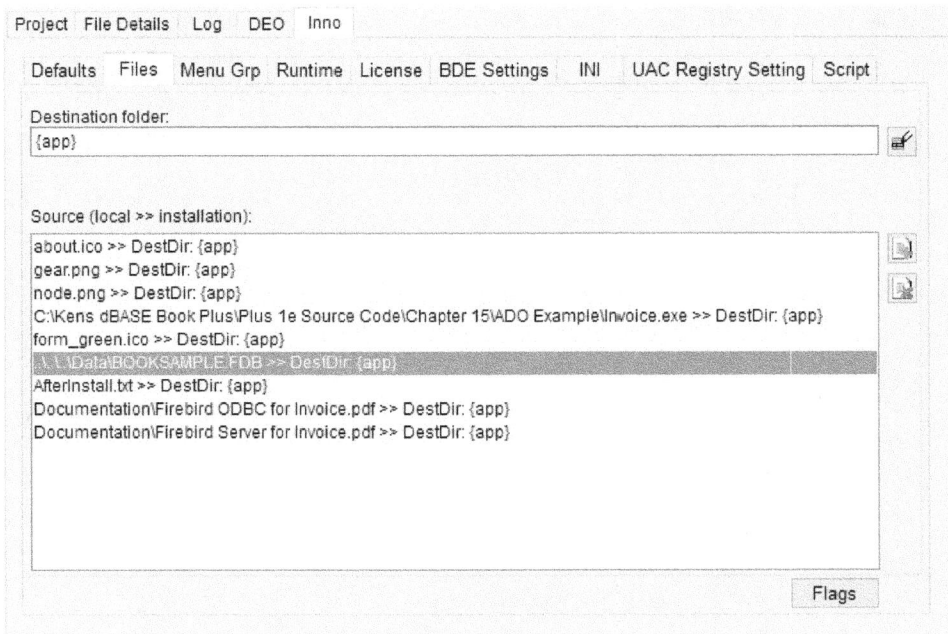

Figure 15-15

As we want the database to be placed in the "Data" folder, click the database filename ("BOOKSAMPLE.FDB") if it does not have focus, in the "Destination folder:" entryfield, add to the end of "{app}" the text "\Data". Click the button to the right of the entryfield, and the screen should change to reflect this:

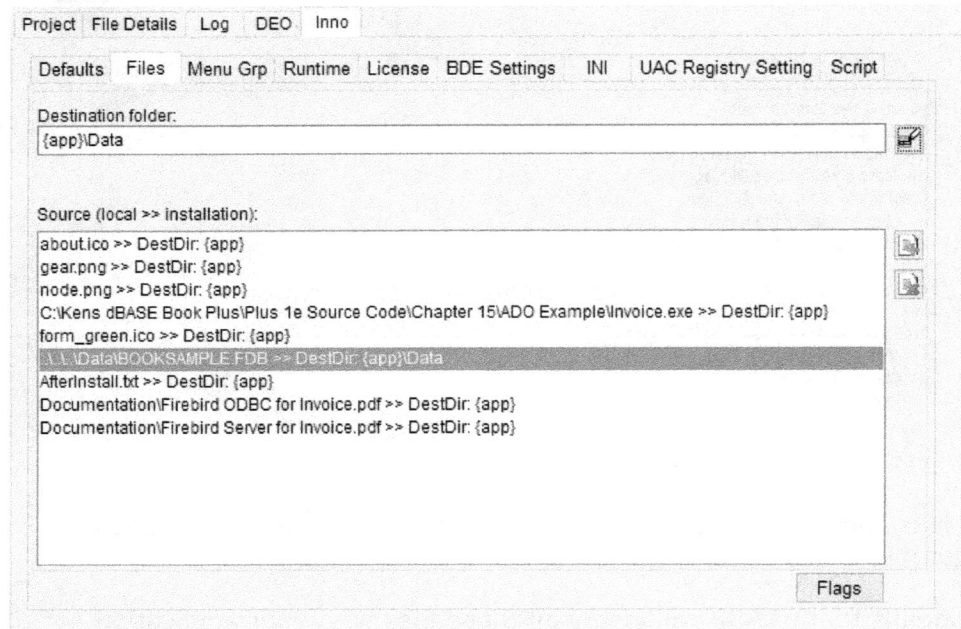

Figure 15-16

Repeat for the two PDF files, only change them to be stored in the "\Documentation" folder.

If you click on "Menu Grp", you should see something like this:

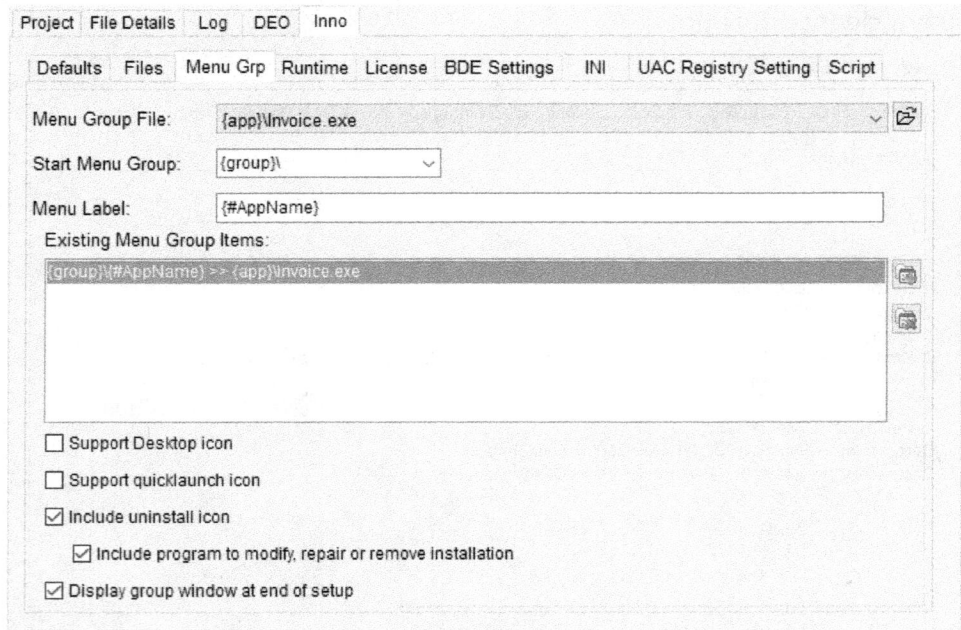

Figure 15-17

For now we will leave this, as there isn't anything we need to do – the default settings are pretty good.

The "Runtime" page is important. Because we chose not to include the runtime in the executable, we need the runtime files – but if we used the "Include Runtime Engine?" option we would install the runtime AND the BDE, which we don't need:

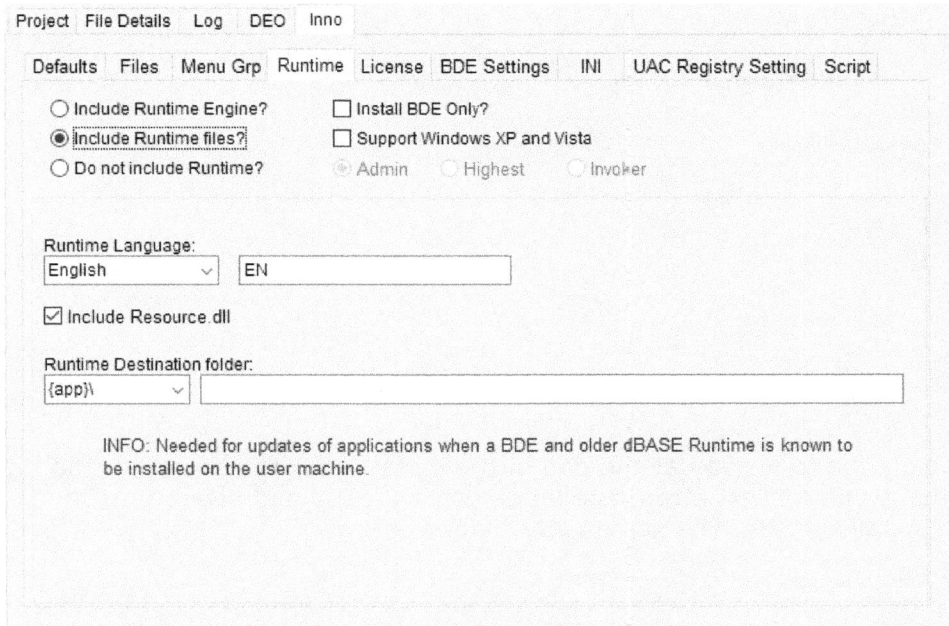

Figure 15-18

If you need to install the full runtime, you should note that with dBASE Plus 10 there is only one runtime installer, if you are using dBASE Plus 8 or 9, there are different installers based on language, as well as an "ALL" option. You should always be sure to download the most recent runtime installer(s) for your version of dBASE.

Click the "License" tab – we need to include the "AfterInstall.txt" to provide explanations at the end of the installation.

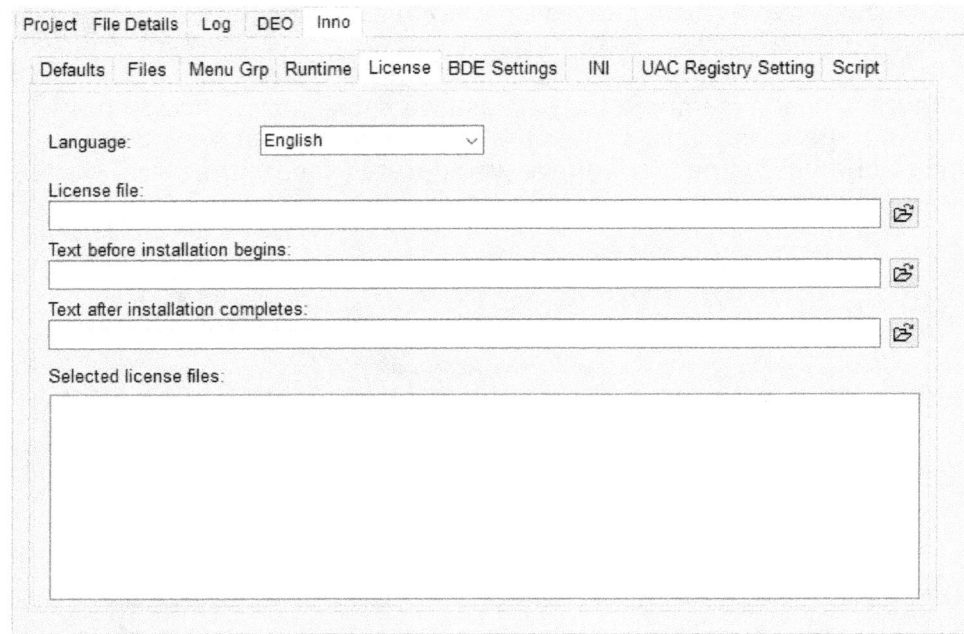

Figure 15-19

To set the file to display at the end of the install, click the button to the right of the entryfield "Text after installation completes:", and select the "AfterInstall.txt" file. The screen will change to:

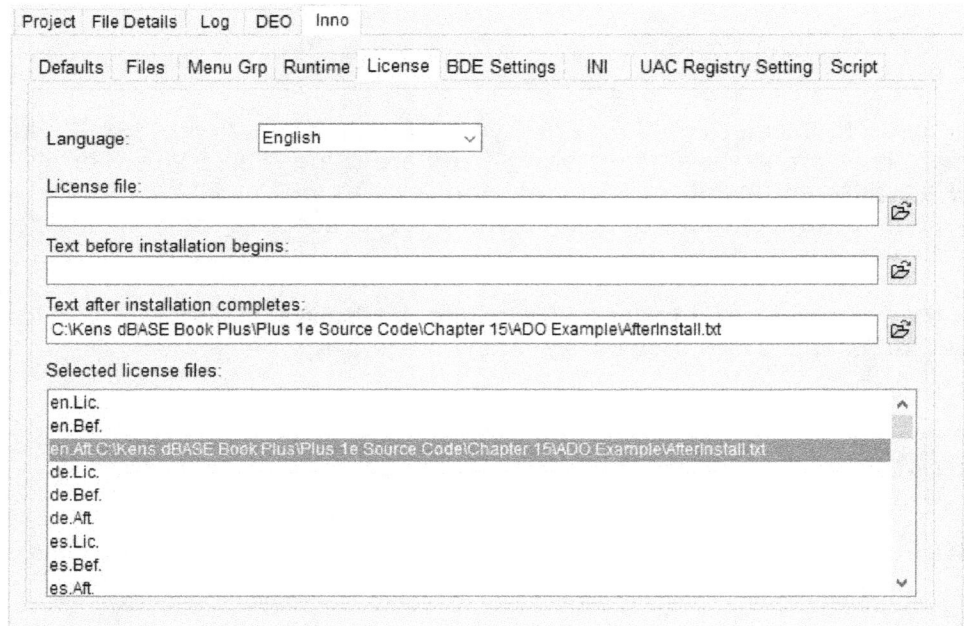

Figure 15-20

This appears fairly complex – it is designed to allow for multi-language installations.

We're going to skip over the "BDE Settings" tab –we're not deploying the BDE. *(For details on BDE Settings, see The dBASE Book, 3rd Edition, Chapter 28.)*

The default for the INI tab is this:

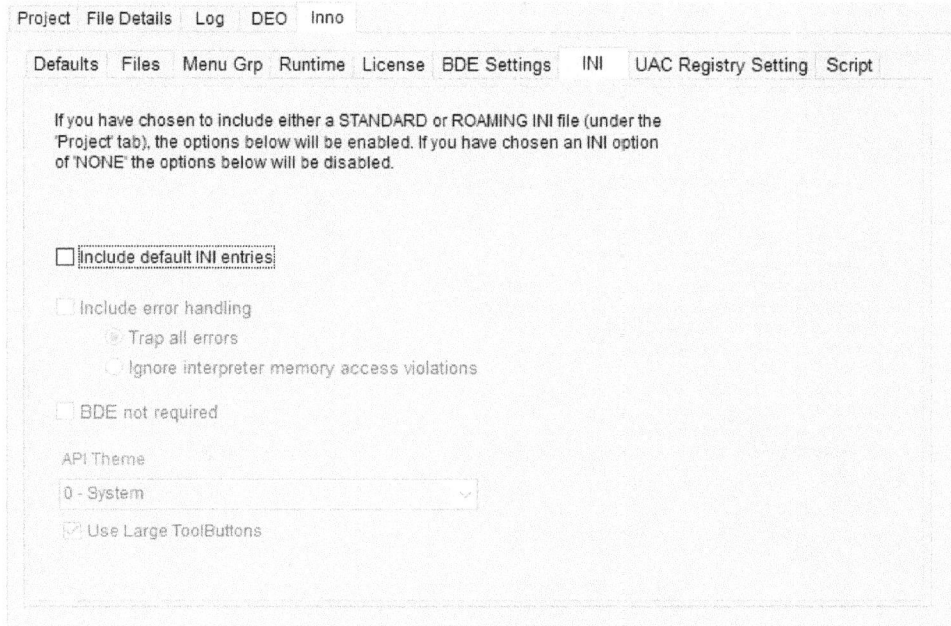

Project File Details Log DEO Inno

Defaults Files Menu Grp Runtime License BDE Settings INI UAC Registry Setting Script

If you have chosen to include either a STANDARD or ROAMING INI file (under the 'Project' tab), the options below will be enabled. If you have chosen an INI option of 'NONE' the options below will be disabled.

☐ Include default INI entries

☐ Include error handling
　　◉ Trap all errors
　　○ Ignore interpreter memory access violations

☐ BDE not required

API Theme

0 - System

☑ Use Large ToolButtons

Figure 15-21

It is a good idea to include the default entries, and since we're not using the BDE, we could check the "BDE not required" checkbox –this is not absolutely necessary because we checked the box on the Project tab that said we were not using the BDE, but it can't hurt.

We'll leave the defaults for "UAC Registry Setting" (see later in the chapter for a description of what this is about), and move on to "Script".

Before we look at the "Script" – the ADO Connection String entries for the application's .INI file are missing. Unfortunately the Project Explorer does not provide a way to add our own items to the .ISS file – as soon as you tell it to generate the script any additions are overwritten.

When you first click on the "Script" tab, the screen is pretty empty. So before doing anything else, type a name in the entryfield, such as "Invoice.iss", and then click the disc button to the right of the entryfield (the ScreenTip says "Generate script with settings").

You should see something like:

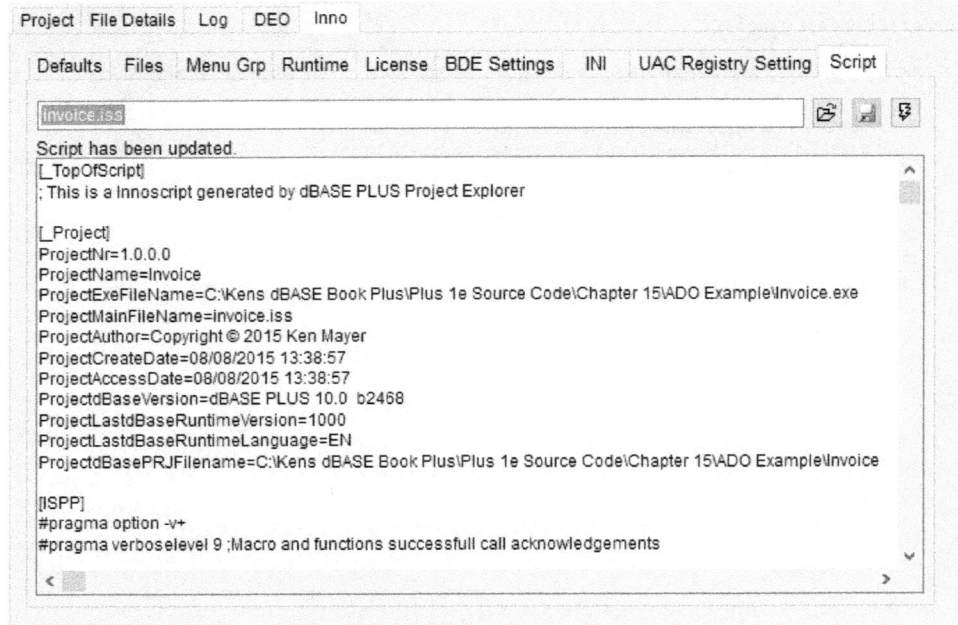

Figure 15-22

Scrolling down you will see that there is quite a lot there. This is, however, a read-only view – meaning that you cannot modify the script from here. You can add files to be deployed, and so on, but anything added by you will be overwritten by the Project Explorer as mentioned earlier.

If you want the ADO Connection strings to be written into the .INI file for the application, you will need to add them manually. If you then change anything and rebuild the .ISS file you will need to add this information. My recommendation is to perhaps keep the instructions in a separate document somewhere in case you need to copy and paste them back into the .ISS file. Save the project and close it.

You can open the .ISS file in Inno Setup by double-clicking it in the Windows File Manager. If you then scroll down to the [INI] section, you can add the following code (note that each statement must be on its own line, starting with the keyword "Filename"):

```
; Add other keys needed, including the ADO Connection Strings
(without password)
Filename: {app}\Invoice.ini; Section: Connections; Flags:
UninsDeleteSection
Filename: {app}\Invoice.ini; Section: Connections; Key: 0; String:
BookSample_ADO
Filename: {app}\Invoice.ini; Section: Connections; Key: 1; String:
BookSample_ADO_RO
Filename: {app}\Invoice.ini; Section: BookSample_ADO; Flags:
UninsDeleteSection
Filename: {app}\Invoice.ini; Section: BookSample_ADO; Key: Provider;
String: MSDASQL.1
Filename: {app}\Invoice.ini; Section: BookSample_ADO; Key: Persist
Security Info; String: False
Filename: {app}\Invoice.ini; Section: BookSample_ADO; Key: Data
Source; String: BookSample
```

```
Filename: {app}\Invoice.ini; Section: BookSample_ADO; Key: Mode;
String: ReadWrite
Filename: {app}\Invoice.ini; Section: BookSample_ADO_RO; Flags:
UninsDeleteSection
Filename: {app}\Invoice.ini; Section: BookSample_ADO_RO; Key:
Provider; String: MSDASQL.1
Filename: {app}\Invoice.ini; Section: BookSample_ADO_RO; Key: Persist
Security Info; String: False
Filename: {app}\Invoice.ini; Section: BookSample_ADO_RO; Key: Data
Source; String: BookSample_RO
Filename: {app}\Invoice.ini; Section: BookSample_ADO_RO; Key: Mode;
String: Read
```

When the install is run, then these will be added to the appropriate part of the .INI file.

From inside Inno Setup, you can build the setup file, which will be placed in the default folder "Output" when you do this.

Using Inno Setup (Only)

The following set of instructions will set up an install script manually using just Inno Setup for the same application that is defined in the previous set of instructions. I personally prefer using Inno Setup directly, but not all developers do.

Before starting you would still need to build the executable. If you use the Project file from earlier in the chapter, and simply build the executable, everything else should be okay.

The following is the complete script with some notes inserted (in regular text). Note that there is a lot of line-wrapping going on. Each "line" starts with a specific keyword such as "Name:". This file is in the samples as "Install_Manual.iss":

I removed the heading comments, and we start with the standard Setup section.

```
[Setup]
SourceDir=C:\Kens dBASE Book Plus\Plus 1e Source Code\Chapter
15\ADO Example
SetupIconFile=C:\Kens dBASE Book Plus\Plus 1e Source
Code\Chapter 15\ADO Example\form_green.ico
AppId=Invoice
AppName=ADO Invoice Example
AppVersion=1.00
AppVerName=ADO Invoice Example Version 1.00
AppCopyright=Copyright (c) 2015 Ken Mayer
DefaultDirName={pf}\Invoice
DefaultGroupName=Invoice
PrivilegesRequired=admin
ShowLanguageDialog=false
; Display this file after the install is
; complete:
InfoAfterFile=AfterInstall.txt
```

The Types and Components sections of the script are used to define how files are deployed based on the Code section at the end of the script.

```
; Define types as Server and Client:
[Types]
Name: Server; Description: Server Install -- Data and program
files on network drive
Name: Client; Description: Client Install -- Local
workstation, installs program only, sets up references for
data, ODBC, etc.

; Components:
[Components]
Name: Server; Types: Server; Description: Server Install
Name: Client; Types: Client; Description: Client/Workstation
Install
```

What directories should be created, and with what rights?

```
[Dirs]
Name: {app}\Data; Components: Server; Flags:
UninsAlwaysUninstall
Name: {app}\Documentation; Flags: UninsAlwaysUninstall
```

List the files that need to be installed, and where to.

```
[Files]
; Images/Icons
Source: about.ico; DestDir: {app}; Flags: IgnoreVersion
Source: gear.png; DestDir: {app}; Flags: IgnoreVersion
Source: node.png; DestDir: {app}; Flags: IgnoreVersion
Source: form_green.ico; DestDir: {app}; Flags: IgnoreVersion

; Executable -- compiled with NO BDE and EMBED RUNTIME flags:
Source: Invoice.exe; DestDir: {app}; Flags: IgnoreVersion
; dBASE Runtime files:
Source: C:\Program Files
(x86)\dBASE\Plus10\Runtime\PlusRun.exe.dll; DestDir: {app};
Flags: IgnoreVersion
Source: C:\Program Files
(x86)\dBASE\Plus10\Runtime\PlusR_EN.dll; DestDir: {app};
Flags: IgnoreVersion
Source: C:\Program Files
(x86)\dBASE\Plus10\Runtime\plusrun.exe.manifest; DestDir:
{app}; Flags: IgnoreVersion

; Documentation:
Source: AfterInstall.txt; DestDir: {app}; Flags: IgnoreVersion
Source: Documentation\Firebird ODBC for Invoice.pdf; DestDir:
{app}\Documentation; Components: Server; Flags: IgnoreVersion
Source: Documentation\Firebird Server for Invoice.pdf;
DestDir: {app}\Documentation; Flags: IgnoreVersion

; Database
Source: C:\Kens dBASE Book Plus\Data\BOOKSAMPLE.FDB; DestDir:
{app}\Data; Components: Server; Flags: IgnoreVersion
```

The INI section defines what goes into the INI file.

```
[INI]
; "Standard" entries in the ini file:
Filename: {app}\Invoice.ini; Section: Toolbars; Flags:
UninsDeleteSection
Filename: {app}\Invoice.ini; Section: Toolbars; Key: Standard;
String: 0
Filename: {app}\Invoice.ini; Section: Toolbars; Key:
StandardFloat; String: 0
Filename: {app}\Invoice.ini; Section: Toolbars; Key:
StandardStyle; String: 0
Filename: {app}\Invoice.ini; Section: Desktop; Flags:
UninsDeleteSection
Filename: {app}\Invoice.ini; Section: Desktop; Key: Maximized;
String: 0
Filename: {app}\Invoice.ini; Section: Desktop; Key: StatusBar;
String: 0
Filename: {app}\Invoice.ini; Section: CommandWindow; Flags:
UninsDeleteSection
Filename: {app}\Invoice.ini; Section: CommandWindow; Key:
Open; String: 0
Filename: {app}\Invoice.ini; Section: DataEngine; Flags:
UninsDeleteSection
Filename: {app}\Invoice.ini; Section: DataEngine; Key:
DefaultEngine; String: None
Filename: {app}\Invoice.ini; Section: AppTheme; Flags:
UninsDeleteSection
Filename: {app}\Invoice.ini; Section: AppTheme; Key: Type;
String: 0
Filename: {app}\Invoice.ini; Section: Tools; Flags:
UninsDeleteSection
Filename: {app}\Invoice.ini; Section: Tools; Key:
LargeButtons; String: 1

; Add other keys needed, including the ADO Connection Strings
(without password)
Filename: {app}\Invoice.ini; Section: Connections; Flags:
UninsDeleteSection
Filename: {app}\Invoice.ini; Section: Connections; Key: 0;
String: BookSample_ADO
Filename: {app}\Invoice.ini; Section: Connections; Key: 1;
String: BookSample_ADO_RO
Filename: {app}\Invoice.ini; Section: BookSample_ADO; Flags:
UninsDeleteSection
Filename: {app}\Invoice.ini; Section: BookSample_ADO; Key:
Provider; String: MSDASQL.1
Filename: {app}\Invoice.ini; Section: BookSample_ADO; Key:
Persist Security Info; String: False
Filename: {app}\Invoice.ini; Section: BookSample_ADO; Key:
Data Source; String: BookSample
Filename: {app}\Invoice.ini; Section: BookSample_ADO; Key:
Mode; String: ReadWrite
Filename: {app}\Invoice.ini; Section: BookSample_ADO_RO;
Flags: UninsDeleteSection
Filename: {app}\Invoice.ini; Section: BookSample_ADO_RO; Key:
Provider; String: MSDASQL.1
```

```
Filename: {app}\Invoice.ini; Section: BookSample_ADO_RO; Key:
Persist Security Info; String: False
Filename: {app}\Invoice.ini; Section: BookSample_ADO_RO; Key:
Data Source; String: BookSample_RO
Filename: {app}\Invoice.ini; Section: BookSample_ADO_RO; Key:
Mode; String: Read
```

Files to delete when an uninstall occurs (although the .INI file is often not uninstalled because it is often changed when the application runs).

```
[UninstallDelete]
Type: files; Name: Filename: {app}\Invoice.ini
```

This is the Code section – it defines pages to be displayed, and allows you to interact with the user:

```
; -----------------------------------------------------------
-----------------------------------
; Code to set up/create pages so we can get the path to the
network where the
; application is/should be installed ... This code is based on
code provided ages ago for
; Ken Mayer by Jonny Kwekkeboom for another application.
[Code]
var
    NetDirPage: TInputDirWizardPage;
    cNetDirDefault: String;

procedure InitializeWizard_NetDir;
var cTitle, cLabel, cDesc: String;
begin
  { Create the pages }

  cNetDirDefault := '{app}';
  cTitle          := 'Select Directory on Network Drive';
  cLabel          := 'Choose directory on the Network Drive
where application files are installed.';
  cDesc           := 'Choose the folder on the network drive
that has the data, most likely F:\Invoice';
  NetDirPage      := CreateInputDirPage( wpSelectDir, cTitle,
cLabel, cDesc, False, '' );
  NetDirPage.add( '' );
  NetDirPage.Values[0] := '';
end;

function GetNetDir( Param: String): String;
begin
    Result := NetDirPage.Values[0];
end;

procedure CurPageChanged( CurPageID: Integer);
begin
    case CurPageID of
        NetDirPage.ID:
        begin
            NetDirPage.Values[0];
            ExpandConstant( cNetDirDefault );
```

```
        if NetDirPage.Values[0] = '' then
            NetDirPage.Values[0] :=
                ExpandConstant( cNetDirDefault );
        end;
    end;
end;

procedure InitializeWizard();
begin
    InitializeWizard_NetDir;
end;
```

Once you save this and compile it, you should have a working install routine that will install the data on the server, as well as the application, and for individual client computers (as in client/server network), the application and necessary files.

Just like with the Project Explorer, this does not automate the installation of the ODBC Drivers for Firebird, or the Windows ODBC setup *(see below)*, but if you provide careful step-by-step instructions for your users, all should be well.

This is not a super "pretty" install routine, I did not put in all the bells and whistles that I did in <u>The dBASE Book</u>, I was focusing specifically on this example application.

Completely Automating the Process
Of course, one could insert the standard installers for the Firebird Server software and the ODBC Drivers for Firebird (see Chapter 2), and perhaps provide some guidance to the user (add something in a document that goes with the installation to ensure they know what to do with it) – you would need to put these in both the [File] and [Run] sections. And as it turns out, there is an additional tool for Inno Setup that I was unaware of until I had completed (or mostly) this chapter that can help set up the actual Windows ODBC instructions (see below, Inno Setup Studio).

Since there are 32-bit and 64-bit versions of the installers mentioned above, you could use the Inno Setup options to deploy the appropriate version, or you could just use the 32-bit installers (the software should work fine), no matter which version of Windows you are installing to.

Omer-Pitou mentioned "Inno Setup Studio" to me, and says that once your .ISS script is created (either through the Project Explorer or manually as shown above), if you download and install Inno Setup Studio, you could then open the script in that, and there are options for creating an ODBC profile, it shows all of your ODBC connections in Windows, and you can select the ones to have created by your script.

I chose not to deal with this, as it is not part of the standard dBASE installation, and this chapter has already gotten quite lengthy. It is worth exploring though, if you have the time.

Project Explorer Updates

The following is based on the dBASE documentation that lists changes in the software. Starting with dBASE Plus 8, the following changes were made to the Project Explorer:

1 New Support for the *useUACPaths* registry entry for an application during installation.

   A new tab was added under INNO called 'UAC Registry Setting' which includes three radio buttons. This gives the user three options with regard to adding registry settings during the installation of their program.

   The options are:

   1 Do not create application specific registry setting for *useUACPaths*. *(Allow embedded UAC setting or the runtime engine registry setting for useUACPaths to control UAC support.)*
   2 Create application specific registry setting with *useUACPaths*="Y" on Windows Vista or newer? *(This will override the runtime engine registry setting and the embedded UAC setting.)*
   3 Create application specific registry setting with *useUACPaths*="N" on Windows Vista or newer? *(This will override the runtime engine registry setting and the embedded UAC setting.)*

   These settings are saved in the .prj file under [INNO]

   UACRB= (options are 1, 2 or 3 – corresponding to the options above in order.)

2 Support for maintaining path setting for runtime installer executable.

   Created a property that keeps track of where the Runtime installer executable is and saves it in the .prj folder under INNO as dBaseRuntimeInstDir=<path and .exe name of runtime installer>

3 Bypassing the Inno Script Generator all together *(unable to make any updates to the program for future releases)*.

   This involved adding new support files under the dBASE/Plus/Runtime and dBASE/Plus/Bin/dBLCore/ProjExp directories.

   Now when a new script is generated the Inno Setup Compiler will open with the new script *(instead of using the INNO Script Generator as a go-between app)*.

Most or all of these changes will be pretty easy to work with. The concept of UAC Paths was discussed all the way through The dBASE Book *(3rd Edition)*, so the first change above just places the ability to tell the installer how to handle the UAC Path settings.

The third item in the list (Inno Script Generator) was due to the fact that this third-party tool is not something that dBASE, LLC can modify, and it was easier to no longer rely on it – instead the developers created some new files to help with generating the Inno Setup script, without using that tool.

Things to Remember with UAC

When files get installed, if the application is defined as a UAC app (which dBASE apps are by default), running the executable copies files to specific file locations.

The .INI file is copied to the path:

```
C:\Users\USERNAME\AppData\Local\AppFolderPath
```

Where "USERNAME" is the name of the logged in user and "AppFolderPath" is the path to the application (i.e., MyCompany\MyProgram). This is the path of the .INI file that is used, and modified (if the application modifies the .INI file). The file in the folder with the .EXE is the original, and is not updated by the .EXE.

This can get a bit strange. When I was working with the Samples folder for dBASE Plus 10, and the FISH application, I ran the executable just to check it out. The original path for the samples folder is:

```
C:\Users\USERNAME\Documents\dBASE\Plus10\Samples
```

When I ran the executable, the .INI file was placed in this path:

```
C:\Users\USERNAME\AppData\Local\Users\USERNAME\Documents\dBASE
\Plus10\Samples
```

(All of that being one path ...)

Imagine how much fun it was finding it so I could clean up after. I mention this just to remind you that the paths can be interesting.

Other Changes/Concerns

Windows XP Support Gone

Probably the biggest change for some developers is that when Microsoft announced that they were dropping support for Windows XP, it meant that the folk at dBASE, LLC decided to follow along. If you are using **dBASE Plus 9** or later, you need to be aware that any application you create *will not* run on Windows XP. All versions of Windows since *(starting with Windows Vista and moving forward to Windows 10)* should be fine, but Windows XP is not going to be something you can count on. It is probably a good idea to convince your clients to move to a newer version of dBASE.

Include Object Code in Project?

Gerald Lightsey and I went back and forth on this issue *(privately)* when I was working on The dBASE Book, a couple of years ago. Gerald believes very strongly that it is important to include the object code in a project when setting up an application for deployment.

I am not quite sure what issues Gerald has run into with this, but wanted to at least address it here. When you have the source code in the Project Explorer, every time you build the executable, the source code is recompiled.

When you deploy the application, the Project Explorer deploys, not the source code, but the object code (the compiled version of the source code -- .pro, .wfo, etc.). If your application uses DEO (Dynamic External Objects), then you can specify which folder(s) the object files are distributed to. This was shown in the book. I have not seen a case, except in some emails from Gerald, where this did not work properly.

That said, if you run into a situation where an object file is not being distributed properly, you can include the object file in the list of files in the project, and specify the DEO location for that file. *(See The dBASE Book, 3rd Edition, Chapter 28 for more details.)*

Gerald also wanted to point out that files such as PDF files can be included in the lists of files to be deployed, and using DEO settings can be installed with your code and other files to DEO folders if needed, which implies that other files should also work the same way.

Sample Code for This Chapter

The following is a listing of the sample code in the "Chapter 15" folder, if you downloaded it from my website. You may use the code contained in these forms for your own applications if you desire, with the caveat that credit be given appropriately.

- ADO Example folder – Contains the application from Chapter 6.
- AfterInstall.txt – Text file to display after the application is installed.
- Invoice_Manual.iss – manual version of Inno Setup script for the ADO Application.
- Invoice.iss – Inno Setup script created by the Project Explorer for the ADO Application.
- Invoice.prj – Project to build application.
- Invoice.rsp – Response file used to build the executable.
- ADO Example folder → Documentation folder – contains files used for documenting the rest of the setup for ADO Sample application.

Summary

As you can see, deploying an application takes patience and time. It is of course helpful if you have multiple computers that you can test on, so that when you have your executable read for deployment, you can test it before taking it to (or sending it to) your client(s) for final deployment and then finding out there was a problem.

Special thanks for this chapter, in no particular order: the dBASE, LLC team for helping me figure a few things out, Rick Miller and Omer-Pitou from the newsgroups ...

The Appendices

Like any book of this nature there is material that doesn't really fit into the main text that really ought to be included somewhere ... that's where we're at now. These appendices include an interesting mix of information that you may find useful.

Appendix 1: Resources Available

dBASE developers have available to them a large quantity of resources, including newsgroups, libraries of source code, freeware applications where you can download and "borrow" code, tutorials and a lot more. This appendix is literally a list of places to go to find assistance with building your applications. I have updated it – all the sites listed here should work as of publication date. I removed a couple of sites from this appendix from the previous version as the sites appear to have disappeared *(as they sometimes do on the web)*.

dBase, LLC

These are the people who own and are developing and selling dBASE PLUS, dQuery, and a few other dBASE-based applications. You can find an overview of the company at:

```
http://www.dbasellc.com/
```

And specifically you can find information about dBASE and other products at:

```
http://www.dbase.com
```

If you need to purchase dBASE, need to talk to Customer Support, etc., this is where you would go. There are links on the website for email addresses of who to talk to for specific situations.

Newsgroups

One of the most useful ways of gaining help when trying to develop an application is through the free newsgroups out there. There are two that are specifically dBASE oriented.

dBase, LLC. provides free newsgroups for support. These include a place to report bugs and post wishlist requests, which get read by the R&D team, but also a lot of different newsgroups *(including some that are language specific – German, etc. so that users who don't speak English have somewhere to go)*. Details on these newsgroups are available from the dBASE website:

```
http://www.dbase.com/dBase_NewsGrpForums.asp
```

The dBase newsgroups are monitored by members of the dBASE community as well as members of the R&D team. Answers are given by anyone: dBase personnel and the dBASE community (other users). One can learn a lot from these newsgroups.

dBASE PLUS Tutorials

In the time before Borland sold dBASE to dBASE, Inc. *(now dBase, LLC)* and after Visual dBASE 7.01 was released, there was a period when there was little support for dBASE. I worked with various developers to create a tutorial. Professor Michael Nuwer took that tutorial, ran with it and improved and enhanced it. Over the years he has added modules to the tutorial to assist in learning more about how to create dBASE applications. While my name is still associated with this, it is really more Michael's creation than mine anymore.

The main tutorial can be found in the dBASE Knowledgebase (see below) and was put there with Michael's permission, but you can also get to other tutorials and modules for the main tutorial at Michael's website:

```
http://www.mnuwer.dbasedeveloper.co.uk/dlearn/
```

dBASE Knowledgebase

In earlier versions of dBASE (everything after Visual dBASE 7.5 and before dBASE PLUS 2.5) the CD included a copy of the dBASE Knowledgebase, which was installed on your hard drive when you installed the dBASE application.

The Knowledgebase is still available on the dBASE website and you can view it either by going to the "Help" menu in dBASE and selecting "Knowledgebase", or going straight to it:

```
http://www.dbase.com/dBase_Knowledgebase.asp
```

dBASE Users' Function Library Project (dUFLP)

The dUFLP, which is referenced in various places in this book, is a vast library of freeware dBL code created by many authors over a span of nearly 30 years. The code is redistributable with your applications with the only caveat being that the comment headers for the programs or functions you use are left intact, specifically the name of the authors of the code *(we believe strongly in credit where credit is due)*.

The dUFLP was created by myself years ago when I was a developer working with dBASE IV, release 1.1. I got code from a variety of sources and put it in a single procedure file. Over time it got too large and unwieldy, so it was split up to smaller files. Over the years many developers have contributed code, helped fix bugs or enhance existing code in the library, making it a huge open-source dBL project. Instructions for the use of the library are both on my website and in the readme.txt file included in the collection of code.

The name: *dBASE Users' Function Library Project* was created so that we could pronounce the acronym as "duh-flop". It's a silly thing, which was meant to be silly and I wouldn't want to change it now.

The current version can be downloaded from my own website:

```
http://www.goldenstag.net/dbase#dUFLP
```

If you decide to use this library of code you should follow the directions given for setup (see "Readme.txt"), then you can use the form "Library.wfm" to get an understanding of what is in the dUFLP – this is a vast library of code and this form can help you find a specific item you need.

dBulletin

Jean-Pierre Martel created an online newsletter that is a great resource to the dBASE developer community called dBulletin. The newsletter was discontinued some years back, sadly. The authors were people from all parts of the international dBASE community and there are often translations of some of the English articles to other languages and it is worth checking out. The main page for the dBulletin newsletter is:

```
http://www.jpmartel.com/bulletin.htm
```

There are other sites around the globe that also host the newsletter, but this is the primary source (links can be found at my website noted above under the "dUFLP" heading).

dBASE Related Websites

Various other people have websites of interest and are quickly noted below:

- **Ken's dBASE Page** – my own dBASE related website:

  ```
  http://www.goldenstag.net/dbase
  ```

- **Golden Stag Productions** - Ken's Business website *(the business is closed, but I left the site up)*:

  ```
  http://www.goldenstag.net/GSP
  ```

- **The dBASE Webring**: Sponsored/hosted by Francois Ghoche (in France), this is a webring that allows you to view related websites – in this case, all about dBASE:

  ```
  http://www.fghoche.com/dbasering.htm
  ```

These are just a few of the various websites out there. You may want to spend some time exploring to see what else is available *(the web-ring will be useful for that)*!

Other dBASE Books

Since the first Edition of this book was published, a German author, Ulf Neubert, has stepped forward with at least two books on dBASE and may be working on more. If you can read German, you might go to Ulf's website and check out his books:

```
http://www.ulfneubert.de/autor/dbasebuecher/index.html
```

I have published <u>The dBASE Book</u> *(3rd Edition)* and <u>The dBASE Reports Book</u> (which takes the information in the Reports chapters of the previous book and expands them in much more detail).

Details on where to purchase my books can be found here:

```
http://www.goldenstag.net/dbase/dBASEBooks.htm
```

Appendix 2: A Brief History of dBASE

This is an extension to the history in <u>The dBASE Book</u> *(3rd Edition)*. Rather than including the whole history here, I figured I would continue the history beyond where the previous one ended.

2012   Late in the year, dBASE released dBASE Plus 8. This occurred very close to the same time I was putting the finishing touches on <u>The dBASE Book</u> *(3rd Edition)*, and figuring out my distribution channels. Rather than trying to incorporate the changes in dBASE Plus 8, I decided to publish. At the time I was frustrated, since I had no idea that this release of dBASE was coming out at that time, and vowed I was done writing books on dBASE, as the amount of money I was getting in royalties didn't really match the amount of effort that went into writing.

dBASE Plus 8 was released with a completely new look, ADO Database classes, and more.

2013   In November of 2013, dBASE Plus 8.1 was released, with many fixes.

Somewhere in here dBASE started producing a set of tools for developers that might be used outside of dBASE. These have been through several release cycles, but I have not used any of the, so cannot speak to a lot of detail. Looking at the Support pages for dBASE:

- dBFUtilities:
  - dbfInspect
  - dbfImport
  - dbfExport
  - dBFCompare
- dBDOS: Designed specifically for people using DOS versions of dBASE under Windows ...

2014   This was a busy year with dBASE Plus 9 being released, and then subsequent updates to dBASE Plus 9.51 released November of 2014. This was mostly a bug-fix version, very few new features, but it is pretty stable, and much of the work on this book has been done with this version.

2015   dBASE Plus 10 went into Beta, with a lot of effort involved in some new interface classes (ListView, a new Grid), enhancements to the Project Explorer and dBASE itself, to make deploying an application easier (and for those apps using the ADO Database classes – deploying without the BDE easier).

I also decided to start working on this book ...

July 21, the announcement that dBASE Plus 10 is now available was sent out in email.

Toward the end of July, a "Hot Release" for dBASE Plus 10 came out, which fixed some serious issues that needed to be addressed.

In the middle of August, dBASE Plus 10.1 was released with a variety of fixes that needed to be completed.

Mid-end of August, I wrapped up this book, and started working on getting it ready for publication.

Appendix 3: Source Code Editor Abbreviations

In Chapter 1 there is a discussion of the ability to use abbreviations in the Source Code Editor by typing a keyword or abbreviation and then pressing Ctrl+B to expand these out. The following is a list of the abbreviations that are in the default abbreviations file:

Abbreviation	Expands to:
adodatabasedn	ADO Database (three lines)
adodatabasecon	ADO Database with connection string (four lines)
adotabledn	ADO Table object (three lines)
adotablecon	ADO Table object with connection string (four lines)
adoquerydn	ADO Query with databaseName (four lines)
adoquerycon	ADO Query with connection string (four lines)
adostoredprocdn	ADO Stored Procedure with databaseName (four lines)
adostoredproccon	ADO Stored Procedure with connection string (four lines)
alttable	ALTER TABLE command
appendfile	APPEND FROM command
appendarray	APPEND FROM ARRAY command
appendmemo	APPEND MEMO command
array	new array()
array2	new array (two dimensional)
assocarray	new assocArray()
build	BUILD command
class	class / endclass (three lines)
copytoarray	COPY TO ARRAY command
createindex	CREATE INDEX command
createtable	CREATE TABLE command
database	new database() (three lines)
date	new date()
date1	new date(<date>)
date2	new date(<msec>)
date3	new date(<year> ... <seconds>)
date4	new date(<year> ... <timez>)
designer	new designer()
designer1	new designer(<object>)
designer2	new designer(<object>, <filename>)
docase	DO CASE / CASE / CASE / OTHERWISE/ ENDCASE (8 lines)
dowhile	DO WHILE / ENDDO (three lines)
dountil	DO / UNTIL (three lines)
exception	class exception / endclass (three lines)
field	new field (three lines)

Abbreviation	Expands to:
filecreateR	new file() / oFile.create with read-only
... lots of variations, "W", "A", "RW" ...	Same – variations for creating a file
fileopenR	new file() / oFile.open with read-only
... lots of variations as above	Same – variations for opening a file
forend	FOR ... / ENDFOR (three lines)
forstep	FOR ... STEP ... / ENDFOR (three lines)
fornext	FOR ... / NEXT (three lines)
fornextstep	FOR ... STEP ... / NEXT (three lines)
function	Function (name) ... / return (three lines)
header	Multi-line header for beginning of a program (Filename, ClassName, Purpose, and more). (17 lines)
if	IF / ENDIF (three lines)
ifelse	IF / ELSE / ENDIF (five lines)
listcov	LIST COVERAGE ...
listmem	LIST MEMORY ...
liststat	LIST STATUS ...
liststru	LIST STRUCTURE
locate	LOCATE ...
number	new Number()
object	new Object()
oleautoclient	new oleAutoClient()
preifelse	#IF / #ELSE / #ENDIF (five lines)
preifend	#IF / #ENDIF (three lines)
preifdef	#IFDEF / #ELSE / #ENDIF (five lines)
query	new query() (with database, etc.) (four lines)
replacefromarray	REPLACE FROM ARRAY ...
tryall	try / catch (exception e) / catch (dbexception db) / endtry (seven lines)
trye	try / catch (exception e) / endtry (five lines)
trydb	try / catch (dbexception db) / endtry (five lines)
with	With (oObj) / endwith (three lines)

Many of these commands have parameters laid out for you, for example, the abbreviation "copytoarray" expands to:

```
COPY TO ARRAY

FOR
WHILE
FIELDS
```

Or "build" expands to:

```
BUILD <filename>, <filename> ICON <filename> SPLASH <filename> TO
<exe-filename> [WEB] [INI ON  OFF  ROAM] [UAC]
```

(This would be on one statement in the Source Code Editor, the insertion point would be between ON and OFF in the INI section.)

Some commands insert blank lines (for example "dowhile" will expand to three lines – one of them blank).

You can add your own abbreviations if you wish by editing the file. Examine the other entries in the file and you can see how this works.

A simple example might be the standard dUFLP header – for this example, calling it "dUFLPHeader":

```
/*
       ------------------------------------------------------------
       Programmer..:
       Date........:
       Notes.......:
       Written for.:
       Rev. History:
       Calls.......:
       Usage.......:
       Example.....:
       Returns.....:
       Parameters..:
       ------------------------------------------------------------
*/
```

You could copy all of this into the abbreviations file, and create something like:

```
dUFLPHeader=/*\n      ----------------------------------------------
----------------\n   Programmer..: |\n   Date........: \n
Notes.......: \n   Written for.: \n   Rev. History: \n
Calls.......: \n   Usage.......: \n   Example.....: \n
Returns.....: \n   Parameters..: \n   ---------------------------
--------------------------------\n */
```

All of the above would be "one line" – no line breaks inserted into it (don't press enter). The "\n" starts a new line, and the location of the vertical bar (|) is where the cursor will be when this is expanded out. If you save this, and then in the Source Code Editor, type "dUFLPHeader", press Ctrl+B – it will expand out to the header shown above. *(I tested this, and it works exactly as expected.)*

NOTES:

Appendix 4: Using MySQL with dBASE

When I started working on the second chapter of this book, I had started to work with MySQL, but ended up finding myself uncomfortable with it. I know a lot of developers use it, and since I had already written up the instructions for setting up MySQL with dBASE and ADO, I felt it would be useful to have here. I am trimming out some of what is in Chapter 2, as it seems redundant, the goal here is to include just the items involved in setting up MySQL.

One thing to note is that ADO will work with both OLE DB and with ODBC drivers. This is important, because while MySQL does not have OLE DB drivers, it does have ODBC drivers.

Installing the MySQL Server

You first must download the MySQL Database Server software from:

    http://dev.mysql.com/downloads/windows/installer/

Scroll down this page and download the installer. You will be asked about creating an account or logging in, but at the bottom there is a link that says "**No thanks, just start my download.**" Click that link.

The installer appears to be 32-bit only, but apparently it includes everything you need.

Accept the License Agreement and move on.

If you are planning on doing development using the MySQL workbench and such, you can install the full package from here. However, for our purposes we are going to assume that you want to use MySQL with dBASE. In that case, change the option to: "Server only". Click the "Next" button.

Click the "Execute" button to download and install the MySQL Server software.

When the process completes, click the "Next" button.

From this point you will need to configure the server software. Click "Next" again, and you should see this screen:

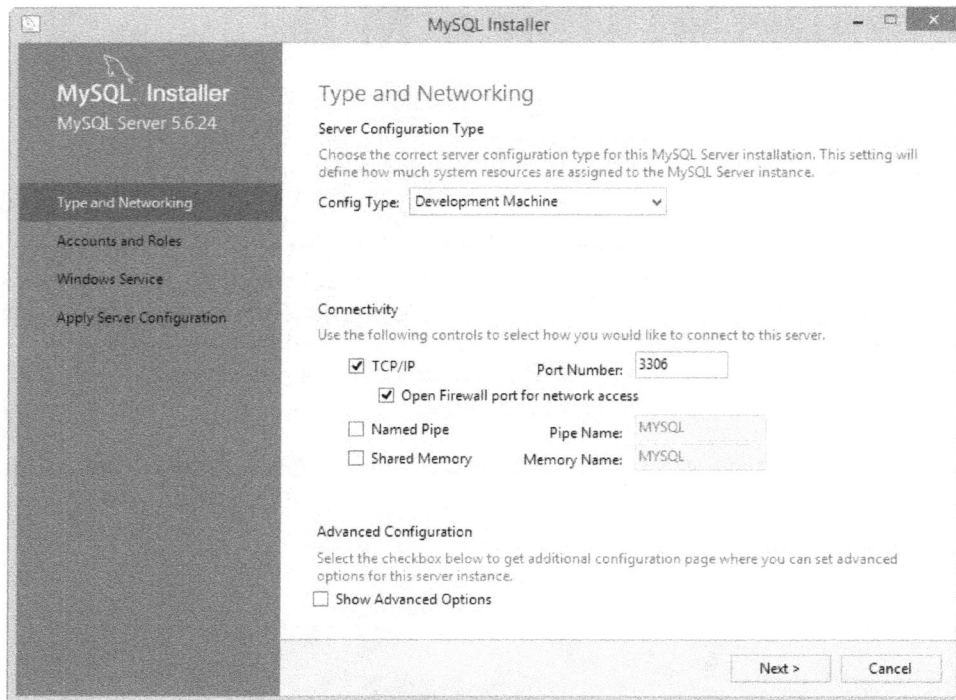

Figure A4-1

You should not change any of these settings, except for the "Open Firewall port for network access" – it is a good idea to turn this off. If it is on it will allow access from outside your computer through the firewall software you have installed *(you are running a Firewall, aren't you?)*. The TCP/IP settings are required for ODBC drivers to work properly.

Click the "Next" button, and we will set up users, which is important to be able to access the data.

It is required that you have a "Root" account – this is a super-user account that has all rights for the database server. You can then create additional accounts, if you wish – these other accounts can be given rights levels.

The root username is, by definition, "root". You need to give a viable password, which the software will verify by having you enter it twice. **Be sure to write this down where you can find it again.**

It is a good idea to have at least one user account besides the "root" user. Click the "Add User" button, and you will see:

Figure A4-2

Create a viable username (something that makes sense, you will remember, etc.)

I am using "dBASEBook1" for this user.

Host – the host is important. If you are on a network, you can limit the user to accessing the data from just the local machine, or you can allow them access from any computer on the network (the default, "All Hosts"). For my personal network, I am not concerned of anyone getting in here, so I am going to leave this setting.

Role – we will leave this as "DBAdmin", but if you click the down arrow you will see many options for the role you can assign to the user.

Enter a password and repeat to confirm. **Again, be sure to write down the username and password!**

Click "OK". If you wish to create other users, you can now, or you can do this at a later point.

Click the "Next" button.

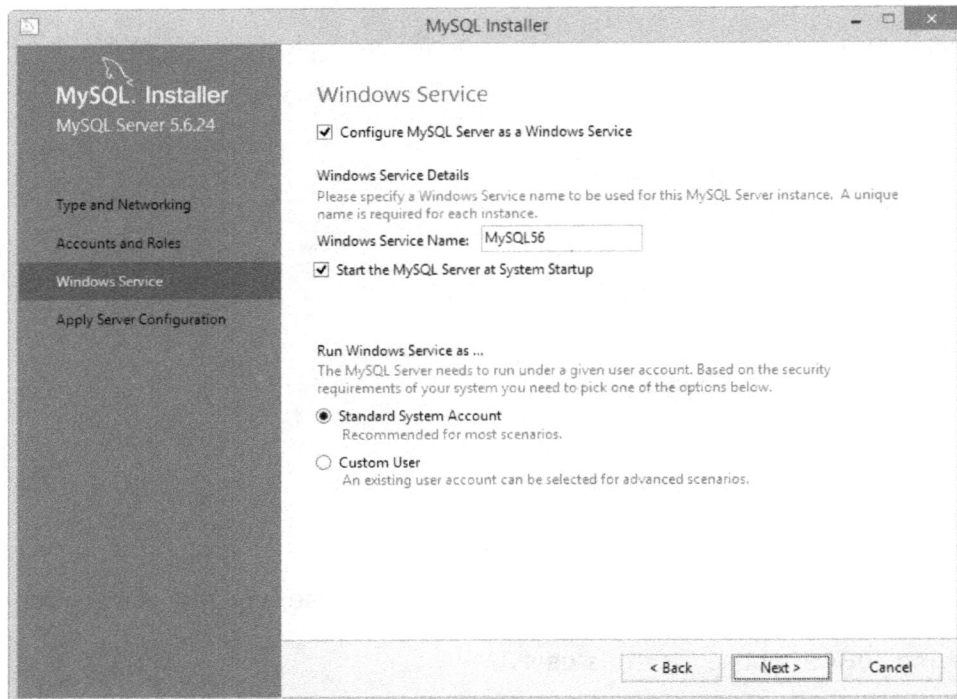

Figure A4-3

For this screen default settings are given, we're going to use the defaults. You can, if you uncheck the "Start the MySQL Server at System Startup" checkbox, and then manually start MySQL Server when you need it.

Click "Next".

On the next screen click "Execute", and MySQL Server will be configured. Click "Finish".

Click "Next", and then "Finish".

In the Control Panel for Windows, you should be able to see MySQL Server running as a service:

```
Control Panel\System and Security\Administrative Tools
```

Double-click "Services" in the window, and you will see (if you scroll through all services available) the service name (using what is shown in the screen shot above, "MySQL56"). You can, if you wish, turn it off from here by double-clicking it …

Installing MySQL Connector

Apparently there is a quirk if you are using Windows 64-bit, in that you must install both the 64-bit and 32-bit drivers for MySQL. If you are working with a 32-bit installation of Windows, this obviously would not be an issue. In addition, apparently the *current* ODBC drivers for MySQL are not ones that work with the Borland Database Engine (BDE). If you wish to work with the BDE, you must use the 3.51 drivers. For ADO the current drivers will work.

The (dBASE) Help instructions state to search using Google for "ADO MySQL Driver" to find what you need to download and install. I did this and found the drivers at the MySQL website:

```
https://www.mysql.com/products/connector/odbc
```

Download this by clicking the link. If you are using Windows 64-bit download the 64-bit drivers, if your version of Windows is 32-bit, download the 32-bit drivers.

Once it is downloaded (this was pretty fast on my connection), find where it was downloaded to and run the .MSI file (Microsoft Installer). I chose a "Typical" install, from the screen with the options for different types of installation.

Once this has completed, **if you are using 64-bit Windows**, you will need to go back and download and install the 32-bit installation as well (also a "Typical" install).

Once you have installed the ODBC driver(s), you need to set up the ODBC side of things before you try to work with MySQL in dBASE.

ODBC Setup

For this example we're going to set up the default "test" database in MySQL. Later details will be given on creating your own database, with your own database name, and the ability to save the database where you want it to be stored.

Find the Control Panel in your version of Windows (in Windows 8, bring up the charms on the right side of the screen, go to "Settings", and then "Control Panel").

In the Control Panel, select "System and Security", and then "Administrative Tools". Select "ODBC Data Sources", and if you are running 64-bit Windows, select the 64-bit version.

You should see a window very much like:

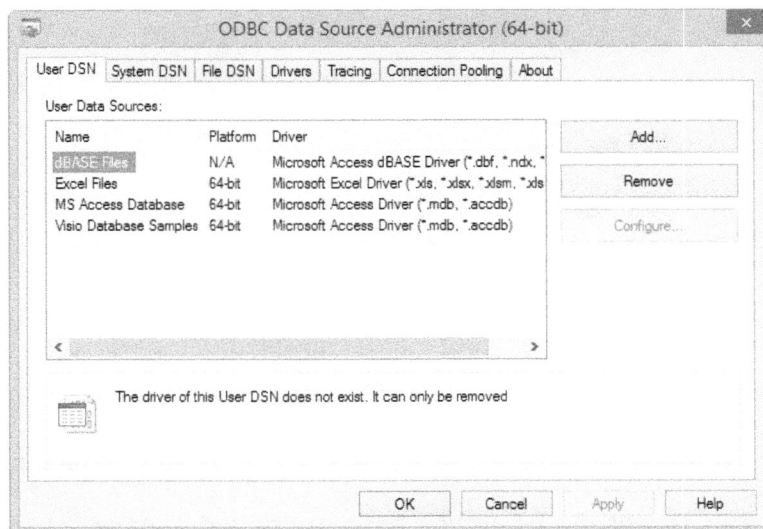

Figure A4-4

Click the "Add..." button to add a new ODBC Data Source.

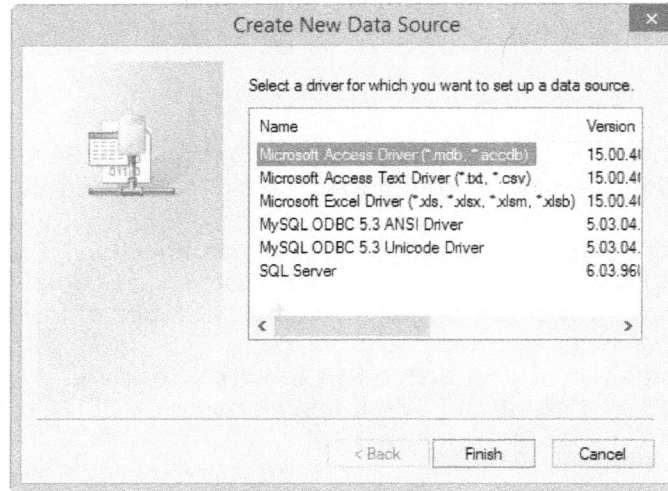

Figure A4-5

The MySQL website suggests that Unicode is what most users should use, so even though part of me says that I should use ANSI (which is standard Windows), I will follow the recommendation by the folk at MySQL/Oracle.

When you select the driver and then click "Finish" you will be asked for more information:

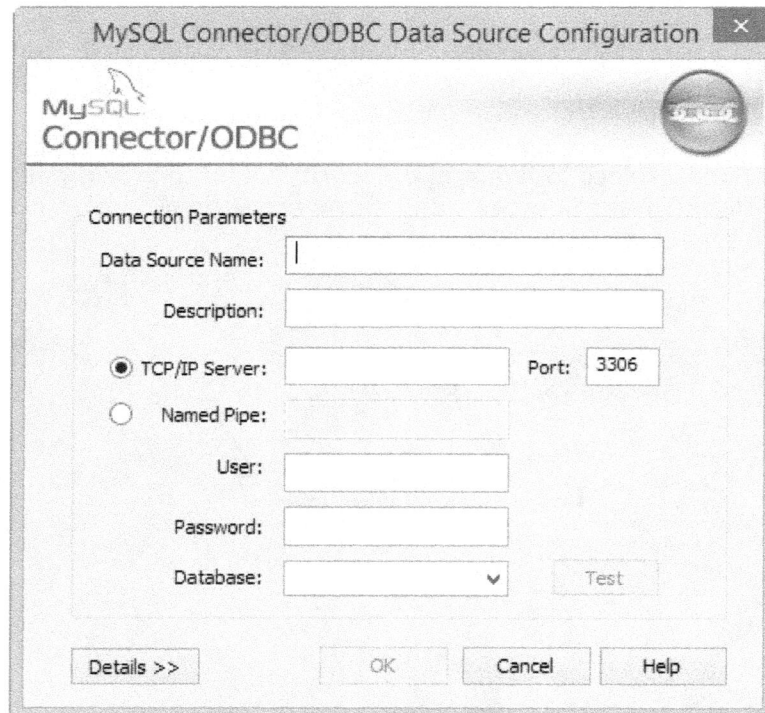

Figure A4-6

Data Source Name: The name of the database (I am using "Startup" for this).

Description: This is a useful when you have multiple databases.

TCP/IP Server: 127.0.0.1 *or* localhost
This is the standard "home" address on your own computer. If you are working on a network, and storing the data on a server, you would want to work with your network administrator to get the correct IP address.

Port: 3306
This appears to be the default.

User: This must be a Windows user, for this we are using "root", but this is a very powerful user – you should be careful.

Password: Fill in the password you created when setting up the server.

Database: In the combobox select "test", or simply type "test".

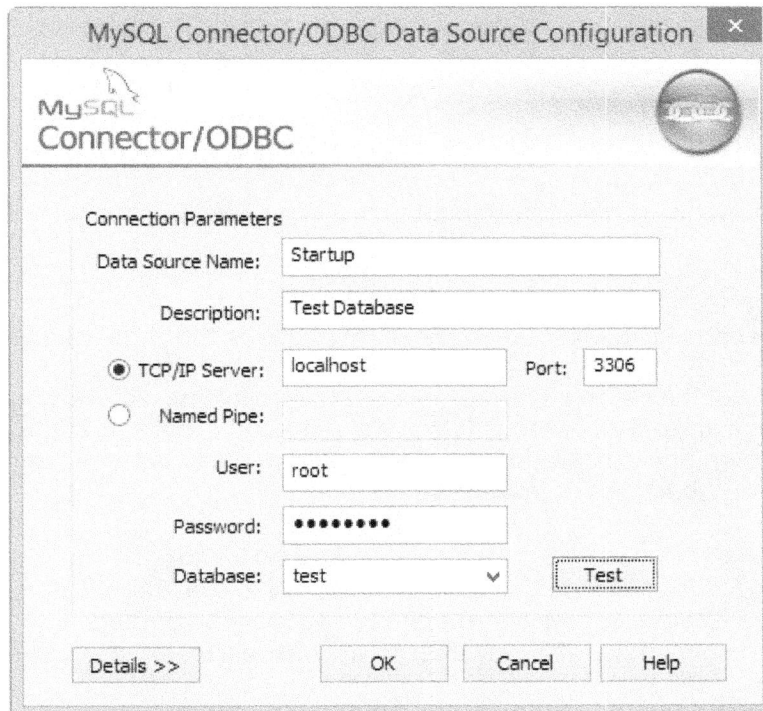
Figure A4-7

The screen should look like Figure A4-7 (above).

Before you click "OK, you should click the "Test" button. You should get the message: Connection Successful. Click "OK".

The ODBC Data Source Administrator should now include your connection:

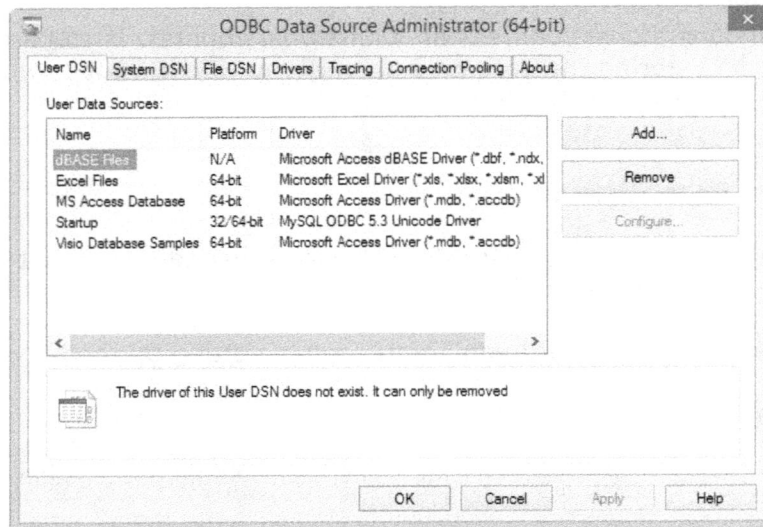

Figure A4-8

Clicking "OK", will close the ODBC setup screen.

The database is stored (by default) on a Windows 8 computer here:

```
C:\ProgramData\MySQL\MySQL Server 5.6\data\test
```

This is because the internal name (in MySQL) of the database is "test".

The next section of this chapter will deal with setting up your own database, with your own name. By having this control, you can create multiple databases, give them names appropriate for the applications you are developing, and quite importantly, back them up easily.

More Control Over Your MySQL Databases

One of the difficulties of this sort of database is that the primary tools that come with the database server can be difficult to work with. Luckily there are developers out there who have come up with easier-to-use tools.

EMS Database Management has a SQL Manager software package (including a freeware version) at:

```
http://www.sqlmanager.net/products/mysql/manager/download
```

Thanks to Ronnie MacGregor for pointing this out. There are other programs as well. I have chosen to try this one.

There are other software packages available that have been mentioned by users in the newsgroups for dBASE:

- Navicat (http://www.navicat.com/download)
- Workbench (part of the MySQL Server suite)

For this example, we will use "SQL Manager Lite for MySQL". Once it is downloaded and isntalled you can easily create a new database by using the "Create Database" button, which brings up this dialog:

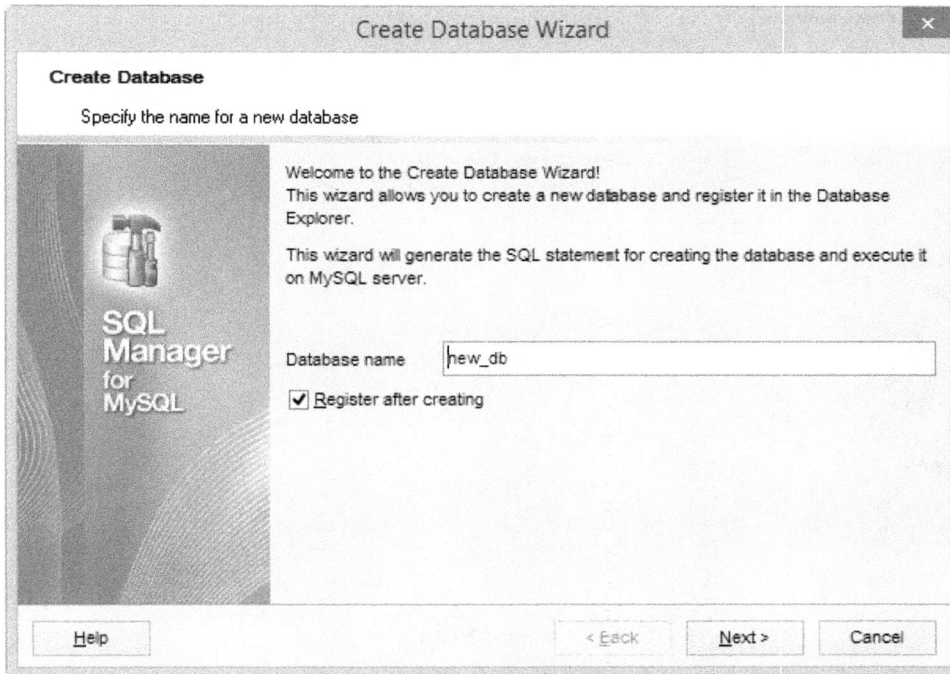

Figure A4-9

Enter your database name (for this example I will call it "BookSample").

Click the "Next" button, and you will see:

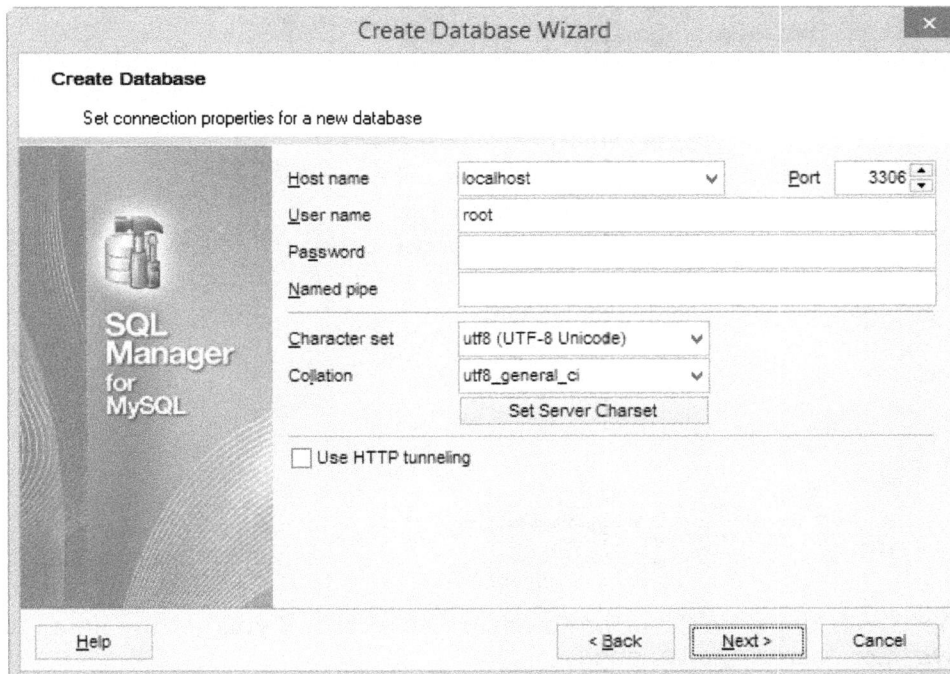

Figure A4-10

Enter the root user password, and click "Next".

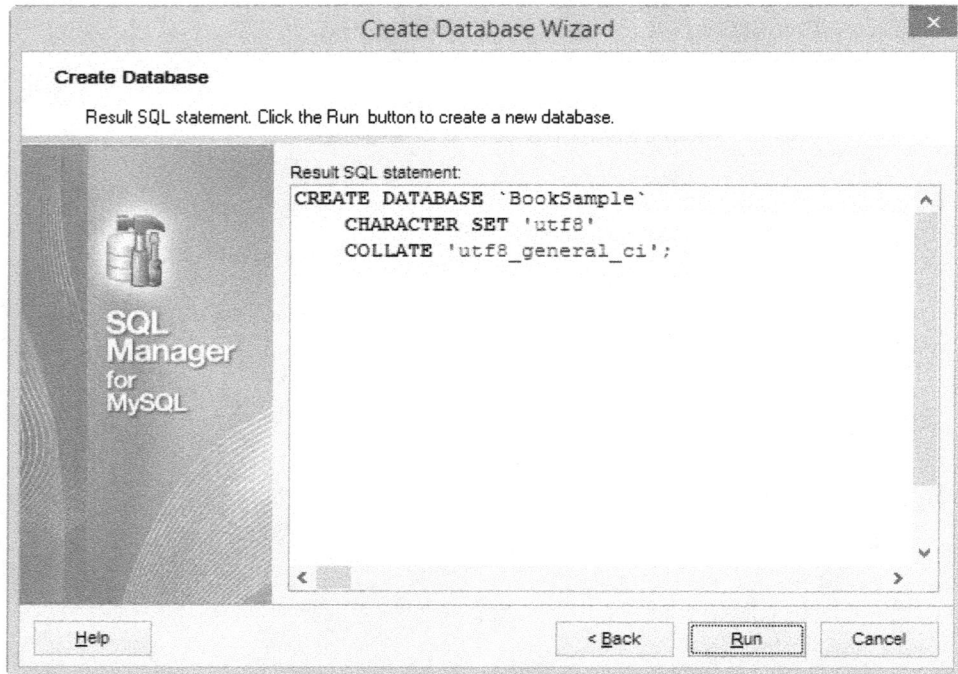

Figure A4-11

Click the "Run" button, and the database will be created, you will see this screen:

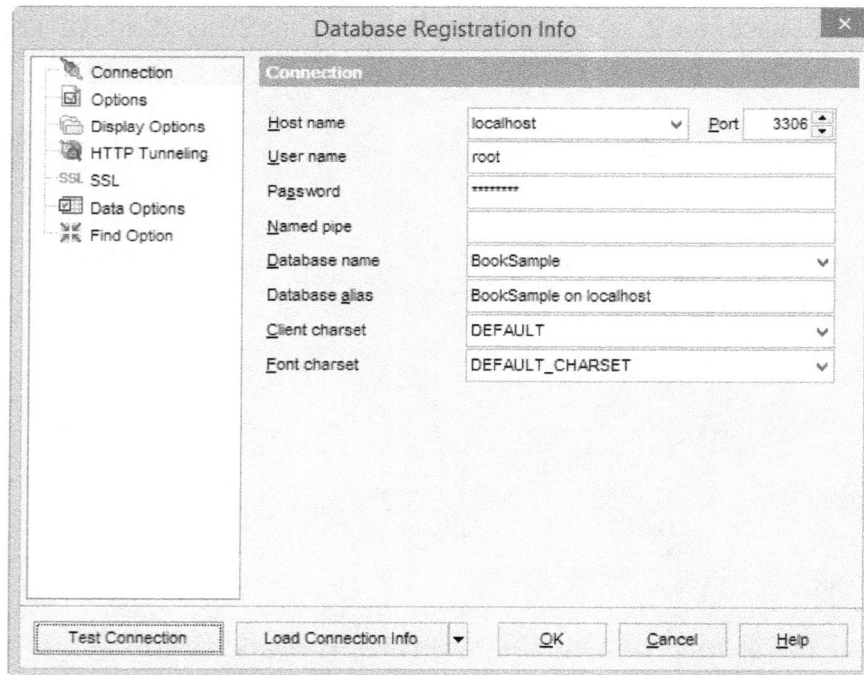

Figure A4-12

Click the "Test Connection" button to ensure all works, if you get the small dialog that says "Connected!", all is good.

Your new database will be created in the same location as the test database:

```
C:\ProgramData\MySQL\MySQL Server 5.6\data\booksample
```

Once you have done this you will need to set up the ODBC Connection to this new database. Follow the instructions given earlier in the chapter, the combobox that was used in Figure A4-7 (page 303) to select "test" will now include the "booksample" database *(or whatever you named it)*. Users can be added with the "SQL Lite Manager for MySQL" software, and so on.

From here you can create tables, and more.

It should be noted that you could probably move the database folder, but you would then need to modify the MySQL initialization file: My.ini, and change this information:

```
# Path to the database root
datadir=C:/ProgramData/MySQL/MySQL Server 5.6/Data
```

To point to where your data is stored. It may be simpler to leave this and just know where the data is stored on your hard drive so you can then back it up, etc.

Setup Connection in dBASE

The steps for this are the same for MySQL as they are for Firebird, and are discussed in Chapter 2.

Creating Tables in Your Database

If you are familiar with dBASE tables, you will find SQL Server databases (including MySQL) use different field types, and some field types you may be pretty familiar with using either don't exist or don't work exactly the same way.

The table designer in dBASE does not seem to create viable tables in MySQL, even if you use only the field types that are acceptable. You will probably need to use a third party tool such as the "SQL Manager for MySQL" that I used in the example above to create a database. This software lists a huge number of field types (SMALLINT, MEDIUMINT, etc.) that gets a bit odd. The idea of the table below is to show the equivalency of fields. This list is based on code in the "DBFToMySQL.wfm" form in the (dUFLP), by Claus Mygind in 2007:

dBASE (Level 7) Field Types	MySQL Equivalent
Character	VARCHAR
Numeric	DECIMAL
Memo	LONGTEXT
Logical	INTEGER
Date	DATE
Float	FLOAT
OLE	LONGBLOB
Binary	BLOB
Long	SMALLINT
Timestamp	TIMESTAMP
Double	DOUBLE
AutoIncrement	*(None – not directly)*

There is more information on field types for MySQL at:

```
http://dev.mysql.com/doc/refman/5.7/en/data-types.html
```

MySQL has many field types not listed in the table above. The online manual for MySQL gives a huge amount of detail about these field types. You may wish to do something different than is shown above. This table is aimed at dBASE developers who are familiar with the DBF table structure, trying to find a way to do something similar to what they are already used to.

Field equivalencies will vary from SQL Server to SQL Server, so the equivalencies shown above may not work for your database server, indeed, you may need to experiment.

Migrating DBF Data to MySQL

If you have a database application already working, but wish to convert it to another database server, such as MySQL, things may get interesting.

First, moving the data and table structures may take some work. dBASE level 7 tables have an AutoInc field (AutoIncrement) – if your application uses these, you will need to change the field type (to INTEGER), and create code (or use code in the dBASE Users' Function Library – dUFLP – a free library of dBASE code – see the appendices of this book) to handle this functionality.

With MySQL, in the dUFLP, is "DBFtoMySQL.wfm" – a "wizard" program designed to walk you through moving the data. However, to use this, you will need to be working with the BDE, which means using the older ODBC drivers for MySQL. I have no experience using this form and cannot speak to how well it works, but it is worth checking out.

You can write your own code to migrate the data, or use the form mentioned above. If you do this via your own code, you may want to look at the UpdateSet class in dBASE, or even just using the COPY TABLE command, although I have a feeling that may give you some difficulties.

Special Notes – MySQL

I had actually had a goal of this appendix covering many different database servers, but most of the developers out there, if they are using SQL servers, are apparently using either Firebird or MySQL, so I was not able to get a lot of information.

Blank Date Fields

"Prior to dBASE 8, dBASE could handle empty date fields in a rowset. However, when dBASE 8 came along, the rowset comes back empty. It appears that if a date field is null or empty then it corrupts the whole rowset. If all of the date fields have a value, then the rowset is correct.

This was later fixed in dBASE Plus 9.xx, but you have to check the "Return SQL_NULL_Data for Zero Date" option in the advanced section of the ODBC connector for MySQL for it to work as expected." – John Noble *(posted in the dBASE Newsgroups)*

NOTES:

Index

B

C

D